Poly

THE CUBEO

THE CUBEO

Indians of the Northwest Amazon

SECOND EDITION

Irving Goldman

UNIVERSITY OF ILLINOIS PRESS

Urbana   Chicago   London

Illini Books edition, 1979

Originally published as no. 2 in the series Illinois Studies in Anthropology

© 1963, 1979 by the Board of Trustees of the University of Illinois
Manufactured in the United States of America

Library of Congress Cataloging in Publication Data

Goldman, Irving, 1911–
  The Cubeo Indians of the Northwest Amazon.

  (Illini books edition)
  Bibliography: p.
  Includes index.
  1. Cubeo Indians. I. Title.
F2270.2.C8G6 1979   980′.004′98   79-13079
ISBN 0-252-00770-0

To Hannah

Acknowledgments

I wish to thank the Social Science Research Council of Columbia University for financing my field work in Colombia. I am indebted to the Colombian government under the administration of Dr. Eduardo Santos for extending every courtesy and aid. The administration of the *Comisaría del Vaupés* was most generous with its hospitality, counsel, and aid. I owe a great deal to the distinguished Colombian educator, Dr. Augustín Nieto Caballero, for sound and friendly advice. To my teachers, Franz Boas and Ruth Fulton Benedict, I owe more than I can express in words. Finally, I can never thank enough the subjects of this study for their friendship, their patience, and their tact.

For encouragement in writing this work I wish to thank Dr. Alfred Métraux. I am grateful to Professor Oscar Lewis of the University of Illinois for a critical evaluation of the manuscript, as well as to Dr. Donald Lathrap, also of the University of Illinois, for helpful suggestions.

Contents

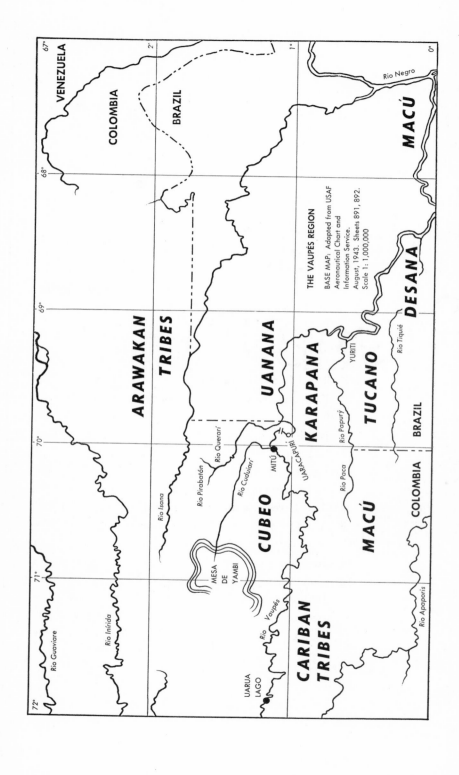

Introduction

No region of the South American tropical forest can claim greater anthropological interest than any other. The entire area of the two great river basins, the Orinoco and the Amazon, is still an anthropological terra incognita. Of its hundreds of tribes most are known only by name; and where more than the name is known it is not the full life but a scattering of information about assorted customs and a handful of word lists that is most often available. The region is an ethnographic swamp where few features rise clearly and vividly above the surface. Whoever undertakes to survey the data confronts a morass of customs dispersed over the vastness of the Amazon Basin with no easily discernible patterns. A few major studies are landmarks and serve as guides to social systems and to cultural patterns. Yet many of these landmark studies are but the surveys of explorers and museum collectors, indefatigable and observant, but understandably preoccupied with the survey in space more than with the study in depth. More recent studies have greater depth, revealing more fully the structure of social life. But of such studies there are few. So slight is our knowledge of this, one of the great natural areas of primitive man, that both kinds of study, the survey of traits and the intensive study of a society, are eminently justifiable. The survey plots the broad features and their variations; the intensive study provides the patterns of tribal life.

One of the astonishing and saddening oversights of twentieth-century anthropological research has been its still-continuing neglect of the lowland South American tropical forest and savannah. Before too long we shall recognize this oversight as tragic, because Indian life in the entire area is rapidly disappearing. When it is gone what will anthropology have lost? It will have lost patterns of cultural life, forms of religious life, forms of social structure, and profiles of personality types, not to mention knowledge of countless customs that have no precise counterpart elsewhere in the primitive world. From what we now know, the Amazon Basin, taken as a whole, contains an extraordinarily wide range of variations on every human cultural institution. It represents countless combinations of a common pool of similar cultural traits spread over its area of over 2,500,000 square miles.

The region of the two river basins, really one great Amazon Basin, provides a common lowland setting within which to study human and cultural variability and potentiality. Here we find a common economic adaptation of root horticulture with its strong emphasis upon bitter manioc (*Manihot utilissima*) as a source of carbohydrate, supplemented by fish protein. For more refined ecological analysis the region also offers the distinction between tropical forest and open savannah as well as gradations in form of forest and in elevation of land. Throughout the region a common economic base supports a variety of social and cultural systems with the exception of states or protostates. For the student of social structure the great attraction of the region is its variety of "smaller" structures. Relative simplicity of social structure cannot be explained away simply as a tropical forest adaptation. The West African states and the example of lowland Maya indicate that a tropical forest environment can support complex social and cultural systems. Even more pointedly, the archeology of the mouth of the Amazon suggests some "high" culture phase in the region even if only relatively short-lived (Meggers and Evans, 1957). The Amazon Basin may, indeed, have supported far greater populations in favored areas than is indicated by present Indian populations. Orellana, the first to descend the Amazon from the headwaters of the Napo River in Peru, was impressed by the unbroken line of houses along the river. He noted villages of 500 houses and unbroken lines of dwellings up to five leagues (13 miles) long.[1]

---

[1] Friar Carvajal, who accompanied Orellana, reported: ". . . the territory occupied by the subjects of this great overlord named Machiparo, which in the opinion of all extended for more than eighty leagues . . . there was not from village to village (in most cases) a crossbow shot and the one which was farthest (removed from the next) was not half a league away, and there was one settlement that stretched for five leagues without there intervening any space from house to house" (Medina, 1934, p. 198).

Thus, if we are to answer the evolutionary question of how complex social systems develop we shall have to turn to a more thorough study of social structures. In this respect, the Cubeo, who inhabit the northwest corner of the Amazon Basin, offer an example of a social structure with "advanced" features of integration and hierarchy that have, however, never quite taken hold.

Tropical forest life is not so much sylvan as it is riverine. The rivers facilitate the ceaseless flow of peoples, of splinters of communities, and of tribes along an intricate water network that binds together a virtual subcontinent. Thus, in the Amazon Basin one finds cultural traits and languages far from their ancestral sources. Not only are tropical forest cultures composite, but occasionally the tribes themselves are made up of ethnically and linguistically distinct segments. Along the river routes there are few barriers. Tribes that have adapted themselves to one corner of the basin have little difficulty in adjusting to a new location a thousand miles or more away, for even where ecologies differ the changes are neither abrupt nor drastic. Forest peoples moving on to the plains along the Orinoco Basin, for example, still have the familiar river and sylvan pattern along the river edges. Climate, vegetation, and fauna are everywhere about the same. The ease of movement and the similarity of environment account for the deposition of a common groundwork upon which all Amazon cultures are built.

One of the features of the common groundwork that defines the tropical forest as a major culture area includes slash-burn horticulture with bitter manioc as the principal but by no means the only crop. Bitter manioc offers a high yield per acre but it exhausts the soil after three to five years and demands, therefore, some kind of community circulation in which people move on, or recirculate within, a fixed zone, until new forest growth has replenished the soil. Bitter manioc, a perennial, grows readily in the Amazon Basin, but it demands a complex and time-consuming procedure for removing its poisonous prussic acid content. Manioc cultivation is almost everywhere women's work. Thus it sets a common pattern of sexual division of labor as well as a basic technology. Along the margins of the Andes, maize supplants or supplements manioc as the food crop and sets its own patterns. Maize, for example, may be regarded as a masculine crop, in which case its cultivation is more readily ritualized. But whether maize or manioc is the staple of plant diet, the tropical forest tribes, with the exception of many Ge-speaking peoples, are given over to chicha, a beer of manioc, maize, or other carbohydrate plants. Almost everywhere narcotics and excitants, stimulants and vision-producing drugs are valued for their ritual effects.

No common psychological pattern, to be sure, encompasses the area. Yet the Cubeo ritual pattern, with its exaltation of intoxication and of frenzied emotional experience, is far from uncommon in the tropical forest. In religion the Amazon Basin is a region of the shaman and of minor cults rather than of priests and of the worship of important deities. Tropical forest religion is small in scale, a feature that is parallel to and assuredly related to the decentralization of social life.

Compared with the Andes, tropical forest communities by and large are small. In many regions community size is unduly small because of severe population decline since white contact. In the Northwest Amazon, the subarea of the Cubeo, the multifamily single house is the common residence. The sense of family and of kinship are very strong, making of religion and ritual largely domestic affairs, with cults of the dead and initiation rites of outstanding importance. Considering the importance of crops, horticultural ritual is strikingly undeveloped. Here we can point to a fruitful field for the study of the commonly accepted functionalist doctrine that magic and religious ritual tend to surround areas of uncertainty such as farming. In the case of the Cubeo one can state with confidence that the lack of rite in farming is related to the strongly secular position of the women as horticulturists and not to the lack of hazard in farming. Manioc cultivation is no less uncertain than yam cultivation in the Trobriand Islands. Uncertainty, after all, is not necessarily an objective condition. Existence is uncertain for all peoples and each society has the choice of underscoring those areas of life where it believes the fears and uncertainties to lie. Since the tropical forest is one of the major world areas of the *couvade,* the rites by which the father plays a part in parturition, it might seem as though it were the fate of the newborn infant more than the fate of the crops that is at the heart of their concern.

There is the fundamental question of the relation of the tropical forest to the "high" cultures of South and of Central America. On this there is still not much to say. Yet the problem of relationship cannot be ignored. One cannot divide lowland and highland into totally distinct and unrelated worlds. The archeology of the lower Amazon calls attention to cultural developments either related to or parallel to the marginal areas of the Andes. Highland and lowland share many traits such as maize, chicha, coca, textiles, and complex basketry. The jaguar "cult" of the Northwest Amazon may well be part of the Central American and Andean jaguar distribution; perhaps the Cubeo ranked clans and ancestral cult are also part of the Andean picture. However, where there is a cultural relationship it is probable that it moves in either direction. The lowlands took from the Andes; it is likely that they gave as well. Perhaps a close study of social conditions in the tropical forest could shed specific light on the spectacular historical developments in the Andes. The way in which the Cubeo maloca, the multifamily residence, tends to become a sib ceremonial center for those sib members who have broken away from it illustrates, for example, a possible process of ceremonial center formation.

Questions of culture history are inevitably to the fore when one compares the tropical forest with the Andes. But even as a separate entity the tropical forest area commands culture-historical interest. Cubeo social structure, for example, suggests some of the ways in which small social units such as extended and joint families and lineages grow into and combine to form more complex and more highly integrated social systems. Segments of one tribe attach themselves as entities to other tribes adopting a new language. Federations of segments are formed by various combinations of adoption, adhesion, and fission; these bind themselves together by ceremonial ties and not by ordinary political means of suprachieftainship. Other processes are at work elsewhere in the region. Thus it is not difficult to imagine that detailed comparative studies of tropical forest social structures could provide a rich foundation for the reconstruction of modes of social evolution, within a fixed range of social integration. As native Africa is a natural laboratory for the study of nascent states, the South American tropical forest as a major culture area is a natural laboratory for the study of variations in a small community, and lineage and clan organization.

In the foregoing discussion my intent was to provide the reader with a broad problem setting in which the Cubeo are viewed generally as a tropical forest culture. Since tropical forest anthropology is not too widely known this seemed a useful thing to do. However, the Cubeo are more specifically a part of the Northwest Amazon subculture area. The Northwest Amazon is designated as a subarea of the tropical forest in the *Handbook of South American Indians*. Not a sharply delineated area, it includes several of the major languages of lowland South America: Arawakan, Cariban, Tucanoan, Witotoan, and Macú. Of these language groups, Tucanoan (the language of the Cubeo), Witotoan, and Macú are restricted to the Northwest Amazon and were until recently listed as unclassified languages

(Beuchat and Rivet, 1911; Mason, 1950). A new classification now places Macú with Tucanoan in a Macro-Tucanoan subfamily, and both, together with Arawakan, in a larger Andean-Equatorial family. In this new classification Witotoan is, together with Cariban, part of a Macro-Cariban subfamily under a larger Ge-Pano-Cariban family (Greenberg, 1960). Culturally, the Tucanoans fall into two groups, an eastern one to which the Cubeo belong and a western one about which we know relatively little. Information on the Arawakan and Cariban tribes in the area is somewhat fuller, but still lacking in necessary detail on social structure and cultural patterns. The Witotoans are somewhat better known through the work of Whiffen and of Preuss, while the Tucuna, who speak an isolated tongue, have been professionally described by Nimuendajú. The present volume on the Cubeo attempts a more comprehensive account of the social life and social structure of a Northwest Amazon tribe. Thus the characterization of the area based upon criteria other than those of material culture rests mainly upon our knowledge of the Witotoans, the Tucuna, and the writer's field work among the Cubeo. The presence of well-developed patrilineal sibs among the Cubeo, Witotoans, and Tucuna, elaborate initiation rites, secret rites involving sacred trumpets, the use of bark-cloth masks in mourning ceremonies, and the single large house constituting the community are some of the traits that set this area apart. All of these traits, it should be said, occur outside the area as well but not in quite the same combination.

By cultural criteria the Achagua also belong in the Northwest Amazon area. This large group of Arawakan-speaking peoples, occupying an extensive area on the Colombian-Venezuelan border along the Meta, Vichada, Guaviare, and Orinoco rivers, bears some striking resemblances to the Cubeo (Steward and Faron, 1959, p. 356 ff.). These Arawakans share such traits as the exogamic patrilineal sibs, the communal dwellings, and the secret male cult of the Tucanoans. Economy and material culture are also similar, although in the tropical forest such similarities are of no great significance since they seem almost to blanket the region. Even so, on the score of subsistence the Achagua have the distinctive maize and bean complex of the highlands while the Tucanoans and their Arawakan neighbors have maize but not beans. Since patrilineal sibs are not common in the tropical forest, the Northwest area stands out strikingly in this respect. Prior to 1940 patrilineal sibs had been identified among the Witotoans only (Whiffen, 1915). The writer reported them for the Cubeo of the Cuduiarí on the basis of his field work (Goldman, 1948). Nimuendajú, in a report published in 1950, independently identified the social organizations of the Vaupés River as patrilineal sibs, and more recently a young Colombian anthropologist, Marcos Fulop (1954), described a patrilineal sib organization with a phratric grouping among the Tucano Indians. Work on the patrilineal Yagua and the Tucuna was also done after 1940. Before 1940 Kirchoff (1931), using the then best available information, had incorrectly characterized the Northwest Amazon region as based upon bilateral kingroups that favored patrilocal residence.

If we are to conceive of the Northwest Amazon as a geographic region then the Macú must also be included. Macú is a catchall name for very simple nonhorticultural peoples whose center seems to be the Rio Negro but who have been moving westward into the Vaupés-Caquetá area (Métraux, 1948). There they have either been assimilated in the Tucanoan- and Arawakan-speaking tribes or have lived among these more powerful tribes as servants or "slaves" or in some other symbiotic relationship. The *Bahúkiwa* sibs of the Cubeo acknowledged Macú ancestry and may well have been, as Koch-Grünberg has claimed, one of the assimilated Macú groups. The Macú are shorter in stature than the other Indians in the region. They lack fixed residences, the hammock, and the canoe. If the Macú languages are truly, as Greenberg (1960) has suggested, Macro-Tucanoan, they are not an altogether alien group among their more culturally advanced neighbors. The Macú, however, have not been studied at all so that we do not know whether they are to be considered a remnant of very early nonhorticulturists or as uprooted people who had given up farming. The tropical forest has a number of examples of the latter case. *Bahúkiwa* traditions, on the other hand, refer to a prehorticultural period.

Since our knowledge of the tribes of the entire Northwest Amazon drainage, including the basin of the Rio Negro, is so slight, too much importance cannot be attached to "Northwest Amazon" as a subculture type. However, the entire Northwest Amazon region, which includes an area somewhat greater than the cultural area designated in the *Handbook of South American Indians* (Steward, 1948), has unusual potential interest, potential in the sense that the ethnological problems it poses can become real only after further field work has clarified the state of cultural patterns and cultural institutions there. This northwest quadrant of the Amazon Basin is open to the entire lower Amazon and has, at the same time, contact with the eastern margins of Andean cultures as well as with the southern margins of the Circum-Caribbean cultures. That is to say, on its northern and western flanks it is subject to influences from more highly developed societies. In reconstructing tropical forest culture history, note must be taken of the extraordinary ease of cultural transfers over the entire area. For this reason alone knowledge of total cultural systems seems essential. As matters stand now, much reconstruction must be based upon the very unreliable foundation of trait comparisons. What has been of special interest in my study of the Cubeo has been the way in which some widespread cultural traits, particularly masked dances, harvest rites, and sacred trumpets, have been taken up and fitted into distinctive cultural patterns with a focus in an ancestral cult.

The Northwest Amazon region is bounded on the south by the Amazon, from where it is joined by the Rio Negro eastward to where the Marañón issues from the Andes. The Guaviare River is its northern boundary, the Andean cordillera bounds it in the west, and the Rio Negro in the east. The principal rivers of the region are the Caquetá, Apaporis, Tiquié, Papurý, Isana, Vaupés (known in Brazil as the Caiarý), Cuduiarí, Querarí, Aiarí, Tie, and Guainía. All drain into the Amazon. Ecologically, the Northwest Amazon is sharply differentiated only from the neighboring Andean region to the west and to a lesser degree from the open prairie or llanos on its northern side. Eastward it fades into the flatter and lower-lying forests of the Amazon. Its southern margin is fixed only by an arbitrary river boundary. It is a densely wooded region of tall trees closely packed and interlaced with vines and lianas. At the river edges the forest growth is lower and more brushlike. It is also an elevated region whose streams are punctuated by hazardous cataracts. On the Vaupés, between Yuruparí and the Rio Negro, Dr. Hamilton Rice (1910) counted 30 major cataracts and 60 small ones. The cataracts (*cachoeiras*) are for the Indians focal points of residence. Traditional sites, they often mark tribal and sib boundaries. Every cataract has its petroglyphs that depict mythical figures still known to the Indians. In some areas, as I have observed, the residents of the *cachoeiras* freshen the petroglyphs from time to time with deepening incisions. The rapids are more of a navigational hazard to the European traveler than to the Indians, who are expert canoemen and whose light craft is easily portaged. Dr. Rice, who knew a good deal about the Amazon, declared the Cubeo to be the most expert canoemen on the river. I can also testify to their coolness and skill in navigating their small dugout canoes, that have only an inch or two of freeboard, through the twisting boulder-strewn channel of a thundering rapids.

The land slopes abruptly eastward. In its western part the area is often a tumble of ravine-cut hills, exposed rock, and swamp. The Vaupés flows past high, open, uninhabited mesas. Scattered hills of

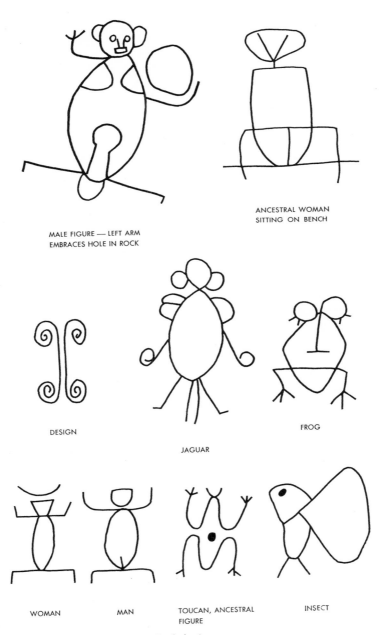

MALE FIGURE — LEFT ARM
EMBRACES HOLE IN ROCK

ANCESTRAL WOMAN
SITTING ON BENCH

DESIGN

JAGUAR

FROG

WOMAN   MAN   TOUCAN, ANCESTRAL
                       FIGURE

INSECT

Fig. 1. Petroglyphs on the Cuduiarí.

igneous rock dot the country. These hills seem to have little interest for the Cubeo, but the mesas with their sandstone caves are held to be the dwellings of dangerous demons.

Fish are generally abundant and are represented by hundreds of species. The favorite of all tribes is the aracú, which the Indians commonly smoke to preserve. The piranha and the river anaconda are the constant river hazards. The piranha seem always to be present, as can be proved by throwing animal entrails into the river. The waste is hit by the fish almost instantly and devoured within minutes. The Indians, however, do not dread either the anaconda or the piranha, but when preparing to bathe they circumspectly drum the surface of the water with their cupped hands to drive these creatures off. The river anaconda reaches a length of over 20 feet and is regarded as dangerous only in the vicinity of submerged trees, which it uses for leverage in seizing a victim and pulling him under. However, children who play constantly in such waters are aware of the hazard but are not afraid, nor are their elders anxious for them. I heard of no specific cases of injury from either piranha or anaconda. The man-eating cayman of the sluggish llanos rivers is absent here and the smaller cayman is a minor hazard.

The Northwest Amazon has its share of tropical forest game, although, as Lord Wallace observed (1870, p. 446), the Amazon is a mammal-poor region. The jaguar is feared in its supernatural aspect only. The peccary, until recently hunted by a group of men armed with spears, is acknowledged to be dangerous and aggressive when challenged. The tapir will also charge when annoyed, but neither animal fills the Indian with dread. For the rest, the forest game is small and shy. It consists of the small red deer, the rodents such as paca, capybara, and agouti, the raccoon-like coati, monkeys, and armadillo. River otters are common but are not molested. When they surround a canoe with their excited barking the Indians greet them with a discreet silence and wait for them to submerge again. Bird life is rich but of small economic importance.

All visitors to the region have described vividly their unpleasant encounters with its insect life. The Indians are made equally miserable by the swarms of pium gnats and sand flies. Careless scratching of an insect bite produces dangerous ulcerations. I have seen Indians who had lost several square feet of skin from such spreading ulcers. Chigger (*neguas*) hygiene is a preoccupation of all residents of the Northwest Amazon. The Indians are expert in expelling the spherical sacs with a deft pressure from a stick or knife blade. In the forest the sting of the red ant bothers the naked Indians more than the clothed visitor. On the other hand, the leaf-cutter ant is a specialist on clothing. I was once covered by a swarm of these ants while asleep. When I had carefully removed the last of them I was left with but a leather belt and a few tatters of trousers and shirt.

The anopheles mosquito is generally absent in the Cuduiarí region where I did my field work. On the whole, the health of the Cuduiarí Indians is good. Carate (purú), a skin pigment disorder apparently of spirochete origin, common everywhere else in the Northwest Amazon, was far less in evidence on the Cuduiarí. Children suffered from worms and other intestinal parasites but infant mortality was not particularly high. There were no epidemics during my stay. The recollections of the Indians about serious illness go back to the 1918 influenza epidemic that apparently ravaged the native populations in the region. Women, in particular, suffered from the painful purulent conjunctivitis, which they attributed to insect molestation in their manioc gardens. The bloated abdomens of children whose diet is too generous with carbohydrate and deficient in protein is a common sight along the Vaupés, but is less evident on the Cuduiarí, where native life and diet is still almost intact. As for the Cuduiarí itself, the people at the mouth of the river, the higher-ranking *Hehénewa* sibs, seemed generally more sturdy, vigorous, and aggressive than the Indians who lived upstream.

Dr. Hamilton Rice, who explored the Vaupés in 1907–08, observed that the most physically powerful Indians came from the Cuduiarí. He noted men who were six feet tall and over, strongly built with thick arms and powerful torsos. Actually somatological variability is considerable on the Cuduiarí, ranging from marked mesomorphy to moderate ectomorphy. But this observation of mine is not based on measurements. Dr. Rice (1910) has published a physical description of the Cubeo based upon anthropometric observations. I quote from it:

Their color is an olive brown corresponding to No. 4 of Broca's scale and seems invariable, a conclusion based on a comparison of the scale with many hundreds of subjects on parts of the cuticle least exposed to sun and pigmented decoration. The eye is dark, palpebral fissure narrow, not oblique, pointed at its external aspect, and the upper lid so heavy at times as to suggest the puffiness of oedema; but the eye by no means conforms invariably to so Mongolian a criterion, closely resembling the European eye in many other cases. The hair is black, lanky, coarse in the male, fine and glossy in the female. The faces are escutcheon-shaped and hairless, the chins rounded and receding, noses from straight and busque to hooked and Chinese flat types, region of cheek bones flat, lower lips large and inclined to turn slightly downward. The ears are not large, lobes absent or slightly developed; heads of the brachycephalic type; though I have noticed cases of extreme dolichocephalic variations. Teeth are generally poor.

Dr. Rice also commented on the capacity of the Cubeo Indians for great exertion on a minimum of food and rest. I can corroborate this judgment. I accompanied Indians on canoe trips when we paddled for as long as 17 consecutive hours with little rest or nourishment other than a handful of manioc meal in water. There was usually no urgent necessity for such exertion or privation. The Indians customarily eat lightly when traveling, and if there is any chance of reaching home rather than camping out or imposing upon the hospitality of another sib they prefer to keep going. However, it was not unusual for strong young men to topple from their canoes in a dead faint upon reaching home. Revived by the river they scrambled ashore, secured the canoe, and entered the house with the appropriate vigorous air, effectively concealing their acute fatigue. It is in fact characteristic of the Cubeo to make light of their accomplishments and not to yield readily to physical weakness.

Ethnographically, the Northwest Amazon was first fully brought to light by Dr. Theodor Koch-Grünberg, ethnographer and museum collector. Koch-Grünberg's systematic survey of the region at the turn of the century covered all main tribes and their settlements along the principal rivers. He spent many weeks on the Cuduiarí among the *Hehénewa* sibs of the Cubeo, and ascended the Cuduiarí to the limits of its habitation (1909). His published reports are invaluable even though he never stayed long enough in one place to get a deep grasp of the culture. He was, however, an excellent observer and reported fully on language, custom, and material culture. I did not read Koch-Grünberg before going to the field so that my observations are totally independent. It is a source of satisfaction, therefore, that our observations agree closely on most details. Koch-Grünberg's information was deficient on social structure and ceremonial patterns. It is in these two respects that my study represents a carrying forward of the work he so ably began. I have drawn freely upon his published works to fill in gaps in my own information on the Cubeo and of course for the rich data on surrounding Tucanoan, Arawakan, and Cariban tribes. His was the pioneering survey of the entire region, whereas mine is a relatively limited study of a single community. Koch-Grünberg died among the Indians of the Northwest Amazon in 1924, his ethnographic work prematurely cut off.

The first scientific observer to report on the Indians of the Vaupés was Alfred Russell Wallace (1870), who was there in 1853. While his interests were mainly those of the naturalist, he found Indian life to be interesting and he recorded tribal distributions and physical conditions of life as well as many customs. It is to Wallace that we owe the first report on mortuary endocannibalism among the Cubeo. Curiously, this information has never been properly authenticated. Wallace learned about it at second hand, as did Koch-Grünberg many years later. I observed what I thought to be this custom, but I could not verify that the bones being prepared for imbibing with chicha were human. The annoyance of the Indians when I accidentally came upon them while they were reducing bones to meal and pouring it into the chicha at the conclusion of a mourning ceremony led me to suspect that the bones were human. In response to my questions, however, no Cubeo would confirm my conjectures.

Wallace (1870, p. 354) traveled up the Vaupés to the mouth of the Cuduiarí River at the rapids of Uaracapurí, where he observed a community of several malocas. He did not enter the Cuduiarí, reporting only that to his knowledge no European had ever gone up that river. As for the Vaupés, this river, particularly in its Brazilian reaches, had in Wallace's time already become an important artery of European trade. Along the Isana River Wallace noted that the Indians were living in European-style dwellings. The Cuduiarí then had the reputation of a totally wild region. The Cubeo Indians seen by Wallace were still wearing large circular wooden plugs in their ears. By 1903, in the time of Koch-Grünberg, this form of male ornamentation had already been given up.

Curt Nimuendajú surveyed the Isana, Aiarí, and Vaupés rivers in 1927. In his notes, published posthumously in 1950, it is revealed that he correctly identified Tucano and Cubeo descent groups as patrilineal clans. He did not, however, enter the Cuduiarí, and his information on that river, being secondhand, is not too reliable.

My own field work on the Cuduiarí began in September 1939 and continued through June 1940. (Goldman, 1948, is a preliminary report.) The Cuduiarí had the advantage of being relatively accessible and as yet almost completely unacculturated. I decided upon the Cuduiarí after a survey of the Cubeo communities along the Vaupés.

CULTURE CHANGE

Cubeo culture has been subjected to acculturative influences from two sources, one from other Indian tribes and the other from European, Colombian, and Brazilian missionaries, settlers, traders, and latex extractors. Cultural interchange among Indian tribes in the Northwest Amazon region is, of course, an old and intricate process, the details of which are as yet incompletely known. At one point or another Cubeo culture resembles virtually that of any other tropical forest tribe of the Amazon Basin. But to point this out is simply another way of calling attention to the common underlying character of all tropical forest cultures. More specifically, one is aware of the strong Tupían influences observable in such traits as the large communal house, a system of fortification, slavery, extended patrilineal families, and the practice of giving a child the name of an ancestor. The Tupían intrusion up the headwaters of the Amazon and its tributaries is probably quite old. Of more recent date and a more striking example of acculturation from native sources is the Arawakan influence. In the relationships between Arawakan-speaking tribes and Tucanoans there has been the opportunity for massive interchange of cultural features, for apart from the ordinary modes of cultural influence, of trading, visiting, and intermarrying, entire social segments, usually sibs, it would seem, have been accepted as entities into one another's tribal organization. Since sib relations in the region are founded upon intensive reciprocal ceremonial participation, it is inevitable that entire ceremonial complexes will be exchanged once a foreign group has been drawn into the social structure. That the social structures will also become mutually compatible may be taken for granted. The student of Cubeo is almost instantly aware of the Arawakan influence, in vocabulary and in religious concepts. The Cubeo culture hero *Kúwai* is the Arawakan *Kówai*. The term for jaguar and for shaman, *yaví*, is shared by Tucanoans and Arawakans. As Koch-Grünberg was the first to observe (1909, I, 129 ff.), the complex mourning ceremonies among Cubeo and among Arawakan-speaking tribes are also remarkably similar.

It was Koch-Grünberg who called attention to the rapidity of culture interchange in the Northwest Amazon. On the Papurý River he encountered Tariana Indians who were giving up their native Arawakan, having just arrived from the Isana, and were beginning to speak Tucanoan (1909, I, 116). Similarly he reported that a Cariban-speaking Umaua group had settled among Cubeo of the upper Vaupés and had begun to speak Tucanoan (1909, II, 65). On the Cuduiarí River the *Hürüwá* had given up Arawakan in favor of the dominant Tucanoan (1909, II, 81). On the Querarí River the *Djurémawa* had also yielded up Arawakan for Tucanoan (1909, II, 66). Macú also had assimilated both to Arawakan and to Tucanoan (1909, I, 50, II, 98). How fleeting these language shifts can be is brought out by Koch-Grünberg's example of an Arawakan group that had assimilated to Tucanoan and was almost immediately shifting back to Arawakan, so that the young people were still Tucanoan speakers while their elders were already back to Arawakan (1909, I, 116). Where Arawakan and Tucanoan coexist, Koch-Grünberg has observed, Arawakan becomes the language of ritual and Tucanoan the everyday language (1909, II, 182).

In general the region of the Vaupés, the only part of the Northwest Amazon that I can speak of from personal knowledge, exhibits a high degree of cultural cosmopolitanism. Many Indians are multilingual because of the frequency of intermarriage with other linguistic groups and the love of the Indians for travel and intertribal trade. Not only do the Indians have some knowledge of the standard languages in the region, but they also employ the *lingoa geral*, a lingua franca based on Tupían, and many are conversant with Spanish and Portuguese. As they adopt languages the Indians also adopt new customs; these are always welcomed, almost in the same way in which women eagerly acquire from one another new varieties of manioc, or in the way in which men and women collect and try to cultivate almost anything that grows. This, in short, is not a region of cultural conservatism. Having freshly arrived from an ethnographic survey in the Colombian Andes, I was literally overwhelmed by the contrast between the secretiveness and wariness of the highland Indians and the openness and friendliness of the Cubeo.

Of course, the question of cultural relations between Tucanoans and Arawakans is one of great complexity and uncertainty. We have only the most general knowledge of these relations; but even this provides a very useful background for understanding the nature of Indian-white relations and of Cubeo acculturation. The essential point in this background would seem to be what I have called the Indian's cosmopolitanism. I speak now only for the Indians of the Cuduiarí. There, it has seemingly provided a strong measure of immunity against the potentially overwhelming effects of European contacts.

The Northwest Amazon has been subject to persistent white influence from the sixteenth century onward.[2] As early as 1557 Francisco Perez de Quesada founded the community of Mocoa on the Caquetá River. The Dominicans entered the region in 1550, the Franciscans some 20 years later. Prior to their expulsion in 1767 the Jesuits founded many missions on the Orinoco, on the Meta, on the Casanare, on the Guaviare, and on the Vichada. On the Vaupés proper the first mission was founded in 1852 at Carurú by P. Gregorio, a Carmelite.

---

[2] For historical background consult: Archivo do Amazonas, 1906; Bauer, 1919; Coudreau, 1886–87, II, 153 ff., for missions on the Vaupés; Gumilla, 1791; Koch-Grünberg, 1909; Martius, 1867, I, 591 ff.

He succeeded in bringing together a village of some 300 Indians. By 1881 the mission was disbanded and the Indians returned to their original communities. At about the same time the mission of Santa Cruz dos Cobeus was established at Mitú *cachoeira* near the Cuduiarí. Missionary activity in the region has been generally discontinuous but nonetheless energetic; and while Christian doctrine has left only a vague imprint in native religious practices it has succeeded in acquainting the Indians with new ideas of dress and in disturbing their convictions about some practices such as cannibalism. For a period between 1875 and the early 1900's there was a flurry of nativist agitation in the Vaupés. Between 1875 and 1878 an Indian from the Isana River, called Anizetto, reportedly a hermaphrodite, led a messianic movement against the whites until he was arrested by the Brazilian authorities. In 1880 a shaman who called himself Vicente Cristo led another messianic movement along the middle Vaupés. Koch-Grünberg observed that the native messianic leaders were always Arawakan-speaking (1809, I, 39). There is nothing to suggest that any of these movements ever took strong hold on the Indians. On the Cuduiarí tangible evidences either of Christian influence or of native messianism were slight in 1940.

European commercial penetration started slowly but reached a sudden expansion with the rubber boom that subsided shortly before World War I. The Putumayo, where thousands of Indians perished in the rubber camps, was a notorious and baleful focus of white influence (Hardenburg, 1912). From then on the Indians and the whites along the Vaupés were in constant contact and in frequent conflict. On the lower Vaupés in Brazilian territory many Indian tribes had taken on the outward appearance of the mestizo, or caboclo as he is called in Brazil, as early as 1852, when Wallace was there. The upper Vaupés in Colombian territory retained its true Indian character for very much longer. The Cuduiarí was still very strongly native at the time of my field work in 1939–40.

Only close study will reveal how far acculturation has gone even among those Indians most closely associated with the whites on the main streams. There the Indians wear the dress of the mestizo, live in European-style shacks, and celebrate the Christian holidays. They also carry out native ceremonials, not, to be sure, with the traditional elegance, but strongly enough to suggest that a good deal of native life goes on beneath the shabby surface of ragged clothing, poor housing, and the litter of cheap manufactured utensils and ornaments.

The resistance of the Indians of the Cuduiarí to cultural loss and breakdown may be attributed in the main to relative isolation, but in part, I believe, to cosmopolitanism, to the capability of the Indians to adopt foreign objects and foreign customs without losing their sense of identity as Indian. As long as the point of view remains Indian, the culture may change but it will still retain for the Indian a distinctive and satisfying pattern. It is when the clear identification as Indian in the cultural sense is lost that change is likely to mean breakdown.

Cosmopolitanism is but one general factor in a process of culture change that is exceedingly intricate and subtle, in which there are no clear-cut stages but endless gradations in the transition from Indian to the new cultural and psychological entity that emerges. Another general factor is the white agent. On the Cuduiarí the white man does not intrude directly upon the Indian's daily life. The missionary expects the Indian to come to him at the mission station. Even then the missionary effort is a patient one. Mainly it goes through the children who are educated at the mission school. Mission Indians and tribal Indians lead different lives but they are not mutually antagonistic. Between them there is a gradation but not a gap.

The commercial white man, the rubber collector (*balatero*), or the trader has only a limited interest in the Indians. The Indian, having completed his contract work in the rubber forest, returns to his own community and is instantly enmeshed in the tribal life. But even in the rubber forests his associates have been fellow Indians, of foreign tribes, to be sure, but to this experience the Indian has been well accustomed. As for the white employer, he is often less a carrier of European culture than he is a frontiersman, a distinct tropical forest product himself. He is partly Indianized and he is generally the husband of an Indian wife.

Among the Mundurucú of central Brazil, as vividly described by Robert Murphy (1960), an anthropologist, work in the rubber forests and the contractual production of farinha, a manioc flour, for the white man were potent factors in the disruption, indeed in the virtual obliteration, of the native culture. To compare Mundurucú with Cubeo is to set off a society that has become ugly and disordered with its meager hoard of cheap objects of white manufacture with a well-ordered and fundamentally satisfying way of life. Unlike the Mundurucú, the Cubeo have succeeded in withstanding both the rubber forest and manioc trade. Far from being overcome, the Cubeo have been able to use the income from labor in the rubber forests and from the sale of farinha to further their own cultural objectives. Murphy tells of the insatiable longing of the Mundurucú for the trinkets and gadgets of the white trader. For these objects of intrinsically little value the Mundurucú yielded up much of their freedom and culture. Perhaps, in their case, the addiction to the white man's trinkets was already a sign of social disorganization, a substitute for the native values that had already been lost. The Cubeo, too, desired trinkets, but in moderation. Native ornaments were still preferred. As for household utensils, the Cubeo were spared the degradation of the five-gallon gasoline-tin water bucket and the flimsy metal pots. With only minor exceptions all native crafts were fully alive. What seems to have immunized the Cubeo against the pernicious effects of overtrade with the whites was the vigor of the social system, that demanded a heavy commitment of time and effort in the production of manioc beer for intersib gatherings, and the binding nature of ceremonial gift exchanges. When the basic patterns of Cubeo social life are broken they, too, will undoubtedly follow the miserable road of the Mundurucú, who once shared a common culture with them.

Throughout the region a first step in culture change is observable in dress and in housing. When the Indian takes to living in a small mestizo-style house and to wearing European-style clothing he has taken a long step toward cultural transformation. Dress and housing impress him as key signs of cultural identification. On the other hand, when he acquires a steel machete, a shotgun, fishhooks, or ornaments he usually does so to enrich his own way of life. The change in house form is the more significant because the long maloca is not only a residence but a ceremonial center to which most of the traditional ceremonies have been adapted. These ceremonies cannot be easily conducted in the small square house. With respect to dress there are stages of acculturation. Nudity is a mark of total unself-consciousness. As late as 1903 there were still sizable Indian populations in the upper Vaupés and all over the Cuduiarí where the women were totally naked and the men wore only the perineal band of dark bark cloth (Koch-Grünberg, 1909). In the first change that occurred, the women began to wear petticoats in the presence of white visitors. This concession to the white man's sensibilities involved no important change in outlook. It was, if anything, a reflection of traditional cosmopolitanism. Subsequently, the women accepted the petticoat as ornamental, wearing it constantly and dressing up in a fresh petticoat for native ceremonies. This is the present situation on the Cuduiarí and along much of the upper Vaupés. Those women whose outlook had become more Europeanized turned to the dress and to covering their breasts. Men's clothing styles followed a similar sequence. Most men who have worked in the rubber forests have acquired trousers and have learned to wear them when they visit the administrative center of Mitú. Some men have learned to wear trousers and a cotton tunic at home. For ceremony, however, they wear only the perineal band, now made of trade cloth. For women the skirt has replaced the ornamental ceremonial apron, but for men ceremonial participation in trousers means an important change in outlook in which the ceremony has become secularized. I learned this from young Indian men, visitors to the Cuduiarí, who, wearing the cotton trousers and tunic of the mestizo, insisted in explaining to me that they were taking part in dances "just for fun." In the truly solemn ceremonies on the Cuduiarí I saw no man in European dress.

The use of Spanish or Portuguese is another sign of change in cultural identification. But here, too, the process is complex. Indian cosmopolitanism is traditionally multilingual. Wives often speak distinct dialects of Tucanoan or else speak Cariban or Arawakan. Children learn the language of the mother first and then learn to speak Cubeo. The Tupían lingua franca has been a traditional trade language between Indians as well as between Indian and white for a very long time. Thus, the Indian who has learned Spanish and Portuguese is simply extending his multilingualism. These European languages have also come to play an important role in native interrelationships. Spanish and/or Portuguese has become the customary language of violent drunken quarrels among men at a drinking party. Used in this context the insults and threats in a foreign language are less ominous, and easier, therefore, to disregard than the same words uttered in the native language. The Cubeo usage is as with us: the foreign phrase used scatologically modifies the impact. Thus, in this respect the Cubeo adoption of foreign European phrases is a matter of enriching the native culture and is far from being a mark of cultural breakdown. I met only a few Indians on the Vaupés and none on the Cuduiarí who had given up their native speech in favor of Spanish or Portuguese.

The use of European personal names offers another example of adaptation to the native cultural pattern. Among the Cubeo, personal names come from the traditional genealogy of the sib. They have a sacred character and are not used freely. Knowing a person's sib name is a sign of intimacy and such intimacy is not readily yielded up. I did not learn native personal names for weeks, and even at the end, one of the more embarrassing questions I could ask was simply a person's sib name. In common discourse kinship designations were used. The native name is not so much an appellation as it is sib identification. The headman of the *Bahúkiwa* sib was the first to tell me his name. He uttered it in a whisper close to my ear. Thus, for the Cubeo, being endowed with a Spanish or Portuguese name is one of the most exciting and valued gifts he can get from a white man. It is a benefice he cherishes far more than the white man can possibly appreciate. It has a double value, as a gift and as a free medium of appellation. I met no Indian no matter how unacculturated who did not have a European name. To have value the name should be bestowed by a white man. When I bestowed names upon newborn children, as well as upon youngsters who were still unnamed, I was asked to give the genealogical references for the name from my own family line. I learned of no Indian child on the Cuduiarí who had a European name that had not been bestowed upon him by a white man, and the Indians remembered the genealogical references. It cannot be said that the possession of a European name gave the Indian an actual sense of kinship with the white man, for which far more than a name would be required. But the name did serve to offset to some degree the conventional estrangement between Indian and white.

On the whole, culture change on the Vaupés and along its tributaries has been gradual except for those instances where missionaries have brought Indians together into a mission village. In 1940 the European economy of the Vaupés had no strong interest in a "civilized" Indian. The exploitation of wild rubber — there were no cultivated rubber plantations in the region — was on a small scale for which the labor of "wild" Indians was altogether suitable. Nor did the undeveloped economy of Mitú call for disciplined Indian labor. At the level at which the economy of the Vaupés had developed in 1940 the Indian was of greater value in his native state, simply because as an Indian and completely self-sufficient he was at least no burden upon the meager resources of an underdeveloped frontier area.

Many Indians of the Cuduiarí had visited Mitú, the capital of the Comisaría of the Vaupés. Mitú was established as the capital in 1936. Before that it was a small trading center and missionary station. After 1936 it began to acquire the features of an important administrative center (Plazas Olarte, 1944). By 1939 it had an administration building, a school for Indian children, a medical dispensary, a new missionary order, partly Colombian and partly French, a radio station, a landing wharf for a monthly military hydroplane, and a police garrison. The population, numbering about 1,000, consisted mainly of Colombians, a few Brazilians, and a floating group of Indians drawn to the administrative center by curiosity or by some business. Many Indian women lived there as wives of white men.

While the Indians of the Vaupés and of the Cuduiarí were not altogether comfortable in Mitú, because of their shyness in dealing with its white residents, they had no reason not to regard it as a friendly place. The *Comisaría* protected their labor rights, supervising terms of contract and entertaining their complaints of unfair treatment. When an Indian completed his term of labor he was "paid off" in the presence of an official in charge of Indian affairs. The Indians regarded the government as fair. The *Comisaría* provided medical aid to those Indians who came to seek it. At the same time it respected native life and interfered with the Indians as little as possible. Although the Cuduiarí is readily accessible from Mitú it was entered only rarely by administrative personnel. When I lived among the *Bahúkiwa* some 15 hours by canoe from Mitú, I had the sense of total isolation from this administrative center. The normal everyday life on the Cuduiarí was completely Indian. In the time of Wallace there had been bad blood between Indians and Colombians, but by the time Koch-Grünberg arrived relations between the Cubeo and the government had already become peaceable.

In Mitú I met Mandú, headman of the *Bahúkiwa* sib of the middle Cuduiarí. He had come to seek medical treatment for his young son, who had injured his knee in a fall. The headman and I became friends and he invited me to visit. When I promptly accepted his invitation I was surprised to find that he had already begun to build a house for me and that the Indians had expected me to settle among them. He had discussed the matter with his people, he told me later, and they had agreed that it would be good to have me live among them. The reasons for wanting me never became too clear, but I came to believe that they thought I would offer them some protection from the pressure of the labor recruiters.

I was informally "adopted" as the younger brother of Mandú. For a while people were amused to address me by an appropriate kinship term. In time this jest lost its freshness and I came to be regarded simply as *pakomá* (kinsman). Nevertheless, I was considered to be a member of Mandú's household even though I had a house of my own alongside the maloca. Mandú sent his older wife, with whom he was no longer living, to serve as my cook. With Mandú's household I had all the privileges of informality. My relations with other households were friendly but more restrained. Since I did not contribute an appropriate share of fish and game to the household, or to the maloca as a whole, I felt obliged to reciprocate food and services with periodic gifts of cloth, tobacco, fishhooks, and ammunition. At one time during a drinking party at which I was not present, a son of Mandú distributed all my trade goods to the guests "in my behalf." However, during the period of many weeks when I no longer had trade goods my status in the community was as before. I still could count upon food and services.

I participated to some degree in the male life of the community and came to learn the language and the culture as much by slow enculturation as by questioning. I had no principal informants because no one would serve in that capacity. All were willing to talk, to explain matters to me, but only in the accustomed atmosphere of easy and genial chatter. The people I knew best and the household of Mandú, in particular, were paradoxically the poorest systematic informants. They were most impatient and most easily vexed with the informant role. They regarded the open notebook and the persistent line of questioning as counter to our relationship. For prolonged and probing investigations I called upon the head of a *Bahúkiwa* subsib. Even this man was a very patient informant only when he was my guest among the *Bahúkiwa*. On his home grounds we were back on small talk. In Mitú I could talk to Indian women more freely than I could on the Cuduiarí, where my relations with them had to be more correct. My house alongside the maloca was an informal social center which children and unattached women felt free to visit without invitation. The children taught me things they thought I ought to know about native customs. This was a privilege they had which adults, with their acute tactfulness about criticizing, intruding, or imposing upon others, could not exercise.

The Indians placed no serious obstacles in the way of my studies. They would not explain or discuss openly a ritual act at the time it was going on because to do so would be to counteract its effects. They did not, however, mind answering questions later and in a more general context. Moreover, they expected me to preserve the proprieties of tact in asking questions about domestic matters. Sex was a difficult subject, as were invidious comparisons. The Cubeo are not eager purveyors of gossip. After trouble had erupted in the open one could ask for and receive a discreet and sober account of some domestic difficulty. At the same time that the Indians imposed upon me their own reserve they were also sensitive to any evident disappointment when my questions went unanswered. Thus, if I persisted I often could get an answer, but I had to follow protocol, since personal relations among adults are rich in decorum and social etiquette. I also had available to me the more informal channels of the play pack of children, which delighted in passing on some household gossip, as well as of old women, whose verbal bawdiness was in marked contrast to the customary verbal restraint of the men on sexual matters.

I chose to stay in one community and to benefit from the intimacy that such an identification gives one. Had I chosen to move from one sib to another I would have had a better account of the formal principles of social structure but at the expense of a knowledge of the patterns of cultural life. My choice of the *Bahúkiwa* among all the Cubeo sibs was partly, as I have explained, fortuitous, but the site, halfway up the Cuduiarí, had its advantages in giving me some command of events along the entire river.

The reader, however, will understand that this study has a special perspective. Although I have made some effort to present "Cubeo," the point of view is unavoidably that of the *Bahúkiwa*, a low-ranking sib and perhaps even an alien sib of probable Macú ancestry. Strictly speaking, a Cubeo perspective can be only an artificial composite pieced together and generalized from the distinctive perspectives of each of its principal sibs. I would imagine that the Cubeo presented from the point of view of the *Hehénewa*, a high-ranking sib, would bring out somewhat more emphasis upon social status and upon the authority of the headman. One wonders how the Cubeo would appear if studied from the point of view of those of its sibs now along the Querarí that were once Arawakan-speaking; or if studied from the point of view of those Cubeo-speaking sibs that now form one of the phratries of the Tucano tribe.

The theoretical position of a study is best understood from what the writer does with the material. What he claims to be doing with it is far less important. My own theoretical viewpoint will emerge from the text and more explicitly from the final summation or conclusion. At this point it should be sufficient to say that my purpose is to present the Cubeo in terms of fundamental principles of social structure and in terms of basic cultural patterns. I have chosen a level of description and of analysis that lies between the idiosyncratic and the universal. The detailed account of person and of personal reaction is an example of the idiosyncratic, and the analysis of a culture as an apparatus for the satisfaction of "basic human needs" is an example of the universal. The idiosyncratic and the universal approaches are pancultural. One deals with individual responses that can occur in any society, the other deals with cultural functions that are true of all societies. The level of description chosen here is intended to set the Cubeo apart as a particular social and cultural type and yet to allow bases for cross-cultural comparison with other societies on its cultural level.

Finally, it is necessary to say that this study is incomplete. It had been my hope to do a restudy. When this hope did not seem realizable it was obviously better to submit an incomplete report on the Cubeo than not to submit one at all.

1

The Cubeo Community

The Cubeo Indians occupy a string of settlements along a small stretch of the Vaupés River from Uarúa Lake upstream to Uaracapurí and downstream to near the Brazilian border, as well as along several of the Vaupés tributaries, namely the Cuduiarí and the Querarí and Pirabatón. The tribe consists of some 30 or more patrilineal, exogamous sibs[1] that are grouped into three unnamed confederations or phratries of unequal size that are also exogamous. Although the bulk of the Cubeo now live on the smaller streams — the Cuduiarí, in particular, being heavily populated — the broad Vaupés, that joins with the Rio Negro to enter the Amazon, is regarded by the Indians as their main stream and as their source. Their leading sibs still live there. Native traditions place the emergence of all the Cubeo sibs at two Vaupés sites, at the turbulent cataracts of Yuruparí and of Uaracapurí. From there the people moved up the nearby tributary streams, the Cuduiarí, the Querarí, and the Pirabatón, a tributary of the Querarí. The traditions record that the first people displaced groups that were already living along these streams and, in this respect, square with historical observations that pressures of enemy Indian tribes, and, lately, the more potent pressures of white colonizers, have been forcing the Indians to leave the main rivers and take shelter in the more distant and constricted feeder streams, or else face physical or cultural extinction. The more timid and the more humble of the sibs have

[1] Following the usage of Lowie (1920, p. 111), "sib" is synonymous with "clan."

always tended to occupy the narrow headwaters of tributaries while the strong and the top-ranking sibs have favored the large rivers and their mighty cataracts. But while these strong and proud sibs in their exposed positions were able to withstand enemy Indians, they have succumbed more to Colombian and Brazilian missionaries and traders. Thus, the sibs that the Indians refer to as our "head" are now the most acculturated, and the low-ranking sibs the least.

I estimate the population of the Cubeo at under 2,500. This is a crude figure based on a calculation of somewhat under 100 persons per sib on the Cuduiarí, the only river that I had occasion to explore along its entire length. Population was undoubtedly greater in the past. On the Cuduiarí there were 29 main residence sites,[2] each averaging some 30 to 35 people, some only a few minutes by canoe from their nearest neighbors, but for the most part they were separated by at least an hour of steady canoeing. This is high population density for the region. On other rivers in the region, houses are separated by at least half a day's journey by canoe. A severe influenza epidemic swept the region in 1917–18 and took a heavy toll of lives, the Indians say. A number of sibs whose names are still remembered are now extinct. The Colombian government census of 1938, which did not tally tribes, listed some 7,000 Indians for the entire *Comisaría del Vaupés* (Colombia, 1942). This figure, too, is surely an estimate, since an accurate head count is virtually impossible. During the period of my stay among them, the Indians, in a state of alarm over rumors that their young men were all to be conscripted for labor in the rubber forests, were understandably nervous about censuses and genealogical explorations so that my own efforts at counting were severely handicapped.

The term "Cubeo" is a Europeanization of the Tucanoan word *kebéwa*, that means, literally, "the people that are not." It is a jest name applied to them by some other Tucanoan-speaking tribe. Most Indians were not aware that they were called "Cubeos," while those who understood what it meant did not like the name. Strictly speaking, there is no tribal name. A man will always identify himself by his sib name, never by phratry and never by tribe. In the course of discussions with the ethnologist on native conceptions of "tribe" the Indians offered some self-designations. The most common was *pamíwa* (first people). They also offered *pwănwa* (people), and then referred to other tribes as *apépwänwa* (other people). I doubt, however, that any Cubeo Indian has ever spontaneously declared himself to be a

---

[2] There is a list of these communities at the end of this chapter.

pamíwa or a *pwănwa*. The group of exogamous sibs that form a phratry are spoken of as *kwináwü, únhiwü,* or *kwinánokauwü,* all terms with the general meaning of "one kinfolk" or "the same kinfolk." However, I have also heard the expression *nuhénokauwü* (my own kinfolk) used to refer to both tribe and phratry.

If tribal designation is vague, the native concept of tribe is only a little more definite. Tribe refers more or less to a common identity of language, descent, and custom. One of the Cubeo phratries was, in fact, once Arawakan. To become tribesmen they adopted the language, customs, and traditions of the Cubeo. Other sibs appear to have been at one time Macú as well as sections of the Tucano "tribe." There are no formal bonds of tribe and there is no acknowledgment of tribal overlordship. Cubeo social structure is segmentary, the patrilineal sib being the basic segment. Every sib has established relationships with other sibs to regulate marriage, ceremonial participation, friendships, and hospitality along traditional lines, but also to some degree along lines that suit its own particular interests.

The phratry is a more sharply defined and a far more important social aggregate than tribe. A phratry is a confederation of sibs that are closely bound by rules of exogamy, by common residence along the same river, by a tradition of common origin and descent, by a graded order of rank that assigns to each sib its place in a social hierarchy, and, finally, by a series of ceremonies, solemn as well as secular, such as drinking parties at which each sib entertains its fellow sibs. Withal, there is no phratric overlordship, no phratric council or other agency to consider policy for the phratry as a whole.

What gives a phratry cohesiveness is the pattern of relations that the individual sibs, each acting individually, have formed with one another. The most important of these relationships is the rule of exogamy. By adhering to a rule of exogamy the sibs regard themselves as "brothers," for fraternity is based on the kinship principle that brothers cooperate and share the same rules of exogamy. Most sibs in a phratry have been joined together from the traditional beginnings or the time of first emergence, others are newcomers who have been adopted into the cofraternity of sibs. Adoption is the prerogative of an individual sib. A sib adopts an alien group as a subsib and automatically gives it a place and rank in the phratry. The phratry is no homogeneous federation of fraternal sibs. It is differentiated by rank, by historic background, and by geography. Sibs of the same historic background and of similar rank who are neighbors on the river feel closer to one another and form, therefore, an unofficial but still evident inner circle. Normally, rank, historic background, and propinquity coincide and so the informal clusterings are strengthened. Thus, when one speaks of sibs within the phratry it is necessary to distinguish between "close" sibs and "distant" sibs. As the discussion of kinship will show, these distinctions between "close" and "distant" sibs are actually expressed in kinship usages. Among the Cubeo, relative ranking of sibs is not as formally expressed as it is among the Tucano tribe. Among the latter, all the lower-ranking sibs of a phratry are junior siblings and are addressed by the term "junior sibling." The highest-ranking sib is "older brother" to all the other sibs (Fulop, 1955).

The basic segment is the sib. A sib is an exogamic, patrilineal, and patrilocal descent group that claims to share a line of descent through males (with some exceptions) back to a founding ancestor at the beginnings. The sense of sib is that of a local group capable of sharing a common residence and of regarding itself as a fraternal kingroup. Sib members may be, and often are, dispersed. This, however, is, in the Cubeo view of things, an abnormal situation. Sib identity, in any case, is never lost. Even women who must marry "out" are forever members of the paternal sib. The sib, as we have already said, has a name. It has a headman, a common residence or sib center, and is on any crucial issue autonomous politically and economically. It may break out of the exogamic grouping of the phratry by moving away and joining another phratric organization. This, however, it will be very reluctant to do. Sibs are not static entities and that is why one cannot obtain an exact count of their number. Fission is an ever active process and reveals itself in what may be called "phases of separation." Within a common residence site most families live in a long house, called in the region a maloca. Others live alongside the maloca in smaller houses. I have called the occupants of the smaller houses "Independents" because of their expressed intention to remain somewhat outside of the jurisdiction of the sib headman.

Some sib members live at a nearby but distinct site with very considerable autonomy, but recognize the main maloca as their sib center. These people are still more estranged from the sib and I have called them "Satellites." The Satellites may estrange themselves to the point of complete separation. They then assume a sib name that is a compound of the original sib name with a new designation and so take on the status of a subsib. A subsib has a strong sentimental attachment to its parent sib, but in all other respects it is autonomous. A Satellite may also give up its satellite standing by rejoining the parent sib. Subsibs are held together by sharing a common sib name and a common genealogy. This is true whether subsibs have been formed by fission or are aliens who have been adopted by a "parent" sib.

A sib is formed of patrilineal lineages that go back no more than three or four generations. Since a sib itself is small, a lineage is of minor importance. The most significant component units of a sib are the fraternal joint families and the nuclear households. A group of brothers of the same father are held together by very firm ties of common upbringing and regard themselves as very close to one another. The households of this fraternal group are distinguishable, not jurally but *de facto*, as separate entities within the sib. When a sib splits, it is the fraternal group that offers the most ready line of cleavage. Finally, there is the nuclear household, a most important unit that occupies its own "compartment" in the maloca, maintains its own hearth, and is capable also of asserting its autonomy. A nuclear household may break from the common residence group of the maloca and establish itself as an Independent, but that is about as far from the sib as it can go. It is not a truly self-sustaining unit. When it does break away, the separation is a consequence of serious disaffection, from the Cubeo point of view, an example of social pathology. Detached nuclear households often become vagrants, imposing upon the hospitality of related sibs.

What I have presented is an outline of Cubeo social organization that encompasses a descending order of subordinate and component segments, from tribe to nuclear household. There is another social concept that falls somewhat outside of this structure. That is the concept of community. The community is the common residence group, based, to be sure, upon the sib, but not exclusively so. Common residence creates its own norms of behavior.

THE COMMUNITY

The concept of community offers perhaps the most advantageous entry into the character of Cubeo social structure; it exemplifies almost all social relationships and relates them to the physical factors of location, economy, and material culture.

From the air, a community appears as a small semicircular island pressed against a thread of river in an otherwise unbroken expanse of tropical forest. The air view emphasizes the isolation and self-containment of each community. Along a well-populated river such as the Cuduiarí the communities resemble rough-shaped beads widely spaced along the thin strand of the sinuously curving river. The river literally binds the communities since, in the main, communities

along the same river belong to a common phratry and share, therefore, rules of exogamy, origin traditions, and mutual obligations of
hospitality.

Close up, a community is revealed as a clearing of a dozen acres
or so hacked out in a crude semicircle from the banks of the river.
Since the river may rise some ten feet or more in the rainy season the
clearing is always on the high bank and will necessarily follow in its
shape the contours of high land. The maloca stands toward the river.
A house is not aligned according to absolute directions, but always
with reference to the river, which the Cubeo, in contrast to other
tribes in the region, insist upon keeping in view. No house will have
its front door facing the forest, though its rear door may. In some
cases the rear door abuts almost on the very edge of the manioc cultivations.

A residence site is commonly called *tavá*, a term that appears in
the naming chants and that I have rendered in free translation as
"soil." A related term that is also used is *taibo* (a made place), a clearing. These two terms refer then to that part of the territory that has
been prepared both for cultivation and for housing. A more inclusive territorial term is *makáno*, that embraces the uncleared forest
and can also mean "forest." Still another term for a residence site is
hobónu, based on *hobá*, a cleared place for planting. More commonly,
however, the manioc cultivations are called *hawabó* (food place).

Within the requirements of contour and with leeway granted to
accommodate individual community preferences, clearings tend to
conform to a common plan. The maloca is the hub from which the
outer edges of the clearing are plotted with approximately equal
radii — footpaths — leading to the bitter manioc cultivations. The
manioc cultivations form a broad outer belt of the clearing that, in
poorer communities, begins very close to the rear or rear side wall
of the house and that in prosperous and more prideful communities
is at some distance. In the latter communities, the zone of plantings
begins far enough away so that the women at work in their manioc
gardens are out of sight and out of sound, only the plumes of white
smoke from each garden signaling silently that a woman is at
work there. No matter how confined the total clearing, the house
rests within an inner clearing of secondary cultivations and, ultimately, within a totally cleared space or plaza. The maloca is more
or less at the center of these three concentric zones. The river (*hya*)
itself is a fourth zone.

These four zones have their social counterparts in that they may
be identified as male and female, although, it should be said, the

Cubeo do not themselves make this identification. The outermost zone, that of manioc cultivation, is largely a female province. Men make the clearing, but women work in the gardens. A woman's garden is virtually her private domain. A man enters it upon a woman's invitation. A husband goes there to help with some heavy task or for casual sexual intercourse. There is extra spice to marital coitus in the garden because it is the traditional place for adultery and so the Indians associate it with licentious passion. Men do not ordinarily wander over to the manioc gardens. When I wanted to see the women at work in their gardens I was not free to go without an escort, who was usually the husband himself or sometimes the headman. In the latter case, the headman courteously informed the husband, and everyone else if the husband was away. Frequent visiting was definitely discouraged. Women could not help but attribute sexual significance to a man's visit and would deride the notion that a man was interested in watching them farm.

This outer zone, then, has a decided sexual connotation that is both erotic and social. Women give birth in their manioc gardens and during male cult ceremonies they may take shelter in the gardens. Nursing babies are brought to the manioc gardens regardless of sex, but from walking age on, no boy will think of playing in the vicinity of the gardens. Manioc is a strictly secular crop for which there are no rites, despite its overwhelming nutritive importance and the usual hazards of cultivation.

From the sexual point of view, the zone of secondary cultivation is a mixed one. Secondary crops include sugar cane, tobacco, *mihí* (kaapí, a vision-inducing narcotic), coca, calabash, gourd, squash, melons, yams, sweet potatoes, and sometimes maize. There are also cultivated trees — orange, lemon, pupunha (*Guilielma speciosa*), pineapple, plantain, and banana. Men exclusively cultivate tobacco, *mihí*, and coca, women exclusively cultivate bitter manioc; all other plantings are mixed. If a plant, onions, for example, is taken from the whites and the Indians have seen a white man grow it, they then regard it as a proper male cultivation. Maize is an old crop that belongs to women but not all communities grow it. Among the *Bahúkiwa* and its neighboring subsibs no maize was planted.[3] This

---

[3] When Koch-Grünberg was on the Cuduiarí, in 1903, he observed that the upriver communities grew only maize and no manioc. For bitter manioc, he said, they came to the lower Cuduiarí communities (1909, II, 82). During my survey of the river I found no community without manioc. On the other hand, maize, which had already begun to disappear in the time of Koch-Grünberg, had become quite scarce and no longer entered into the regular diet. On certain ceremonial occasions it was made up into tortillas. Mainly it was used in native beer and as

secondary zone produces supplemental crops only. Gourd provides household dishes, while tobacco, *mihí*, and coca are for ceremonial purposes.

The plaza consists of two clear spaces, a front plaza that is at the entrance to the house, and a rear plaza that is an extension of the kitchen area. The front plaza is a ceremonial site. It serves for the staging of dance formations and is a gathering place of the men.

Ideally, a front plaza is large, clear, and clean. Its appearance speaks for the quality of the house, for its prosperity, for its high morale, and for the excellence of its headman. It is the headman who will insist that the plaza be kept clean. Women are not barred from the front plaza, but it is definitely a male zone with sacred connotations. The medicine man does his curing on the front plaza. By contrast, the rear plaza is a female zone and is secular. It is often littered with the debris of past meals and abandoned and broken household utensils, shards, and frayed basketry. The women assemble here for their own gossip. During important ceremonies, when the sexual demarcation is accentuated for ritual purposes, it is the rear plaza where women guests are received. The rear plaza is demarcated even when the house is still a mere skeleton under construction. A visitor then may have no obvious clue as to which is front and which is back. If he should make an approach by way of the rear plaza he will not be received until he realizes his error and comes around to the front. In just such a situation I have seen the occupants of a house ignore a guest who made this *gaffe*. When he did recover and came around to the front he was received with as much formality at the bare frame of the house as he would have after it had been fully completed.

Finally, the river. The river is sacred to the sib, and is in that sense a male zone. Men fish in the river and hunt along its shores. They hide the sacred ancestral trumpets along the shore and bathe to the music of the trumpets before dawn to receive strength from the ancestors. Ordinary connubial coitus takes place well before dawn at the river's edge, where chances for conception are considered to be better. Again, to call the river a male zone is not to say that it is restricted against women. Women have access to the river for bathing and for washing. But it is not their domain.

During the early part of the day, from just after sunrise until the high heat of the early afternoon, a community gives the appearance of being altogether deserted, or, if the men are not hunting or fishing that day, it appears to be an all-male community. The men are then

---

chicken feed. The *Bahúkiwa*, cited by Koch-Grünberg as maize growers, had no tradition of having cultivated anything but bitter manioc as their principal crop.

in or around the maloca, loafing, jesting, or in jovial groups working at small manufactures such as basketry. It is the wives and their daughters who are dispersed, each in her separate garden, and who then return in the heat of the day, tired and subdued, to a house that is gay with the laughter and chatter of the men.

In the recent past, no more than a generation or two ago, the inner zone of the community was separated, indeed virtually isolated, from the manioc gardens by a ten-foot-deep defensive moat set with sharpened stakes. Tree trunks crossed its steep walls to serve as narrow foot walks for the sure-footed women. At night, or in anticipation of an enemy, the footbridges were withdrawn. The house and the plaza then were an inner citadel. The moat protected against surprise attack. When enemies were sighted or their presence announced by the angry growling of the dogs they were met as far from the residence as possible, and the moat served as a defensive line to cover retreat. The strategy then was to lure the attackers to fall into the moat while the defenders slipped across their secretly placed bridges. If the people felt themselves to be overwhelmed they scattered to safety through the dense forest, abandoning house and possessions. (Houses still have an escape port at a side wall facing the forest.) But if they were confident they left the women and children behind in the house with a small guard. I had the privilege of this guard duty on one occasion. I was instructed to cover the escape of the women and children if need be. Fortunately, there was no need.

The canoe landing is little more than a level stretch of beach where a canoe can be pulled up out of the water. It is also the site for bathing, for drawing water, for washing manioc roots. It is a port. One rarely comes upon a community by land. Visitors pause at the landing to wash, adjust their apparel, and freshen up face and body paint before beginning the climb up the path leading to the plaza. Like the plaza, the orderliness of the canoe landing denotes the state of morale of a community. Some householders have carved steps into the clay bank, lined them with split logs, and provided a rail. Guests are never received at the landing. Courtesy requires that guests be allowed the privacy of arrival, and the hosts discreetly retire to the plaza to await them. There are ceremonies in which the arrival of spirit beings is an important feature. On such occasions the men who are to enact these beings use the canoe landing for donning masks and for other preparations. On these occasions, too, the canoe landing is a sanctuary from which all unauthorized persons discreetly retire.

Before dawn the canoe landing is the favored place for marital coitus. First building a small fire, the couple bathes; they have coitus and bathe again. The ancestral spirits add power to the water, that promotes pregnancy. Because of its connubial use the canoe landing is thus a sanctuary of another kind, at night restricted to those who are going to use it for the proper purpose. When the last married couple has left, the young men take over. They bathe off the canoe landing, sounding the ancestral trumpets that have been hidden somewhere along the river bank. Regular bathing with the horns gives strength and sexual potency.

People arise for the day's activities sometime before dawn. Thereafter, the canoe landing is the scene of secular activity, women and girls drawing water, men readying their canoes for fishing, and the young play pack frolicking. In the high heat of the day the women return from their manioc gardens to bathe and refresh themselves. In effect, there is a secular and a sacred period in canoe landing activities. The secular part of the day is from dawn to a tropical four o'clock in the afternoon, when the first guests may be expected to arrive if there is a drinking party or a ceremony. The sacred part is from after four o'clock until dawn. Even on ordinary days, activities slacken at the river by late afternoon. On ceremonial days the distinction of a sacred and a secular period holds strongly.

BOUNDARIES

The clearing delimits the effective area of habitation, but not the full area of a community. This territory runs along a stretch of river and is usually demarcated by a *caño* or creek. On the Cuduiarí these small tributaries run into the main stream at almost regular intervals. A principal habitation is ordinarily along the main stream, which is the preferred site. However, the requirements of slash-burn horticulture necessitate a periodic circulation allowing for three to five years at each site. Depending upon the particular conformation of the land with respect to the danger of flooding, a community may be able to move along the banks of the main stream, preparing its new clearing adjacent to the old. It may, on the other hand, be forced to move up a *caño*, with its connotation of lower status. If it is required to spend a period in a *caño*, it has a cyclical existence, of being in a relatively poor state when it is off the main stream and returning to an epigone when it re-establishes itself on the main stream. When I came to live among the *Bahúkiwa* they had just come from a *caño* phase and were in an expansive mood at having moved onto the Cuduiarí proper again. *Caño* dwellers are self-conscious; they entertain less and are reluctant to have visitors. I was never invited or encouraged to visit a *caño* dwelling house. I was always told that they did not care to have visitors.

When a headman dies his house is ordinarily abandoned and the new headman undertakes to build a new maloca, since one requirement of the office is his ability to enlist his sibmates in working with him. Abandonment of a house, however, changes mainly the outlines of the clearing if a new site is chosen for the new maloca. A new maloca may be built alongside the old, in which case there is no change at all. Sometimes the new headman decides that the old site was the victim of evil forces and a new clearing is built. But against such a fear is the desire not to abandon still-productive manioc plantations. At all events, a new clearing is normally close enough to the old to ease the transition from last harvest to new harvest. When a site is moved the last harvest is drawn from the old, and cuttings from the old *chagra* (plantation) are planted in the new. Thus there is a transitional period when the community is actually working both clearings. The Cubeo regard this transition period as a difficult one, and until they are drawing a bitter manioc harvest from the new clearing they will be too preoccupied to hold drinking parties. Fruit trees on the old *chagra* are harvested as long as they bear fruit.

The extent of a community's territory is such that it will be able to circulate within it more or less permanently, reoccupying after some 15 years land that has become reforested and so workable again. Boundaries are along a river only. Past the line of cultivation the forest is an undifferentiated darkness.

The traditions of the Cubeo indicate that they were originally dwellers along the Vaupés, the main stream, and that they later moved up the smaller tributaries such as the Cuduiarí and the Querarí. The present distribution of sibs is also interesting in this connection in that high-ranking sibs live along the main stream or along the mouths of the tributaries, whereas the lower-ranking sibs occupy the headwaters of smaller streams. Sib status is definitely associated with location along a river. The back reaches of creeks deep in the forests are the refuge of the weak, whereas the strong occupy a stretch of river that has majesty either by sweep of water or by the character of its rapids. The main site of a sib that has become dispersed is always in a conspicuous part of a river whereas Satellites and Independents often move up small creeks. Father Antonio Giacone of the Salesian Mission has observed that the Tucano (referring to the tribe) never constructed their malocas in creeks but only along the main river. Occupying the main streams, he noted, they regarded themselves as the superior of all other Indians who were driven back into the headwaters (Giacone, 1949, p. 5).

Thus the movement of Colombian settlers down the Vaupés River had a markedly disturbing effect upon the Cubeo by dispossessing them from their ancestral river. The first-ranking sibs, however, did not leave their sites at the rapids from whence their ancestors are supposed to have emerged. But in staying on they succumbed most rapidly to the European influence.

Despite their strong orientation toward the river the Cubeo also make use of footpaths. Near the mouth of the Cuduiarí, for example, a trail leads to the Querarí. There are, in fact, many paths in the region that provide short cuts between rivers. Raiding parties come on foot to avoid detection, and paths are used for short journeys. The Cubeo Indian, however, is not, by preference, a walker.

SIZE

The size of a clearing is variable, to a degree, depending upon the number of households and their ambitions for entertaining and for trade with the whites. A headman's household, which is always the most ambitious and is, therefore, the most productive, requires approximately two acres of manioc land for an annual yield of 400 baskets (50–60 pounds per basket). Most households among the *Bahú-kiwa* averaged only 200 baskets of manioc a year and utilized accordingly a manioc garden of one acre. A sib center community of 12 households requires more than 12 acres for manioc cultivation as well as several acres more for the plaza and subsidiary cultivations, if the full burden of entertaining is left to one or two households, as is often the case. Satellite communities are often as small as three households and their clearings are proportionately smaller.

The Cubeo community is always small, rarely reaching a population beyond 16 households, a household in every case being limited to a nuclear family. The size of community seems to be a result of a complex series of adaptations of many elements to one another — architectural, ecological, sociological, and psychological. The architectural factor is that a community must be dominated by a single maloca. The largest maloca in the Northwest Amazon region is a 16-household dwelling with eight compartments ranged along each long wall. The smaller dwellings of the Independents can augment the size of a community. The fact is, however, that an Independent household has usually been formed for personal reasons, such as a quarrel with the headman, rather than for reasons of crowding. The Cubeo believe that one roof unites a community while several roofs divide it.

Size of maloca is adapted in some measure to cultivable terrain. We have already noted that seasonal flooding and the requirement of good river frontage limit the availability of land for relatively permanent cultivation. But these are highly variable factors. Along the Vaupés, a deep river basin that can carry a great volume of water, there are vast stretches of dry land that have become the sites of civilized population centers. There is no doubt that from terrain alone the Vaupés could have supported far greater Indian populations than it did at the time of first contact. Along the Vaupés the limiting factor seems to have been social. On the Cuduiarí, on the other hand, land contours are such as to divide frontages into much smaller segments. On this smaller stream, terrain has been a more significant factor in limiting community size. But even on the Cuduiarí, land utilization is subject to strong social considerations. One consideration is that sibs must retain their traditional boundaries. This means that with slash-burn horticulture the sib territory must provide, as a minimum, a three-step cycle in which a community returns to its original land after 10 to 15 years. The well-situated tract must then be at least three times the average land requirement at any given time.

There is still another consideration, and that is the distance of manioc gardens from the residence. When they prepare a clearing, the Cubeo bear in mind the distance a woman will have to trudge with her burdens of manioc, a baby, and firewood. That is why the gardens are laid out along a semicircle. Bitter manioc is a cumbersome crop. It needs reasonably dry soil and it makes heavy demands upon the time and energy of a woman for its cultivation, transportation, and preparation. Whatever can be saved from travel time is an advantage.

The thesis of ecological adaptation, however, can be argued most successfully in the abstract. If one notes the actual events in the life of a community, then the processes of community growth and community fission appear in quite a different light. The balance of forces of fusion and of fission that hold community size to its stable limits in harmony with the natural environment are not entirely economic. They often include personal factors. To state this more precisely: the economic factor affects fusion strongly but has less direct bearing upon fission. Satellites, for example, are urged to return to the fold, guests are urged to stay on, and daughters are invited to take up residence in their own sib if there is ample land. Splitting, on the other hand, occurs because of personal quarrels and rarely because of a feeling of land shortage. A social structure, to be sure, that facilitates fission by providing a place for each new segment within a phratry is well adapted to the ecology of rivers of the size of the Cuduiarí; but the adaptation may well be fortuitous. The Cubeo do not plan it that way.

Among the factors affecting community size the tradition of the maloca appears to be the most significant. Whatever the terrain, there it stands as a maximum dwelling for 16 households. It would be of value to study the distribution of such single-house communities to determine the conditions to which they may have been originally adapted. Giving, as they do, maximum occupancy for a minimum of space they seem well suited to the relatively cramped terrain of small rivers along a flood plain.

The problem the maloca poses for community growth may be put this way. A single maloca in the Cubeo view is an ideal community. As the community grows, the maloca is enlarged to its maximum size. Any further increase results in the construction of a small-size dwelling nearby. But now there are two social units of unequal size and the small unit stands apart. Its ultimate fate can be only reabsorption or further cleavage. The construction of equal-size small malocas only emphasizes fission more strongly. It would thus seem that while a tradition of small dwellings lends itself to expansion by aggregation, a tradition of unity based upon common residence under one roof must devise a new tradition if it is not to impose thereby a rigid limit to community size. In the Northwest Amazon region a tendency can be observed for one maloca to become a social and ceremonial center for scattered smaller groups who are themselves incomplete communities. Among Tucanoan- and Arawakan-speaking peoples in the region Koch-Grünberg often found such scattered small communities that identified themselves as belonging to a main maloca some distance away (1909, I, 58, 332, II, 21). But while a maloca may become a center for dispersed sibmen, who owe it nothing but an affiliation by sentiment, it cannot, in traditional Cubeo terms, become the center of a large community made up of many houses.

In this respect, however, native attitudes seem to be changing. The *Bahúkiwa* headman, for example, who was interested in adapting the life of the community toward the standards of the white man, described himself to me as *capitán y generál*. He then added that he planned to have a community of many houses and he would be chief over them all. He used the term *habókü*, which means a man of great influence, rather than the milder term *kenámi upákü* (owner of the house). He was not the only one to speak this way. Elsewhere along the Cuduiarí I met Indians who spoke of the advantages for personal autonomy of smaller residences. The Satellite community of the *Bahúkiwa* subsib was in the process of establishing itself fully in small, square-shaped, individual household residences.

SANITATION

A well-run community, as we have already observed, is clean and orderly. The maloca is swept regularly and is neatly maintained. Except for an accumulation of kitchen debris at the rear of the house, the grounds, including the plaza, the canoe landing, and the path from the canoe landing to the house, are kept orderly and clean. The headman, responsible for the appearance of the community, commands the women to clean up house and grounds in anticipation of visitors. Normally, the women of his household, wife and daughters, sweep the central corridor as well as the kitchen zone at the rear and the front reception area. A headman's wife does not command assistance in general cleaning chores. She requests it and it is most unlikely that a woman asked to help would refuse. When the women take to cleaning they do so with gaiety and vigor, as is appropriate for a collective undertaking.

The Cubeo regard disorder as a sign of low morale, so that a house that has become untidy will surely be restored to order in expectation of company. A large maloca is almost invariably clean if only because it is a firm and effective headman who will have founded a large maloca in the first place. When a guest arrives unexpectedly, the woman who first presents him with the formal offering of boiled capsicum peppers apologizes for the condition of the house. Since there is always some advance notice of a guest's arrival, the women have some time for tidying. Cubeo etiquette is rather demanding that guest and host make the effort to appear at their best when they meet.

Sanitary standards of a Cubeo community are very high. The Indians protect the river from pollution. They dump in it only waste meat such as entrails — but these are immediately devoured by the piranha fish. No one defecates near the river. People go off into the brush, that lies at no great distance from the house. When a child has been toilet trained it, too, will go off to the brush for its excretory functions.

A dump is maintained near the river bank. During the rainy season the household waste products are washed into the river. But at that time the volume of water is high. During the dry season the dump is at a distance from the water and is kept sanitary by action of the sun. The dump receives the body wastes of the very young children.

THE MALOCA

The maloca (*kenámi*) is no mere shelter or sleeping barracks. It is a vital social center, the very focus of social and religious life. Under its great gabled roof all ceremony takes place, the dead are buried, food is prepared, and almost all implements and articles of use are manufactured. The Cubeo are largely an indoor people. Children play outside and there are occasions when the older men sit on the plaza in the shade of the house. But in the main, adults spend their leisure time indoors, lounging in hammocks. Guests are received at the doorway of the house, the hosts standing always within, in the formal exchange of greetings. Having been welcomed at the door, guests are ushered to low benches set at an angle near the doorway and facing inward.

When I came among the *Bahúkiwa* they were on the upswing, having come from a creek site to the main stream. In the new site they had put up several smaller houses and the framework of a large 12-compartment maloca was in place. This large house, of standard size, was 75 feet long, 55 feet wide, and 21 feet high. The eaves of the hip roof extended six feet past the low side walls. The new house is always the work of the headman. It is started on his initiative and the work is carried on with his active encouragement and under his direction. The leadership qualities of a headman are precisely reflected in the maloca, in its size and in the care that is taken in its construction. The headman is known as *kenámi upákü* (owner of the house). The house is his, in the sense that one who is not willing to accept the authority of the headman will not live in the house. A house, the Cubeo believe, cannot tolerate dissension. Whatever the genealogical relationships of its residents, they are the equivalent of a joint family. The Cubeo are decidedly uncomfortable if the atmosphere of a house is lacking in familial warmth. If necessary, they will overlook discourtesy, uncooperativeness, and sullenness in the expectation that such behavior will be only a passing phase. Nevertheless, they are acutely sensitive to one another's moods and before too long one sullen individual will have infected them all. Then someone will move out and all sense the impending dissolution of their community. The smaller house that will now be built alongside does not remove the source of dissaffection. It stands rather as a reminder that they have not been able to get along with one another. The headman is responsible for the morale of the house. He is aware that its architectural features contribute positively to morale.

The larger the maloca the more comfortable it is. It is cooler, less smoky, freer of insects, and, offering more space per inhabitant than smaller houses, it presents a more orderly appearance. In my observations along the river I have found the smaller malocas to be less tidy than the larger ones.

A sib center, unless it is in a state of perilous social disintegration, will have a large maloca with some 12 compartments. Such a maloca provides minimum accommodations for dances and for ceremonies that will draw upon all or a large part of the phratry. Since higher-ranking sibs entertain more than do lower-ranking sibs they must have larger malocas. Thus, size of maloca tends to correlate with the social standing of the sib. The small maloca is an open acknowledgment of social inferiority. The Satellites all have small malocas housing from four to six families. Such a community may be economically self-sufficient, but it is socially and ritually underprivileged. It can attend ceremonies but is unprepared to carry out ceremonies on the

Fig. 2. Children helping in housebuilding.

proper phratric scale. Some Satellite communities have small malocas of the standard design, but most build a house that has a square floor plan with a four-sided roof and a single entrance. The distribution in the region of this square type of house is not well known. It is an old design but it may be of European origin. The advantage to a Satellite community of the square house is that it cannot be mistaken for a small maloca; its identity as Satellite is clear. It expresses in a more subtle way the point of separation from the parent sib house without conveying any implication of total cleavage. When a Satellite puts up its own standard-design maloca it is usually on the way to achieving social and ceremonial autonomy that will qualify it as a subsib. The square houses lack a dance floor and must regard the main sib house as the ceremonial center.

The oblong design of the standard maloca provides the following spaces: living quarters along the side walls, a dance floor down the central corridor, a reception foyer and burial ground at the front end, a communal kitchen and women's quarter at the rear. The living quarters are formed by the uprights supporting the roof. A 12-household house has two parallel rows of seven uprights each along each side wall. These uprights are placed so as to form a series of living spaces along the sides. At the center of each such space is a hearth formed of three pottery cylinders with pinched-in sides that resemble hourglasses.

Each family hangs its hammocks from its posts, which are shared with the adjacent families on either side. Each person has his own hammock; and at night each compartment is blocked off by the hammocks that have been strung at all angles from the four posts. The hammock arrangement is not formal. Children's hammocks are lower, and husband and wife are apt to take a parallel position from outer post to inner post as being least subject to disturbance. The rule is not invariable. However, once a hammock position is set it tends to remain fixed. During the day all but one or two lounging hammocks are rolled neatly and tied to a single post. There are no partitions of any kind, and no provision for privacy. Coitus, as we have already noted, takes place outdoors, as do all toilet functions. The privacy of the space of each household is, however, fully recognized, even by toddlers. People visit one another and lounge in one another's hammocks, but usually by invitation. Freest in the in-house sociability are blood siblings. Each household has its own storage facilities, a shelf built above the hammocks just under the roof, and the thatch of the sloping roof, which is a repository for any article that can be thrust into it. From the posts are hung plaited or bark-cloth baskets, and calabash bowls in which the people keep their small possessions. Most houses have a flooring above the main supporting beams to provide storage space for farinha.

Malocas are commonly decorated. The front walls at the narrow end are painted with representations of bark-cloth masks that are used in funeral ceremonies, while the interior posts flanking the dance floor receive geometric designs. The *Bahúkiwa*, whose ancestry may have been that of the more primitive Macú, do not decorate their houses. The bark-cloth mask designs depict spirit beings, and while their representations on house walls have no specific magical function they do convey to householders the atmosphere of contact with friendly beings. Similar representations are common as petroglyphs. The geometric designs on the house posts are similar to those on dancing tubes, and portray simply an atmosphere of ceremonial gaiety.

Ordinary cooking is done over the household hearth, and simple meals are eaten around it. Manioc is prepared at the rear end of the central corridor, where the women wait their turn to share the large communal manioc oven, a circular ceramic plate on pottery supports, that has been provided by the headman's wife. Most evening meals are eaten communally in the central corridor.

Allocation of space in the maloca follows no precise order of status, but as a rule older and socially less active households occupy the rear compartments near the kitchen area, while a headman prefers a central location on either side.

At night a fire is kept going at the center of each compartment, and on chilly nights the occupants vie for the comfort of the space just above the fire. The people sleep fitfully. Someone is always up to tend the fire and to crouch over it for extra warmth. The day begins several hours before dawn and ends several hours after nightfall.

THE FACTOR OF CORESIDENCE

While community and sib are normally coextensive insofar as their male occupants are concerned, there are, nevertheless, permanent male residents of alien sibs in many communities. Widows, for example, return to the parental community with their children. There are some cases of matrilocal residence as well. These exceptional but not rare cases provide information on the role of coresidence in regulating social behavior. The question of coresidence is of special interest in the Northwest Amazon region because among tribes that do not have sibs but are organized on the basis of patrilocal families it is coresidence rather than kinship that has been reported to be the governor of exogamy (Kirchoff, 1931). In a sense this seems to be true of the Cubeo as well.

Among the *Bahúkiwa*, for example, a widowed younger sister of the headman had taken up residence with her sons and daughters and had assumed, as was her right, the status of household head. She prepared chicha for the in-house drinking parties and she contributed chicha to the drinking parties organized by the headman for the entertainment of the phratry. As a consequence she had a voice in sib affairs. Her children were cross-cousins to their *Bahúkiwa* generation mates and, therefore, according to the rules of kinship, marriage partners. They were, in fact, addressed as *tcimá* (cross-cousin). The boys, however, were reared with the male play pack, normally a sibling group, and were initiated into the *Bahúkiwa* ancestral cult. Because of the close association of these boys with their *Bahúkiwa* age mates, the expectation in the sib was that the widow's boys would not marry *Bahúkiwa* girls but that the widow's daughters could, if they wished, marry into the *Bahúkiwa*. One of the widow's sons, a boy reaching marriageable age, explained his position as follows: "How can I touch the sister of one who is like my brother?" The headman thought that such a marriage was possible, but it would be embarrassing because the boys were living together "like brothers." The widow thought it was all foolish. Her fondest hope was for all her children to marry right into the sib or at least into the phratry and so be with her. However, she, too, conceded that it would probably not happen that way. I also heard of the case of an orphan who had come to live in his mother's sib and who later eloped with a girl of his mother's sib. This marriage proved to be unpopular; some people called it "incest." The older men considered it to be proper but awkward. Apart from this case my list of marriages documents only community exogamy.

Community exogamy is not a "law" but a convention that has grown out of the tradition of the localized sib. The rule of sib exogamy, on the other hand, is inviolate regardless of residence. The Cubeo invariably identify social intimacy with fraternity. They have granted asylum to alien groups on their river by adopting them into the phratry on the theory that aliens intermarry but truly friendly people do not. Ceremonial friends become as "brothers" and will avoid sexual relations with one another's sisters. Within a community, the only fully established patterns of behavior are those of fraternity. Thus, a sib alien can be either a guest, that is, a transient, or become assimilated — not adopted — into the fraternal group. It is the men who are drawn into the sibling group. The position of a girl resident in an alien sib depends upon whether she has a brother. If she has a brother, his associates, who regard him in a brotherly way, will probably respect his sister as one of their own. If she has no brothers in the community she has still to overcome the reluctance of men to take a wife from nearby. This, too, is no minor obstacle, since an orthodox marriage must ceremonialize the tearing away of a woman from her own community.

THE COMMUNITY OF THE RIVER

The river forms a wider community of related sibs. With some exceptions the sibs have aligned themselves along a river on the basis of degree of closeness and of rank. Sibs that have segmented from a parental sib ordinarily occupy an adjacent site. The river is the most important territory. It is a highway and a link between related sibs, the source of ancestral power, and the economic zone of the men, fish being the main source of animal protein. Even most land animals are hunted along the river banks.

The orientation of the Cubeo is toward the river and not toward the forest. Whereas the forest is undifferentiated terrain, the rivers are known to every turn and outcrop of rock or other feature. The river is the source of the ancestral powers, of benefits as well as of dangers. The forest is a source mainly of dangers. The river is literally and symbolically a binding thread for the people. It is a source of emergence and the path along which the ancestors had traveled. It contains in its place names genealogical as well as mythological references, the latter at the petroglyphs in particular. For these reasons of sentiment and of symbolic association as well as because of the clear economic value of the river — hunting as well as fishing — the Cubeo have cause to feel that those living along the same river should be people of common descent and, therefore, of common exogamic grouping. It is not accident but strong intent that has grouped the phratries along the same river. Those who join a river will accept membership in a phratry. On the other hand, it is accident that has interrupted the sib homogeneity of the rivers. The *Hürüwá* sib is an intruder on the Cuduiarí River and belongs more properly on the Querarí. It is now the only large alien group on the river. Since it is an established affinal sib it cannot be incorporated into the Cuduiarí phratry as were the apparently alien *Bahúkiwa*. But the *Hürüwá* are drawn into the round of drinking parties and so have slid into what is a pattern of intraphratry activity. Here again we have an example of the pull of propinquity. The Cubeo welcome and respect neighborliness.

The river has its natural boundaries. These are the segments of river demarcated by rapids and by the tributaries or creeks. A boundary is from one such feature to the next, from a *cachoeira* (rapids) to a creek, from a creek to a creek, but rarely from *cachoeira* to *cachoeira*. A boundary defines only sib territory. There is no phratric territory as such. If there is phratric and tribal territoriality it is because each of the sibs undertakes to defend the principle in terms of its own interests. A sib may adopt a stranger and in this way incorporate it into the phratry. It needs no permission to do this. On the other hand, a sib may appeal to phratry mates for help in warding off by force unwanted intruders. Boundaries do not close a river to traffic. The river is always an open highway for travel, and travelers may fish and hunt along it freely. They may not put up fixed installations such as weirs or show other signs of residence such as fishing a particular spot with regularity without permission. Men regularly fish only within the sib limits. The discussion of boundaries, it should be explained, does not flow naturally from the Cubeo. It is drawn out by the ethnographer. The Cubeo are not jealous of boundaries and they rarely have issues over them, but they do know them. Occasionally someone violates the common law of courtesy of the use of fish weirs and keeps the barrier closed beyond the allowable period. The Cubeo cannot and do not attribute this unmannerly act to gluttony. Gluttony is an incomprehensible notion to them. They attribute it either kindly to forgetfulness, in which case there is no issue, or to unfriendliness, in which case there is a quarrel and an effort is made to tear down the barrier. On the forest side there are no boundaries at all except for the clearing itself. It is not land but river frontage that is valued.

CANOEING

So much of a man's time is spent in a canoe that no description of native life would be complete that did not relate the Indian to the river as a canoeman or that failed to bring out the motor rhythms of canoeing. Motor rhythms are patterned, the rhythm of paddling and the characteristic rhythms of the dance showing particularly striking parallels.

Paddling follows a definite though irregular rhythm. The prowsman on a long trip is keeper of the stroke. Paddling is noisy. On the downstroke the stem of the paddle just above the blade is struck against the gunwale to set the rhythm. Frequent changes of stroke are common. In pulling away, the first stroke is slow and strong. This is followed by a brief pause, the blade just out of the water, the stem resting against the gunwale. The helmsman, who steers with a broader-bladed paddle, uses powerful slow strokes that are one to two or three to those of the prowsman. When inertia has been overcome the stroke is accelerated, often to a furious tempo. The oarsman's back bends lower and his stroke is sharp, fast, and shallow. A fast beat is not kept up for long. The paddlers rest, permitting the canoe to continue on its own momentum. Unless exhausted from a long trip the mood of men in a canoe is gay. They burst into spontaneous shouts of *he ee ee*, sing, and joke loudly. Each passing bird is addressed, as "Where are you going?" With the paddle held as a gun they aim at the bird, pretend to shoot, and shout, "Now he is dead!" On one occasion we chased a covey of herons downstream for about two hours for amusement. The birds followed the river course, flying some 100 yards before settling on a branch. Striking paddles against the canoe and beating an empty gasoline tin, we drove the birds to the communities. The Indians shouted, "We sent you herons, why didn't you shoot them?"

The most important canoe positions are those of stroke and of steersman. A woman traveling with men always steers, the lighter work. She may even nurse her child while steering. Among boys, each wants to be a steersman because it is easy. When the people are in no hurry canoe positions are informally assigned; children then occupy the stroke position, in a large canoe sitting side by side. They also steer. On a long journey the prowsman or stroke is always the strongest man, while a woman, or the oldest or weakest man, is at the helm. Intermediate positions are filled by considerations of balance, each canoe known for its own balance characteristics.

All the Indians know the river and its currents. Downstream the canoe is piloted along the currents that sweep out from creeks, calling for frequent crossovers; the center of the river is usually avoided because of the sun, the Indians preferring the shade of the shoreline. Going upstream the canoe hugs the shore and in rapid currents the men pull it along by seizing creepers. During low water, punting poles replace paddles, and sometimes the riders get out and push. High water offers cuts through the forest. I have timed these short cuts against the regular passage downstream and found that there is no actual saving. Threading through jungle lagoons in a large canoe is time-consuming, but is less monotonous and tiring than the direct passage. These passages lead often through dense brush that tears the skin, and where a clumsy move shakes down hordes of stinging ants, or the canoe has to be pushed through narrowly spaced trees. Sometimes the canoe is portaged across a hillock. The forest passage is made with light, quiet strokes in keeping with the silence Indians observe in the forest.

Canoes range in size from a one-man capacity to up to one ton. Each man makes a personal fishing canoe. Some prefer a four-man capacity, but the small one-man canoe is most popular. Every community has at least one large cargo canoe with a capacity ranging from a half to a whole ton. Usually made by the headman, it is for the use of all, for long trips, for transporting cargo such as farinha or palm leaves for roofing, and is the festive canoe that transports women and children to drinking parties. The headman is the owner but the canoe is taken freely by sibmen. Paddles are individually owned and are kept in the house, never in the canoe, but are freely borrowed.

Women do not own canoes, a canoe belonging always to its maker, but women have use of the large canoe. They do little unaccompanied traveling. I have rarely seen a woman alone in a canoe; she is accompanied at least by a child. A woman in a canoe alone is suspected of running away or of a rendezvous with a lover. Women walk great distances, but a man is ashamed to walk if he can go by water. A man who does not own a canoe is regarded as lazy and inept, and some boys who have never learned to make a canoe are scorned by the girls and find it difficult to marry.

Canoes don't last long. Unless properly seasoned, the wood is cracked by the sun, and such canoes split quickly. Short splits are calked with pitch, stuffed with a rag, or smeared with clay. I have been in canoes that required constant bailing; but as a rule an old canoe is left at the canoe landing house for the children to play in. Finally it is sunk in shallow water at the canoe landing, where it serves as a receptacle for manioc set to soften. Good canoes are brought into the house and are used as chicha containers during a drinking party. On the Cuduiarí, Koch-Grünberg saw canoes ornamented on the inside with painted designs, as well as paddles with painted motifs on the blades (1909, II, 89). By 1939 such embellishments had disappeared.

The Cubeo are careless in mooring canoes, and they float away but are always recovered. No canoes have ever been reported as stolen. A week may pass before an owner of a lost canoe goes to look for it. He waits until he needs it, for there is never any doubt that he will recover it. Away from home, a canoe is moored completely out of the water.

COMMUNITIES ON THE CUDUIARÍ (upstream from mouth)

PLACE NAME	SIB	PLACE NAME	SIB
1. Kakómba	Hehénewa	16. Xiábewa	Pedíkwa
2. Kuridí kenámi	Hehénewa	17. Kuraría	Kenánikauwü
3. Tcípakoríba ª	Hehénewa	18. Abúhakü	Kenánikauwü
4. Okóhambü	Bahúkiwa	19. Xwévebo	Hürüwá
5. Vekókü	Bahúkiwa	20. Bedébo	Hürüwá
6. Ewáhubo	Bahúküdjauwü	21. Kobéhowa	Pyéndo-Hehénewa
7. Hurédo	Bahúküdjauwü	22. Avyákoríba	Hürüwá
8. Nyáparatainto	Bahúküdjauwü	23. Kwitóro	Wadjá-Hürüwá
9. Yavíbi	Bahúküdjauwü	24. Bedébü	Hürüwá
10. Kiráda	Bahúkiwa	25. Toróhambü	Hürüwá
11. Úbo	Pedíkwa	26. Hokóbü	Kenánikauwü
12. Mákavekü	Bahúkiwa	27. Horáharía	Hürüwá
13. Makatóta	Bahúkiwa	28. Hudjíbü	Bahúkiwa
14. Toídibü	Pedíkwa	29. Mátakwe	Pyéndo-Hehénewa
15. Monékenpaunwa	Pedíkwa		

ª A small Korówa settlement is at Urupera between 3 and 4. It is, however, only a fraction of a Querarí River sib and not a full community.

2

Economic Life

ECOLOGICAL SETTING

The Northwest Amazon region abuts on the eastern slopes of the Cordillera Oriental and has an average elevation of some 200–300 meters. Many of its rivers flow quickly and the terrain generally lacks the flat and swampy character of the lowland Amazonian rain forest. The headwaters of the Cuduiarí are within the territory of the Cubeo and apparently arise in a high savannah, an eroded plateau laced with caverns and supporting on its remarkably flat surface only a meager xerophytic vegetation. There are other highlands in Cubeo territory along the Vaupés. Of no economic value to the Indians, the highlands form for them a setting of mystery because of their strangeness and their desert quality, and are held to be the domain of mythological beings.

The Cuduiarí is a narrow river that runs swiftly past several cataracts into the Vaupés. At the peak of the dry season it is barely navigable along its full length. At that time a large canoe is pushed across several inches of water and the river course is beset with sandbanks. The smaller tributaries or *caños* dry up altogether, stranding their low-status occupants seriously. Perhaps this is one reason why the Cubeo associate social standing with frontage along a big river. The Cuduiarí is an intimate river — along much of its length the trees and creepers that line its banks reach overhead to midstream to form a bower. The opposite shore is close at hand and the entire

49

river can be traversed downstream in two days and upstream in four.

The Vaupés, the main stream, is a mighty river, also swift, rocky, and guarded by cataracts than can be perilously "shot" in high water and portaged at other times. It is a deep river with distant banks, in places resembling a sea.

During the two "dry" seasons, *ihibo* (October–December, February and March), the Indian communities are perched on high banks, in many places clayey and sources of ceramic clay. Access is difficult; the steep, often slippery slopes are hard to manage unless the people have troubled to provide wooden steps or a handrail. At the height of the June, or great, rains, the flood reaches to the clearing, and the river is brought close. A community with its plantations is then an island, the low-lying country a vast lake.

The Cubeo are more pleased with low water than with high. High water, to be sure, does not threaten cultivations, which are always on high ground, and flooding facilitates river travel, yielding shorter routes over ordinarily sinuous turnings of the river. But the seasons of high water (*ilákoro*) (May–August and January) bring relative scarcity even though bitter manioc is an unfailing crop. Fish and game are then most difficult to catch. At the bottom of low water, fish are scarce but game, drawn to the dwindling streams, is now abundant. The peak seasons, when game and fish are both abundant, are after the beginning of the rains, when the rivers are filling in November, and at the conclusion of the rains in July, when the rivers have begun to fall off. The Cubeo render *ihibo* as summer and *ilákoro* as winter. They also refer to seasons as *kwaíno* (falling river) and as *edávaiya* (growing river).

Thus, while the Cubeo normally do not experience famine or, for that matter, serious deprivation at any season, the periods of glut are short, one falling roughly between October and December, and the other a minor dry season between February and April. During these seasons fish need only be scooped out of the drying streams, game — tapir, peccary, deer, capybara, and paca — crowds the river banks, and the manioc yield is at its peak. These are favorable seasons for ceremony — initiation into the ancestral cult, fish dances, deer dances, mourning rites, and the most frequent round of drinking parties.[1] The seasons, however, lack abruptness. The rains increase and then decrease. Neither economic nor ceremonial life need be precisely geared to a season.

While the Cubeo are a true riverine people, knowledgeable about

---

[1] The year is reckoned from the dry season, since this is the time when manioc gardens are extended or new clearings started.

every turn and landmark of the waterways, their utilization of forest products is also extensive. From the forest they derive mainly raw materials for construction: woods, fibers, and leaves for roof thatching; and some food produce: wild fruits and berries, ants and grubs. Forest foods are supplementary and minor contributions to the diet. In a sense, game are riverine too because they are hunted along water courses. Only occasionally do hunters enter the forests on foot. They prefer to go by canoe, entering the smaller *caños* to catch animals as they come to drink. Hunting is important; the flesh of game animals — the tapir in particular — is highly appreciated and never fails to add a festive note to a meal. On balance, however, it is fish and other water creatures that furnish the main source of animal protein to the diet.

Fishing is the daily masculine routine; hunting is spasmodic, undertaken according to circumstance, as when someone has observed a herd of wild peccary or fresh tapir dung. As a break in the monotony of everyday work, and when the appetite has become jaded with fish, a hunting party is an enlivening experience.

The Indians do not complain about the corner of nature they occupy. They recognize and accept periodicity, times of glut and times of scarcity. Abundance is pleasing to them and scarcity does not alarm them. They expect it to pass. The Indians believe that they are living now in a "golden age." In the past, before they had learned farming and all the techniques of hunting and fishing, they were always on the verge of starvation and lived on tree saps and bark, their traditions say.

Once, while gathering roots, according to one tradition, they came upon the *aúnhokü* (manioc) tree, a tree that had leaves of the manioc plant. Manioc tubers fell from it. They had never encountered such a tree and did not know what to do with it. Agouti (*Bwü*) came along eating. An old man asked him what he was eating and Agouti replied he was eating manioc. The manioc at that time had no skin. The tree grew in a clearing with no growth around it. It was guarded by many animals. The old man thought, "What are we going to do?" Then along came *Húbükokü* (a rodent), and he told the people to clear a *chagra* and to plant. "Now, let us cut down the tree," he told them. The old man made a *chagra* and the people cut down the tree with stone axes and puño teeth. When the tree had fallen, all the animals came to eat. The old man then saw that one branch held plantains, another sugar cane, another *turú* (poison), another *pudjú* (a potato-like tuber), and another *yapika* (sweet potato). They then cut off each limb and planted it.

From *Kúwai*, the culture hero, the people learned how to fish with hook and line and how to hunt with bow and arrow and with the blowgun. The Indians say that in ancient times they did not hunt the tapir. It was not until they acquired guns that they learned how to kill tapir. Other animals they did not eat because of religious taboos that are no longer in force. Paca and armadillo were devourers of human corpses and were hence forbidden; eating sloth would make people lazy; and finally, all animals whose names were represented in the sib genealogies were taboo to members of that sib.

PRODUCTION

The Cubeo do not value abundance of food for its own sake. Plenty is, to be sure, widely enjoyed as a break in the daily routine. It is not valued for its promise of satiety, for the Indians customarily eat moderately, but for the opportunity it offers for a gay feast. A big catch of game or of fish excites the people because it does not occur often. There is no desire to overdo, however, and no more is brought than will be consumed directly or can be safely preserved by smoking and drying. Since, at best, smoking preserves meat for only a week or two in the tropical climate there is not much point in increasing a fisherman's or a hunter's "take." Social status is a minor issue in food production since feasting is essentially intrasib, whereas social status comes into play most sharply between sibs.

In short, there are no strong motives to stimulate hunting and fishing other than appetite and desire for variety. The pressure in production falls upon the women. If we are to speak of "surplus" at all in Cubeo food production it can be only in connection with the manioc crop, which is regarded as the woman's contribution, even though it is the men who make the clearing. The limiting factor in manioc production is not land as much as it is labor and morale. A large community under a forceful headman can clear a good deal more land than is needed for subsistence. In the case of manioc, subsistence can be measured precisely by the amount that is converted directly to manioc cake (*áuno*) and to tapioca porridge. "Surplus" is what is converted to chicha (*unkúndye*) and to farinha. There can be no doubt but that the machete, now universal in the region, improved the standard of nourishment considerably. The real limitation upon production is woman power. Since women carry through all phases of manioc production, from planting and harvesting to conversion into the final product, they are the ultimate "bottleneck." A woman working only to prepare manioc as food is already fully occupied.

To produce farinha, which is mainly for trade, and chicha, which is mainly for sociability, she draws upon what is normally her "spare" time. She gives up the evening hours of rest, moments of gossip, play with her breast baby, and food foraging in the brush, which she regards as a pleasant diversion from the back-breaking manioc routine.

A Cubeo woman cannot be coerced to work any more than a man can be. Her willingness to work hard depends, in the case of a married woman, upon her regard for her husband in the first place, but also upon her general relations with the community at large. The Cubeo know that a lazy woman is a disaffected woman and they are conscious, accordingly, of the social importance of marital felicity. The only control the community has over a domestic situation is by maintaining a generally high level of good feeling. Needless to say, Cubeo women are not and do not consider themselves to be abused. A woman who does not care for her husband will leave him or, if her laziness is deep-seated and represents a grievance against the community as a whole, she will urge her husband to leave with her. The fact is, the feeling against indolence or apathy toward work is so strong that even a thick-skinned person can sense the unvoiced community disapproval. Thus, in the absence of strong political authority the productivity of a Cubeo community depends in the main upon all of the subtle factors of kinship, sexual attractiveness, and satisfaction, and of public morale. An unproductive community is normally not underprivileged by virtue of location or of tools but simply by its own lack of social health.

FISHING

Fish are abundant and there is hardly a day when fish are not part of the diet. The basic Cubeo meal consists of manioc cake and fish. Every male, from puberty to the grave, is a fisherman. Fishing is the regular masculine routine. Most fishing is individual — a man sometimes accompanied by a young son in a small canoe fishing with hook and line, or a man (also accompanied by a young son) fishing in shallows with bow and arrow. An Indian fishes his own stretch of river at a preferred place. If a man wishes to join another at the same place there is no quarrel, since fishing is never competitive. There is some rivalrous display of a catch but only a good-humored kind. Unlike gardening, which follows a rigid routine, fishing is flexible; a man follows his hunches and preferences, the seasons, and the species of fish and their habits. Some fishing is by torchlight, at night. The men do not necessarily leave for the river at the same time, nor do all the men fish on the same day. A man who has had no luck one day temporarily loses interest in fishing. He turns to other activities, perhaps to hunting or to making household implements, or he may do nothing. As the season begins to taper off one fisherman after another gives up. The last to stop is the most successful. The Cubeo believe that a dispirited fisherman will catch nothing anyway. When all have stopped fishing the community hungers. After about a week of poor meals the women nag, but the men do not move until they have received a sign. The sign usually comes from the young male play pack. When the men have retired to the maloca to sulk, the youngsters turn their play fully toward the river. They take out canoes, and they set lines along the shore. For this they win immediate praise from the women, who say, "Look, the boys can catch fish but the men cannot." The boys patrol the river. One sights a school of fish and rushes into the house shouting, "The fish are coming." The men run to the bank to see. Then with great hilarity and good-natured pummeling of the boys they take to their canoes and the fishing cycle resumes.

Periodically, the routine of individual fishing is interrupted by organized collective fishing parties. The organizer is often the headman, but any man who has a plan will enlist a party. Summer is the season for fishing parties, when fish can be trapped in a shallow pool and stupefied with fish poison. Fishing parties are festive and noisy. The young play pack attends them, and the catch, which may be large, is collective. Each fisherman secures his own catch. When the party returns they distribute the total catch to all households. The distribution, according to an important Cubeo principle, is personal and never anonymous or generalized.

Fishing a shallow pond requires equipment and preparation. One man locates the place and asks his fellows to join him in fishing it. Several, or all, contribute sections of splint fencing that forms the weir. One party undertakes to put up the weir while another manages to gather and prepare fish poison. The men, as always, work efficiently together with a minimum of formal direction. Most have been members of a common play pack so that teamwork is automatic. Each household head has brought his own canoe into which he loads his "own" catch. Some shoot with bow and arrow, others use a dip net, and some thrash about seizing the dulled fish with their hands. Such fishing is never solemn. The men joke, they address each fish, and when they have tired of the sport they stop. A man may take secret pride in his individual catch, but he is expected to behave as though he were lampooning rivalry.

Another and somewhat more restrictive form of collective fishing is with basket traps in conjunction with a weir. Some household head may have traditional rights to a *caño*, inherited from his father or uncle. He invites men of the sib to place their baskets at the *caño* when the fish are running, usually at the start of the dry season. All sibmen may share this privilege although the obligation to invite holds strictly only within the joint family of brothers. In any event, the catch from the basket traps is eventually shared among all households in the sib.

The technology of fishing is fairly complex, involving skills in making and in maintaining equipment and, of course, expert knowledge of fish and their habits. Nowadays all Indians use commercial fishhooks. All else is native. A father teaches his son by explaining, by showing, and primarily by allowing the boy to accompany him. The basic instruction is individual and direct. A boy who has no father learns from a paternal uncle or grandfather, but he will often not be as deft as one who has his own father as a teacher. An important supplementary mode of learning is within the play pack. Here, unsupervised by adults, the boys practice what they have learned from their fathers, listen to one another's criticisms, and exchange information. The laggard has a chance to catch up.

Because the best fishing is during low water, great stress is laid upon skill in handling the fishing bow and arrow. Every boy toddler is provided by his father with a miniature bow and set of arrows and is set to practice at a fixed target on terra firma. Grown boys practice with adult equipment along the river bank, aiming, if they possibly can, for fish. A boy is always welcome to accompany his father as a companion on a fishing trip, but if he wishes to be a partner he must be reasonably adept. The Cubeo may treat some work as fun but they never confuse it with play. Needless to say, the boys attend very closely to the task of learning river skills.

Every man makes his own equipment — a fishing canoe, line, fish net, basket traps, splint weirs, bow and arrows. There is some trade in these items, but no one is regarded as having reached adult status who is unable to equip himself with these necessities for fishing. Skill in making equipment is acquired by careful observation of others and by helping. As a boy reaches manhood he prepares his equipment, calling upon and freely receiving assistance from elders and from more deft age mates. Fishing lore is acquired gradually.

The Cubeo say that all men are equally skilled at fishing, although to an outside observer differences seem obvious. Leadership in fishing is to them a matter of initiative and personality, not of skill.

Yet a leader of a fishing party may, indeed, ask an elder to come along as an expert. The fact is that expertness is very casually shared, as each fisherman narrates at the end of a day what he accomplished and how he accomplished it.

After a great catch, fish are dried and smoked for several days on wooden racks set up outside the house. The entire sib gathers, each man selects a dried fish, mounts it on a stick, and dances with it. The dancers wear a headdress of splints that is shaped to resemble a fish basket and is called *nyukáro*, and also carry dance staffs decorated with feathers of the great fishing birds, the heron and the river eagle. They sing songs (*máopwa*) honoring the fish. There may be as many as four or five such festivals during the course of the year. I was told the greatest come when the winter rains have stopped. After the dance they feast on the fish. Curiously, I never witnessed this fish festival, called simply *upaúeteno* (festival). The Indians explained that they only have the festival when they are in the mood. The dance is not intended to increase the supply of fish.

Not all communities were as well situated for fishing as were those of the Cuduiarí, a well-stocked stream. Other tribes in the area often used distant streams, camping out for long periods of time, living on fish and preserving some of the catch for use at home. Koch-Grünberg, in his travels, encountered many Indians far from home, fishing strange streams (1909, II, 27 ff.). On the Cuduiarí the problem of shortage was felt mainly by the upstream communities at the very bottom of the dry season. These people, however, were then free to fish along unoccupied stretches of the Cuduiarí, camping out or accepting the hospitality of phratry mates for fishing sites and for shelter. If they went to another stream it was generally to the sites of in-laws, where they also had hospitality rights. Thus, kinship, including the affinal and the maternal ties, provides a completely reliable mechanism for interchange of territorial resources.

HUNTING

Hunting is a secondary masculine pursuit. Whereas every adult male is a fisherman not all are hunters. Hunting attracts naturally the most vigorous age groups, men in their late teens to about 30, although there are no age restrictions that would bar an old man from joining a hunting party. Hunting may have been more prominent in the past, when only native weapons, spears and blowguns using curare-tipped darts, were fashionable. Today the Indians hunt with muzzle-loading shotguns that only a few possess because of the expense and trouble. A hunter is not disposed to take risks with his small store of shot, powder, and percussion caps, and, since a man does not like to return empty-handed, a hunting party is formed only when its organizer is reasonably certain of success. As in any collective undertaking, any man who wishes to may join a hunting party. However, most parties that I have observed consisted of blood brothers or other sibmates who habitually hunted together. Hunters, of necessity, have a strong feeling for teamwork. The Cubeo are excellent marksmen, cool and courageous.

The big game is the tapir (*vekü*), who is awaited at a salt lick near a small stream. The tapir follows a customary route to the salt lick, arriving quite late in the afternoon. He has worn a trail as deep as a ditch in the soft earth. Among the maze of these deep pathways fresh tracks and fresh dung are the signs of current use. A man who has seen fresh tracks reports it. The hunters go out to kill a particular tapir who has already been observed, so that they may speak of him in personal terms.

Communities differ in hunting customs. Some use dogs to chase the animal through the forest. The *Bahúkiwa* method, which seemed quite successful, was to rendezvous with the tapir at his salt lick. The Indians are fond of tapir flesh, which is tender and tasty. I participated in only one tapir hunt with the *Bahúkiwa*. A large female was killed, toward dusk, as she nibbled on salted earth. We camped nearby, spending a good part of the night eating spit-broiled steaks and cutting up the animal for transportation home. The limbs came as entire pieces, and the rest of the flesh was cut into strips and neatly packaged in palm leaves. The men were very gay. They amused themselves by inserting sticks into the tapir's vagina. As the animal had been killed in the territory of another sib we stopped at the sib house and, as is customary, gave away about half the meat. The *Bahúkiwa* hunters were pleased at the opportunity to display both generosity and evidence of success. The remainder of the flesh was distributed at the home sib, each hunter making a personal presentation of a portion of meat. The Cubeo utilize nothing but the flesh of the tapir.

Hunting, in summary, is a distinctive pursuit and marks one for prominence. An aspirant for the headmanship is ordinarily a hunter. He pleases the community because he enlivens the diet and has surrendered some of his leisure in its behalf. In a special category is the hunter of the dreaded jaguar. Such a man is interested in sport and in prestige. The jaguar hunter may be solitary or he may invite a few close friends to accompany him. He brings home the hide for a trophy, for which there is no further use, but the teeth form a girdle that is a mark of high status. Jaguar hunting is strictly voluntary and is not a formal test of manhood. During my stay among the *Bahúkiwa* the headman's son — an aspirant for the position — killed a jaguar with a steel-tipped lance and accepted modestly the moderate acclaim of the community. His explanation was that he wanted to experience what it was like to kill a jaguar.

GARDENING

I have no statistical means for comparing the relative contributions of men and women to the food supply. The general rule is that men provide the bulk of the protein, women the bulk of the carbohydrates.

The Cubeo unhesitatingly regard the man as economically most important. This is surprising, since manioc in its multiple uses as food, chicha, and trade goods is not only the staff of life but the source of intrasib activity, status, and general well-being. My informants pointed out, however, that it is fish which is the important food, and besides, they added, it is the men who make the manioc clearing. Nutritionally they are right. Bitter manioc is a poor food, rich in starch and deficient in protein.

An important distinction between the labor of men and women is in the nature of their economic effort. That of the woman borders on drudgery. Hers is the steady routine of planting, harvesting, washing, scraping, grinding, operating the tipiti press, and, finally, forming the manioc cake and baking it.

On days when only subsistence manioc — that is, the manioc cake — is to be baked, a woman devotes half of all the daylight hours to its preparation, including time in the garden. Her preferred routine is to spend six hours on alternate days in gardening. On the day she gardens, she also spends two or more additional hours in processing the roots. On the second day, however, she works only four hours on manioc. She spends, on the average, 12 hours on manioc over a two-day period. If to this is added hours spent in preparing chicha and farinha, the annual average comes close to nine hours a day. By contrast, men's labor is more flexible in its demand upon time and the quality of effort. However, it would be erroneous to overstress the distinction. There is, after all, variety in the manioc cycle as well.

Women customarily go to their manioc gardens at the same time, leaving the maloca an hour or so after daybreak and after breakfast. Each smears her face with red pigment both as ointment against sunburn and as preventive magic against the jaguar. A woman is usually accompanied by an unmarried daughter, who is both helper and chaperon, a dog, and her breast baby. Her equipment is a machete (in the past it was a digging stick), a portage basket, and a tray upon which she rests her baby.

With the machete she cuts the long root at the base of a mature manioc plant and then loosens the earth so as to pull out the cluster of tubers. Each root yields an average of six tubers, two of which are large, two medium, and two small. This phase of the work is difficult but the woman moves quickly and silently. She does not sing at her work. Her daughter, assistant and apprentice, tears each tuber from the root, scrapes it clear of earth, and drops it in the basket. When a basket has been filled the woman gathers up the stems of the manioc plant, trims them of their leaves, and stacks the cuttings neatly in small heaps. She burns the leaves to add ash to the soil. She does not replant the cuttings immediately, but allows them to lie for several days. After an accumulation a woman devotes a morning to replanting. She breaks up the soil of the segment she has harvested and forms it into small mounds, into each of which she puts a number of trimmed cuttings, setting them in at a sharp angle. She works segments of garden that are about 25 yards square. After replanting, the earliest harvest will be after half a year, but full maturity takes two years. Each 25-square-yard segment yields from 50 to 60 pounds of manioc, or one basket load.

Among the *Bahúkiwa*, for whom I have productivity figures, the household of the headman harvested 400 baskets of manioc annually. Another household that had three adult women harvested 500. One old woman had a minimum yield of 150 and all other households averaged close to 200. Ten households produced 2,550 baskets, or some 75 tons of manioc a year. A basket of manioc converts into two large manioc cakes. In the headman's household of seven people three cakes were eaten every two days, leaving a "surplus" of close to 30 per cent for use as chicha and as farinha. On the other hand, households producing 200 baskets annually are close to the subsistence line.

The point of this digression into production figures has been to show how exigent are the demands upon the woman's labor. The women feel that they cannot afford to interrupt their labors or they will fall behind. Nevertheless, childbirth, illness, ceremonies — women do not garden on the day of a ceremony — and the press of other activities such as accompanying men on prolonged trips for hunting (in the nature of a respite for a woman) take their toll of labor time. Women do not complain of having too much to do. On the contrary, I have heard the grievance that the manioc garden is too small.

A woman is proud of two aspects of her work in gardening: total productivity and the quality of her manioc cake. Productivity reflects favorably upon her own efforts and, even more important, upon the efforts of her husband, who makes the clearing. The quality of manioc cake depends upon the quality of the tubers and upon the variety of manioc cultivated. Women are knowledgeable about manioc. They are familiar with many varieties, their food qualities as well as their characteristics of growth. They are experimental as well. When women from different communities meet, they talk about manioc farming, exchange information, and very often exchange cuttings. Thus, a garden includes five or six varieties of manioc. The *Bahúkiwa* cultivated eight varieties, one of which, a yellow variety, they had obtained from Indians on the Amazon below Manaos. Like any good farmer, a woman in the course of time eliminates poor strains for better ones. Many women have personal recipes for a manioc cake blended from several varieties of tuber. Gardening, being a woman's domain, is a totally secular activity. If crops grow poorly the women

Fig. 3. Preparing manioc.

place the blame upon the material conditions. The woman, then, is more than a mere toiler in the garden. She qualifies as agronomist as well.

Women return from their gardens in the very early afternoon. They pause at the rear door of the house only long enough to drop the machete, and without putting down their burdens of manioc and infant, go directly to the river to bathe themselves and to wash the tubers. This is a pleasurable hour. Refreshed from the heat of the morning, the women play with their infants and jest with one another. Washing the tubers is a simple task of dipping the entire basket into the water. A light midday meal follows the washing, and the routine of processing the tubers begins. The woman may start with fresh roots, but for a more tender manioc cake she will allow the roots to soften for several days either in the house or in the river.

The first step is peeling. The woman seats herself at her own household compartment, her back braced against a post, her legs stretched out stiff and straight before her into the dance corridor — the public alley of the house. The manioc basket is at one side and a tray at the other. She bites the butt end of the tuber to break the skin, and using teeth and fingers pulls off the readily peelable skin. This phase of the work is leisurely. Women who are not at the moment occupied come by to chat and help casually in the peeling. A woman's daughters sit with her and help. Enough is peeled for one manioc cake — that is, one half of a basket.

The next step is the most arduous and least liked — grating the peeled tubers on a wooden board (*pediba*) that has been set with abrasive stones. A woman can usually shift this work on to her daughter or her daughter-in-law.

The scraping process is as follows. The woman sits with her feet stretched out straight before her and slightly spread. She sets the grate on her legs with its far end braced against a house post, the forward end pressed against her abdomen. She takes up two large manioc tubers from a tray, one in each hand, and scrapes vigorously with alternate arm movements with the hardest pressure on the forward stroke. The action is vigorous, involving not only full arm movements but the bending of the back from the hips. Young women of marriageable age work rapidly and continuously until bathed in sweat. When worn down to a size where it cannot be conveniently scraped any more, the tuber is thrown aside and two others taken up. Finally, a collection of scraps is assembled into a single bunch clutched in both hands and scraped down virtually to the very bottom. This is a break in the work rhythm since both hands are used together and the movement is slower and altogether less vigorous. Usually, except when she is very strong and young, the woman interrupts her scraping for a rest or change of occupation. For example, the work may be staggered. If the mother begins the scraping and the daughter continues with the peeling, the daughter, when she has finished peeling, will take over the scraping, while the mother prepares to begin the next process. The manioc mash that has accumulated at the far end of the board is removed by hand and thrown into a basket tray, and the liquid drained off into a pot to be poured out.

A substantial part of the poisonous liquid of the manioc has been removed in the scraping on the grater; the mash is further dried by pounding it through a tightly woven basket sieve. A tripodal frame is set up and the sieve set on it at a woman's waist level. The pounding, also strenuous work, requires vigorous motion of the arms, back, and shoulders. With both fists clenched the woman attacks the mash, using her arms as pistons in a crisscross motion. The mash is frequently turned. As this work is done standing up, the woman has a chance to limber her legs. Because of the height at which the sieve is set little girls are not very efficient at the pounding, and only help out for a little while. When the mash is relatively dry after a thorough pounding it is put into a long tubular squeezer (the tipiti). The woman grips the lower end of the flexible tube between her knees, and bending the top toward her, fills it with the mash from the sieve. When full, the squeezer is hung from a projecting beam at one of the house posts. Through a loop at the lower end of the squeezer a long pole of heavy wood is inserted, the fulcrum end going through a few twists of heavy rope around the post. This phase of the work affords the woman a rest from the strenuous labor of scraping and pounding. She may sit on the pole, adjusting the pressure by the distance from the fulcrum. A woman is sometimes joined by another, who helps her sit on the pole. The liquid starch that runs down the sides of the squeezer is collected in a pot set for it. The pot is covered with a layer of ash that absorbs the volatile prussic acid, and the clear starch is used as the base for a porridge.

The mash, free of much of its prussic acid content, is finally formed into a cake upon the flat circular oven at the rear of the house. The baking is leisurely and as women wait their turn at the communal oven they enjoy some sociable moments.

A good housewife prepares a fresh manioc cake daily since the cake tastes best when fresh, moist, and warm. On the second day a cake is dry and considerably less palatable. Thus, under ordinary conditions, the routine of manioc preparation is daily. However, a woman who has daughters to help her can prepare a surplus of mash that, covered with banana leaves or stored in a circular bark bin, holds over to the next day. Whatever time a woman spares from manioc cake preparation is immediately absorbed by other duties, among them the making of chicha and farinha, which is simply the manioc routine all over again. When a woman prepares manioc for chicha, however, she has the help of her husband, but only at those stages that are totally distinct from manioc cake preparation. The Cubeo tradition is for men to take no part in *áuno* production, once they have made the clearing. Still, men do help their wives in peeling the manioc tuber. Since the knife has begun to supplant the teeth as a peeling implement, men, who are the most expert in handling knives, feel somewhat more free than formerly to help — but not without embarrassment. I once walked into the house and saw the headman sitting amiably beside his wife and peeling manioc with a knife. Were I a proper Cubeo I would have managed to appear as though I had seen nothing. But the sight was so unexpected I stared. The man flushed and dropped the knife and tuber. Then he collected himself and explained that his wife was not well and so he felt he should help her. He assured me, as his wife smiled, that he never did this ordinarily.

Whereas all women share the same general manioc routine, individual circumstances differ. A young married woman with young children has no one to help her and must work very hard in contrast to an older woman with several daughters who can relieve her of much of the work. A woman with many sons and no daughters has a very heavy burden. The men provide her with a very large garden, they eat heavily, they are sociable and plan drinking parties. An old woman living alone prepares her own small manioc cake ration, and worries rather that she can call on no man to enlarge her manioc garden. Yet in all these individual circumstances one observes leveling factors as well. The household with very young children eats less, has less need to entertain, and has smaller trade needs. The household with grown daughters eats more, entertains more — suitors and their parties for example — and has great needs for trade goods, skirts, and ornaments for the girls. The household with many men has greater access to trade goods through their wage labor and saves on farinha. An old woman living alone may eat with her close kin and so devote her manioc production entirely to farinha, if she desires. There are no significant differences in manioc cake consumption. Families differ only in the rather small prestige of owning trade goods and in providing drinking parties. While prestige is not a negligible factor in motivating production it is secondary to subsistence needs.

Compared to manioc, all other subsistence horticulture is of trifling significance. The list of Cubeo cultivations besides manioc is a lengthy one, but except for the pupunha palm there is nothing on it that adds bulk to the diet. Crops cultivated by the Cubeo include bitter manioc (*kerika*), yam (*nyámu*), sweet potato (*yapika*), maize (*karáiye*), and tabena (*mwa*), as well as the following unidentified tubers: *kwaiváryo, waiwari, moá, pudjú, kanéka*, and *kabéka*. In addition there are sugar cane (*kavámene*), pineapple, (*ihibo*), banana (*djwéye*), plantain (*óne*), pupunha (*uné*), gourd (*horóbe*), calabash (*hahámu*), coca (*patú*), tobacco (*butci*), and capsicum (*bya*). The pupunha palm is important only as an ingredient in chicha. Gourds serve as vessels, and yams, sweet potatoes, sweet manioc, and maize barely supplement the diet. Sugar cane has become a most important ingredient to chicha, and every community grows several varieties of melons. Most of the starchy tubers the Cubeo grow are used to lend variety to chicha, not to the solid diet.

The Cubeo, as I have already observed, have a very strong feeling for domestication. This covers plant as well as animal life. They are eager to plant anything that comes recommended and to follow the advice of experts. Some have planted coffee shrubs, although no one drinks coffee and they have no other use for the bean. One man built an immense box on stilts which he filled with earth so that he could plant onions safe from pests. Neither he nor anyone else in his community cared for onions. Sugar cane, as already noted, is mainly a male cultivation, but all other food products except for manioc may be grown equally by either men or women. No plant is neglected and the busiest woman seems to have time to look after her plantings, which may be scattered all over the secondary clearing or inner plaza. The produce of these scattered plantings, a melon or two, a handful of sweet potatoes, are often given as gifts from one household to another. Children, too, have their plantings.

Finally, every household has chickens, descended from stock brought in by white settlers. Chickens belong to women, mainly, I believe, because that is what the Colombians and Brazilians thought was proper. Although the Indians take good care of the chickens they do not ordinarily eat them, regarding them either as pets or trading them to the occasional white man who comes by. In some communities, chickens roost in nearby trees — others provide roosting places in the maloca. A few communities rear ducks in the same manner, and some Indians have experimented valiantly with rearing pigs as pets.

The trade element in Cubeo experimentation with plants and animals is important but not, to repeat, the exclusive interest. I had been living among the *Bahúkiwa* a short time when they learned of my liking for fruit. I was constantly presented with fruit, some wild and some cultivated. I usually made some payment in the form of a small gift. Word spread along the Cuduiarí. One morning I saw a fleet of a dozen canoes or so, each heaped high with bananas, plantains, pineapple, lemons, and oranges, coming to the community. It was all for me, brought in the expectation that I would reciprocate with a gift. This transaction, however, was an unusual one, for normally the Indians have no market for any food product but dry manioc — farinha. They have no great taste for fruit and grow more than they normally consume for the sheer satisfaction of growing it. Lemons, for example, are used by women to prepare a hair wash.

MANUFACTURES

Cubeo material culture is rather elaborate for a tropical forest tribe, but not as fully developed as is that of the more westerly tribes that have a cotton technology. Material culture has been treated by Koch-Grünberg and is, moreover, fully covered in the *Handbook of South American Indians*. I shall confine myself then to a discussion of manufactures as it bears upon an understanding of Cubeo social life.

There are few products made jointly by men and women. Men ordinarily make all objects that are of wood or fiber, while women specialize in ceramics. Thus, the great bulk of material equipment has been made by men. This includes the house, all baskets and trays, hammocks, canoes, signal drums, ceremonial objects, musical instruments, weapons, and fishing gear. Women make pottery, including the large ceramic plate of the manioc oven and the hourglass-shaped pottery hearthstones. They also prepare gourds as dishes and water containers since these supplement pottery dishes. There is a small basket (*póbü*) in which personal articles are kept, and this is made by young girls as well as by men. The only product that is jointly made is the *pediba*, the manioc grating board. Men make the board, execute a design on it, and women insert the bits of stone that form the grating surface. Whatever is made is either as a specific gift or to replace an object or utensil that is no longer serviceable. Men work slowly and for short intervals, so that the completion of a simple basket is often a matter of several weeks. Every man has at his side, so to speak, a number of unfinished objects which he hopes to get at before too long.

The sexual division of labor in manufactures is rather firmly maintained. I learned of few objects in use that were not made by a member of the proper sex. Young men are drawn to pottery making, but they may handle clay in a playful manner only. They make pots and dishes in strange shapes, working rather expertly. Such dishes are given to children as toys and are soon destroyed. Children, boys and girls, play with clay, making small animal or human figures and quickly destroying them. No permanent clay figures are ever made. Serious pottery work is an annual affair, undertaken by the women when the falling river has exposed the clay banks. All at once the women working together renew the household ceramic ware.

Manufacture is most often a group activity, and like all group activities is regarded by the Indians as a pleasurable recreation. The exception to this rule is perhaps housebuilding, which is often strenuous. Even then, when the exertion of the task has broken the spell of good feeling, the men stop and turn to another task. A large maloca can be a very long time in building. Among the *Bahúkiwa* a house begun when I arrived was not yet complete when I left almost a year later. A house must be built by a group working together not only for technical reasons, but in obedience to the principle that all who are going to live in it must work on it.

Building the communal house is a major technical and social enterprise. It tests the capabilities of the headman and the morale of the community. The true maloca is a solid structure built with great care, skill, and concern for details. Temporary houses may be slipshod in construction, but when a house is slipshod it is either clearly designated as temporary or it will be a cause of shame. Every part of the house is built with the greatest care, but nothing reveals more clearly the Cubeo concern for combining structural integrity and aesthetic design than the lashings that hold all the materials together. The most conspicuous lashings are those that bind the main beams. The builders start with temporary house posts and with temporary lashings. Finally, when the entire structure is in place, an expert lasher goes over the entire inner structure, replacing the beams and rebinding them in a consistent pattern, using carefully chosen lianas. The Cubeo are painstaking in all crafts, but the maloca is their supreme creation. I was able to observe almost every stage in the construction of a maloca among the *Bahúkiwa*. I do not recall that a single bundle of roofing thatch was laid under pressure or under duress. Men worked on the house only when they felt cheerful and dedicated to the work. The man who felt out of sorts dropped away and returned only when his spirits had improved. Dependency upon mood was one of the most important factors delaying completion of a house.

Even so, the magnitude of the technical problems is not to be underestimated. The mere assemblage of material is a complex, arduous, and time-consuming task. Construction materials are not always close to hand. The *Bahúkiwa* fetched roofing thatch from the mouth of the Cuduiarí in what was technically the territory of the *Hehénewa* sibs. Their house of 12 compartments consumed 560 bundles of thatch, and, since each canoe could transport only five bundles, over a hundred canoe loads were needed, a task that would normally be spread out over many months. The *Bahúkiwa* headman was able to borrow from the *Comisaría* a large cargo barge and in this way a great deal of time was saved. Even so, a large party of several households camped for weeks on the lower river during a dry season, gathering and preparing the parana palm thatch (*tciná*). Altogether, thatch gathering consumed 50 days of the time of at least half the community. The practice is for the headman to institute a "crash program" to get each phase of the work well under way. His problem is to fit each phase of construction into the routine of daily and of seasonal life with minimum disruption. Strictly speaking, the decisions are not his. His is the technical voice, but he will do nothing without discussion with the household heads. Roofing can be cut during the two dry seasons and can never be finished in only one. Gathering, trimming, and binding the parana palm leaves into sheaves is the only housebuilding task in which women share.

The headman, together with his firmest supporters, that is, his own sons and blood brothers, has the specific responsibility for erecting the central framework, the three pairs of heavy posts that will support the main weight of the roof. Others may help in this if they wish but they have no specific obligation to do so. The inner framework of three pairs of heavy posts forms the inner box around which the rest of the house is built. The timbers must be carefully chosen and then well dug in, while the parallelogram must be very carefully laid out. The floor plan is laid out with long sticks, and right angles are very accurately estimated. The rest of the framework including the ridgepole is a collective enterprise and is the second stage of construction. Roofing is the third stage. When enough roof has been laid down to provide even a bare shelter, the close kin of the headman move in. The walls and the two great doors that can be swung up are built long after the house is fully occupied.

Much of a man's spare time is devoted to preparing string of one sort or another — fishline, hammock strings, binding ropes. The most common material is from the miriti palm. The palm leaf is boiled in water and allowed to soak until long, strong fibers can be drawn from it. These fibers have extraordinary tensile strength and, therefore, have wide use among the Indians. The lower and thicker part of the leaf is slit with a knife or broken by hand to expose the fibers, which are then stripped off in one smooth, continuous motion. The man holds the leaf pinned to the ground with his great toe and pulls the fibers upward. Essentially it is men's work but women and children help in pulling out the fibers. After the fibers have been allowed to dry by exposure to the air, several are joined together and rolled on the thigh into a string. Occasionally a woman helps her husband roll fishline. The end of the string is gripped between the great toe and its adjacent member and allowed to pass under the frontal arch of the foot and so is held firm. Rolling twine is leisurely work. Men rarely make more than they need for a particular purpose. Fishline is coated with resin. This will not only strengthen it and make it easier to handle, but, the men told me, the resin darkens the line so that it will not be seen by the fish.

The Cubeo have no true category of specialist. That is to say, they expect all adults to possess the skills for making all ordinary household articles that are on the roster of sib manufactures. They must, of course, contend with differences in aptitude. They do so by giving the inept the fullest technical help, either by advice, or, if necessary, by virtually making the article. But even when total aid is given, the object is considered to have been made by its owner with help. Items of public use, and these include ceremonial equipment and musical instruments, require special proficiency and are made by the headman and by aspirants to the office. The headman then is a specialist, but his specialty is in esoteric objects for public use.

TRADE

The entire Northwest Amazon area is a vastly complex trading network. Objects of every description, household implements, ornaments, musical instruments, ceremonial objects, plants, pets, and magical substances are in constant circulation from tribe to tribe, from sib to sib. Indians who are in contact with the trading centers of Colombians and Brazilians are often middlemen, pumping manufactured goods into the stream of trade — cloth, salt, fishhooks, guns, machetes, as well as cheap ornaments. There are at least three kinds of trade. One, with the whites, is commercial and is of increasing importance. A second is intertribal, in which specialties are exchanged. Each tribe has its recognized expertness and its products are sought after. The third, intratribal, is less economic and more in the nature of a social exchange in which people acquire objects they can readily make for themselves.

Trade with the whites is centuries old in the Amazon Basin. Since World War I it has been largely stimulated by European interest in Amazon rubber. In the Northwest Amazon, rubber tapping is a small enterprise, between wars. Even so, it has exerted a great influence upon native life. Almost every Cubeo adult male on the Cuduiarí had spent some time in the service of a *balatero*, where he learned to speak some Spanish or Portuguese, depending upon which side of the border he worked on, and where he acquired the taste for European manufactures and the wherewithal to acquire them. By now almost every Indian regards the machete, the muzzle-loading shotgun, steel fishhooks, cloth, and even trinkets as necessities. He acquires these objects by selling his labor. Farinha, which represents the labor of the women, provides another source for trade goods. Farinha does not leave the area. It is the main food supply of the Indian rubber tappers. A coarse meal of manioc, farinha is dipped in cold water to make a moderately nourishing if unpalatable gruel. The Indians use it among themselves only as an emergency ration on a long journey. They dislike it as a food. The *balateros*, admiring it as a remarkably cheap provender, contract with the Indian women for all they can produce. Every grown Indian woman I met was under verbal contract for a number of *paneros* of farinha. Three *paneros* of farinha, representing 12 baskets of manioc or the equivalent of about three weeks of manioc cake supply and about 12 days of labor, are traded by women for objects that have cost the trader about 50 cents. One woman showed me a pair of cheap metal earrings for which she had paid two *paneros* of farinha. The more experienced and the more extroverted women do better. They have learned to bargain and they enjoy this form of trade. Farinha has become an integral part of the Cubeo economy and of its social life, as later chapters will show. There is also some minor Indian-white trade in other foods — chickens, fish, and fruit.

This commercial trade has come to develop standard values, partly because of administrative measures to protect the Indian against undue exploitation but mainly because of the nature of European business. The Indians are now aware that in their dealings with the whites their labor and their products have a fixed value with some leeway for bargaining. Direct commercial trade, object for object, is almost exclusively the province of the Indian women. This is not a new role for them because they also are active in intertribal and intersib trade. Because women do not have as much contact with whites as do their men they still inject into the commercial trading much that is traditional.

The traditional attitude is that any exchange is part of a patterned social relationship. An exchange establishes a linkage between the principals and each is aware of his obligations and of the showing he must make. The obligation is of generosity, the temptation to give somewhat more than one has received. The impression to be made is that one does not haggle over objects. An exchange between a man and a woman who are sexually eligible to one another introduces the additional element of flirtatiousness. All of these elements enter into and complicate and enliven the farinha trade. The more experienced men are able to adapt to commercial methods, but since it is improper for a man to conduct his wife's business for her he will stand aside when she is trading her farinha.

I never witnessed the intertribal trade, but when I pointed to an object and asked who had made it or where it had come from, its provenience and the nature of the transaction were always known. Manioc grating boards, for example, generally come from the Isana River. The Cubeo often traded European articles for tribal manufactures, less because they needed the tribal object than to satisfy another Indian's need for the European article. A Macú once wanted matches and gave a small basket for a box. The Macú baskets are highly valued, but in this case the initiative was with the Macú. An important principle of native trade in the area is that an object asked for must be surrendered. One must be careful, therefore, not to ask for something the owner might be reluctant to part with. Thus the *Bahúkiwa* headman asked me as a condition of my staying in his community not to offer to buy ceremonial objects. "If you ask for them," he explained, "we shall have to give them to you. How shall we replace them?" Thus, there is an element of delicacy in intertribal trade. At the same time there is a compulsion to engage in trade so as to give significance to the meeting of people of different tribes. In sum, while intertribal trade eventually satisfies the requirements of the Indians for specialized objects they would not ordinarily have, each individual transaction responds to motives that are often only indirectly economic. Trade objects circulate readily. Thus, a set of calabash dishes that had only just been acquired from the Karapana Indians was traded to the Desanas for a tray. The Cubeo seem to prefer the trade article to the domestic product. Finally, it should be said of intertribal trade that much of it follows the lines of inter-marriages, in which objects are transferred in the course of normal affinal exchanges.

Within the tribe, objects tend to be exchanged largely in accordance with principles of kinship and blood brotherhood. However, as sibmen visit along the river they learn which objects and whose skills one may properly admire. The object is asked for, or in a sense contracted for, and a genial nonhaggling discussion settles the terms of the exchange. Apart from farinha, a special case, food rarely enters the channels of native trade. Koch-Grünberg's information that up-river people acquired manioc from the downriver *Hehénewa* does suggest trade in food. He gives no details, however (1909, II, 82). I never observed or heard of native trade in food, other than casual and small-scale exchange of secondary crops. Maize, for example, is a trade item, but then it is hardly a foodstuff on the Cuduiarí.

PROPERTY

With respect to land it is dominion rather than ownership that we deal with. A tribe has dominion over a territory, a phratry over a river or over sections of a river, and a sib over a smaller segment of river frontage. Dominion is sanctioned by traditions of origin which narrate precisely where the first ancestors came from, and their sub-sequent travels and settlements. On the strength of these traditions people can say, "This is our land." A group that has been displaced from a traditional territory may adapt its traditions to new conditions, giving itself a new origin myth. But as long as the traditions hold, the claim to dominion over the territory is not surrendered. Place names are part of the traditional claim to a territory. They identify ancestral sites, and, more particularly, fishing sites, old orchards, and manioc plantations.

Since there is no tribal or phratric administrative organization, concepts of tribal or of phratric dominion are matters of general sen-timent rather than of concrete claims. Only a sib is truly concerned with its territorial integrity. There is little cause for a sib to fear encroachment on its territory. There have been instances of one sib taking over the territory of another, but these instances, as the Cubeo interpret them, were of hostility against the people, not of desire for their land. I found no evidence of land hunger among the Cubeo.

The phratry, with its extension of kinship along a large section of river, provides for amicable settlements of boundary disputes; these arise, however, over river use only, never over cultivated land. There is no thought more repugnant to the Cubeo than that one should cultivate land that has been cleared by another. When a woman dies her manioc plots are left to be grown over after the mature tubers have been harvested, so strongly do the people feel about the intimate relationship between land and its cultivator.

Within the sib territory, male household heads arrive at individual or, more often, joint decisions as to the total clearing and the allocation of household manioc plots within it. An individual may select any part of the sib territory for a clearing, although by tradition and for reasons of convenience the plots are contiguous and the clearing is one large space. Preparation of a clearing is most often a collective effort supervised by the headman. Even as they begin to prepare a clearing the household heads discuss their individual allocations and stake out a location. There are two ways in which the cultivation of a clearing can be organized. The preferred way is for the headman to organize a collective work party, including all household heads. If this cannot be arranged, either because of lack of agreement about a joint move or because some male household heads are away in the rubber forests or in some other work, the move is made gradually. Then the headman and his close associates are the first to move to the new location. They start the clearing by preparing their own plots, establishing a bridgehead, so to speak, for the rest of the sib. This method of moving over to a new location indicates how little anxiety the Cubeo feel about getting a choice location. When the later arrivals come they can count upon help from the headman and the earlier settlers in preparing their own clearings. The general clearing begins initially as a narrow semicircular band so that each plot is about the same distance from the house. The band is then widened by each household in accordance with its needs for new land. Annually, during the short dry seasons, a household head and the other adult males cut down and burn over the timber, outward from the *chagra*, to extend the cultivations. Manioc can be harvested at from six to 24 months. A providential family allocates one section of a field for a two-year harvest.

A manioc cultivation is always spoken of as belonging to a woman. A woman says, "This *chagra* was made for me by my husband" (or "my son" or "my brother"). She is the sole administrator of the plantation and may assign sections of it to her daughters, to her daughters-in-law, and to guests who have come for an extended visit. The

relation of the men to the manioc cultivations is as follows. By working jointly in making a clearing the men are fulfilling, in part, a sib
obligation. This is of minor importance, however, as compared
with the specific obligations and the ensuing relationship between
a man and a woman. No bond between a man and a woman is of
greater importance and richer in sentiment than that set up by the
making and cultivating of a manioc garden. Every garden plot defines
a relationship between a specific man and a specific woman. A woman without a man can have no garden. A man without a woman has
no clearing to make; he can have subordinate status only in another
household. Each side gains status from the arrangement. The only
firm bond is that between husband and wife. A widow has only a
frail claim upon the labor of her brother, whose primary obligation
is to his own household, where his wife keeps jealous watch over her
own *chagra*; for a woman's pride is deeply involved in the size of
her manioc clearing. The Cubeo regard the size of clearing as a sign
of a husband's affection for his wife. A widow has a better claim upon
an unmarried son. As we shall see, between unmarried brother and
unmarried sister a semiconjugal relationship develops over the material holding of land.

We have spoken of a reciprocity in status involved in the manioc
chagra. There is also a specific and related economic reciprocity. By
making a clearing a man obligates his wife's production. The preparation of manioc cake is never spoken of as a wifely obligation, but
chicha and farinha are. The point of economic reciprocity as it sometimes emerges in the course of conjugal quarrels is entirely one of
status and not of so fundamental an issue as food. If we are to speak
of male-female reciprocity on matters of food the issue is between
the male flesh foods and the female cultivated foods. Although a
man obligates his wife's labor for chicha and for farinha he evidently
does not obligate all of it, for a woman will suddenly declare that
she is cosponsoring a drinking party by a contribution of "her"
manioc. Moreover, it is part of the status of a wife that she can freely
contract part of her farinha production for personal objects, such
as cloth and trinkets. If there is a formal principle governing this kind
of connubial economic arrangement I did not learn what it is.

The point to emphasize with respect to manioc cultivations, then,
is that the issue in possession of land is not simply that of subsistence.
It would be unthinkable for a Cubeo to allow a sibmate, or phratry
mate for that matter, to hunger if he had any food for him. When a
solitary woman laments that her *chagra* is exhausted and no kinsman
is moving to make another for her, the fear she voices is not that she

will lack food, but that she will lack a role in chicha preparation and be deprived of trade goods. Her fear is for loss of status.

The *chagra*, to summarize, is a well-defined item of property. It is the domain of a particular woman, in the sense of economics, in the sense of status, and, as mentioned earlier, as a kind of sanctuary. No other land in the community has this character of particularity. All other cultivations, including pupunha orchards, belong to the cultivator, but the land on which they are grown has no standing as personal property. Whereas the manioc gardens of a household have contiguity, to the point where a son clears a plot for his wife adjacent to that of his mother, the variety of its other cultivations are scattered over the entire settlement.

With respect to all secondary crops, there is also very clear recognition of ownership. Each planting has its known owner, who may be a man, a woman, or a child. Ownership rights are scrupulously respected, and no one would consider disturbing another's plantings without permission. Tobacco, coca, and *mihi* are generally grown for the community by the headman, but are recognized, nevertheless, as his plantings. He also contributes to the community all of his pupunha harvest. But it is precisely because he contributes to the community that his ownership is clearly acknowledged. The point, of course, about Cubeo property relations is that generosity and sharing go along with the assertion of individual rights. The privilege of the individual as a *giver* is thereby respected. The least formal sharing involves sugar cane. It is understood that everyone is entitled to the simple refreshment of a freshly cut stalk of cane. Even so, adults who do not have cane of their own prefer an invitation. Children, on the other hand, do not stand on ceremony. Yet even a very young tot who is cutting a stalk does so with the announcement, "I am now cutting the cane of my older brother," or whatever the kinship connection may be.

On the river, the masculine domain, the men have staked out sites for placing weirs and fish traps. The setting of weirs is the one territorial issue that disturbs the harmony between sibs along a river. Weirs are commonly set in a *caño*, in which case they are a purely intrasib matter. If, however, men block the main stream they are obligated to allow fish to pass through periodically. "Sometimes they forget," I was told, "and then we go and tell them. But if they are mean then we go at night and break up their weirs." Such disputes are not common. Within the sib the issue is not of weir rights but of specialization in fishing methods. A man develops a preference for weir fishing, he troubles to prepare the cumbersome equipment and use it, and, as the others do, he shares his catch with the community. Weir sites are inherited by a son so that there is some tendency for this specialty in fishing to descend in certain families and not in others.

In objects there are two main kinds of property rights, those of the community and those of the individual. Community rights are in all objects made for public use by the headman or his wife, such as a large canoe, great chicha urns, the manioc oven, the sugar cane press, and guest benches. Of a somewhat less public nature are ceremonial objects and musical instruments also made by the headman or by an aspirant to his office. The first group of objects are fully in the public domain and subject to constant use. The second group are in the possession of their maker and are brought out by him alone on the proper occasion. Full individual ownership resides in all other personal possessions: household utensils, canoes, weapons, trinkets and ornaments, all trade goods from Europeans, and items of clothing. Disposition of these objects is subject entirely to the discretion of the owner.

Infants also own property and their rights are more or less respected. Sometimes a planting is set in an infant's name by the parent or grandparent. A mother commonly dedicates a brood of chicks to her nursing child. The feeling is that, as with ornaments, possessions confer human status. That is, a person should own things. If the child is old enough to understand possession it assumes charge, more or less, otherwise its possessions are administered by its mother. I have negotiated, for example, the purchase of chickens owned by children. In one instance a mother prevailed upon her little boy to sell me a chicken. After the sale was made, however, the child wailed miserably so that I felt obliged to make him a gift of it. His mother kept the purchase price and announced that she owed the child the value of the chicken. When the child does not understand the transaction, its mother announces publicly the facts of ownership and her intentions to make restitution.

The attitude of the Cubeo toward personal possessions is best described as casual. They are not indifferent to objects but they regard strongly proprietary feelings as improper. Their attitude toward ownership is governed by the important status principle that giving is honorific. Among sibmates objects circulate freely, the closer the tie between people the more active the exchanges. Sisters exchange ornaments and trinkets and men borrow freely from one another with or without permission. They seem to be most free with objects of economic utility, such as a canoe, weapons, implements, and somewhat more possessive with objects of personal adornment. While the former objects circulate most freely within the sib, the latter tend to circulate more among blood siblings. Consonant with this attitude of casualness is an almost total lack of anxiety about loss of property. An improperly secured canoe drifts away and the owner makes no immediate effort to retrieve it. It will come to rest somewhere downstream, he reasons, where a sib or phratry mate will secure it or even bring it back. Children have access to cherished possessions of their parents and when there is damage or loss it is considered improper to scold. The young son of the *Bahúkiwa* headman asked for a prized clasp knife. The father, reluctantly to be sure, gave the child the knife. The next day the child had lost it in the river and the father accepted his loss without comment.

On one occasion a visitor from an upriver sib rose to leave, after having spent most of the day in amiable talk, and in a most casual voice said, "I will take my spear with me." A young man then went to his quarters and fetched the spear, which the visitor took as he departed. The young man explained that he had been at this man's house during a drinking party. He saw the spear and admired it and took it home without saying anything about it. Theft to the Cubeo is not a matter of purloining an object. It is entirely a matter of attitude. They ask, in a manner of speaking: Is the taking of an object an act of friendship or of hostility?

INHERITANCE

Land, as already mentioned, is not an important issue in inheritance, mainly because the question of who has prepared a clearing for whom is too vital a matter for the Cubeo. A woman would find it unsettling to work land that a man not of the proper relationship had prepared. Daughters, of course, will work the land of a dead mother as they had worked with her when she was alive. Some personal objects are buried with the deceased; others, such as a woman's pots and a man's fishing gear, are destroyed. Some property, however, is inherited. Sons inherit from the father, daughters from the mother. Valuable and important objects go in inheritance, minor objects are destroyed, and symbolic objects are buried with the dead. The right to bequeath an object within the family is fully recognized. Ceremonial objects confer status and must go to the proper heir. I learned of no irregularities or disputes in the inheritance of ceremonial regalia. A man's gun and machete are valuable items and go to the son, but if the widow should remarry it is proper for the son to present them to her new husband on the principle that the economic balance of the household should be maintained.

FOOD

Food passes among close kin and rarely goes outside the sib. The household is, of course, the primary food-sharing unit. Its members eat all informal meals together and up to a point where it becomes arrant discourtesy the members of a household are privileged to take all their meals separately. The maloca group, nevertheless, is the common body that shares the formal evening meal. The setup of the maloca is such that only small quantities of cooked food can be prepared over a household's hearthstones. Manioc cakes and large quantities of food call for the use of equipment that is the property of the maloca, having been presented to the maloca by the headman or by some aspirant to headmanship. No household, however, has to share food merely because it has been prepared on common equipment. The common equipment stands as a reminder that the maloca is indeed a single house occupied by a single family. People eat together because they are conceptually a single family. When members of a household are cross with others in the maloca they prefer to eat alone, for it seems absurd to the Cubeo to eat with someone with whom you are angry. Ordinarily, however, households breakfast alone; they may or may not have a midday bite with other households, and they will ordinarily take the evening meal, the major meal of the day, together. Unmarried girls eat with their parents; young men, however, enjoy the hospitality of each married brother's household. Independents, those members of the sib who are of the community but not of the same maloca, eat their ordinary meals separately and join the maloca for a gala feast, when there has been a great catch of fish, or when tapir or wild pig has been brought in. On such occasions a portion of the food may be sent to the Satellite communities, or the Satellites may be invited to come and take part.

The following observed event illustrates some of the principles of distribution of game. Four hunters had shot and brought back four peccary, one animal each, as is customary. Three of the hunters were blood brothers, but of two different mothers, and the fourth was their father's brother. Among the brothers, two were unmarried. The youngest of the unmarried men presented his peccary to his mother, who singed it for him before he took it down to the river for butchering. The others made no formal presentation of their game but did their own singeing and proceeded to the river's edge to prepare their animals. When the animals had been butchered, the wives of the married hunters and the mothers of the unmarried hunters carried off the first cuts of meat, the internal organs, and scraps. (The stomach and intestines are not eaten and are thrown immediately into the river.) Each woman took the meat from the animal belonging to "her" man and boiled it at her own hearth. Then all the boiled meat was heaped upon clean banana leaves at the household of the mother of the older unmarried hunter. She was an old woman no longer a part of the household of her husband. She was chosen to be honored by her son because of her ordinarily underprivileged situation. The entire community was invited to eat. The hosts and their households took a portion of this meat aside and ate alone, to emphasize clearly that they were givers. When this meat had been eaten, portions of the remainder, haunches, were distributed to those households that did not ordinarily provide animal game, in this case the household of a widow and the household of an old man. The older woman who had been honored gave, on her son's behalf, to the widow; the elder of the hunters presented a haunch to the old man. The greater part of the meat was appropriated by each hunter's household for smoking. This meat belonging to its respective hunter was then shared with the rest of the community at the collective evening meals. Each of these households, however, had the privilege, of course, of eating as much of the meat as it wished at any other time.

Wild fruits, grubs, and ants, that is to say, foodstuffs foraged by women, are consumed more informally. Fruits are simply heaped upon the floor of the maloca to be eaten at will. When women bring in grubs and ants, that are commonly roasted on the communal manioc oven, those who wish to join the informal feast gather about the oven and help themselves. Foraged foods are not regarded as meals but as tidbits. There is still another form of informal eating. When a man returns home from any strenuous activity he is immediately given some food by his wife or mother.

Food has symbolic significance for all people. The Cubeo always attach social meaning to the exchange of food. Food does not pass casually from person to person merely as a means of assuaging hunger. People visiting other sibs carry food with them because unless they are drawn into the life of the host sib in such a way as to give them true family status they cannot count upon being fed. The *Bahúkiwa* were endlessly annoyed with me because a visiting trader or labor recruiter could count on having a meal with me. "Why do you feed him when you don't even know him?" they would ask incredulously. For some time thereafter the attitude toward me would be one of reserve, perhaps of suspicion, as though the meal had established a relationship between me and the "enemy." Because, at their insistence, I lived among the *Bahúkiwa* as an "Independent" in a small hut of my own I shared only in the festive meals. But when I traveled with them and took part in what they were doing I shared in the food of whatever household I happened to be most closely associated with in the current activities.

Men give game and fish to their wives and to their mothers. If there is to be a further distribution to other women the wives and mothers usually make it. When a man gives fish or game to a girl whom he may marry he will have declared his intentions. In ceremonial friendship, food exchange between men and women is a most important token of closeness of relationship. In food preparation the Cubeo follow the common tropical forest pattern: women boil, men bake and broil.

The visitor to a maloca is given a pepper pot (*bya*) in which to dip a bit of manioc cake. This offering of the pepper pot is a token of feeding; it may even be refreshing to a weary traveler but it is not food; it is in lieu of food. The casual visitor is received into the coolness of the house and is offered the visitor's bench near the door. When he is seated, the headman's wife appears with a small pot of boiled capsicum peppers which she sets on the ground before him. She withdraws after inviting him to eat. She then comes back with a tray on which is a manioc cake or a portion of one, sets this before the pepper pot, and withdraws. Then each woman of a household brings forward her own pot of peppers and adds manioc cake to the tray of the headman's wife. When the guest is alone with the pepper pots he leaves the bench, and, crouching, dips small bits of manioc into the pepper pot, taking care to taste of each. He does not eat as though hungry, but solemnly, just tasting. He returns quickly to the bench and the women come forward and remove the pots. That is the extent to which a guest is fed. The offering of *bya* and manioc cake has a precise meaning. It is enough food to betoken hospitality. On the other hand, the peppers are of a class of excitant substances that are suitable for the atmosphere of excitation when guests are entertained. Food formality is most marked among the elders and most relaxed among younger men either not yet married or newly wed. I have seen such young men visiting another sib mock the formalities of the pepper pot with their age mates and even join in a family meal. When they do so they make it clear that they are jesting.

Within the maloca there are two eating arrangements. One, within the household, is informal, and the other, collective or maloca-wide, is formal. In informal eating, husband, wife, and children of both sexes eat together, crouched about the small pot of prepared food or sitting in a hammock. Such meals are usually light and rarely consist of fresh fish or freshly caught game. It may be a pepper pot into which preserved fish or meat has been flaked or a dish of dried meat chopped fine, with dry peppers. If it is the morning meal, taken just upon arising an hour or so before dawn, it is a *mingau*, a tapioca porridge sometimes mixed with crushed pineapple. There is not much eating between meals. If men have been working hard they refresh themselves with sugar cane. Youngsters, however, eat as often as they like, and that is most of the time. Youngsters are free to draw upon the household larder, but much of what they eat they have foraged for themselves, fruits, sugar cane, small game, and fish. A youngster, however, will take only manioc cake prepared by his own mother.

The main meal, taken just before sunset so that it concludes shortly after sunset, is usually formal and separates men and women. A collective meal, it is eaten in the center of the dance corridor. The men crouch in a tight circle around the cluster of pots that each woman has set down. Their sons are before them in an inner circle. Women and girls sit in an outer circle behind their fathers and husbands. The men eat first and when they have finished they rise and return to their hammocks while the women and girls then move in to finish what is left over. The Cubeo are not voracious eaters. They eat almost daintily and are amused at the uncouthness of those who eat as though they were hungry. When I ate with them I always left the table hungry. I never saw any Indian eat to repletion even when great quantities of food were available. The method of eating, with the women waiting hungrily behind them, is perhaps a deterrent to gorging. It is my impression, however, that the Cubeo associate excess only with drink and associate food with moderation. That is to say, excess is pertinent to intersib gatherings, moderation is the keynote within the closer community of kin that is the sib.

People eating together are gay though not boisterous; even the older men, ordinarily solemn, unbend. The younger men laugh, tease one another, remember with amusement an incident in the catching of the food they are now eating. The women join in the laughter most generously and the men gallantly pass back to them morsels of food on bits of manioc cake. The normal movement of food at this point is from a man to his wife, daughter, or sister. But in the spirit of jest he will pass food to another woman. This will provoke mirthful calls of "ha, your sweetheart." No man would be so foolish as to pass back food to a woman with whom he might be having an affair even though this is a permissible jesting occasion. If he is really "cutting up" he will choose an old woman and so draw upon truly licensed ribaldry. When the women are left with their portion they carry on in the same convivial spirit. Household meals by contrast are solemn. When a meal is finished they rinse the mouth with water, using the fingers to scrub the teeth, and finally they wash their hands in a "finger bowl" of water. In some upstream houses, though, I noticed hands being wiped on the house posts.

Guests who have come for a drinking party or other ceremony will ordinarily eat very little for the duration. At the mourning ceremony, which lasts three full days, the hosts prepare a few corn cakes and tie these to the house posts for a hungry guest. But they prepare no more than about one corn cake for every three guests or so. Moreover, by tying the cakes to the house posts rather than serving them in a dish they are clearly indicating that this is not a meal. If people wish to eat during these three days they must bring their own provisions. Needless to say, a person hungry enough to ask for food will be fed; and at the protracted mourning rites there is a certain amount of scrounging upon the food resources of the hosts, but of an informal and almost underhanded nature. Women feel freer about passing food to one another and the men surreptitiously nibble at it. The Cubeo expect an adult male to tolerate hunger under any circumstances, and not to feel hunger at all during a ceremony. They expect women to live up to this standard but partially, and they are completely tolerant of the young, who may or may not eat on these occasions as they see fit.

Eating is considered a social activity occurring in a number of specified social settings, all of which involve Cubeo notions of intimacy. The sib is the normal outer limit of intimacy with respect to eating. However, guests may be temporarily assimilated into the sib if they take part in all of its activities, such as the woman cultivating a borrowed manioc garden and the man hunting and fishing. When they have been so assimilated they may eat as sib members do. The eating problem involves the overnight guest. There is no taboo against inviting even an overnight guest to join in a sib meal. It is rather that host and guest alike regard this as a most delicate matter. It is embarrassing to eat with people who are not intimates. Most often I have seen guests huddled in a corner eating a cold supper of old manioc cake and some dried fish they have brought with them. They are surrounded by a wall of privacy since the hosts will not look at them and they will not look at the hosts while they are eating. Before I understood the Cubeo sentiments about eating I inadvertently caused a visiting woman acute embarrassment. She and her husband, passing by downstream, had paused among the *Bahúkiwa* to pay a courtesy call. The woman was hungry and drew some provisions to eat. She then noticed that I was looking at her as she ate, so she turned her back. Puzzled by this, I asked the *Bahúkiwa* headman what it meant. He said, "That is the way some people are." When the woman heard me ask, she reached in among her things and fetched out a mat which she set around her like a screen. From behind the screen she completed her meal.

The Cubeo seem to regard food as markedly secular, and this may explain why the sick who are supernaturally afflicted must avoid all foods except for some manioc cake.

The play of young boys often involves food. The young male pack fishes for minnows, traps small game, and forages in the nearby forest for ants, grubs, and fruits. They share all food equally, except that a boy aspiring to be a leader takes a smaller share for himself. This attitude of leadership has its counterpart among adult males. Within the maloca a leader — not necessarily the headman — makes a point of sharing the food he has with the sib even if it is no more than a small fish. Those who are not leaders and who do not aspire to leadership consume small catches of game and fish in the household, reasoning that they have only enough for one family.

In view of the symbolic significance of food, its involvement in leadership and in social intimacies, it is not surprising that a good part of social and individual pathology should involve disturbances of conventional patterns of sharing. Two kinds of disturbance came to my notice; one, the more common, a pathological nonsharing, and the other a pathological stealing of food. Nonsharing appears early in the male play pack and continues, I suspect, into adult life. Food disorders affect males far more because only they are expected to uphold the amenities of food sharing. Like their mothers, girls are attached only to a household, forming no play pack. If they forage for foodstuffs it is in company with their mothers and for the use of the household or the sib. Some boys in a play pack take the share of food that has been given them and hide behind a tree, crouch behind a bush, or turn their backs while eating. They are even stealthy in eating food that they have obtained by their own efforts. A boy once came to my hut and asked for food. I gave him a banana. He crawled under a table, turned his back to me, and gulped it, while his companions were outside the door waiting for him to come out. I am certain they knew what he was doing, but even the youngest Cubeo boy has learned the courtesy of ignoring poor manners in others. I doubt that any nonsharing goes unobserved and I expect that the nonsharer is not too concerned with being unobserved. Often enough, boys will quarrel about the distribution of food, but never with a nonsharer. They sense the significance of the gesture and are embarrassed by it, waiting for the delinquent to finish. He rejoins them and their play resumes as though nothing had happened. Elders will not correct nonsharing among children because they regard what the boys do in the play pack as a matter of no adult concern. I was never aware that the children themselves ever rebuked or punished a nonsharer in their midst. The nonsharer always received his portion. The play pack leader, who does not hesitate to censure a member for indecent sexual behavior, is comfortable in his role as a giver and will not censure a nongiver. He understands, to be sure, that nonsharing is a form of deliberate estrangement from the intimacies of the group, but he also knows that no headman will censure a household head who chooses to become an Independent or a Satellite. Similarly, the nonsharer may estrange himself from the play pack but the play pack will not ostracize him. Among the *Bahúkiwa* the flagrant nonsharer was also the boy who ran away during the ancestral whipping rites. Every example of a case of nonsharing that came to my attention (five or six only) was that of a boy who had no father. Orphan boys are deprived of one of the more pleasurable intimacies of receiving a portion of fish or game that a father brings home. A man's son is the first to greet him when he beaches his canoe. He is given a fish or a bit of meat, which he prepares by broiling or baking and shares with his play pack. He has the status of a giver. The orphan child, in these circumstances, has the lower status of a receiver and is denied a food intimacy. The nonsharer acknowledges at the same time a status of subordination as well as of estrangement.

Among adults, nonsharing is more disturbing and more consequential. A man who does not share food eventually refuses to do his share of work. Such a person is called "one who does nothing." A household head who is angry or out of sorts will not join the sib meal but will gather his family around him at the household hearth for a private meal. A mood is respected and the incident passes with little notice. If it is repeated, it is assumed that the nonsharer will soon move out and become an Independent. Nonsharing does become a touchy issue when food is scarce. We were experiencing hungry days during the height of the rainy season, most meals consisting of manioc cake dipped in peppers, fortified occasionally with a minnow. One late afternoon a household head entered the maloca with a string of two fish. Momentarily all eyes turned hungrily and happily toward him, only to encounter the averted eyes that told plainly that he was not going to share. The man walked directly to his own hearth and gave the fish to his wife, who was awaiting him there with the children. She took the fish in silence and quickly set about preparing it, never once turning her eyes out upon the maloca. The house filled with an appetizing aroma that it had not experienced for many days. Everyone pretended not to notice it. The little family sat glumly around its pot of fish, eating in silence and with averted eyes, observed only by the young children, who did not, however, venture near. One man made an effort to break the melancholy spell that had fallen over the maloca. The effort failed. A visitor to the maloca the next morning, however, would have been unaware that the previous night had been a miserable one.

During this same period of hunger I also saw a household head prance into the house holding before him one little minnow. He chanted in a comic vein a little ditty to the effect that he had singly caught this monster of a fish and that now his wife would prepare it and all would feast, putting an end to their hunger. With a grand gesture he gave the fish to his wife, who giggled merrily and, helped by the women, prepared it. The meal that followed was about the gayest I had attended. This is correct procedure. A responsible household head does what he can to boost morale. The nonsharer has a deadly influence upon a house and in the end he will have to leave. The Cubeo know very well what nonsharing means: He does not like us.

No one will be asked to leave his own kingroup except in a fit of anger. Just as the boys of the play pack will only stand aside as their nonsharing comrade gulps his food privately, so the adults will do nothing but pretend not to notice the nonsharer in their midst. "He does not have to share his food if he does not want to," they say in extenuation. When the nonsharer refuses to do his share of the common work, he adds to the sense of grievance against him, but the crisis is subacute. It becomes acute when his wife no longer goes to the manioc garden and asks other women for manioc cake. Then it will be said, "He has a lazy wife, they are not good." At the next drinking party they quarrel, all the resentments are aired, and the dissaffected household departs. I was told, but could not verify it, that in the end chronic nonsharers are killed by sorcery. Such people, it is said, become wanderers, imposing upon the hospitality of kin and of friends. Since they are basically uncooperative they annoy everyone until someone in a fit of anger decides to put them to death.

THE ECONOMIC SYSTEM

The Cubeo economy may be characterized as essentially inelastic, sustenance-oriented, and egalitarian. In these respects it contrasts with parallel root horticulture economies in other parts of the world, such as in Oceania and Africa. In those areas economies are generally in the service of social status and of political power and are, consequently, dynamic, fostering social and economic inequality. Among the Cubeo, on the other hand, and in the South American tropical forest as a whole, social status is a minor issue in production, while the headman, who in Oceania and in Africa plays a commanding role in economic distribution, has here only the most diffuse economic functions.

The relative inelasticity of an economy is, needless to say, a function of many factors. In the case of tropical forest horticulture, the nature of crops, soils, methods of cultivation, and tools are all relevant. Even more significant, however, are such factors as the social organization of production, including such fundamental matters as the division of labor, as well as the nature of political controls. The motives of production are of greatest importance. Motives of status and of political power provide, all other factors being equal, for an expanding economy. When the aim of production is mainly to provide sustenance and to maintain a limited network of lateral (as opposed to hierarchical) exchanges the economy tends to remain in equilibrium with its customary standards of community size. Such an economy is conservative and traditionalistic.

With respect to physical factors, Cubeo manioc horticulture has come close to reaching a productive limit in terms of yield per acre. The yield from *Manihot utilissima* normally ranges from six to ten tons per acre. Among the *Bahúkiwa* I estimated the acreage yield to be between five and six tons, a productivity that reflects considerable agronomical skill and effort. Any substantial increase in aggregate production would have to come more from expanded acreage, for which the land is available, than from more intensive cultivation of present plots. Acreage expansion, however, is limited by a combination of social and cultural conditions as well as by the peculiar nature of bitter manioc itself. As is well known, the ease of cultivation of bitter manioc and its relatively high yield is offset by the great effort required to rid the tubers of hydrocyanic acid. I have already described the processing of manioc from raw tuber to a cake and its heavy demands on the time of the women. Bitter manioc is a cumbersome crop and the load of 50–60 pounds that a woman carries home from the garden represents her carrying capacity. These are the technical problems. They are not inherently formidable, except in terms of the traditional sexual division of labor of the Cubeo. The men who make the original clearing can call upon group labor and they have the spare time. If increase in manioc cultivation were only a matter of preparing a clearing it would be relatively easy for any community to double its present zone of planting. The Cubeo, however, must calculate the size of a clearing in accordance with how much land the women of a household, working independently, can cultivate. On her part, the woman does not cultivate more than she can handle in the course of her accustomed routine. In manioc cultivation each household is autonomous; and while a woman can call upon the help of another woman when she is not well there is simply no collective or cooperative organization to help harvest, bring in, and process the crop. The headman who has the authority to direct the masculine work party that prepares the clearing has no jurisdiction over the work of the women. And neither does anyone else.

Nor does the nature of demand place much pressure upon manioc production. Under ideal conditions at least two-thirds of the manioc crop is for food. The rest is divided between chicha and farinha. Since the Cubeo are moderate eaters and do not have the custom of feasting outsiders, the demand for manioc as food is inelastic. There is only a little more elasticity in the demand for chicha. Although the drinking party is a principal means for binding the sibs it cannot be said that increasing the quantity of chicha consumed at a party or adding to the traditional number of parties would promote additional sib cohesiveness. In this instance a law of diminishing returns may be said to operate.[2] In any case, since each sib assumes some of the responsibility for entertaining the others, the burden of supplying the chicha is phratry-wide. The poorer sibs entertain less often than do the richer ones.

It is in the production of farinha that some elasticity in demand may be expected. Farinha, as the Cubeo equivalent of a "cash crop," pays largely for vanity articles, ornaments that have no traditional sanction, but also for cloth petticoats, that have now become customary apparel. However, this aspect of production for the market is also socialized. The goods a woman acquires from the sale of her farinha are largely committed to the intricate network of gift exchanges that apply between husband and wife, brother and sister, and between ceremonial friends of opposite sex. In a general way

---

[2] See the chapter on the drinking party.

the production of farinha by women is a partial counterpart to the work of the men in the rubber forest. The man takes most of his earnings in "capital goods," muzzle-loading guns, machetes, fishhooks, matches, knives, thread, needles, ammunition. The remainder goes to a few vanity items for himself and in gifts for his wife, sister, and female ceremonial friend. It is these gifts that a woman is obligated to reciprocate through her farinha trade. Since these gift exchanges involve traditional relations of status equality they quickly achieve a relatively stable equilibrium. Only a small part, then, of commercial exchange leaves the traditional channels of lateral circulation of goods. As for "vanity" purchases, they form no part of any institutionalized expression of social prestige. The issue for the Cubeo is rather one of a limited degree of self-indulgence. For a woman, in particular, the privilege of indulging a fancy for some trinket and freely contracting her farinha for it is an essential part of her sense of domestic well-being. It is an expression, on the one hand, of her autonomy, and, on the other, of domestic felicity. A dissatisfied wife does not indulge her personal vanity more; on the contrary, she produces less.

Another important element in production is the attitude toward labor. For the Cubeo all effort must be inherently satisfying. Women accept more drudgery than do men, but they no more than the men would accept the bitter peasant philosophy that hard and unrewarding work is man's lot. Men and women alike are accustomed to a variety of effort. They do not care to drive themselves beyond the onset of boredom or of fatigue. All work patterns are based upon short and diversified rhythms. I have demonstrated this in the work cycle of women. It is even more marked in the work cycle of men. Food gathering and preparing does demand continuity and completion. The hunter must complete his chase, the fisherman must return home with a suitable catch, and the housewife must complete her daily ration of manioc cake. Even so, there are many opportunities for rest and diversion that the Indians take. They would rather eat less than work more. In the course of a year there are many holidays. Among the *Bahúkiwa* these averaged almost one a week. On the occasion of a drinking party women do not go into the fields either on the day of preparation or on the day after. In manufactures, which form part of the domestic economy, the pace of work is very slow. Men, who make the baskets that are important home utensils as well as major items in trade, work very sporadically. There is no compulsion to finish something quickly. Thus, on the whole, the Cubeo work habits also contribute to general economic inelasticity.

There is no formal provision in Cubeo economy whereby food-stuffs, utensils, or productive equipment can accumulate dispropor-tionately in any one household or in any one community. There are well-to-do communities and there are poor communities, the differ-ences between them being due, however, almost entirely to their own state of morale, but also to differences in location. Location, as has been noted, follows the formal but functionally inconsequential ranking of the sibs. Upriver sibs may have some disadvantages in fishing during the dry season. On the other hand, they have ad-vantages in hunting. Tapir, for example, are more numerous upriver on the Cuduiarí than downriver. Moreover, occupants of a river do have the privilege of fishing anywhere along its length. In this respect, the most important point to emphasize is that the Cubeo acknowledge the right of all who are not enemies to the available food resources. The economic domain of the tribes in the Vaupés area is, in fact, an extensive one. The sib territory is of course the economic center, but there is also available a vast periphery of supplementary economic zones. On the score of friendship and of bilateral kinship men acquire hunting and fishing rights in many different rivers. Thus, in his travels Koch-Grünberg met sections of tribes, including Cubeo, very far from their home base. The hospitality of the house is proverbial in this region and such domestic hospitality has its counterpart in a hospitality of the river or of the forest. It is the privilege of families to travel about, visiting community after community where they have either a kinship claim or a friendship claim. Everywhere the men are welcome as fishermen and as hunters and the women are assigned gardens. So long as visitors join the economic round they are welcome. It is even more accurate to say that they are eagerly welcomed, for nothing contributes more to the state of contentment of a community than the desire of others to join it. The issue, of course, is economic hospitality and not freedom of trespass. The right of trespass is the right to enter and to use an economic domain without taking formal cognizance of those who have a stronger or more traditional right to it. Such rights among the Cubeo are nonexistent. The rights of hos-pitality, on the other hand, obligate those who have entered a non-traditional economic domain to engage in the traditional forms of reciprocity that bind sibmen and phratry mates. When hunters kill a tapir in the domain of another sib they are not obligated to "pay tribute" but they do have a sense of obligation to give some of the meat to the host sib as part of a pattern of food reciprocity.

Underlying this relatively unrestricted access to food resources are two cultural conditions. One is that food for the Cubeo symbolizes the amity of the highly knit sib community; the other, and a related condition, is that the total economic product is divorced from considerations of status and power. Thus, the Cubeo cannot think of economic advantage as a political advantage over others, and, conversely, they cannot regard the economic advantage of others as a threat to their own autonomy. Economic equalization through the various formal channels of distribution is taken for granted. There are no sanctions or techniques deliberately designed to promote equality, but simply provision of sustenance for all persons within the network of kinship and friendship.

3

The Sib

The Cubeo sib is a unilineal descent group whose members regard themselves as being descended from common ancestors but cannot establish an actual genealogical relationship. Sibs are named, normally localized, exogamic, patrilineal, and patrilocal. They are bound into unnamed exogamic phratries within which they occupy an order of rank that expresses the sequence in which they emerged during their mythical first emergence. Sib members claim descent from the male of an ancestral brother-sister pair. Each sib bears a name that in some cases is the name of the sib founder, but in any case is the name of an Ancient, that is, an early ancestor. The first ancestors are called *Beküpwänwa* (the Ancients). The sib is the center of the social structure, the focus and regulator of all main social, religious, and economic activities. It is the only true political unit since only a sib has a headman. A person's identification is only by sib. The strongest feeling that the Cubeo have for the sib is that it is a family in which the males show the strongest solidarity because they are the ones who live permanently together. The women never lose their sib identity, and when a married woman returns home, as a widow, divorced, or with a husband in tow, she may take up a position in the sib that is sociologically equivalent to that of a male head of household. She takes her place in the informal council of household heads and takes her turn in giving drinking parties to her sibmates.

Since my study of the Cubeo sib system is incomplete, being based on information from a few sibs only, the principles of sib nomenclature can only be hinted at and not definitely established. One principle, that of eponymy, seems to hold for sibs of high social standing. But my information on this point is limited to only one of the phratries. In this phratry, composed of sibs along the Cuduiarí and the Vaupés, the two top-ranking sibs bear the names of Ancients who were the very first men to emerge from the traditional emergence site. The founders of the *Órobawa* and of the *Aúnbwawü* were, respectively, *Órobakü* and *Aúnkü*.[1] These men, it is said, named all the other sibs of the phratry that emerged after they did. I could not discover the source of these names. They may have been from the genealogical list of the two top-ranking sibs, in accordance with the current principle that when a new sib is adopted into the phratry the adopting or sponsoring sib endows its members with names from its own genealogical list. However, Cubeo traditions suggest diverse origins for the sibs so that it is unlikely that a single principle will explain the sib names.

The first ancestors of the sibs, other than the top-ranking two, had names that were not the same as the sib names. The founder of the *Bahúkiwa*, for example, was *Bwü* (Agouti) and the founder of the *Hehénewa* was *Djurédo*, but later Ancients took as personal names the sib name itself, thus establishing in subsequent generations the principle of eponymy. In later generations, *Bahúkü* becomes a leading *Bahúkiwa* Ancient and *Hehénakü* a leading *Hehénewa* Ancient. Any Ancient may also be referred to generically by the sib name, so that one may speak of a specific *Bahúkü* or *Bahúko*[2] or of a generalized *Bahúkü* or *Bahúko*, meaning in the latter instance an Ancient man or woman of the *Bahúkiwa* sib.

A proper sib name must have some eponymous quality. Some sib names are descriptive, such as *Mánapwänwa*, meaning "Trail People," a derogatory reference to people who arrived on the Cuduiarí overland like the Macú instead of decently along the river by canoe. These people reject this name in favor of a subsib name which has the orthodox merit of having been bestowed by the founders of the phratry. Cubeo sib names are normally descriptive only insofar as personal names are descriptive. The legendary method by which the first sibs got their names from a higher-ranking source stands for the Cubeo as the model by which newcomers are brought into the phratry. An adopted sib is given a name that has in its stem the name of the adopting sib. All the sibs of the *Hehénewa* are differentiated by a descriptive prefix, while the sibs of the *Bahúkiwa* are differen-

---

[1] There is a full list of sibs following the present discussion.
[2] The suffix *kü* is masculine, *ko* is feminine.

tiated by a suffix. From the *Hehénewa* traditions it seems likely that
they were originally an independent tribe, probably Tucano, that
had joined in with the group of sibs that were headed by the *Órobawa*
and the *Aúnbwawü*, bringing with them their associated sibs. The
sibs that carry the *Hehénewa* stem with their descriptive prefixes are
also known by names that are compounded of the prefixes as well.
Thus, the *Byarí-Hehénewa* are also known as *Byarídowa*, and the
Pyéndo-Hehénewa as *Pyéndowa*. According to Koch-Grünberg, the
Órobawa regard themselves as a branch of the *Hehénewa* and are also
known as *Ólaba-Hehénewa*. His information was that the *Hehénewa*
were the "true" Cubeo and that the *Bahúkiwa* were intrusive Macú
(1909, II, 87). The actual history of the sibs is clouded in uncertainty.
We can be reasonably sure only of a composite of several distinctive
peoples or "tribes." The few *Wathariwa* sibs in my list are also
named in a fashion similar to that of the *Hehénewa*.

Each sib also possesses a list of personal names that constitutes its
traditional genealogy.[3] These are names that all sib members must
bear. They are called *aínheme* (*ain*: anaconda; *heme*: tongue) to indicate their origin from the speech of the anaconda, the animal form
in which all first ancestors emerged from the earth. In these names
there is a note of prestige, in that some names are illustrious, being
part of the earliest genealogies, while others, having been added later,
are less important. Since only one name can be held at a time, names
are allocated in order of seniority, but not, insofar as I know, within a
senior line. Names with an honorific connotation circulate within
the sib, and not by lineage. They are transmitted in alternate generations, going from a deceased grandparent to a grandchild. It should
be said at once that while the notions of sib rank and of the distinction between more honorific and less honorific names suggests a structured system of social status, the social significance of status hierarchy
is not great. The Cubeo have the skeleton of an aristocratic system
that is fleshed with an egalitarian ethos.

Personal names are often those of birds, insects, and beasts, less
commonly of fish. In the recent past, it is said, sib members did not
eat the flesh of any creature whose name was then being carried by
a sib member. This taboo is no longer in force. The explanation
given is that hunting is more important now and they do not wish
to deprive themselves of animal meat.[4] Without a proper sib name,

---

[3] There is a list of *Bahúkiwa* names at the end of this chaper.

[4] On the other hand, there is the tradition that in the past they lived by hunting, fishing, and gathering rather than by farming. If this taboo did indeed exist
it may have lapsed for the same reason that other ceremonial observances have

a child will not grow, the Cubeo say. Growth is an attribute of the Ancients. The giving of a name is one of the ways in which the growth magic of the Ancients is utilized. These names from the sib genealogies are not used freely, the Indians preferring to use Christian names and to address one another by a kinship term.

The sib has permanence and it has continuity with the past. The "history" of each sib is known and is recited at all major ceremonial occasions.[5] In narrating sib "history," distinctions are drawn between original sibs, later comers, and the newest-formed sibs. Since ancientness is honorific and the Cubeo have a sentiment of egalitarianism, these distinctions are underplayed. But when people have been drinking and quarreling the matter of ancestry will be brought up.

The tradition of phratric organization is that all its member sibs are kin. Tradition holds, too, that once all sibs of the same phratry were united under a single headman. But this tradition may refer to the scheme of sib rank and the acknowledgment of the leading sib as the "head" rather than to an actual political organization. On the other hand, since there is little doubt but that tribal organization in this region of the Amazon is highly fluid, with smaller segments forming new enlarged formations and enlarged formations breaking up again into smaller and relatively more stable sib segments, the tradition of the phratry as a political unit cannot be dismissed.

The Cubeo distinguish between *kwináwü* (one kin) and *abéwetema* (they are not ours) in referring to their own phratry and to an opposite phratry. In the past, there may have been at least four phratries, since the traditions speak of one group of sibs as having amalgamated with another. Previously these two groups had intermarried, it is averred. According to one version of the origin myth the sibs of a phratry are all descended from a single water anaconda called *Pwénte ainkü* (Anaconda person), who divided himself into segments, the head becoming the leading sib of the phratry, and each subsequent segment forming the remainder of the sib hierarchy. A variant version states that pairs of anacondas emerged from a crevice among the rocks of a rapids, shed their skins, and formed a brother-sister pair. Subsequently, the sisters married out and the brothers took wives from people they met in their wanderings. The first pair to emerge were the head sib, and they gave names to all that followed

lapsed, out of simple neglect. Also to be considered in this connection is the common Cubeo view that the life of past generations was more severe than it is today.

[5] The text of the *Bahúkiwa* "history" follows the sib list in this chapter.

them. Either version accounts for sib hierarchy. In the first version the Cubeo visualize the phratry as the body of the anaconda spread along a river with its head anchored at the site of emergence and its tail lying upstream to form the lowest-ranking sib. In the second version the sib pairs moved upstream and located themselves according to the sequence of their emergence. The theme of common descent that sanctions exogamy and confraternity is conveyed not by a common anaconda ancestor, for the Cubeo would not doubt that all human beings were descended from anacondas, but rather by common emergence from the same site. All sibs of the same phratry should ideally have emerged from the same rapids. But even among those having emerged from the same rapids there are still distinctions of relative closeness depending upon whether they emerged from the same hole or from adjacent holes. It would seem that the origin myth must be in harmony with current social relationships and that a particular version is employed depending upon the present state of affairs. When a sib is newly admitted into the phratry it must adapt its own origin traditions to the common mythical theme of emergence in the form of an anaconda at a preferred emergence site.

From the *Bahúkiwa* I heard at least three versions of the story that placed the *Hehénewa* within the phratry. One said that the *Hehénewa* were really strangers, having emerged somewhere along the Papurý River. They heard the *Órobawa* sounding the ancestor trumpets, and attracted by the music — a sign of identity — they came

Fig. 4. Petroglyph: *Kúwai* and *Aínkü* (scale: 1″ = 6′).

to the true emergence site of Uaracapurí, where they were received by the Órobawa, who bestowed upon them the name *Hehénewa*. This version would account for Koch-Grünberg's information that the *Hehénewa* are also known as *Ólaba-Hehénewa*. Another version suggests a closer relationship by making the point that the *Hehénewa* had wanted to emerge in the same place with all the others of the phratry, but because other sibs were hostile to them they came out instead at the Papurý and then journeyed to join their kin. A third version is simply that the *Hehénewa* and *Bahúkiwa* were once alien groups that joined into a confederation after the *Hehénewa* had befriended the *Bahúkiwa*.

The theme of hostility in the *Hehénewa* emergence was explained by informants in the following way. The first people were very fierce and those that came out of the emergence hole wanted to prevent others from emerging. The *Órobawa*, having come out first, made a hole for the others to come out of. Those they willingly allowed to come out formed with them one group. Those that came out despite opposition formed another. Subsequently both divisions were rejoined.

The *Pedíkwa*, a branch of the *Hehénewa*, also tell that they had been prevented by the hostility of the other sibs from emerging at Uaracapurí and so they emerged at the Papurý. They came out in the form of a single anaconda who cut himself into many parts, each of which became a parakeet (*kúdjuru*). The parakeets flew about looking for food and settled at a lagoon at *Yaibabü* near the Mitú *igarapés*, an affluent of the upper Cuduiarí. After a time, they cut a path through the forest and arrived at *Pedíwa*, a rock on the Cuduiarí where they built a house and became the *Pedíkwa*. A more honorific version of this tale that the *Pedíkwa* also tell is that, having come to *Pedíwa*, the site of a major rapids on the Cuduiarí, they re-emerged. Since, they insist, they had never taken human form until they had re-emerged at *Pedíwa*, they feel justified in claiming that rapids as a true emergence site and they have the distinction, therefore, of now residing, as does the *Órobawa* head sib, at an original emergence site. An unknown people, the tradition relates, had been living at *Pedíwa*, now known as *Toídibü* (Painted rocks — petroglyphs) but moved away when the *Pedíkwa* re-emerged.

The *Bahúkiwa* explain their relationship to the *Hehénewa* as follows: *Bwü* (Agouti), the Ancient of the *Bahúkiwa*, was leading his people from the Vaupés up into the Cuduiarí when they encountered the *Byari-Hehénewa*, a now extinct subsib of the *Hehénewa*. They fought and all the *Bahúkiwa* were killed except for one boy, who came to be known as *Bwübekúdjo* (*Bwü* the Ancient). The *Byarí-Hehénewa* took him captive. Sometime later, the *Hehénewa*, coming to visit their kin, determined to rescue the boy. They did so, killing off the *Byarí-Hehénewa* who were holding him. They released *Bwübekúdjo*, giving him two *Borówa* (Macú) women as wives. The *Borówa* were then servants of the *Hehénewa*. The Macú women bore *Bwübekúdjo* ten children. It was from the males of this sibling group that the *Bahúkiwa* sib was reconstituted.

This concession of kinship alliance with the Macú stigmatizes the *Bahúkiwa* as an inferior sib even though the descent is still in the male line. Normally, Cubeo used *Borówa* women sexually but did not marry them. The *Bahúkiwa* do not concede that they are *Borówa*. And I learned early in my stay among them that nothing was more offensive than to even hint that someone was *Borówa*. The *Hehénewa* had told Koch-Grünberg that the *Bahúkiwa* were *Borówa* who had assimilated themselves to the Cubeo and were still to be regarded with contempt (1909, II, 136). No *Hehénewa* made this observation to me, but possibly out of courtesy since I was living with the *Bahúkiwa*.

The origin of the *Bahúkübwauwü*, a subsib of the *Bahúkiwa*, is also attributed to an act of kindness by a fellow sib, in this case at the hands of the second-ranking *Aúnbwawü*. In the course of an attack on them, all but one *Bahúkiwa* girl were killed. She was succored by the *Aúnbwawü*, among whom she lived until she married. The narrator claimed that no one knew whom she had married, a lapse of information of utmost importance, since the point of the story is that despite patriliny a woman can also re-establish a sib. She bore eight children and they and their descendants took the name of *Bahúkübwauwü*. Descent then reverted to patriliny.

The Cubeo view of the phratry, as revealed by the traditions, is of a grouping of essentially autonomous sibs into a loose fraternity that takes its sanction not from descent from a common ancestor but emergence from a common place. The genealogical relationship determines sib identity, but it is geography that determines phratric identity. The principal idea that is expressed is that the closer the sibs were spatially at the time of emergence the closer should be their present fraternal bonds. Thus, the traditions draw fine distinctions between emergence from the very same crevice on the rocks, from the same rapids, and from the same river. Unfortunately for our interest in reconstructing tribal history, the traditions lack consistency. This inconsistency reflects perhaps the ethnic heterogeneity of the region, which, together with the lack of a central source for tradition, places upon each sib the responsibility for describing its own history. To be sure, the custom of reciting a sib origin tradition at the regular drinking parties that bring the sibs of a phratry together has probably had the effect of eliminating major discrepancies. I suspect that there are two kinds of sib traditions, those that are recited publicly and so have official standing and those that are talked about and ruminated about within the privacy of the sib or at small multi-sib gatherings. I do not, however, have a collection of official origin traditions. Another reason for discrepancies is that the origin traditions are the most important sanctions for regulating current relationships among sibs. If sibs are close now it is, in Cubeo thought, because they were close in the past; if they are distant now it is surely because of some event in the past, at the time of emergence. The more friendly sibs feel toward one another the closer do they bring together their first origins. When they quarrel they call attention to the initial distance in their origins.

Nevertheless, there are orthodox versions of sib histories that do acknowledge differences in origin. The sibs of what I call Phratry I form two divisions, according to some traditions. One group of sibs is sometimes referred to as *Yavimanawa* (Children of the jaguar).[6] This group, consisting of *Órobawa*, *Aúnbwawü*, *Hehénewa*, *Watharíwa*, *Byá-Watharíwa*, and *Byá-Hehénewa*, is supposed to have emerged together at *Yavíbebo* (Place of the jaguars), a site at the Uaracapurí cataract. The remaining sibs of the phratry had different origins and are not, as far as I could learn, identified by a distinctive name. The *Yavímanawa*, according to this particular tradition, form the core of the phratry, while the others are secondary members. The distinction is not without significance. The rule of exogamy, of course, holds for all members of the phratry. All phratry mates will refer to one another as *pakomá* (kinsman), and will entertain one another and offer ready hospitality. Sibs that are close in origin entertain one another more frequently and can depend upon one another to honor drinking party invitations.

In short, the relationship among the sibs of a phratry is far from uniform, but ranges from a degree of closeness akin to that holding among common residents to such distance that the rule of exogamy can be called into question. The *Hehénewa*, for example, discounting *Bahúkiwa* assertions of closeness, claim that they are so distant from

---

[6] This reference to "Children of the jaguar" has, of course, an honorific reference. There is, however, another usage that is derogatory and that is when it is applied to the Macú. Giacone (1949, p. 88) reports that Tucanos, Tarianas, and Desanas say that the Macú are not people at all but are *filhos da onca*.

the *Bahúkiwa* that intermarriage is possible. The *Bahúkiwa*, for their part, deny this. I could obtain, however, no record of a marriage between the *Bahúkiwa* and *Hehénewa*. I am inclined to attribute such discrepancies to considerations of prestige. The high-ranking *Hehénewa* emphasize distance, the low-ranking *Bahúkiwa*, closeness, between their respective sibs.

The Cubeo phratry is particularly interesting because of its hierarchical organization. Ranked sibs suggest a hierarchical social structure and hence a political organization of some complexity. Neither, as we have already observed, is actually present among the Cubeo. Insofar as I could determine, the leading sibs of a phratry had no actual jurisdiction over any of the lower-ranking sibs, nor was there any formal way in which the rank order of sibs was expressed other than by listing, and by some prestige privileges that allowed only the high-ranking sibs, up to and including the *Hehénewa*, to wear the quartz cylinder pendant on their breasts. Among the low-ranking *Bahúkiwa* no one possessed the jaguar-tooth or the armadillo-vertebrae girdles either.

The hierarchy of sibs is consistent with a kinship stress upon seniority of birth that distinguishes older and younger siblings, but it seems at variance with a very strong feeling for equality, with the absence of deferential behavior, and with other marked symbols of social status. There are, nevertheless, intimations of rivalries within the phratry among sib headmen, in which one accuses the others of seeking power over the phratry. White influence may be responsible for this, since the authorities hope to be able to deal with a single chief rather than with each small sib. Even so, it may well be that the groundwork for phratric leadership has been laid down by the hierarchical organization. We do have a tradition that the *Hehénewa* once made an unsuccessful military effort to establish political authority over the entire Cuduiarí.

The character of the Cubeo sib is such that it is a moot point whether we are dealing with a true patrilineal sib or with a patrilineage. From the Cubeo point of view, the descent group has lineage features. It is small, it is generally localized, its members have the strongest feelings of kinship identification, and they claim not merely descent from a common ancestor but they produce genealogies to establish such a connection. At some time during the year, an old man gathers all the young males, from the age of six on, together in the evening and each night for a month teaches them the sib genealogy. The genealogies, however, begin from the past and never actually connect with the present. The interest of the Cubeo in present genealogies is not strong, so that they have only a general, albeit a strong, feeling that the family lines presently in a sib are related. What keeps the sib from being a lineage is then the technical fact that the Cubeo cannot link up their present descent lines with their ancient descent lines.

One is tempted, therefore, to think of the Cubeo descent group as a transitional form, hovering between sib and lineage. At first glance the distinction between sib and lineage seems to hang by the technicality of how sophisticated a people are about genealogies. Yet this sophistication is a matter of major importance. Sib continuity and growth is a relatively simple matter of transmitting a sib name and a line of descent with an origin myth to give historical sanction. Lineage continuity and growth, on the other hand, demand motivation as well as the capability for maintaining accurate or presumably accurate genealogical records. Societies organized upon aristocratic lines can do this readily. Egalitarian societies, on the other hand, can have small lineages or large clans and kindreds but they cannot readily support large or historically deep lineages. The Cubeo have a shadow aristocracy only, not enough to sustain the necessary degree of genealogical sophistication. On the other hand, if the Cubeo could not sustain the growth of lineages neither could they sustain the growth of sibs. Two social conditions seemed to stand in the way of the enlargement of sibs. One was the inherent fissility of the sib, the other was the organization of the phratry. The phratry allowed the sibs to split without endangering their survival by virtue of being too small.

The basic social organization that provides for autonomous confederation of small units conforms readily to the requirements of easy absorption of new groups. The modes of group-binding, such as exogamy, the cycle of drinking parties, and the segmented forms of ceremonial participation that allow each sib to function as a ceremonial unit, are also admirably adapted to rapid assimilation of foreign tribes without benefit of a central administration. In cases of assimilation, all the necessary joint activities to which the sibs of a phratry are bound will inevitably encourage a common language. Just as the phratric organization allows for easy binding of autonomous sibs into a convenient fraternity that provides for peace, cooperation, and sociability, it allows as readily for fission without serious disruption. From these observations it may be inferred that the history of the Northwest Amazon region has been one of constant formation and disruption of sociopolitical entities. What a tribe is at any time is a core of sib segments that may have persevered through time and then have drawn to them new sibs from peoples speaking the same as well as other languages. The Cubeo tribe, as we have already observed, seems to be an aggregate of Tucanoan-speaking, Arawakan-speaking, and "Macuan"-speaking peoples. A particular sib that belongs to one tribe today may incorporate itself into another tomorrow.

It is possible that sib formation in the Northwest Amazon region has been an outgrowth of this process of repeated assimilation of new groups. The reasoning behind this assumption is as follows: patrilocal extended families need only assert and maintain a tradition of common origin and then live up to the requirement of maintaining a firm group identity, within a confederation, to make the transition to sib or clan. The suggestion is, however, that sib formation cannot be accounted for merely by the growth of extended patrilocal families or by the enlargement of lineages — because of the ease of fission — but rather as a response to quite another process, that of confederation in which the identity of the joining segments is retained. A confederation of descent groups heightens the probability that all will defend their autonomy by asserting their identity of common descent.

THE SIB AND PHRATRIC ORGANIZATION

The sibs are listed in approximate order of rank. This rank order should be considered as provisional, since it represents mainly the *Bahúkiwa* view of sib rank.

PHRATRY I

Órobawa   The leading sib; they still live at Uaracapurí on the Vaupés, the site of a rapids from which they first emerged. Their first male ancestor was called *Órobakü*. According to one version of the origin tale, he was the head of the anaconda from which all Cubeo are descended. He then named all the sibs of the phratry that followed after him. Koch-Grünberg identified them as *Ólaba-Hehénewa* and hence as a branch of the *Hehénewa*. Nimuendajú listed them as *Órobawa*. According to my information, they are most closely linked with the *Hwáni-Hehénewa* and with the *Aúnwewa*, the easternmost or most downstream community of the Cubeo.

Aúnbwawü   The second sib, occupying the next site upstream on the Vaupés at Urania. Their first ancestor was *Aúnkü*. Some informants said that *Aúnkü* was the last to emerge but was granted second place by *Órobakü*. In any case, their position on the Vaupés gives them second rank. They are regarded as very closely linked with the *Hehénewa*. In 1940 they were reduced to four households. Some had taken up residence at Pindaíva on the Cuduiarí. Nimuendajú's reference to the *Ambo-mamára* on the Cuduiarí, whom he did not visit personally, may refer to this Cuduiarí group. The Vaupés group is not mentioned in either his or Koch-Grünberg's lists.

Hehénewa   In the present social structure, the *Hehénewa* represent the largest grouping of sibs of this phratry. From the traditions, it is not unlikely that the *Hehénewa* were once an independent tribe which joined with other groups to form the present phratry. When Koch-Grünberg visited them in 1903 he came to regard them as the "true" Cubeo. They have, even today, the highest prestige on the Cuduiarí and are, to my knowledge, the only group on this river authorized to wear the quartz cylinder pendant. According to native traditions, they came originally from the Papurý River and were not Cubeo but Tucano, known as the *Xwéve-Hehénewa* or *Toucan-Hehénewa*. Their origin site on the Papurý is known as *Wahúdja impemáni*. They were adopted into the phratry by the *Órobawa*. The story goes that the *Hehénewa* heard the *Órobawa* sounding the ancestor trumpets. They were attracted by the music — a sign of kinship — and when they came close they were adopted. Another version of the tradition emphasizes the close kinship of the *Hehénewa* with the other Cubeo sibs that emerged ·at Uaracapurí. This notes that the *Hehénewa* had the intention of emerging at the traditional site but were prevented from doing so by the hostility of others. Therefore they emerged at a distance and came to join their rightful kinsmen later. The *Hehénewa* now occupy sites all along the Cuduiarí, but are concentrated on the lower Cuduiarí and have a maloca on the Vaupés near Urania close by the *Aúnbwawü*.

Byá-Hehénewa   A subsib of the *Hehénewa* who live at the mouth of the Cuduiarí.

Wathariwa   The *Bahúkiwa* regard them as distant members of the phratry, linking them rather more closely with the *Hehénewa* and the *Aúnbwawü*. They emerged at *Byátankwe*, a rapids on the Vaupés. Their first Ancient was called *Kwábebo*. They still live on the Vaupés at *Uacuréwa*, near Tatú *cachoeira*, and at *Umari* just below. Koch-Grünberg located them above Uaracapurí falls, an upstream location more appropriate to their standing in the phratry.

Byá-Wathariwa   A subsib of the *Wathariwa* on the Vaupés.

Urérariwa   Perhaps a subsib of the *Wathariwa* on a small stream of the Vaupés.

Bahúkiwa   They list their emergence site as *Impenáni* on the Uaracapurí falls of the Vaupés. Their first Ancient was *Bwü* and his sister was *Onpwéndoko*. They now consist of several subsibs occupying sites along the middle Cuduiarí. Koch-Grünberg referred to them as *Bahúna* and identified them as a Macú group (*Borówa*) who wandered into the Cuduiarí and became fully assimilated into the Cubeo, giving up their original language. *Bahúkiwa* traditions do, indeed, refer to an episode in the history of the sib when, having been virtually wiped out by an enemy raid, the last survivors married *Borówa* women and so regenerated the sib. They deny any imputation, however, that they were ever low-caste *Borówa*. The term Macú, which is the colloquial form of *Borówa*, is commonly used in the region as an epithet. The *Bahúkiwa* regard the *Órobawa* as their "head."

Bahúküdjauwü   A subsib of the *Bahúkiwa* living just downstream from the *Bahúkiwa*, at a site commonly known as Yasitara. They had originally been one with the *Bahúkiwa*, but separated from them when they came up the Cuduiarí and established a Satellite community up a small tributary, Cucúra *igarapes*.

Bahukuonówa   A subsib of the *Bahúküdjauwü* living near Yasitara on the Cuduiarí.

Bahúkübwauwü   A subsib of the *Bahúkiwa* who are also known by the derogatory connotation of *Mánapwänwa* (Trail people) or *Mánawa*. According to the traditions, they were not Cubeo but a nomadic group, perhaps Macú, who had come to the Cuduiarí overland, and whose emergence site was the Querarí *mirí*, a small tributary of the Cuduiarí. The *Bahúkiwa* adopted them and gave them personal names from their own sib genealogy.

Pedikwa   A subsib of the *Hehénewa* on the Cuduiarí above the *Bahúkiwa* sites. According to the traditions, they came originally from the Papurý River with the *Hehénewa* and then settled at Itapinima or *Toídibü*, at which rapids they had a second emergence. They say their first Ancient was *Djurédo* of the *Hehénewa*. They did not like him and so they separated. They are also known as *Pedi-Hehénewa* because they emerged at *Pedíwa*, a rock at Itapinima. Koch-Grünberg encountered them in the same site they now occupy. He says they were once enemies of the Cubeo. They now include five Satellite communities living upstream from them on the Cuduiarí. They are also known as *Piátokaüo*.

Kenánikauwü   A subsib of the *Pedikwa* on the upper Cuduiarí at *Piramirí* and at *Abúhakü*. They used to live at *Toídibü* but broke off and moved upstream. They do not appear on either Koch-Grünberg's or Nimuendajú's lists.

Kenámbwawa   A subsib of the *Pedikwa* living on the upper reaches of the Cuduiarí.

Utciwaiwa   Their emergence site was the Yuruparí *cachoeira* that is upstream and at some distance along the Vaupés from Uaracapurí. Having come from a different emergence site they were originally not in the phratry. They were drawn into the phratry by a pact of friendship with the *Bahúkiwa*. They now live at the mouth of the Mirití *igarapes* below the Yuruparí falls on the Vaupés. Koch-Grünberg found them on the Dyi *igarapes*, an adjacent tributary of the Vaupés. They may be the same as the *Bucíbowa* mentioned on the Vaupés by Nimuendajú. Their first ancestor was called *Utcíwehwedi*. They are also included as a sib in one of the phratries of the Tucano tribe.

Baryáwatiwaiwa   A sib that emerged from Yuruparí *cachoeira* on the Vaupés and is related to the *Utcíwaiwa*. They are also known as *Baryáwa* and still live on the Vaupés.

Piaráwa   A sib that emerged at Uaracapurí rapids, from a particular site called *Mumikü*. They live at Mirití *cachoeira* on the Vaupés and at the headwaters of the Muchú, a left-bank tributary of the Vaupés. They have some personal names in common with the *Hehénewa* but are most closely associated with the *Kompainyewa*. Koch-Grünberg found them on the left bank of the Vaupés at a site called *Naibö*, where they were known in the *lingoa geral* as *Tokandira-Tapuyo*. He recorded their self-name as *Olá-Piaráwa*. Nimuendajú incorrectly placed them on the Cuduiarí.

Pyéndo-Hehénewa A dissident sib of the *Hehénewa* group, maintaining no friendly relations with the other *Hehénewa*. Their close sib ties are with the *Pedíkwa* and the *Kenánikauwü*. They occupy several sites above Patú at the headwaters of the Cuduiarí, the main maloca being at Querarí *miri* (*Enpanáwe*). They are also at *Abúhudjo* on the Yuruparí *miri* and are known also as *Pyéndokauwü*.

Hwáni-Hehénewa A *Hehénewa* subsib on the Vaupés at Paraná *picuna* and at Tukano *cachoeira*. Their origin site is *Impenáni* of the Uaracapuri *cachoeira* and they are, therefore, closely related to the *Órobawa* and the *Aúnwewa*, in contrast to the *Hehénewa* proper, whose emergence was actually on the Papurý.

Aúnwewa A subsib of the *Aúnbwawü* on the Vaupés at *Upyaria* just above Mitú. Nimuendajú incorrectly placed them on the Cuduiarí and referred to them as *Aweéa*. They are also listed as a sib of a Tucano phratry.

Kompainyewa Closely linked with the *Piaráwa*, they live at Pindaíva on the Vaupés just above Urania near the Yuruparí falls. Their emergence site, however, is Uaracapurí.

Abóxo-Hehénewa A sib on the upper Querarí mentioned by Koch-Grünberg, on which I have no information.

Ambomamára A sib on the Cuduiarí mentioned by Nimuendajú, on which I have no information. From the name it would appear to be a subsib of the *Aúnbwawü*.

Byari-Hehénewa An extinct subsib of the *Hehénewa*, who had lived on the Cuduiarí as well as at Uarúa Lake on the upper Vaupés. They were also known as *Byarídowa*.

Papuli-Hehénewa A sib living on the Cuduiarí during the time of Koch-Grünberg's visit at Suriburoca but now extinct. They came from the Papurý and were closely linked with the Tucano tribe of the Tiquié River.

Kenámbwawa A sib on the upper Cuduiarí, presumably a subsib, along with the *Kenánikauwü*, of the *Pedíkwa*.

Phratry I consists of two divisions that represent distinct origins. In the past these two divisions may have been intermarrying, because even now, although the entire phratry is exogamic, informants disagree as to the proprieties of intermarriage between the two divisions. The dominant division from the point of view of prestige and of numbers is known as *Yavímanawa* (Children of the jaguar) and includes the *Órobawa*, *Aúnbwawü*, *Hehénewa*, *Watharíwa*, and their subsibs: *Byá-Hehénewa*, *Byá-Watharíwa*, *Pedíkwa*, *Kenánikauwü*, *Utcíwaiwa*, *Pyéndo-Hehénewa*, *Hwáni-Hehénewa*, and *Aúnwewa*. The second division has no name and consists of the *Bahúkiwa* groups, the *Piaráwa*, and the *Kompainyewa*.

PHRATRY II

Bwoíbowa   The leading sib of the phratry, living at Muchú on the Vaupés. According to tradition, they came from the Isana River originally. They emerged at a rapids called *Aíndoribo* at a site called *Hobónoburúno*. Originally they fought with the *Byówa*, now a sister sib of the phratry. Koch-Grünberg encountered an abandoned maloca of theirs at Uarúa Lake, where they had been living adjacent to the Tucanoan-speaking but non-Cubeo *Pamóa*. The indications are that they had moved in recent years considerably downstream on the Vaupés.

Byówa   A group occupying all of the Pirabatón, an affluent of the Querarí. Koch-Grünberg placed them at the headwaters of the Querarí, but since he had not identified the Pirabatón that may be the river that he called the upper Querarí. They are strongly intermarried with *Bahúkiwa*.

Hürüwá   Members of a foreign phratry living on the Cuduiarí, where they occupy a number of upriver sites, having replaced a *Hehénewa* subsib. They emerged from a site called *Kohédariwa* above Uaracapurí on the Vaupés. Koch-Grünberg met them in the same locations on the Cuduiarí. He claimed they were originally Arawakan-speaking Baniwa who had wandered in from the Vaupés.

Wadjá-Hürüwá   A subsib of the *Hürüwá* at *Kwitóro* on the Cuduiarí.

KoRówa   Primarily a Querarí River sib that had spilled over onto the Cuduiarí at one time. Wallace reported them there in 1853. They are closely linked with, and according to Koch-Grünberg politically subordinate to, the *Byówa*. In more recent times they have settled on the Vaupés, where they have also been reported by Nimuendajú. They also had a house on the lower Cuduiarí. They are known as *KoRókoro-Tapuyo* (Green Ibis Indians).

Waláola   A group mentioned by Nimuendajú as living on the Vaupés. Presumably a subsib of the *KoRówa*.

Mianáwa   A group occupying several sites in the vicinity of the Tukunaré *igarapes* on the upper Vaupés — *Makakinyo, Jacaré, Seima* — as well as at Pirabatón *igarapes*. Koch-Grünberg found a small group of only four families living at the Yuruparí falls on the lower Vaupés. Nimuendajú also found them on the Vaupés.

PHRATRY III

Djurémawa   Nimuendajú has identified them as the *Yiboya-Tapuyo* of the Aiarí River in Brazil. He says they came to the mouth of the Querarí on the Vaupés in 1904. According to Koch-Grünberg, they were once hostile Arawakan Baniwa who had assimilated to Cubeo and are close kin of the *Káua* of the Aiarí. The Uanana, Koch-Grünberg reports, call them *Maxka-Pinopona* (Boa).

Tóriawü   A sib on the Querarí, originally Arawakan-speaking, that claims to have come from the Isana.

Konéntaraboiwü   According to Koch-Grünberg, who referred to them as *Kolátalapoauo*, they were Baniwa Arawakans who settled on the Querarí and assimilated to the Cubeo language. He noted that they were intermarried with the *Hehénewa* of the Cuduiarí. The *Bahúkiwa* also married them. Nimuendajú mentions a *Kowitárabewi* on the Querarí, perhaps the same people, or possibly a subsib, since I have in my lists an unidentified *Kowétarabawü* on the Querarí.

Yániwa A sib at the mouth of the Querarí. Nimuendajú also noted them on the Querarí as *Dyaniwa*.

Yokókübewü A sib on the lower Querarí.

UNIDENTIFIED SIBS

Batóua Koch-Grünberg found them at the mouth of the Cubiú *igarapes*, a tributary of the Vaupés, and called them a small "horde" that had come from the Querarí. I did not hear of them. Nor are they mentioned by Nimuendajú.

Ilhéadowa A group mentioned by Koch-Grünberg and later by Nimuendajú, but not on my lists. Nimuendajú says they were once Macú and placed them on the Cuduiarí, which he did not explore, but which Koch-Grünberg and I did. Koch-Grünberg did not locate them on the Cuduiarí, but recorded a visit of some from Puranga *paraná* on the Vaupés to the *Hehénewa* of the Cuduiarí.

Káua A Cubeo group whom Koch-Grünberg encountered on the upper Aiarí. They lived in a maloca at Yuruparí *cachoiera*. The Siusi called them *Maulieni*. They were, said Koch-Grünberg, originally Arawakans from the Querarí and then became Cubeo-speaking. Since moving to the Aiarí near the Siusi they have returned to the use of Arawakan. They are closely related to the *Djurémawa*, but they are not in my lists.

THE *BORÓWA*

The *Borówa*, who are more generally known as Macú, were once servants or menials of various sibs of the Cubeo. This is no longer the case since, as many Cubeo informants said, the *Borówa* came to be too troublesome and they were allowed to leave. There was fear of *Borówa* sorcery and that was another reason for sending them away. The Cubeo say that the *Borówa* had come to them voluntarily and offered to work for them in return for food, shelter, and protection against enemies. Individual household heads took in individual *Borówa* or a man and wife pair. The *Borówa* did all the everyday work. They fished, their women worked in the manioc garden, they fetched water and firewood. They lived in the house with the Cubeo and were to all intents and purposes members of the household. They even made their own chicha. The Cubeo claim they did not intermarry with *Borówa*, although this statement is belied by a sib tradition that the *Bahúkiwa* were once given *Borówa* wives. The view is that it was improper to marry such lowly people. One man not very long ago had eight *Borówa* men and women attached to his household.

Once the practice of keeping *Borówa* had become established, they were bought and sold in exchange for ceremonial objects, such as wooden dancing staffs. I was told that a *Borówa* was worth one *behórü* (a ceremonial staff). Since the *Borówa* were nomadic and had no strong attachments to any particular place they did not mind moving from one place to another. It would seem that far from being slaves there was a symbiotic relationship between these very crude nonfarming people, who had no settlements or permanent houses of their own, and the Cubeo. The Cubeo do not stress the economic advantages to them of the *Borówa* other than to point out that they helped with all chores. In any case, no Cubeo was released from any of his normal tasks because of the presence of the *Borówa*. The *Borówa* were skilled basketmakers and it was in this economic field that they were most important. Nor was social status too important an issue in maintaining *Borówa*. They were valued mainly because they increased the household. The fact is, the *Borówa* consumed a good deal of manioc produce in the form of chicha. They were notoriously heavy drinkers and when drunk were very quarrelsome.

The question of relationship of the *Borówa* to the Cubeo is still not clear. There is an origin tradition that says that the *Borówa* were the last to emerge from Uaracapurí and for this reason they were held to be the servants of the others. However, this account may simply reflect the Cubeo tendency to relate all people with whom they have close and persistent connections to their origin myths. If the *Borówa* came from Uaracapurí that would be reason also for the ban against intermarriage with those groups that had settled among the Cubeo. As against the tradition that would make the *Borówa* a lowest-ranking Cubeo sib is the information that they spoke a different language and only adopted the language of their households. Along these lines is also the comment that the *Borówa* were a people "without shame," because among them brother and sister (presumably parallel cousins) were permitted to marry. There is still another explanation given by the Cubeo of *Borówa* status and that is that they had been conquered. The *Borówa* are said to live at the mouth of the Querarí but I had no opportunity to visit them.

The *Borówa* have been house servants or field slaves to most, if not all, the Arawakan and Tucanoan tribes in the region. My own information on Macú "slaves" is entirely hearsay, since, as far as I could learn, all the Cubeo sibs on the Cuduiarí had already given up keeping *Borówa*. In 1905 Koch-Grünberg observed Macú "slaves" among the Tucano of Pary *cachoeira*. In this community there were three men who "belonged" to the chief. They lived in a hut of their own in the woods, together with their wives and children. Every day the *Borówa* men came to the main house bringing game, fish, and fruits. They did household chores. The Tucano treated them well, like tame animals, Koch-Grünberg commented (1909, I, 269 ff.). The Macú took part in the small drinking parties. They were not given coca, however (women among the Cubeo are also not given coca), but were given tobacco and chicha. They took no part in the dancing and (this is a very important note) they wore no ornaments. Little Macú girls took care of the children and brought firewood. The girls were at the sexual disposition of the men. The Macú were sold by the Tucano to other Indians. The Tucano told Koch-Grünberg that the Macú "were not people." They did attribute to them, however, the very human arts of black magic.

BAHÚKIWA NARRATIVE OF THEIR EMERGENCE AND WANDERINGS

The text is chanted and narrates mainly place names. Thus the narrative is mainly evocative and is only barely a description of events. The chant is referred to as "a good mouth that is talking" (*meákamótewu yavaiwü*). It means simply that the people are talking good things. In the following rendering of the text, information in parentheses is explanation and not translation. A free translation follows the text.

pwéntewü — the people came out

tcúntcauwa — and shed (their anaconda skins)

hahádami — they went forward

waré borikapindo — the place of the star ray (the name of a rock that has a hole through which a star ray entered)

opéko tamána — crossing over the milk (a reference to a rock forming a bridge over rushing water called milk [*opéko*])

emíntakori — the passage of minnows (the name of a rock)

kanúrübo — (a hill named after the *kánuku* tree) and the rapids of four channels

bwühürüküwü — the rock where *Bwü* (Agouti) jumped (a good jumper is now referred to as *Bwü*)

byátakwe — the rapids of the pepper plant (a reference to a rock that was once a pepper plant)

kwábebo — the place of *Kwákü* (a name in the *Hehénewa* genealogies)

boríkabo — the place of *Borikakü* (a name in the *Hehénewa* genealogies — it means the aracú fish)

opéko tavá — the milk of the tree (a reference to a tree called *wanumu* that gave milk; *Borikakü* drank this milk and some of it spilled here)

nahó pwánwa — the place of the worm people (the *nahó* is a worm used as bait in fishing; the reference was not explained)

bwütaunrü — the tree beneath which *Bwü* passed (a tree had fallen across the stream and *Bwü* passed beneath it)

bwütaunrü — the tree beneath which Bwü passed (a tree had fallen across it and it turned into a rock)

waokún — the beach of the monkey (a monkey passed by; an Ancient killed it and it turned to sand) *tarayávikun* — the river bank of the jaguar (a jaguar tried to climb the high bank and failed; an Ancient came along and the jaguar, frightened, dashed into a tree, where it became transfixed)

nyukáhemekun — the beach of the kumari plant (there was a kumari [*nyuká*] bush here; an Ancient cut it down and it turned to sand)

popébünawü — the place of the war club (an Ancient arrived here to drink and met one of his own kinsmen; they quarreled and the Ancient killed his kinsman with his war club [*popébü*])

opéko tavá — the milk of the tree (a reference to a place when an Ancient passed among the others a small calabash of palm milk)

opéko hyáwü — (the name of a rock where they paused again to drink milk)

opéko tankúru — the whirlpool of milk (a reference to a rapids, the place of white waters)

hurébu — the place of the dove (a rapids where a dove flying by fell and turned into a rock)

turúbokun — (the name of a beach where there were many small fish)

mamúwa — the rock of the amári tree

mamúkapindo — (a reference to the part of the rock that projects into the river [*kapindo*])

nebékuwa waibóhateni kríwü — there the Ancients crossed to the other side to live

horóbotabü — they made pottery vessels

ipákarekü waibuhateni kritámeda -- they crosssed a hill and there they lived

ipakaréda hanhánkenaku — the hill of the hán han bird (a fish-catching bird)

opéko kenákuna — milk of the mountain of rock (a rocky outcrop where they paused to drink milk)

hanhánatakuwe — the place where the hán han played (the name of a rock)

marúkubo — the rock of the marúku monkey (they killed this monkey and it turned into a rock)

nakóterarerakun — the high bank with the great round eyes (when one of the Ancients saw this place he looked at it with huge round eyes of astonishment)

emuni dani — they came upriver

wainitenimeda — they passed

wanindona — the narrow passage of the *wanindo* spume

pidári hwaibo — the burrow of *pidári* (a reference to a place at the head-waters of the *wanindo* creek where the water is as black as *pidári* [a dark liquid formed when manioc is left in the water to decay]; here an Ancient made a burrow such as an animal makes and in it left the calabash of milk as a cache)

makánoka pidári kóbo — in the forest of *pidári* he made the cache

opéko maná emenádani — at the milk trail he went out of the river

kríwü máakaraka — to live on a high hill

pindó kavárebo — the bend of *kavárebo* (a rock at the mouth of the Cuduiarí where it enters the Vaupés)

kwitótedo — (a lake near Urania on the Vaupés)

kwitóteku — (the sandy beach of that name)

nyemí hwainéndi — (the place name for what is now Mitú, the capital of the *Comisaría del Vaupés*)

opéko tokóve — the small stream of milk (a creek that was then pure milk but is now only water)

dyarídü — the slippery rock

tuwárü hivéda — the stream of blood (*hivé*, a reference to waters that run red)

toténekribü bekédowa — there the Ancients arrived to stay

putovanimeda — there they explored upriver

nénbudja — and then back

noná hivédera — to *hivéda*

kempaimeda — they returned

opéko haváteni — they drank milk

húwü opéko — the cold milk

tankü wena pianítani — the rapids where they emerged

danáni kríwü — they came to live

opéko teríbobü — where the waters were like milk

kenánhamedo — the lake of *kenáhume* (yellow clay used in dyeing the ceremonial ligatures; the lake is just above Santa Marta)

namúkoribana — the place of the *namúkoriba* fish (near the mouth of the Cuduiarí)

towándaimeda — they reached

wainitanidaimeda — and then they passed

opéko horóbena — an urn of milk (a reference to water that looked like milk, i.e., a rapids)

xuikopwimada — they came upon

neháwükemana — their in-laws

pwü nehóitaro — and already at the creek of grease (a reference to its waters, which were then pure grease)

kerarú kemódakiporu — the place of the closed-off creek (a site above Garaffo Lake)

nohíva paipíbü — above them the whirlpool of Guassí

pwü heniharína — and the fast black waters

apyá bepora — the whirlpool of the tree trunk

hivákapunáwü — (a place name)

makavékü — the place of parrots' wings

hubókiporü — they portaged overland

pwü mavákobe — and quickly arrived at

biarído bupékü — the place of the *bupékü* butterflies

peómbü — the lake shaped like a *peómbo* (a container for curare)

djútuna moró — the place of the many grubs (a reference to a thick mass of grubs they found and cooked into a stew)

miauikü tonwéndo — the high bank where the water rushes with a sucking sound

mumúkü — the place of the tangle of roots

yavikénamü —the house of the jaguars (a reference to their having encountered many jaguars here)

mahópanwa waríndo — (a place name)

waníketawü — the place of the *táwü* fish (a reference to fish that resembled *táwü*, bark-cloth masks worn in mourning ceremonies)

mimikütcundu — the creek of the *mımíkü* bird
unenýkübo — the place of the pupunha trees
                    [Then they began to return and they came to]
wakúdjari — (a creek named after the *wakúdjari* fruit)
tcipédikoriba — (a place name)
tcipéü taváno — (a place name)
püwûdjaribü — the slippery place
kenóha mutútu — the bank of the yellow clay
tuibü — (a place name)
yuparido — (a creek named after a red fish)
veábokutcendu — the hill of the háku fish
hororákipúru — (a place name)
pwánaku — the high bank of mud out of which water seeps
vekókü — the place of the parrots (the present site of the *Bahúkiwa*)
vekúro — the creek of the parrots
nomi tavibo — the circle of women (a reference to a circular trench around
    a house, built by women to ward off enemies)
kurúwatha hutchíndu — he untied himself and escaped (a reference to an
    Ancient who was tied up by enemies during a fight but who untied him-
    self [*kurúa háku*: to untie oneself] and escaped)
kanyapíka — the place of the sweet potato (*yapíka*)
hwanidya — the creek of the pigs (*hwaní*)
ewáhubo — the lake of the birds
miwave — the bird place
emiheria — the creek of the sweet waters
hurédo — the place of the doves
takaikoriba — the place where the maize grew
yavibü kurábü — the buttocks of the jaguar rock (a reference to a sharp
    rock upon which an Ancient sat down to rest; the rock penetrated his
    rectum and killed him)
teviaría — the place of the milk palm
yavihoba — the garden of the jaguar
kamíne — the place where the *kamindü* turned to stone
kwünkwüntoto — the place where *Kwûnkwü* settled (a reference to an An-
    cient who decided not to be human and so turned himself back into an
    anaconda)
véabo munháru — (a place within a creek where there are háku and puño
    fish)
wari pani — the place of *Wari* (a forest monster, addressed by an Ancient
    as "in-law" [*pani*])
konéndobo — the hill of the woodpeckers
komórü kenátakwe — the rocky rapids where *Komóri* lived (a reference to
    a *Bahúkiwa* Ancient)
makapimbo — the parrot beak rock
úbo — the place of *U* (the sloth)
táwü — the place of the bark-cloth trees
udyébo pediwa — the rocks carved with manioc graters (*pediwa*)
namáwa — the place of the deer
kudjúpanwa — the place of the small parakeets
Opómbibekü — (a dwarf whose penis was the length of an arm)

kenánokakü — the place of the stone people (a reference to figures of people in stone in the highlands of the Cuduiarí)

FREE TRANSLATION

The people came out and shed their anaconda skins. They went on to the place of the star ray rock, where they crossed over the milky waters. They came to the rock where the minnows pass, to the hill called *kanúrübo*, and then to the rapids of the four channels. They came to *bwühürüküwü*, the rock where *Bwü* [Agouti] jumped across the rapids of *byátakwe*, at the place of the pepper plants. They came to the place of *Kwákü* the Ancient, and then to the place of *Boríkakü* the Ancient, at the place where he spilled the milk of the tree as he was drinking it. They came to the place of the worm people, and to the tree across a stream under which *Bwü* passed. They came to the rock of the jaguar, where an Ancient killed a jaguar and it turned into a rock. They came to the beach of the monkey, where an Ancient killed a monkey and it turned to sand. They came to the river bank of the jaguar, where a jaguar, failing to scale the high bank, took fright at the sight of an Ancient and dashed into a tree, where it became transfixed. They came to the beach of the kumari plant, where an Ancient cut down a kumari bush and it turned to sand. They came to the place of the war club, where an Ancient, coming for a drink of water, met a kinsman. They quarreled and the Ancient clubbed his kinsman to death. They came to the place called "milk of the tree," where an Ancient passed out a calabash of palm tree milk. There, at the rock called "drinking milk," they drank it.

They came to the place of rushing waters, a whirlpool of milk, to the rapids of the dove, where a dove dropped into the water and turned into a rock. They came to the beach of the many small fish, and to the rock where the amári tree grew. They came to the point of the rock, and there the Ancients crossed over to reside. They stopped here and made pottery vessels. Then they crossed a hill and there they resided, at the hill of the hán han bird. They paused at the rocky hill of milk, the place where the hán han birds played. They came to the rock of the marúku monkey, where they killed a marúku and it turned into a rock. They came to the high bank which the Ancients looked upon with the rounded eyes of wonderment. They went upriver and they passed through the passage of spume, out into the black waters of *pidári*, at the head of the *wanindo* creek. Here an Ancient made a burrow and left in it a calabash of milk. At this place, called "the trail of milk," they left the river to reside on a high hill at the bend of *kavárebo* [where the Cuduiarí enters the Vaupés]. They went on and came to *kwitótedo*, to *kwitóteku*, and to *nyemí hwainéndi* [where Mitú now stands]. There, at the milky creek, at the slippery rock, at the stream of blood where the waters are reddened by the rays of the sun, there the Ancients arrived and there they lived. From there they explored upriver and then came back to *hivéda*.

They returned and drank milk, the cold milk at the rapids from which they had emerged. There they came to live, at the place where the waters were like milk, at the lake of the yellow clay. Then they went on until they came to the place of the *namúkoriba* fish [near the mouth of the Cuduiarí]. And then they passed a rapids that was like an urn of milk. There they came upon their in-laws. They were already at the greasy creek, at the place of the closed-off creek [a site above Garaffo Lake on the Cuduiarí]. Above them was the whirlpool of Guassí and the fast black waters. There, at the whirlpool of the tree trunk, at *hivakapunáwü*, at the place of parrots' wings, they portaged overland and they quickly arrived at the place of the *bupékü* butterflies, at the lake shaped like a container for curare.

They came to the place of many grubs which they cooked into a stew. They came to the high bank where the water rushes in with a sucking sound, to the place of the tangle of roots. They came to the place of the jaguars, to *mahópanwa waríndo*, to the place of the bark-cloth fishes, to the creek of the *mimikü* bird, and then to the place of the pupunha trees. From there they returned and they came to the creek of the *wakúdjari* fruit, to *tcipédikoriba* and *tcipéü taváno,* and then to the slippery place, and then to the bank of the yellow clay, and then to *tuibü,* where the creek of the red fish is, and then to the hill of the háku fish. Then, at a place called *hororákipúru,* they came to the high bank of mud, and then to the place of the parrots [the present site of the *Bahúkiwa* sib]. At the creek of the parrots they came upon the circular trench called "the circle of women" [because it is the women who dug this trench]. There an Ancient who had been tied up by his enemies managed to free himself and escape. Now they continued up the creek to the place of the sweet potato, and they came to the creek of the wild peccary and then on to the lake of the birds and the bird place.

From there they went up the creek of the sweet waters to the place of the doves. And then they went to the place where maize grew and then to the sharp jaguar rock. Here an Ancient, sitting down on the rock, pierced his rectum and died. They went on to the place of the milk palm, to the garden of the jaguar, to the place where the *kamíndü* turned to stone. They came to *kwünkwüntoto,* where *Kwünkwü* the Ancient decided to settle down. [This is the *Bahúkiwa* Ancient who later decided that he did not care to be human and turned himself back into an anaconda.]

The Ancients moved on to the place of the háku and puño fish, to the place of *Wari* the in-law, the hill of the woodpeckers, to the rocky rapids where *Komóri* the Ancient settled down, then to the parrot beak rock, then to the place of the sloth, then to the place of the bark-cloth trees, then to the rocks of the manioc graters, then to the place of the deer, and then to the place of the small parakeets, where *Opómbibekü* lived [a dwarf with an enormous penis]. Finally, they went to the place of the stone people [at the head of the Cuduiarí].

TRADITIONAL NAMES IN THE *BAHÚKIWA* GENEALOGIES

MALE	MALE	FEMALE
Aribahúkü	Kwünkwü or	Bahúko
Arienakü	Kwáhünkwü	Hehénabo
Bahúkü	Míabekudjo	Henéako
Bahúkübeküdjo	Onpóhena	Henákuwa
Bahúküdjitca	Onpwéanba	Iho
Bekübo	Onpwénda	Ihoruko
Bwü	Onpwéndabu	Kokáhenako
Harákü	Onpwéndakü	Kokáiko

MALE	MALE	FEMALE
Hehéna	*Onpwénda kwáhünkwü*	*Miánko*
Itütü	*Onpwéndeva*	*Opwéndoko*
Kokáhena	*Wáhena*	
Kokai	*Wai*	
Kokaídi	*Waikomu*	
Kokaikü	*Waikomúhütü*	
Komóri	*Waimoya*	
Kumúra		

4

Kinship

The focus of Cubeo kinship is the sibling group, of which the
brothers form a permanent body, the hard core, so to speak, and
the sisters an emotionally close but separable group, since they are the
ones who marry out. The sibling group is the model for the extension
of terms of consanguinity throughout the phratry.[1] More people are
addressed and referred to as "sibling" than by any other term. When
the Cubeo speak in Spanish or in Portuguese they identify all their
age mates within the range of patrilineal consanguinity as "my
brother" or "my sister." Their own language differentiates degrees of
sibling closeness, distinguishing lineage brothers, sib brothers, and
phratry brothers. But the linguistic device for drawing these distinctions, by manipulating prefixes and suffixes without altering the
stem itself, seems to be a finely contrived compromise between the desire to embrace all patrilineal consanguineal kin within the bonds of
brotherhood and the need to deal with the actualities of relationships. The Cubeo are very sensitive to terms of address and so they
use terms not merely to designate a precise degree of relationship,
but diplomatically, to create a mood of closeness or of distance. I
believe this diplomatic use of kinship draws mainly, perhaps exclusively, upon the sibling terms, since all other terms of consanguinity
are by comparison of far lesser significance. A phratry brother may
be called by the term appropriate for sib or even lineage brother and
vice versa. When this is done, the speaker indicates by his manner

---

[1] There is a list of relationship terms at the end of this chapter.

or tone of voice that he is being flattering or is jesting. In the solemn terms of address that people use on ceremonial occasions, relation-ships, however, are used correctly.

The stress being on patriliny and on patrilocality, brothers are permanently held together by common residence in the respective degrees of closeness extending outward from hearth, house, com-munity, adjacent community, and the common river as the usual ter-ritory of the phratry. Depending upon the degree of physical closeness, brothers share joint economic and ceremonial activities. In any case they share common traditions and the highly significant bond of common exogamy. The Cubeo offer hospitality to any kins-man whether consanguineal or affinal. However, when men are trav-eling along their own river they are made more comfortable by the thought that they will be stopping over at the house of a "brother." Kinsmen, in contrast to in-laws, are *hiwá*, an apt term that means literally "my group." (*Hi* is the possessive pronoun, *wa* is the suffix indicating the animate collective.)

Brothers of the same mother are, contrary to the traditions of pat-

Fig. 5. Sib group at mourning ceremony.

riliny, the closest of all. On occasions uterine brothers form a common front from which brothers of the same father but of different mothers are excluded. A father expects'his sons to stand by him and not by their mother, who is a sib outsider. Yet the simple fact that a woman keeps her own children close to her side, lavishing upon them all her attentions and affection, and ignoring, as much as she can afford, the other of her husband's children by other wives, creates a basis in sentiment for a maternal attachment that no amount of official sib doctrine can override. The attachment to the mother is recognizable in modes of behavior, such as intimacy or susceptibility to cleavage. Uterine brothers also quarrel and part, but they are unlikely to drift apart as readily as can mere agnatic brothers. However, kinship terms draw no distinction between uterine and agnatic brothers. A woman addresses all her husband's sons by the same term, just as her husband does.

The term for brother of the closest degree embraces lineage as well as blood brothers. Still, a distinction of sorts does enter into kinship usage, through a sister. A girl, as a mother's helper, has a very important role in looking after younger children of the household. Her first responsibility is to her uterine siblings. Like her mother she favors the boy child over the girl. In later years she still calls her younger uterine brother by the affectionate term *tcumi*, while reserving the conventional term, *hiyokü*, for an agnatic younger brother. Women, however, take more liberties, generally, in the use of kin terms than do men. They are particularly free with terms that define nearness and intimacy. Thus, a sister's discrimination between uterine and agnatic brother may be regarded not as official usage but as a special female prerogative.

As to formal principles of kinship, the distinction between uterine and agnatic brothers is of no great importance. Most marriages are monogamous and in most families there are no stepchildren. Headmen, however, are generally polygynous, and it is in their households that the distinction assumes some importance. Since a headman's household is a focal point of sib activity, whatever occurs within it will affect the state of being within the sib and ultimately its unity. Should a cleavage develop among brothers of different wives of the headman it could split the sib. Cleavages develop around rivalry for position. A headman's sons are inclined to model themselves after the father and to seek leadership of the community. Since the mantle of leadership will in any case fall upon one of them they are, in any case, virtually obligated to seek leadership. Thus it appears, paradoxically, that the line of cleavage in a sib tends to form at its very center in all respects, among the blood brothers, who are the sons of the headman, the very symbol and guardian of the unity of the sib. The Cubeo attribute the source of this "fault" in the sib to the unruly and passionate nature of women, that does not adapt itself readily to the requirements of the sib. The women are said to be at fault in having drawn their sons too closely to them and in having divided the sons of one wife from those of another. Men deplore this, yet they concede that it is in the nature of a woman to do so. Much of the formal and ceremonial relationship between men and women seems to be designed to overcome this feminine and maternal influence.

All sibling terms indicate relative seniority. If the terms refer to near siblings, that is, to siblings of the same sib, their seniority refers strictly to relative age. When sibling terms are used among members of different sibs in the phratry, then the forms of senior-junior indicate respect. An older person may then use the senior term in addressing a younger person. Men may use the senior term in referring to a member of a higher-ranking clan, or, apart from formal rank, to pay respect to a phratry mate who has been generous. Among the Cubeo, rank and seniority are marked by giving more than receiving. Thus, a generous and hospitable person can come to be an "older brother." Women pay respect to men by using the senior term — outside the sib — rather freely. It is a pleasing relationship for a woman to have an older brother and for a man to have a younger sister. When a woman addresses a man as "younger brother" she cannot help but endow the term with an almost maternal tenderness. She finds it more comfortable, one might say, to address a more distant sibmate as "older brother."

There is a more formal usage of terms of relative seniority that acknowledges the ranking of sibs. My information of these seniority usages, coming only from the *Bahúkiwa*, is therefore incomplete. According to the *Bahúkiwa*, all men of the head *Órabawa* sib who are of one's own generation are addressed as *mamü*, the stem term for "older brother," while the reciprocal term that is applied to them by the *Órabawa* is *hwa*, the stem term for "youngster." In the case of the *Bahúkiwa* relations with three sibs of the phratry, the *Pedíkwa*, the *Kenánikauwü*, and the *Piaráwa*, the women of the *Bahúkiwa* address the women of these three as *amikó*, the somewhat more distant form for "older sister," and are called in turn *hwainyó*, or "youngster." Though in the case of the *Órabawa* the seniority usage applies only to the men, in the latter case the usage applies only to the women. My informants could not account for the latter usages although they understood the *Órabawa* usage very well. The *Pedíkwa* are, of course, a sib with high status because they occupy a cataract on the Cuduiarí that they regard as an original emergence site. The *Kenánikauwü* are a subsib of the *Pedíkwa*. In the case of these two sibs I would hazard the guess that it is their present association with an emergence site that warrants this respect usage. In the case of the *Piaráwa* I have no explanation other than the suggestion from Koch-Grünberg's information that since they call themselves *Olá-Piaráwa* they may actually be a subsib of the *Órabawa* and hence have a special claim to respect.

In the neighboring Tucano tribe the seniority usages among the sibs of each phratry are very systematically developed (Fulop, 1955). By comparison the *Bahúkiwa* seniority respect usages with other sibs are only fragmentary.

Distinctions of relative age have their counterparts in behavior. Seniority commands precedence in succession to the headmanship in the household of the headman. In all households seniority is accorded respect and ritual precedence. Among children, the eldest of a play group is expected to be leader. When members of a sib come to attend a ceremony at another sib house they present themselves at the door in order of seniority and are greeted by a receiving line also formed in order of seniority. During the early stages of a ceremony, when all is still formal, chicha, coca, tobacco, and *mihí* are also passed among sibmates in order of seniority. Seniority cannot be said to confer authority, however, since the Cubeo are reluctant to endow anyone with authority. Even the headman governs by a principle that is not quite that of authority.

As between men and women, seniority has a different significance, because of the ritual separation of the sexes. In the etiquette of ceremony women take precedence according to the order of precedence of their husbands and not by their own relative age. The wife of a headman has a position vis à vis the women of the house as her husband has in the sib generally. An older sister who has been a substitute mother to all her younger siblings is regarded by them with a mixture of respect and affection. In later years, should she return to the sib as a widow, a divorcée, or with her husband, a ceremonial role is open to her as sib "mother," from whose breast may be drawn the ritual milk that an infant drinks at the time a sib name is being bestowed upon it.

A younger sister has a special role with respect to an older brother. She is often assigned to him for use in an exchange that will bring him a bride. As an older sister is a "mother" to her younger brother so an older brother is *amyóbakü* (older brother-father) to his younger sister. He is her guardian. He may arrange her marriage, or offer her sexually to a friend, if she is willing. It is a special relationship in many respects.

Seniority is of consequence only in the sibling generation. There is no concept of senior line and no recognition in terminology of descendants of older or younger siblings.

Apart from sex and seniority, Cubeo sibling terms also demarcate social distance. They differentiate, as already noted, three degrees of sibling closeness: lineage sibling, near phratry sibling, and distant phratry sibling. They do so, ingeniously, by the linguistic device of using a common root for sibling — this usage is only in the senior term, because only the senior term is important — indicating distance or closeness by the use of appropriate prefixes and suffixes. The root for senior sibling of either sex is *ami*. With the possessive prefix *hi* and the gender suffix *ko* or *kü* (*himámiko, -kü*) it connotes utmost closeness and is applied to older brother and sister of one's own family, including the extended joint family or lineage. Since sib and lineage may often be coextensive these terms are also sib-wide. The term *himámiko* (my older sister) does not apply to a mother's sister's daughter unless she happens to be — via brother-sister exchange marriage — a father's brother's daughter as well. The intimate usage, that is, must also correspond with coresidence. One's own sister, to be sure, does marry out, but in the meantime there has been a long period of coresidence. In any case, there is not the slightest tendency to slur over a nuclear kinship relationship. In the case of father's brother's daughter the intimate term applies only when she is still a coresident. After she has married she falls into the next more distant category.

The second range of kinship intimacy is the most widespread of all, including sib, subsib, and all close sibs within the phratry. It may even be applied to all members of the phratry of one's generation, in which case the third and most distant form of sibling terminology is reserved for those people whom one does not know well. The terms used in this second range are *amiyó* and *amikó*. The suffix *yo* conveys the meaning of "such as" or "one who is of the class of." It is also used in the term *baküdyó* (father's brother) and means literally "one who is in the class of a father." In *amiyó* it means, therefore, "one who is in the class of an older brother." Strictly speaking, the suffix *yo* has no sex gender and if it were applied to a woman would constitute no major linguistic blunder. But since one's contacts are almost invariably with male siblings, the sisters normally at a distance, the term has apparently taken on a masculine meaning and *amikó* is used to specify the female. A term *amikü* does not exist to my knowledge. With the loss of the possessive prefix *hi* some of the intimacy has gone out of the term. Nevertheless, being diplomatic in their use of kinship terms, the Cubeo sometimes employ the form *himámiyo* and so give the term a warmer tone.

Finally, the most distant usage is to employ only the stem *mamü* ("older one") equally to male and female to connote the barest sibling relationship. I never heard this term used because, I suppose, the Cubeo find it too formal. Rather than call a person *mamü* they prefer the more cordial *pakomá* (kinsman). The special respect use of this term for men of the head sib has already been described.

The junior sibling term is rather unusual. I am inclined to regard it as a quasi-kinship term because it has equally a kinship and an age-grade connotation. *Hwainyó* means literally "one who is in the class of youths." Like *amiyó* it can refer to females, but *hwainkó* is the special term for a younger sib and phratry sister. Because it is an age-grade term, the kinship meaning of *hwainyó* is so wide that it has come to mean any person of sib or phratry who is younger either by relative age within one's generation or is of a younger generation. When it is used as the reciprocal for *amiyó*, as a respect term, it refers to one to whom one condescends somewhat as a donor or good Samaritan. It would seem that the Cubeo have developed only the senior term as a true kinship term and have given seniors the prerogative of addressing all their juniors, whether by age or status, simply as "youth." Nor is the term bound by phratry, since it is applied to all grandchildren (male or female) who are not of the lineage. *Hwainyó* also means son-in-law and any nephew or niece. *Hwainkó* is the daughter-in-law. *Hwankü* is a serviceable male form giving it somewhat greater intimacy and thus is limited generally to younger men of one's own sib or of closely related sibs. The abbreviated form *hwa*, a more jocular term, is also used.

BROTHER - SISTER RELATIONSHIP

Lineage brothers and sib brothers are joined by all the strong bonds of a localized patrilineal sib organization. The obligations of lineage brothers toward one another are very little less binding than those of blood brothers, and the obligations of sib brothers, while somewhat less binding, are still considered to be strong. But these brotherly ties are general and taken for granted, whereas the relationship between brother and sister, as indeed that between husband

and wife, is based upon complementarity. Complementarity of necessity entails more precisely structured relationships than does a homologous relationship as prevails particularly among brothers, the importance of seniority notwithstanding.

Among the Cubeo, the brother-sister relationship is modeled rather closely upon the husband-wife relationship, particularly in respect to forms of economic reciprocity. Even in sexual respects there appears to be a quasi-conjugal relationship. The conjugal division of labor is that a man clears a garden and his wife cultivates it. He provides fish and game, she provides the staple, manioc. She brings in forest products that can be gathered, such as grubs, ants, wild fruits, and he supplements it further by such extra cultivations as pupunha, sugar cane, squash, gourd, coca, tobacco, and *mihi*. She makes pottery and he basketry. Under more modern conditions the women secure trade goods from the whites by bartering farinha, while the men barter their labor in the rubber forest for trade goods. The women acquire, in the main, trade goods for themselves, but will always barter something for a husband, son, or brother. Similarly, a man works primarily for his own wants, such as a muzzle-loading shotgun, but will always take part of his wages in goods for his wife, daughter, or sister.

To carry this account of sexual economic complementarity further, we might add that the women prepare all the regular everyday meals while the men take over the food preparation — with the assistance of the women — for the great events when big game (e.g., tapir) or a spectacular catch of fish has been brought in. In ceremonial life it is the role of the men to astonish the women with the mysteries of the ancestor cult and the role of the women to be astonished. One of the functions of ceremonies that maintain mystery between the sexes is to augment the tension of complementarity.

Sexual complementarity is an aspect of adult status. The young are attached to generalized groups only, the boys in a young male pack that attaches itself only loosely to the adult males, while the little girls are charged with household chores under the direction of their mothers. Adult status is reached by a woman when she has a manioc garden of her own, by a man when a woman is cultivating particularly for him. From this point of view, full adult status is gained only at marriage. The Cubeo brother-sister relationship provides for adult status in advance of marriage and, as we shall see, serves to facilitate marriage and often to protect the stability of marriages. Above all, the brother-sister relationship seems to satisfy a very strong need for particularized relationships.

A brother and a sister who are close to one another in age and who show a fondness for one another are regarded as being linked in a bond that is both warmer and more specialized than the normal bonds between a brother and a sister. The girl is spoken of as "belonging" to her brother. The boy prepares a manioc garden for his sister and she in turn barters a good part of her farinha production in his behalf, getting him fishhooks, ammunition, jewelry, and items of clothing. He will always bring something for her. If he wishes to act as host in a drinking party his assigned special sister has a particular obligation to assist in the preparation of chicha. They do not exchange the ordinary male-female foodstuffs since that is strictly a connubial form of reciprocity and the unmarried are part of their parents' household. They do simulate a conjugal relationship, though, in that they reportedly allow themselves the intimacy of external coitus (i.e., without intromission). On the other hand, since the girl has been allotted to her brother to be part of an exchange marriage, he assumes the right to offer his sister's sexual favors to persons of his choosing, although, as in the case of an exchange marriage, he cannot force her to accept a man against her will.

As the Cubeo explain it, the purpose of the brother-sister relationship is to provide for the boy's marriage. Since the most desirable marriages are those in which brothers exchange sisters, a boy, they say, must have a sister assigned to him if he is to have a strong bargaining position. The Cubeo do recognize the validity of a material bride price, but very few families will readily yield a daughter merely for objects. They want a daughter-in-law to replace a daughter. Exchange marriages are complicated because it does not often happen that the exchange can be immediate. The delay in completing an exchange transaction calls for a reliable guarantee that the agreement will be adhered to. For this, several recourses are available. The ultimate recourse is force. The aggrieved party will raid a household that has reneged and hope to abduct a bride, or, more commonly, love magic will be used to lure the girl away. The most assured contract is one involving cross-cousins, since it draws upon the absolute probity of relationship between a brother and a sister, who are always principals in such a marriage negotiation. But even this has a loophole in that the girl must be willing. By and large, it is the attitude of the bride-to-be that the Cubeo regard as unpredictable. If she enters upon a marriage with reservations that are not removed soon after she has been taken to her husband's community she can be counted upon to run home and stir up complications. The special brother-sister relationship is intended to guard against this. On one hand, the assigned sister can be counted on to act in her brother's behalf and to accept the exchange marriage. On the other, if his bride should leave him he believes that he can ask his sister to leave her husband so that accounts will be squared. This arrangement does not work perfectly, but it works well.

Not every young man has a sister assigned to him. The son of a headman who is in line for the succession has preference, as has a favored son, since it is the parents who play an important part in establishing this relationship. In the case of an apparent heir to the headmanship the assigned sister enhances his status in two ways. It makes him part of an adult status economic relationship in that he has a woman "working" for him and it smoothes the way for his marriage.

I could get no term for this rather specialized brother-sister relationship. Ordinary relationships between brother and sister lack the specific economic exchange features. Lacking the intensity of the paired relationship, the ordinary relationship is still charged with considerable emotion.

From the point of view of the sib, the brother-sister relationship may be considered as a source of holding women to the sib even after they have taken up residence in another sib. There is the curious expectation that a woman will some day come back to her own sib. She will do this as a widow or after a break in her marriage. When a young man is on his way to his "affinal" sib to bring back a wife his parents say to him, half in jest, "Try to make your sister come home." The symbolic act of marriage for the Cubeo is the drama of a "marriage by capture." The groom seizes the bride, who protests, and carries her forcibly to the beach and into his canoe. Her outcries bring her kinsmen on the run, who then try to prevent her "abduction" by cudgeling the groom. This dramatic enactment makes the point that the bride is unwilling to leave her sib and that her kin are determined not to let her go. It is a strong demonstration of attachment that soothes the feelings of the sib and particularly of the brother. It satisfies the sentiment that no one wishes to leave the sib.

The relationship between brother and sister may also be considered in the context of the sib origin myth which states that the founders of a sib were always a brother-sister pair who only later entered into exchange marriages. The tradition of the *Bahúkiwa* sib that a woman re-established the sib after all her brothers had been killed by enemies illustrates still again the Cubeo sentiment that a woman really belongs to her sib. Thus a sib has a female ancestress as well as a male ancestor.

PARENT - CHILD RELATIONSHIP

The Cubeo distinguish between father and father's brothers, but do not distinguish between mother and mother's sisters. The term *baküdyó* means "like a father." [2] This distinction conveys rather precisely the actualities of the relationship. Relations between fathers and sons (the daughters are linked in household duties with the mother) are intimate, and one important sign of intimacy is the privilege that a youngster has of taking food from his father before it is brought into the maloca or into the individual household. Boys value this privilege enormously when they are preadolescent. Without a father a boy will be fed by his father's brother but will lack this privilege with food that he had with his own father. The relationship between paternal uncle and nephew is a strongly supportive one, but with restraint in it. A boy does not take or handle objects belonging to his father's brother without permission. With his father's possessions he has the same freedom as with the possessions of his sibmates of his own generation.

Parents and children share an exclusive set of kinship terms and thereby set themselves apart from the fraternal joint family. Even though mother and mother's sister are equated, a woman distinguishes, as does her husband, between her own and her sister's children. The equation of mother and mother's sister is normal clan usage in a classificatory system. Among the Cubeo, this equation is not related either to the sororate or to sororal polygyny. It would seem to correspond rather to the principle of generalizing relationships that are less important and differentiating very sharply relationships that are most important. With respect to the term for "mother," this is not to say that the actual relationship between children and mother lacks real importance, but only that from the point of view of patriliny of the sib the incoming females, such as mothers, are less important. Actually, the feeling for one's own mother is very strong, not only on the part of the daughters but on the part of the sons too. In a polygynous household the sons of the same mother share a close link with one another; and as we have

---

[2] Koch-Grünberg, who stayed with a *Henénewa* group at the mouth of the Cuduiarí, reported that father and father's brother were equated, as were mother and father's sister (1909, II, 82). Since he did not use the genealogical method it is likely that he was in error with respect to both reported usages. The equation of mother with father's sister controvenes, of course, the patriliny of the sib. On the other hand, the grouping of father and father's brother is conceivable since the distinction between *bakü* and *baküdyó* is not great for the Cubeo. In calling attention to this difference of information I should add that the nature of the Cubeo tribe is such that variations in minor usages are perhaps to be expected.

already noted, cleavages between siblings commonly occur at this point, the sons of one mother breaking with the sons of another. Thus, the distinction between terms for father and father's brother is associated with subtle differences in behavior, yet the grouping of mother with mother's sister ignores even greater distinctions in behavior.

The father's sister is *panimó*, a term built on the root *pani*, which means "in-law." Although a woman of the sib, she rates as an in-law because her daughter is normally eligible as a cross-cousin marriage partner. *Panimó* also means "mother-in-law." There are no formal avoidances with a mother-in-law. Ordinarily, because of the rules of residence, a man sees little of his mother-in-law.

Mother's brother (*paniyó*) is a parallel relative to father's sister. He is father-in-law. There are no formal avoidances in this relationship. The important relationship is between a woman and her father-in-law. There is a good deal of restraint between these two. The father-in-law is her mentor on moral issues, and if she commits adultery he will often act in the matter before his son does. Reserve between father-in-law and daughter-in-law is eased after a time but never lapses. The Cubeo defend the unity of the sib by regarding the in-marrying women as permanent strangers. It is the father-in-law as a sib elder who is expected to enforce the separateness. Coupled with this reserve and, in a sense, counteracting it, is the fact that he calls her *hwainkó*. Reserve prevents sexual joking, licentious bodily contact, and other undue levity. It does not bar the father-in-law from beating his daughter-in-law. Father-in-law and son-in-law may refer to one another by the common term, *pani*. Between father-in-law and son-in-law there is only the reserve of unfamiliarity. But when a man does come with his wife to visit her parents he is warmly welcomed as a son and is drawn into all common activities. The visit of a daughter is so exciting an occasion for the Cubeo that the son-in-law is readily tempted in the aura of warmth and good cheer to prolong his stay.

The terms that siblings apply to one another's children are only partially based on considerations of the marriage possibilities between their young. Primarily, the children of siblings are regarded as "youngsters." As juniors they merit generalized terms. Thus, the common terms for nephew and niece within the sib are respectively *hwainyó* and *hwainkó*. The son of a sibling of opposite sex is *pani* — an in-law — but the daughter is not. She enters the household as *hwainkó*. Again we notice the neutral character of the term. *Hwainkó* is not a term of the sib necessarily. The point is, rather, that it is not a term that connotes out-of-the-sib, as does *pani*. Thus, Cubeo usage with respect to daughter-in-law points up again the strength of their feelings about membership in the common residence group.

The problematical relatives are the mother's sister's children. There is no problem if they are also father's brother's children, or if they have been born within one phratry. But since mother's sisters marry into other phratries or into other tribes, their children are in effect strangers who belong to their paternal sib or tribe. They are not included in the kinship system, they are lost sight of, and such parallel cousins one may marry since they do not belong to the phratry.

GRANDPARENT - GRANDCHILD RELATIONSHIP

The two grandparent terms, *nyéko* (*kü*) and *nyekundjó*, refer to all kin of the generation of grandparents and beyond, irrespective of sib or phratry affiliation. Correspondingly, their reciprocals (*panaíhinkü, -ko* and *hipanímekü, -ko*) do not differentiate between a child of the sib or phratry and a child outside the sib or phratry. The grandchild terms are all formed of the *pani* stem from which affinal terms are constructed. *Panaíhinkü* means "my very little in-law," and *hipanímekü* means "of my in-law line." The ignoring of sib lines for grandparents seems to follow from the simple fact that at this generation level exogamy is not an issue.

I could get no explanation from the Cubeo as to why the grandchild should be classed with the affinal line. It may result from the Cubeo interpretation of cross-cousin marriage. Brother and sister negotiate for the marriage to one another of their children and so would be inclined to regard the offspring of that marriage as a contribution from the affinal line to the sib. Often enough, however, I have encountered the use of the descriptive terms such as *himákü-makü* (my son's son) to distinguish between a lineal descendant of the sib and other grandchildren.

Elders of a distant sib of the phratry may be addressed and referred to as "grandparent" even if of one's own generation. Their children consequently are called "father" or "mother." In these usages the reciprocal is always *hwainyó* or *hwainkó* and never a specific "child" or "grandchild" term. Among the Tucano, Fulop (1955) has noted that one of the sibs of a phratry is the "grandparent" to all the others so that all persons of one's own generation in that sib are "grandparents." If this is also the case among the Cubeo of the Cuduiarí then the fact must have escaped my notice. This usage of grandparent

terms is different from the seniority respect usages previously discussed, because "older sibling" among the Cubeo has a formal connotation of respect, whereas the grandparent term is a genial one as
in English.

CROSS - COUSINS

Cross-cousins of the same sex often have a relationship that is
formed by the fact that they have been principals in a brother-sister
exchange marriage. Since their parents, who were siblings of the
opposite sex, were also principals in arranging such a marriage, they
have shared in some of the intimacy of relationship between these
two. Cross-cousins of the same sex have, of course, little contact with
one another, but having so much in common, their relationship tends
to be a warm one. It is a curious relationship, in that it also has in it
a latent threat of trouble, trouble that arises from marital discord.
As already noted, one of the expectations of a brother-sister exchange
marriage from the male viewpoint is that if his wife leaves him he
can get his sister to leave her husband in retaliation. He believes that
he can apply pressure upon his cross-cousin brother-in-law to send
back the runaway wife or face the breakup of his own marriage.
Thus, what begins as a family squabble in one community may embroil a happy marriage in the affinal community. The expectation
that a woman will leave her husband only because her brother wants
her to is in practice a vain hope, unless he has the cooperation of his
male cross-cousin brother-in-law, who urges the woman, his sister, to
return to her husband.

Cross-cousins of opposite sex refer to one another as *hitcimako* or
hitcimakü, the possessive prefix connoting closeness. By contrast,
tcimá has the connotation of distance. The relationship between
cross-cousins of opposite sex is governed by the customs of courtship
and is, therefore, an individual matter.

THE AFFINAL GROUP

Among affinals there are two principal relationships. The most
important is that between parents and children-in-law, the *pani* relationship. This relationship is both consanguineal and affinal since it
includes the children of siblings of opposite sex and reciprocally the
cross aunt and uncle. The Cubeo draw no distinction, incidentally,
between parents and their children-in-law who are of the consanguineal kin and those who may be complete strangers. The emphasis in

this group is on the affinal relationship. Because of patrilocal residence it is the daughter-in-law who occupies a special position. She is *hwainkó* (younger female), a term that receives her with familiarity and some condescension as an in-group member. A daughter-in-law is considered to be at first a replacement for a daughter who has married out, and she lives for a time under the jurisdiction of her mother-in-law, helping her in gardening and in all food preparation. A woman tries to keep her daughter-in-law within her household as long as possible, speaking of her not as her son's wife but as a replacement for her daughter who has been lost to her by marriage. One aspect of the relationship between mother-in-law and daughter-in-law is stereotyped, and that is the tug of war between a woman's desire to keep her daughter-in-law within her jurisdiction and the desire of the young wife to win autonomy by cultivating her own garden. For the rest, the relationship depends upon the interplay of personalities anl upon the circumstance of whether the bride is a foreigner or a brother's daughter or a member of the brother's sib or phratry. When a child has been born and a woman has her own garden, she and her mother-in-law achieve a relationship of greater equality. Terminology does not change, even though the reference to an elderly woman as *hwainkó* may seem incongruous. The term defines the relationship at its inception.

It is the role of a woman to introduce her daughter-in-law to the economic routines and to the local customs of the community, a task that would be inappropriate for her husband. Since the Cubeo often marry women who do not even speak their language or dialect the initial period of tutelage is most important, even though the Cubeo do not stress this feature of what is really an apprenticeship.

The relationship with a son-in-law is governed by the circumstance that he normally does not become a member of the community. At best he will be a visitor who joins in the male activities. His relationship with his mother-in-law is one of restraint rather than of formal avoidance. It is perhaps for this reason that she addresses him as *hwainyó*. His relationship with his father-in-law, on the other hand, borders on intimacy and is predicated upon the equality of men engaged in their common tasks of hunting, fishing, and the conduct of ceremonies. Perhaps it is this equality that governs the use of *pani* or *paniyó* as a reciprocally used term between father-in-law and son-in-law.

The other set of affinal relationships recognized by the Cubeo are those involving spouse's siblings, for whom a variety of terms are applied. The general affinal term is *kodjú* or its plural form *hikódju-*

mana (my in-law group). These generalized terms are most appropriate in referring to members of a phratry into which one has married. They have a connotation of a claim to hospitality and of expectation of further intermarriage. Of this group of terms there is also *hikódjumu,* that is used reciprocally between men — sister's husband and wife's brother as well as sister's husband's brothers and brother's wife's brothers. Across the sexes women call their sister's husband's brothers as well as their husband's brothers *hikápenamu* and are called by these men *hikápenamo.* Women call their husband's sisters *híwemu* and are called by them *dyáko. Dya* is a very general term that may be applied reciprocally between any actual in-laws of the same generation. Finally, I have an alternate term for spouse's siblings, *hiháwükimana,* and the term *kíbü* for brother's son's wife. What may be observed about the affinal terms in own generation is that affinals are generally not confused with cross-cousins. As we have noted, the *tcimá* usage, which has the connotation of "sweetheart" for the Cubeo, is entirely inappropriate when one of them has married. Should a man be courting his brother's wife's sister, who is his cross-cousin, she is his *tcimá,* or rather *hítcimako.* If not, courtesy calls for the use of the affinal terms.

ORPHANS AND STEPCHILDREN

The treatment of orphans and stepchildren underscores the importance of the actual blood tie for the Cubeo. Parents lavish affection only on their own children. While a woman is obligated to look after all her husband's children, this need mean nothing more than that she feed them. That she will favor her own children and neglect or treat the others harshly is more or less expected. A man does not expect his second wife to accept as her own his children by another wife. A girl with a stepmother has a more difficult time than a boy, since women generally favor their sons and are harsh with daughters. The mother is her daughter's disciplinarian in household work. Her son is the little lord of the household, his sister its slavey. Stepdaughters are set the most burdensome tasks while own daughters are then freer to play. Own daughters then make common cause with their mother at the stepdaughter's expense. Since the father does not mix in the female side of the household he can do little to improve his daughter's lot with her stepmother.

A boy with a stepmother is less underprivileged. His is the male prerogative of being looked after by a woman, his mother or his sisters. He has his male play pack for companionship and can look to his father for personal attention. On the whole, a child is at a greater disadvantage if it has lost a parent of its own sex, that is, a girl with a stepmother, a boy with a stepfather. A girl with a stepmother has a hard life of chores and of open neglect. A boy with a stepfather does not have a hard life at all in the material sense. He is deprived more subtly of intimacy with a paternal figure, and this usually shows itself in his own reserve with respect to his fellows. If he has no father at all the effect upon his personality is even more marked.

My direct acquaintance with the situation of a true orphan is limited to the observation of one case among the *Bahúkiwa*. This was a girl from another tribe who had lost both parents and was adopted by the *Bahúkiwa* headman as his "daughter." The little girl, about nine, was addressed as "daughter" but held the status in the household of a servant. She took on the heaviest chores and was almost never free to play. Her lowly status was truly stigmatized by her lack of possessions. She was the only child among the Cubeo whom I had ever seen unadorned, until I gave her a necklace which she was allowed to keep. The children of the household enjoyed beating her as a way of teasing her, rather than wickedly. She took their pinchings and cuffings good-naturedly, on the whole, and had learned to pretend not to notice. Once, in the presence of the headman, her "father," the children were overdoing their teasing. She looked imploringly at the headman. Finally, she caught his eye and he said to her, "It is all right for you to run away." He saw no need to reprimand his own children.

In reading Giacone (1949) on the Tucano tribe I found my observations on orphans corroborated. He, too, reported that orphans do not lack food but that they appear to be melancholy.

CEREMONIAL FRIENDSHIP

A parallel to the brother-sister relationship is the *hikü-hiko* relationship, a ceremonial friendship. These terms, formed by combining the possessive prefix with the gender suffix, connote a relationship of exceptional closeness. The linguistic significance of possessive prefix and gender suffix for kinship terms has already been brought out. The curious feature of *hikü* and *hiko* is that these terms are composed of the two intimate-indicating particles.[3] The ceremonial

---

[3] *Hi* is also the verb stem "to give," but if *hikü* were translated as "giver" — a feasible rendering — it should be possible to say *hihikü*. But this form does not exist.

friendship is an intimate relationship, indeed. The Cubeo expectation of it is that it have a quality of warmth and of privilege, if not
beyond, then at least equal to a close, recognized kinship relationship.
Since ceremonial friends are already sib or phratry mates, their relationship, if it is to have any meaning at all, must make them at least
the equivalent of lineage kin; and that is what it is intended to do.
Ceremonial friendship gives vividness and exclusiveness to sib and
phratry relationships that are often too tepid and too generalized for
Cubeo tastes.

When ceremonial friends are of opposite sex they forgo the erotic
play that even brother and sister are supposedly allowed to indulge
in, asserting, thereby, that theirs is the closest bond of friendship at-
tainable. The relationship is often a substitute for a brother-sister
pairing. Not every sibling line is so conveniently arranged as to provide for a brother-sister pairing. Hence, if no sister is allowed to a
man he casts about for a girl of his age group and asks her to become his *hiko*. If she agrees he acquires the equivalent of an assigned
sister, and she of a brother. They will form a team in an exchange
marriage and they will exchange products. She will provide him with
manioc for chicha, if he wishes to sponsor a drinking party, and she
will prepare farinha for him, which he will use to trade for objects
of white manufacture. He will reciprocate with appropriate gifts
and with making household implements for her. When he is paid
for his labor in the rubber forests he will surely bring cloth and
trinkets for his *hiko*.

To cite one specific example of gift exchange between ceremonial
friends: A man of a *Bahúkiwa* subsib took a sib sister as his *hiko*. He
gave her, immediately, cloth for two petticoats, two boxes of matches,
two decorative combs, two small hand mirrors, thread and needles,
two tins of brilliantine hair dressing, and a bar of soap. In return
she gave him four big chicha serving calabashes, two balls of miriti
twine, and a valuable necklace of silver triangles known as "butterflies." In addition, her father gave her two fishing bows to give to
her ceremonial friend.

The relationship between *hikü* and *hiko* does fill the gap left by
the normal imbalance between male and female siblings. But the
Cubeo do not regard it as a mere substitute for a missing brother
or a missing sister. Men who have sisters assigned to them still seek
a *hiko*, if only to enjoy an individualized relationship of their own
choice. If exchange marriage is not to be a central feature of the relationship, the *hikü* is still entitled to a gift from the groom at his

hiko's marriage and he will expect to have been consulted so that he may consent to her marriage.

Ceremonial friendship should be permanent, the Cubeo say. Whoever breaks it has become an enemy and his soul after death will be that of an insect and not of a human being. Marriage, of course, separates *hikü* and *hiko*, but they visit one another, as do brother and sister, bringing gifts, and they try to arrange the marriage of their children to one another. The *hikü* has the first claim upon his *hiko*'s daughter as a bride for his son.

Between members of the same sex, ceremonial friendship is also the equivalent of a blood sibling relationship except that they exchange gifts in a formal manner. Whereas a man has reason to suspect that his own brother might commit adultery with his wife, he believes that his *hikü* will never cuckold him. Still, when it comes to adultery even ceremonial friends sometimes succumb. Adultery or even flirting with a ceremonial friend's spouse is a principal cause for a break in this otherwise very stable relationship. A ceremonial friend who has been wronged by his partner retaliates by entering the offender's house to break or carry off everything belonging to him except the hammock. This act of vandalism declares the friendship broken. Eternal animosity succeeds it. Women are less inclined to seek a ceremonial friend among their own sex. When they do, they have acquired mainly a confidante. Since women are likely to be dispersed at marriage the pledge against adultery with one another's husband is of no great consequence.

Ceremonial friends advise and assist one another. They feel that they actually have more freedom in their relationship with each other than they do with their own siblings. This may be correct, but I suspect that the Indians exaggerate the closeness of the relationship when talking about it. Ceremonial friends give up the use of their normal kinship designations in favor of the more intimate term.

Most ceremonial friendships are based upon simple reciprocity and so are modeled very closely, or I should say precisely, upon the sibling relationship. They satisfy in the main the longings of youths just before marriage and apparently fade with age. I was told that not everyone has a ceremonial friend but I could get no figures on its extent. Some ceremonial friendships model themselves after unequal kinship relationships, such as uncle-aunt or nephew-niece and grandparent-grandchild. These, I gathered, were not common and were rather aberrant forms of the true relationship. An older man takes a little girl as his *hiko* and is content with an unbalanced relationship in which he lavishes gifts upon her. "When she grows up," the Indians say, "she will repay him." A young man enters a friendship pact with an elderly widow because she has no one to look after her. This relationship, though, is like mother-son, and the woman will provide the young man with chicha and farinha if he has provided her with a manioc garden.

The Cubeo believe that ceremonial friendships persist in the afterlife. As spirits, they walk about arm-in-arm, one informant said, rapturously. The spirit of the friend who dies first hovers about the house until the other dies. It then leads its spirit friend away.

The ceremony for inaugurating ceremonial friendship is a simple one. At a drinking party, friends paint one another with red pigment which they refer to as "blood." Applying body paint to another, picking lice, or removing insect-bite scabs from the body is a gesture of intimacy normally confined to the immediate family. It is this intimacy that makes it appropriate between ceremonial friends.

Ceremonial friends tend to form a network. When a man has taken a girl as his *hiko* he is likely to take her brother as his *hikü*; his own brother will then take her sister as his *hiko* and so on. There are many network possibilities. Men who are *hikü* encourage their children to become ceremonial friends. The friendship network encompasses the phratry, giving to people special privileges of hospitality along the river. The network of kinship already encompasses the phratry, to be sure. But ceremonial friendship interlaces these bonds with the quality of close kinship. This seems to be its special significance. One may also look at the relationship from an economic point of view, noting the circulation of goods through its requirement of gift exchange. The Cubeo, however, are not so much property-minded as they are person-minded. The Cubeo joke about the gift aspect of ceremonial friendship and laughingly say that some people enter into the relationship with many people in order to acquire gifts. They are amused at the thought that a girl with many ceremonial friends will be a burden upon her suitor, who must make a gift to each ceremonial friend. The parents of young people are also burdened because they will be asked for something to be used as a gift. However, it is not goods they seek but intense relationships. It is not that the sib and the phratry fail to provide people with warmth and mutual assistance. The ordinary organization does this to a high degree. It seems, rather, that being virtually surrounded by "brothers" and "sisters" the Cubeo have exalted expectations of warmth and assistance which ceremonial friendship helps satisfy.

KINSHIP TERMS

nyéko Grandmother and all old women of grandparent generation of maternal and paternal lines, as well as older women of an opposite phratry, regardless of generation.

nyekundjó Grandfather and all old men of grandparent generation of the lineage and of the sib, including maternal or paternal lineages.

nyékü "Grandfather": all old men of own phratry or of opposite phratry regardless of lineage.

bakó or *hípako* Mother, mother's sisters, all women married to father's brothers, and all mothers of sib brothers.

bakü or *badjü* or *hípakü* Own father, as well as sons of men of the phratry who are called *nyékü*. (*Badjü* is the affectionate term.)

baküdyó Father's brother and all father's sib brothers.

himámiko My own and lineage older sister.

himámikü My own and lineage older brother.

hiyoko My own and lineage younger sister.

hiyokü My own and lineage younger brother.

amiyó My older sib or phratry brother; includes all male parallel cousins, but only those mother's sisters' sons who are of the phratry.

amikó My older sib or phratry sister; includes all female parallel cousins, but only those mother's sisters' daughters who are of the phratry.

hwainyó "Youngster." It is applied to all children of siblings, to all younger male parallel cousins of the sib and phratry, to all children of sib brothers, and to all of grandchild generation of the phratry who are outside of the lineage.

hwainkó The female counterpart of *hwainyó*. It is also the term for daughter-in-law.

hwankü An alternative form of *hwainyó* generally restricted to younger men of a close sib in the phratry.

hwa A short and colloquial form of *hwainyó* used between younger men of same generation of the phratry without necessary regard for relative age.

mamü A variant form of *amiyó* that is used only between members of different sibs of the same phratry.

mamüko The female counterpart of *mamü*.

amyóbakü Literally "older brother-father." A special respect term a woman applies to an older brother.

himako My own daughter.

himakü My own son.

hipanimeko Granddaughter of the maternal or paternal lineage.

hipanimekü Grandson of the maternal or paternal lineage.

panaihinko Granddaughter (literally "my little in-law") and alternative and more affectionate reference.

panaihinkü Grandson, counterpart of *panaihinko*.

tcumi Generalized affectionate term for male grandchild (literally "little one"). Can be extended as an affectionate term toward any younger male, but only by a woman.

tcúmiko Female counterpart of *tcumi*. Only a woman would use it for a younger sister.

pakomá   Kinsman (male or female) of my own phratry.

tcimá   Cross-cousin of my own sex.

hitcimako   Female cross-cousin (m.s),[a] wife's sister.

hitcimakü   Male cross-cousin (w.s.),[b] husband's brother.

hipánimo   Mother-in-law, father's sister (m.s., w.s.).

hipániyo   Father-in-law, mother's brother (m.s., w.s.).

pani   Generalized term for parent-in-law or child-in-law.

himanípako   Wife (literally "my children's mother").

himanípakü   Husband (literally "my children's father").

tcumípako or *tcumípakü*   These are alternative terms for husband and wife with colloquial connotations.

kodjú   Generalized term for members of a phratry into which one marries.

hikápenamu   Husband's brother, sister's husband (w.s.).

hikápenamo   Wife's sister, brother's wife (m.s.).

hikódjumana   My sibling's spouse, a generalized term.

hikódjumu   My sister's husband (m.s.).

hiháwükimana   My spouse's sibling.

hikópwimana   Wife's brother in an exchange marriage.

hiwemu   Husband's sister.

dyáko   Reciprocal of *hiwemu*.

dya   Any in-law of one's own generation.

kibü   Brother's son's wife.

hiwá   Any relative (literally "my people").

CEREMONIAL FRIENDSHIP TERMS

hikünahu   A very close friend.

hihwimu   My male friend (w.s.).

djuré hwiyo [c]   My female friend (m.s.).

hikü   Generalized term for male friend.

hiko   Generalized term for female friend.

adjuré hwinomwa   Ceremonial friendship between two women.

[a] Man speaking.

[b] Woman speaking.

[c] *Djuré* has the connotation of "sweetheart."

5

Marriage

The rule in marriage is that a wife cannot be taken from within the sib or phratry. She may be taken from another tribe and, of course, from any of the other two phratries. There is no actual prohibition against marrying a woman from one's own community if she belongs to a group that is outside the phratry. As I have already noted, such marriages are not common because of a preference for marrying someone from a distance. Since true friendship is apt to mean brotherhood for the Cubeo, and so is identified with exogamy, the parties to a coresidence marriage, the man in particular, are made to feel as though they were behaving indecently. The only case of a coresidence marriage that I learned about was complicated somewhat by an issue of adoption, but it illustrates the ambiguity of feeling the Cubeo have about such marriages, nevertheless. A boy, born a *Bahúkiwa*, was orphaned and adopted by the *Hürüwá*, a sib of the opposite phratry. He then married a *Hürüwá* girl. Opinion was divided. The boy and his supporters claimed that he was *Bahúkiwa* and so the marriage was proper. The other side argued that since he was raised by the *Hürüwá* he had no business marrying a *Hürüwá* girl. Since the girl's family allowed the marriage to stand we must assume that the boy's position was legally sound. Marriage is preferred between age equals, and since a groom must be forceful enough to make a good impression he will not marry until his very late teens and so neither will the girl. The term for marriage is *nomíkükü*, meaning simply "woman getting."

There is a strong preference for taking a wife from the same sib from which one's mother has come. This establishes a pattern of cross-cousin marriage and creates a very close bond between the maternal and paternal sibs. The *Bahúkiwa*, for example, are closely intermarried with the *Byówa* [1] and the relations between these two sibs accordingly are cordial, even warm, in contrast to the stiff relationships that generally prevail between sibs of opposite phratries. Preferential marriage into the mother's sib arises naturally from the strong bonds of affection and of formal relationship between brother and sister. The principal way in which brother and sister maintain their ties even after marriage has separated them is by arranging for the marriage of their children to one another. We have seen that the grandchild is called a "little affinal," a designation that I have taken to mean that a man, having arranged for his son to marry his sister's daughter, regards the offspring as a contribution by the affinal sib to his own. He has the satisfaction of regarding his sister as responsible for this. She has succeeded in getting something from the "other" sib over to his sib. In this way, exchange, which is the greatest of human binders, is kept active.

From the point of view of the boy, marriage with a father's sister's daughter also seems most natural and certainly convenient. Having had virtually no opportunities for courtship, he does not know where to go for a bride. His father suggests that he visit his aunt in his mother's sib and his mother is delighted that her son will visit her kin. There is no more desirable guest than a boy who is visiting both his father's sister and his mother's kin. The warmth with which he is received should put even the shyest boy at ease. There are, to be sure, other opportunities for finding a bride, but by and large even the most aggressive young men still prefer to go to a community where the way has been smoothed for them. Since Indians travel mainly to visit kinfolk they are more or less bound to marry a woman from a sib from which, if not the mother, then a brother's wife has been taken.

Work in the rubber forests has broadened opportunities for marriage because men from different tribes are brought together and form friendships that allow them to visit one another and to exchange sisters. But even with these opportunities the preference for marriage into the mother's sib is still strong. A boy's parents will have opened the negotiations for him. There is no formal betrothal, but there is a kind of understanding that a particular marriage will

---

[1] There is a list of *Bahúkiwa* marriages at the end of this chapter.

take place, although, it must be emphasized, these are never binding. Marriage is always thought of in terms of a boy getting a wife. A girl thinks a great deal about getting a husband, but her parents prefer not to think about that. The Cubeo know bachelors but not spinsters. Parents of a boy have in mind a little girl somewhere, usually in the maternal sib, as a wife for their son. Unable to bespeak her — a girl is bespoken only as a result of a brother-sister exchange marriage in which her brother has already taken possession of his wife — they keep an eye on her, waiting for her to grow up. She may marry someone else, in which case their disappointment will be keen although they will have no grounds for complaint.

There comes a day when a boy's parents say to him that there is a girl ready for marriage and that he ought to go and see if he can bring her home. If it is not the second stage of a brother-sister exchange marriage they will not say to him that they have already pursued the matter with the parents on the other side, through earlier exchanges of visits or through an emissary. Out of deference for his feelings should he fail to get the bride, they may instruct him as though he were going to broach marriage for the first time. If the girl is "vowed" to the sib his instructions are simply to bring her back, or, failing that, to take back his sister.

The young man sets out with a party of sibmen, some of his age group and some of his father's age group. The parents may come along, because a woman welcomes this chance for a home visit. A party does not necessarily announce itself as a wedding party. They prefer to announce upon arriving that they have come only to visit. If the parents are not to accompany the party, the father assembles the marriage party in the plaza and, in the presence of the entire community, instructs his son in the exchange procedures. If it is the completion of an exchange marriage he recapitulates the history of the earlier marriage, the promises of exchange that have been made, and declares what is due the sib. In an exchange marriage a particular girl has been promised and a substitute has usually been indicated if the girl who has been promised is unwilling. There is also the question of supplementary gifts to the bride's parents, such as a small canoe, a gun, ornaments, and the like, that the father authorizes his son to offer. If this is to be the initial marriage, from which an exchange will follow, the boy is instructed to say which sister or other girl of the sib will be offered. Under any circumstances both bride and groom have the option of deciding that they do not care for one another. This option is no mere formality and many a marriage party has had to settle for a social visit alone because the principals in the marriage were not attracted to each other. It is to avoid this embarrassment that the marriage party does not declare its intentions. They announce that they have come to visit relatives. They are made welcome, assigned to sleeping quarters, and are drawn into the general round of activities of the house. They may stay for many weeks. The groom-to-be joins in the activities of his age group, hunting and fishing with them. He spends part of his time in making gifts for his host's wife, who need not be the prospective mother-in-law, and for the mother-in-law-to-be as well, if he has been a guest in her household. He may make baskets, trays, or a hammock. Every woman treasures an object that a suitor has made. These objects, however, are not presented as marriage gifts but as offerings in return for hospitality.

The courtship itself is a slow process. For some time the prospective bride and groom virtually avoid one another. The young man is attentive to the other girls of the sib, and his own age mates, if single, act as though they are courting the prospective bride. They are all looking one another over. The young man's personality is evaluated, and his skills in hunting, fishing, and crafts are observed. The visiting party, for its part, makes close observations on the bride-to-be. The nature of this opening phase of the courtship in which bride and groom are being "looked over" is such that unexpected matches are sometimes made. It has happened that a boy who has been flirting with his bride-to-be's sister to divert attention from his real objective falls in love with her. Or the sister falls in love with the suitor and seeks her betrothed sister's permission to marry him. This happened among the *Bahúkiwa*. A man, having reached the final stages of courtship with a girl, had arranged the formal elopement tryst with her. At the end it was the sister who appeared, explaining that it was she who wanted to marry him, with her sister's consent. The suitor was not disappointed, and all went well.

If the young man is satisfied with the bride-to-be the party prolongs its stay. Otherwise it leaves quickly. Once it has decided to stay, the groom awaits a sign of acceptance from the girl. One of the first indications of sexual interest that she shows is to run rather than walk in his presence. When the older folk see a girl running when she should be walking they smile knowingly at one another. One day she throws a handful of manioc mash in his face in the presence of company and laughs at him. He pretends anger and moves upon her. She pretends fright and runs off to her manioc garden, where he overtakes her. They have coitus and they are then engaged. She may show her interest in other ways, pinching him or cuffing him as she walks by. If she runs from him toward her manioc garden his quest is over. Since it is the girl who must indicate acceptance by inviting coitus, the young man comes prepared with love charms. One of these is an extract of *úwe*, the plant associated with the ancestral cult, a symbol of power and virility, which he sprinkles upon her when she is unaware. This makes her desire him very passionately. After marriage a man uses what is apparently an antiaphrodisiac charm to keep his wife faithful.

Actually a wedding party is engaged in three levels of negotiation simultaneously, all three of which must be successful. The first is the courtship, the second is the discussions going on between the parents and the elders of the party over the terms of the marriage, and the third is the discussion between the groom and his *tcimá*, his male cross-cousin, the bride's brother. The *tcimá* is involved because a daughter will not be let go unless a return bride can be secured for him. It is up to the groom to promise the *tcimá* his own sister in return. Since no marriage is honorable that does not establish a proper relationship with an affinal sib, a man would be a scoundrel if he eloped with a girl without paying heed to these formal matters. Normally there are no difficulties, since the courtship would not get very far if the *tcimá* or the parents were seriously dissatisfied with the terms of marriage.

It is typical of the Cubeo that the atmosphere in which these three levels of negotiation are conducted is a genial one. Their mode of hospitality assures this by drawing guests fully into the life of the maloca and of the community — the groom joining the age group of his *tcimá*, the elders picking up corresponding social roles in their age group. The wife of a visiting elder is assigned a section of manioc garden. The point is that a guest who is going to spend more than a few days is as near as possible "at home." It is when the people feel at ease in their familiar roles in a new setting that they get down to business. When the marriage party has left with its bride it has also succeeded in strengthening the ties of friendship with an affinal sib and has overcome in practice the general theory that an affinal is a hostile sib of the tribe.

This mood of geniality is not achieved, nor is it sought for, in all circumstances. When the marriage is intertribal the courtship is conducted in an atmosphere of strain that is almost impossible to overcome. The bride's sib cannot be easily consoled at the loss of a daughter. When the marriage does occur they feel that they have been tricked in some way. They resent the girl's willingness to go off; they are mistrustful of the bride price and the promised exchange marriage. These suspicions are not overcome even though they may already have affinal kin in the other tribe.

Among the *Bahúkiwa*, I was witness to some of the events of the full cycle of an exchange marriage involving the neighboring Tucanoan-speaking *Tatúyo*. The opening wedge for this marriage was made by a *Bahúkiwa* woman who had married a *Tatúyo*. One day she reappeared among the *Bahúkiwa* with her husband and young children and settled down for a long wait. She was given a manioc garden and her husband devoted himself to making household implements for the wife of the headman. The headman had two marriageable daughters and two marriageable sons, to each of whom had been assigned, in the traditional manner, a sister whom he would exchange for a bride. One of the daughters, the elder, was very attractive, vivacious, flirtatious, and ardently desired by many young men. She had been married and divorced several times and was accused of having aborted, or killed at birth, several of her offspring. Because she was headstrong and not very industrious, sober-minded folk regarded her as a poor choice for a bride. Nevertheless, she was assigned to the older son, a very capable young man who showed every promise of becoming a headman. By seniority his was to be the prior marriage. Among the Cubeo the problem is to have the sons marry in proper age sequence and not the daughters. The *Bahúkiwa* visitor stated her opinion that such a girl needed a *Tatúyo* as a husband. "A *Tatúyo* could tame her," she said. The *Tatúyo* indeed had a reputation for ferocity because at the time they were still at war with the whites. By contrast with the Cubeo, those I saw were sullen and certainly appeared to be far more aggressive. She added that the *Tatúyo* also had many fine young girls, girls who had not been spoiled by contact with whites. The headman had no sooner grasped the possibilities of such a marriage for his undisciplined older daughter than a party of *Tatúyo* appeared to visit their fellow *Tatúyo*, who, they remarked jokingly, had lived away for so long that they now thought of him as a *Bahúkiwa*. It was a "large" party of eight men of warrior age. They came in two canoes. They were quartered among the various households and they stayed for several weeks, showing great skill in hunting, fishing, and in making implements. No one spoke marriage; but the signs were soon evident in the flirtatiousness of the daughters of the headman and two of the *Tatúyo* youths. When the *Tatúyo* announced that they were now ready to go home, a drinking party was quickly arranged as a farewell. When the *Tatúyo* party had left, it was discovered that the younger daughter was missing and that the older sister, whose "elopement" was taken

for granted, had remained home. When this was discovered the headman and all the able-bodied men he could muster rushed for their
canoes and paddled furiously downriver to intercept the "abductors."
The girl's mother sputtered with indignation at the *Tatúyo* who had
"tricked them" and at her daughter who had betrayed them. This, it
emerged, was a genuine elopement. The older sister, willful as
ever, had no intention of being "tamed" by anyone, least of all by
backwater Indians. Her younger sister was eager, however, and it was
no trouble to get the *Tatúyo* to accept her. In due time the *Tatúyo*
were intercepted. Assuredly they allowed themselves to be intercepted. Since the girl would under no circumstances agree to come
home, the parties had only to settle the conditions of an exchange
marriage. The *Tatúyo* designated a girl, ripe to be taken as a wife at
any time, and by way of apologizing for eloping with the wrong
daughter agreed to add a large canoe. Back home, the headman be-
rated his sister for thinking more of the interests of her *Tatúyo* husband than of her *Bahúkiwa* people.

The elopement postponed the marriage of the older son, who was
eager for a wife and precipitated the younger one into a marriage to
which he had not yet been giving thought, so strong is the Cubeo convention of pairing a brother and sister for an exchange marriage. In
a few months the younger son was sent to "demand" the bride promised. I did not accompany the marriage party to the *Tatúyo*. But when
the party returned with a very attractive young bride they reported
to the satisfaction of the headman that the groom, having first offered
his sister a chance to return home, asked for the bride. The girl was
brought out. He took her by the hand and led her to the canoe. "We
did not even stay overnight," he boasted. Such brusqueness and calculated discourtesy would not occur if the exchange were with the
maternal sib.

Sheer sexual attractiveness is regarded as the wrong reason for
choosing a bride. The point is not only that physical sturdiness and
industriousness are better traits, but that a sexually provocative woman will be a source of trouble to the sib. A responsibility of an elder
accompanying a marriage party is to remind the groom-to-be to pay
attention to the sterling qualities of a bride, that do include, however, such erotically desirable features as large, full breasts, a strong
back, and a clear skin. They would prefer to have her sullen rather
than vivacious.

Formal marriage is signalized by what must be regarded as the
"rite of abduction." The groom seizes his bride and runs with her
to the canoe. She cries out for help and her male kin rush out and

beat her "abductor" with sticks or with their bare hands. His own companions aid him, and if the girl is willing, they get to the canoe landing with no serious damage. This display of ceremonial violence satisfies two Cubeo doctrines, one that affinal sibs are "hostile" and the other that a woman will not leave her sib by her own volition but must be torn from it by brute force. There is also a third notion, namely, that a man be strong enough to capture a bride. I heard many accounts, perhaps apocryphal, of fainthearted striplings who could not bring home a bride. Such stories are often told to tease young bride seekers.

Father Giacone (1949, p. 21), who studied the Tucano tribe, reported no courtship and no marriage ceremony but did note forcible seizure of the bride. Father Giacone's information does suggest some variation in practice among the Tucano. There, the bride is not seized by the groom but by the groom's father, who has been accompanied by some men. They pretend they have come to purchase a canoe. In the midst of their visit for this purpose they carry off the girl and bring her home, unmolested, to the waiting groom. Often, he notes, this is the first time they have met. The girl is timid and retiring, he reports, and the women undertake to cheer her up by inviting her to accompany them on their labors. When the bride begins to work with satisfaction at all her tasks the marriage is considered settled. Some weeks later her parents come to reclaim her and the groom hides her. Her parents are given presents if she is unwilling to return home. At a later visit they repay with gifts of their own.

In general, Tucano and Cubeo marriage practices are alike; the most striking difference is in the fetching home of the bride. Cubeo notions of manhood would be offended at the notion that the father should bring a bride home for his son.

Among the Cubeo, the early stages of marriage are almost invariably difficult for the young couple. They are barely acquainted and the husband is expected to show his wife only the barest semblance of affection so as not to interfere with his mother, whose role it is to assimilate the young bride into her household as a replacement for the "lost daughter." The bride enters her mother-in-law's service, working with her in the manioc garden and in the preparation of manioc. Doing all the chores that she has done as an unmarried girl in her own community but under a strange woman, she is understandably disappointed, even though she is received very warmly. She is immediately locked in a conflict with her mother-in-law for her freedom. The issue is the manioc garden. A woman wants her daughter-in-law to help her in her garden and the daughter-in-law, knowing that her full status as a married woman begins with her having her own garden, must get her husband to get her out of her mother-in-law's household. He, however, knows his mother's will and is also aware that the men of the sib are watching him to see if he will be strong enough to stand up against his wife, the "alien" to the sib.

If the stalemate continues too long the young wife has the means to break it. She runs away. It is a married woman's privilege to run away at any time during her marriage. Her husband will pursue her, but she has many sanctuaries. She can get back to her own community, where she is safe and has the certainty that she will not be yielded up to a pursuing husband and that he has no claim against her parents. The common view is that if a man is not strong enough to hold a wife that is his misfortune. A runaway wife may find sanctuary in any sib, even in one that is closely related to that of her husband. A neighboring sib is only a temporary stopover for a runaway wife. It provides a more neutral atmosphere, however, in which she and her pursuing husband can discuss the reasons why she has run away. It is young brides who most frequently run off. Occasionally a girl is seriously determined to leave her husband and she will then most certainly find her way home, even if she has to go afoot all the way. Ordinarily she expects her husband to intercept her. When he brings her back the headman will say to him, "Take charge of your wife," and the husband will proceed to prepare a manioc garden for his wife. Some young wives provoke a crisis by seducing the husband's brother and allowing the community to find out. Again the headman will say, "Take charge of your wife."

These crises are so common in the early stages of marriage that I am inclined to regard them as quasi-ritual, and as part of a prolonged marriage ceremony at the end of which the wife achieves her proper status as controller of an autonomous zone, her manioc garden, and as female head of household. The act of running away suggests a counterpart to the initial act of "abduction." Both acts acknowledge the unruly role of the alien woman and emphasize the power of the man in restoring order. The man who brings his runaway wife back has scored a victory in the eyes of his sib. This victory absolves him from the onus of seeming to "give in" to the demands of his wife. But if the act of bringing back a runaway wife is a bit of ritual, it must also be stated that it is not devoid of spontaneous and rich human emotion.

Monogamy is the rule and is consistent with the preference for exchange marriage. Polygyny and polyandry, however, are not barred.

Plural marriages are uncommon only because they are not convenient. Polygyny is usually limited to the headman. Two wives (I never heard of any man having more than two wives at the same time) are regarded as suitable for a headman, first because he has the personal qualities to sustain a complex household and second because the maloca will be more orderly if two women are responsible for looking after it. A headman's prospects for getting two wives are enhanced somewhat, since he will almost certainly have had a sister assigned to him as an exchange for his first wife, and his prestige and perhaps affluence will help him get a wife through bride price alone. Brother-sister exchange is preferred, to be sure, but circumstances are such that an enterprising man will find many other ways of getting an additional wife from among widows, divorcées, and orphan children. He will not, however, marry a woman, either widow or divorcée, who has been brought to his community as a wife by a sibmate. A man may well have a surplus sister. These opportunities are available to all men, but it is the headman who is most likely to seize upon them. Koch-Grünberg, noting the common occurrence of polygyny along the Vaupés, commented that plural marriages were harmonious. From what I observed and from what I heard I have a very different impression. Polygynous households are rather turbulent.

If a man has two wives, he must prepare two clearings and set each up in her own household. Even so, my informants told me, the wives quarrel and bear tales against one another to the husband, accusing one another of laziness. The first wife taunts her colleague as being a mere second wife. The second retorts that she would not have been chosen if the husband had really cared for the first wife. Since men take it for granted that women are an unruly element they expect wives to quarrel. A headman, however, should be able to manage them, it is believed.

One man told me that after he had married his present wife he was offered a girl for bride price alone — a shotgun and cloth — and so for three years he maintained a polygynous household. He then decided that it would not work. At first the new wife refused to garden and urged him to come and live at her sib. They did this for a time and he left his first wife at home with their children. After a year he returned with the second wife. He made a large clearing and divided it into two parts, assigning each to one wife. His first wife, he said, cultivated her part but the second did nothing and just sat about the house. One day she departed and he did not chase her. He claimed that he did not understand why she had left since he had not forced her to do anything she did not wish to do.

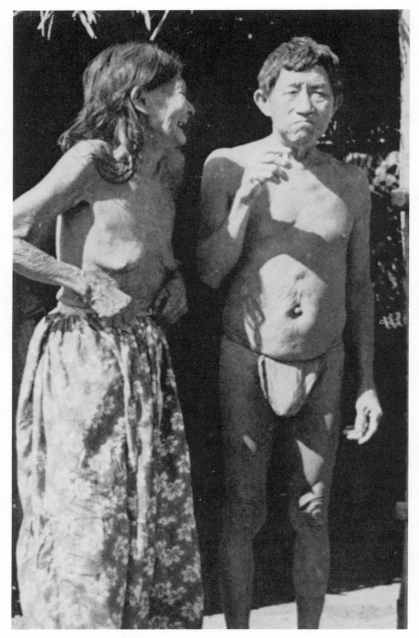

Fig. 6. Old *Bahúkiwa* couple.

The *Bahúkiwa* headman also had had two wives. In his case the second and younger wife succeeded in displacing the older woman. The younger woman insisted that her husband give up sexual relations with his first wife. She bothered him so much that he yielded and told his first wife to leave him. She refused, insisting that she would stay on with her children. An old woman now, she has a grandmother role. A son not yet married has provided her with a small manioc garden. Her relations with the headman and her successor are cool but not unpleasant. That women regard polygyny as contrary to their interests is further indicated by the fact that they are reputed to possess an herb (*pedídya*) which, mixed into a husband's porridge, causes him to lose interest in acquiring a second wife.

Polyandry is rare. I knew of only one case, a man who took his brother into his ménage because the man had been unable to get a wife on his own. This occurred in a small Satellite community and seems to have been an accommodation to what might otherwise have been a troublesome situation of adultery. The woman fed both men and was a sexual partner of the junior husband only when her first husband was away.

Common marital difficulties have their counterpart in Cubeo folklore, as these tales reveal. *Kúwai* the culture hero and his two brothers shared the same woman. When one brother was away fishing or hunting, the other two took turns copulating with her. *Kúwai* plotted to get rid of his brothers so that he would have exclusive possession of her. They were then living at Urania on the Vaupés by a lake called *Marúkuwari* [Lake of the marúku monkey]. In this lake grew a great miriti palm. *Kúwai* asked his brothers to climb the tree to fetch a ball of miriti to make a hammock. Both brothers climbed the tree, after warning *Kúwai* not to start anything. As they climbed, *Kúwai* caused the tree to grow higher and higher and the lake to grow wider. When they reached the top, *Kúwai* cut down the tree. Then a great wind blew up and swept the men and the tree away. One brother was blown to the Cuduiarí, where he formed the river. The other was blown to the Querarí, where he formed the other river. As each man fell, his legs formed the mouth of the river, his outstretched arms two creeks, and his head a whirlpool. *Kúwai* then returned to his wife, who was now living alone. Later *Kúwai*, walking in the forest, passed a *wahókakü* tree. Each time he passed it, it made a sucking sound at him. This happened day after day. Then it seemed to *Kúwai* that the tree was human, so he cut it down and carved a woman out of its trunk. *Konéko*, a bird, came and opened up the woman's vagina. The woman was very pretty and *Kúwai* was happy. He named her "Carved Woman." He took her home as his wife and drove out the other woman. *Mamúwü* came along and asked *Kúwai*, "Are you living alone?" *Kúwai* told him what had happened. This made *Mamúwü* angry and he took "Carved Woman" away from *Kúwai*. Now *Kúwai* lived alone and went about looking for another wife. He sat upon the branch of a tree and wept. Then along came Otter. He asked *Kúwai* why he was weeping. *Kúwai* told him that *Mamúwü* had taken away his wife. Otter then told *Kúwai* where his wife was living. He led *Kúwai* to a beautifully painted house that was under the river. There *Kúwai* saw his wife. He seized her and fetched her home to Urania. One day *Kúwai* saw an angry *Mamúwu* come after him. In fright *Kúwai* leaped up and fled. He never returned. He is now living at Carurú on the Vaupés without a wife.

In another version *Kúwai* cut down a tree and carved it into the form of a woman. He brought it to his grandmother and asked her to make all the body parts that belong to a woman. He returned to find that his grandmother had completed a beautiful woman. This woman did not know where she had come from. She went to the river to fetch water. An anaconda came by and copulated with her. Each day when she went for water the anaconda came and they copulated. *Kúwai* noticed this. One day he watched, and when his wife and the anaconda were copulating, *Kúwai* blew a dart from his blowgun very high into the air. It came down with great force, struck the anaconda in the back, and killed him. *Kúwai* seized the anaconda and cut off his penis. He transformed it into four minnows which he gave to his wife to eat. As she ate the minnows, *Kúwai* told her she was eating the penis of her lover. The woman spit out the food and went to the river to look for her lover, but he did not appear. *Kúwai* then threw his wife away and she became a tree again.

In a third version the saddened wife, awaiting the return of her anaconda lover at the river, was disappointed when only a little anaconda "as thin as a string" appeared to tell her that her lover was dead.

It is perhaps indicative of Cubeo attitudes on marital stability that *Kúwai* is depicted as ultimately unsuccessful in marriage, and, disillusioned with the faithlessness of woman, retires to live in solitude on a nearby hilltop.

The terms for spouse, *himanípako* (wife) and *himanípakü* (husband), denote the important emphasis in marriage. These terms mean literally "my children's mother" and "my children's father." Before children are born husband and wife address one another simply with the common expression *hápyako* (listen!). It would not be correct to say that children "seal the marriage." Children, however, do give a marriage its full status. Until her first child is born a wife may remain as part of her mother-in-law's household. Thereafter she automatically achieves her independence, with her own garden and her own hearth. The equality of the spouse terms is also significant, corresponding to the economic and symbolic complementarity of male and female, husband and wife. Although an outsider in a patrilineal and patrilocal sib, the Cubeo wife is not "inferior" to her husband

The relationship between husband and wife depends largely upon personal factors, to be sure. Still, there are some cultural standards for the people to follow. One of these is the keeping of physical distance in public. One does not observe among the *Bahúkiwa* informal or spontaneous gestures of intimacy between husband and wife. They rarely touch one another in public. This lack of physical contact is all the more marked because the Cubeo are in other respects a tactile people. Men embrace one another, women caress one another, and at drinking parties there is a certain amount of heterosexual body contact. But even then, husband and wife keep their distance. There are, however, specific public gestures of intimacy between husband and wife, but these are formal and are in the nature of obligations. A woman applies decorative paint to her husband, delouses his head, and scrapes insect scabs from his skin. These are all intimate gestures to the Cubeo. They are done in public and only in preparation for a ceremony.

The marital relationship is to be understood, I believe, as falling within the range of respect behavior appropriate to members of different phratries. It is incumbent upon the man, furthermore, to uphold his solidarity with his male sibmates by imposing public distance upon his wife. Male solidarity begins early in life and, in any case, is not readily yielded up after marriage. There is a relationship, as well, between connubial distance, as we may call it, and the frequency of tribal exogamy. In many marriages husband and wife cannot even understand one another fully because they speak different dialects or languages. It would seem that the pattern of connubial distance helps make such marriages more tolerable since there is no expectation of sudden intimacy. Lack of privacy makes it easy for public pressure to enforce the rule of distance.

With time, of course, husband and wife develop more ease, more intimacy, and more affection for one another. These new relationships will be revealed in manner of address and facial expression rather than by touch.

Divorce is easy and rather frequent during the early years of marriage. Most often it is the woman who leaves her husband, for the general reason that she does not like him and, more rarely, because he beats her. If a woman has no intention of going back to her husband she returns home, re-enters her parents' household, and her husband has no further claim upon her. If she is undecided, she claims the hospitality of a neighboring sib and awaits a reconciliation. A marriage is not officially severed, on the woman's part, unless she returns home. She cannot run away with another man and expect to avoid trouble. Men send wives away mainly because they are barren. The Cubeo have no other official view of infertility than that the woman is using an abortifacient. They therefore tend to view barrenness as a hostile act. A wife who is asked to leave has no choice but to do so. Her grown children are expected to remain behind in their own sib, while the nursing baby accompanies the mother.

The most common source of marital discord that may also lead to divorce is adultery. From quarrels that erupt during drinking parties the impression is created that adultery is very common. Almost invariably it is the woman who is blamed, partly because women commonly are sexually aggressive, and partly because that is the least disruptive view to take of the matter; it does least damage to the important male solidarity of the sib.

BAHÚKIWA MARRIAGES

Byówa	14	Tatúyo	3
Uanana	7	Síriana	2
Miandwa	5	Bwébowa	1
Hürüwá	4	Hurédariwa	1
Korówa	4	Karapana	1
Yurití	4	Piratapúyo	1
Djurémawa	3	Tóriawü	1
Konéntaraboiwü	3		

6

Leadership and Authority

Leadership among the Cubeo follows a principle that tends to understate authority. This principle asserts that leadership derives from giving more than one receives. Authoritarian relationships, by contrast, follow an opposing principle, that of receiving more than one gives. Authority, to be sure, can be established on a personal basis of personality and prowess. However, societies that have developed strong authority systems have usually done so by economic means, by inequality in the flow of goods. An authority system based on unequal flow of goods upward, from the community to a chief, is likely to respond quickly to economic development, and at the same time to foster economic growth. The Cubeo theory effectively minimizes the economic impact of leadership. The principle of greater flow to the top creates the condition for an expanding economic-political system, whereas the principle of greater flow from the top down creates the conditions for a static political-economic system. The economic role of the Cubeo headman is confined largely to stimulating the production of chicha. In short, the Cubeo headman gives all of his effort and ability to the community. The community, for its part, has no obligation to give anything to him. Since he has no authority to command economic productivity, for he is not an economic redistributor, he is devoid of significant economic function. At the same time the headman is a secular figure; he has no greater magical or religious powers than any other and so he is lacking in sacred authority. He may be a war leader, but he need not be; and even when he is a war leader, it is a very small party that he commands. Thus, the Cubeo headman is lacking in precisely those attributes that in other parts of the world have traditionally played a prominent part in political evolution.

The two terms, *habókü* and *kenámi upákü*, meaning, respectively, a man of substance and "owner of the house," illustrate the conceptual range in Cubeo leadership. The *habókü* is the leader, whose presence, enhanced by a muscular physique, commands respect, who has undisputed skill in hunting, in fishing, in crafts, and who commands ceremonial lore. He possesses the full range of ceremonial regalia, feather headdresses, necklaces, and girdles. His equipment is of the best quality and in excellent condition. The *kenámi upákü*, on the other hand, is simply the head of the maloca. The *habókü* is apt to be head of the house, but a house head need not be *habókü*, although as a leader he will possess some *habókü* attributes. Thus not all headmen qualify as *habókü*. Those of higher-ranking sibs, such as the *Órabawa*, *Aúnbwawü*, and *Hehénewa*, usually do, and those of lower-ranking sibs, such as the *Bahúkiwa*, usually do not. The existence of a concept of *habókü* is a spur to the ambition of a headman, although the status is honorific only. The *habókü* commands respect everywhere in the tribe, but his authority, such as it is, is limited to his own sib. Sibmen share in the prestige of having a *habókü* as headman. Not every *habókü* is the head of his sib, for in some sibs several men hold the title and their senior is then the headman. In time of war the *habókü* is the natural war leader. Even when not headman his leadership is drawn upon in hunting and in all collective activities.

In the higher-ranking sibs the insignia of *habókü* include, first, a quartz cylinder worn as a pendant, a jaguar-tooth girdle, an armadillo-vertebrae girdle, and, finally, *mápena*, the ceremonial headdress of feathers and monkey hair. The *Bahúkiwa*, who are not privileged to wear either the quartz pendant or the girdles, maintain that *mápena* are the principal insignia of *habókü* status among them, although they defer to the higher status of the insignia of their higher-ranking clans. The *Hehénewa* deride this *Bahúkiwa* claim and insist that without the pendant and girdles no man can call himself *habókü*. The *Bakúkiwa* define *habókü* as an achieved status and the *Hehénewa* as a hereditary status, but only in the sense that it pertains to high-ranking sibs. Within the proper sib any man may acquire the insignia and the status of *habókü*.[1]

---

[1] Apropos of social status, Martius (1867, I, 596) reported caste distinctions of chiefs, nobles, and commoners on the Vaupés. He gives no details. One suspects an exaggeration, although the bases for his view are understandable.

INSIGNIA OF STATUS

Ornamentation is for the Cubeo a requisite for basic status; one might say for human status. The Macú, for example, are sometimes derided as "not human," and it is noted in evidence that they have no ornaments. The very first day a newborn infant is in the house, it is painted with a jaguar design and its mother puts twine cord on its wrists and a seed necklace around its neck. An undecorated child is a rarity, an extraordinarily underprivileged creature. The common denominator of personal ornamentation includes face and body painting with red pigment (*urucú*) and a necklace. The wristlets of children have the magical purpose of fattening the arms, but the necklaces are sheer insignia of status. A popular trade item around Indian tribes is a necklace of silver plates in a triangle shape which all the Indians of the region call "butterflies." Necklaces of various seeds are common for men and women. In the past, ear ornaments and lower-lip labrets were common to both sexes. The Cubeo are proud and sensitive about their personal appearance. They apply pigment with great care, using dye rollers to print a design and pigment applicators that will apply parallel lines. Ornaments are always in good condition and of good quality.

The minimum ornamental requirement for full standing as an adult male is the complex feather headdress, *mápena* (feathers of the red *arara* [macaw]), which actually includes feathers of many different birds mounted on a crown of plaited fiber as well as a rope of monkey hair. These feathers, painstakingly gathered and put together, are handled with very great care, kept in a long fiber box where they are laid away always slowly, ceremonially, and in proper order, to be taken out for a dance. A man who does not own *mápena* borrows from the headman or from another sibmate so that he can take part in certain dances. All men possess some part of the full set of feathers, but only a headman will feel the strong obligation to possess the full set. No one among the *Bahúkiwa* owned a complete *mápena*, but this poverty was not too disturbing to them. The downstream *Hehénewa* were well provided. *Mápena*, however, are not a mark of sib rank.

The *Bahúkiwa* attitude toward *mápena* is ambivalent; their joy in possession is tempered by fear of death because of it. They do not make the headdresses but buy them from other Tucanoan and Arawakan tribes, and they suspect that whoever has sold them the feathers has included a spell that will kill the owner if he should own the full set. One informant explained that the feathers have power that may be too strong for the owner and that is why it is better not to have too much. Some men accumulate outfits of *mápena*. They are certain to die from overdoing, it is said. A host at a drinking party may lay out his *mápena* in a tray at the doorway so that guests may wear them for dancing. It is a point of pride to be able to supply guests in this way. He addresses a guest as follows: "Here it is now, this poor thing that I have. When you put this on you may drink. Our ancestor wore this when he made chicha to drink. He became sick when he did this, when he adorned himself. Other people know how to make this [*mápena*]. He bought it from them."

The girdles of jaguar teeth and of armadillo vertebrae were also possessed only by the *Hehénewa*. They are worn only during ceremonial dances. These girdles are symbols of shamanistic power although they are not shamanistic insignia. The jaguar is, of course, the full-fledged shaman himself. The armadillo claw forms the handle on the special rattle a shaman uses to bring rain. The quartz cylinder (*kenádox*: stone) may also be a shamanistic symbol since stone crystals are part of the medicine man's equipment. But whatever its symbolic significance, it is for the Cubeo the ornament of major prestige, limited to the high-ranking sibs. The quartz from which this pendant is laboriously made and drilled is found, I was told, only on the Tiquié River and is widely traded in the region. The *Hehénewa* claim that their first ancestors brought the *kenádox* with them and that is why they alone may wear them. Koch-Grünberg found these pendants to be widespread among the Tucano, where even children wore them.[2]

HEADMANSHIP

The headmanship, whether of *habókü* status or *kenámi upákü*, normally stays within a particular lineage, although no lineage has a specific and traditional claim to the office. The office may go from a father to his eldest son or from a man to his next younger brother, depending upon circumstances and upon which of these pushes himself forward most effectively. Koch-Grünberg observed that among

---

[2] Martius (1867, I, 599 ff.) observed that the quartz cylinder is a special trait of the Vaupés. He put the source of the stone at the Apaporis and Caquetá rivers and reported that it took two generations to make a pendant. The stone is ground into shape with volcanic ash obtained from the Solimoes River and the hole is bored with a bamboo drill. He saw chiefs on the Vaupés who wore pendants drilled through the long way, an exceptional mark of high status. The size of the pendant, according to Martius, was in proportion to the deeds of the wearer in war and in the hunt.

the Tucano Indians of the Vaupés, succession was from father to son, while on the Aiarí it went from brother to brother (1909, I, 68). The Cubeo combine both methods. The tendency of the headmanship to stay within a lineage conforms to the natural tendencies of sons to model their behavior on their father, and for a group of brothers, who form among the Cubeo a particularly intimate sibling group, to share common interests. Thus, the men of a chiefly lineage behave with a greater sense of responsibility for the welfare of the sib; they follow the pattern of giving and act generally to maintain high morale. If the prospective heirs fail to live up to expectations they cannot succeed to the office. The office is not their automatic due, although coming from a chiefly lineage, their chances for the office are very much enhanced. Competition for the office is regarded as unseemly. Since the Cubeo are most sensitive in their distrust of the authoritarian personality, an overeager contender for the headmanship would most likely jeopardize his chances.

In the case of the headman who is known only as "owner of the house," the model of leadership is, as the title denotes, paternal. His warrant of office is that it is he who has built the maloca. A changeover in the headmanship comes with the building of a new maloca, when a headman has died or when the old maloca needs to be replaced either because of its deteriorated condition or because new manioc gardens need to be planted at a new site. On those occasions, the man who feels confident of his support undertakes to put up the main beams of the new house, with the help of his own brothers and of his sons. For the reasons already cited this man is most likely to be of a line of headmen. When the main posts are in place, the other household heads of the sib are invited to join in the work of completing the house. Those who join will be residents who accept the leadership and authority of the new headman. No man is compelled to join. He may declare himself an Independent, saying he will build his own house. The building of a maloca constitutes an election — one that occurs every five years or so, the period of duration of a house and of a manioc clearing. A headman who has grown unpopular will then find himself replaced, often by a brother or a son. It is as "owner of the house" that the headman is giver, guide, and keeper of order. He is in charge of the hospitality of the house, the receiver of guests, and the main organizer of drinking parties. He is responsible for ceremonies and for all ceremonial equipment, including tobacco, coca, and *mihí*. He is chairman of discussions and arbiter of disputes. He has no authority to order punishment, although his opinion as to punishment carries weight.

No Cubeo headman has rights over person, over life, or over property.

Within the sib, the headman is the firm but gentle father, ever watchful of the welfare of his sibmates. There is, however, another side to the office. As representative of the sib within the phratry he is the organizer of drinking parties in which the prestige of the sib and his own prestige are involved. An ambitious headman urges his people to produce more chicha, to entertain often. His pressure may become burdensome on the people and his influence within the sib is, accordingly, jeopardized. The *habókü* with more commanding presence can push people farther, it is said, than the ordinary *kenámi upákü*. While drinking parties are enjoyed and sibs are conscious of their own heightened prestige as givers of chicha, they suspect that their headman is pushing himself forward too strongly and they resent it. To forestall such resentment a headman urges household heads to join as cosponsors of a drinking party.

The headman is charged with preserving the unity of the sib. While concern with personal prestige is not lacking, this considera- tion of his must be secondary to the welfare of the sib. He must pre- vent splitting of the sib. If a household leaves, the headman is blamed. He is blamed if sibmen's quarrels reach a dangerous point. When drinking parties erupt in violence the women taunt the head- man with his inability to restore order. Yet in asserting leadership the headman dare not be too forceful. Father Giacone has observed about the Tucano Indians that they are docile. The same can be said of the Cubeo. A man will not, in fact he claims he cannot, re- sist a direct command. He will obey and be resentful. No house- holder who had unwillingly submitted to a headman's command would long remain in the sib. Moreover, the Cubeo do not easily tolerate social tension. If the atmosphere in the house becomes un- pleasant someone will certainly move out. Men will not work, hunt, fish, or join in any collective undertaking if the atmosphere is not cordial. Maintaining this atmosphere is perhaps the most difficult charge upon the headman.

The headman who must deal with white tradesmen and with labor recruiters has the additional burden of representing his community against men of very forceful personality. He finds that he dare not submit to the common weakness of docility and must match their forcefulness with his own. A headman who has learned to deal with the white man on equal terms will tend to be more authoritative within his sib as well.

There is much talk in the region about powerful chiefs, but no one has really seen one. In the past, the Indians say, there were chiefs over all the sibs along a river. Koch-Grünberg was told the same thing (1909, I, 264). One is also told that other people have powerful chiefs. I had no opportunity to investigate this, but Koch-Grünberg, who traversed all the main rivers in the region, was always told that the chiefs along another river were strong. The Desanas had only headmen, but they informed Koch-Grünberg that great chiefs ruled along the Papurý and Tiquié rivers. When he got there he found only headmen. If there has been a stronger political organization among the Cubeo in the past there is no suggestion of it now.

The fact is that leadership follows similar principles among all neighboring tribes from whom we have adequate information. Describing the Arawakan Siusi, Koch-Grünberg notes that the headmanship is a hereditary office, going from father to oldest son or to his younger brother. The headman himself passes on the office to someone in his line. His authority is minor and is concerned only with village affairs. It is based on the respect owed to age. The headman among the Siusi, he adds, is a representative, receiving guests and leading all community activities and discussions. He sees to it that the house is kept in order; and if he leaves for any length of time he turns the command over to his brother. He maintains order but he cannot punish. A headman who had long associated with the whites claimed authority over the entire river but no one took him seriously. Koch-Grünberg had the impression, however, that the oldest man in the maloca was the headman (1909, I, 68). This is not quite true among the Cubeo. The Cubeo respect age, but leadership, to repeat, depends upon ability to be a giver, so that a man who has gone too far past his prime is ordinarily ruled out as a headman.

LAW AND JUSTICE

With respect to the administration of justice and of order the headman is no magistrate. He is a mediator, a counselor, and often a persuasive advocate of his own views. It is the entire adult community that must reach a decison. The headman provides for orderly discussion until a decision is reached. Within the sib a primary objective of the headman's efforts is to smooth over difficulties, calm tempers, and restore the atmosphere of congeniality. There are, however, serious breaches of the peace, such as sorcery, persistent adultery, chronic and malicious theft of food, and murder when punishment is called for. In such cases the aim of the headman is not to calm tempers but to inflame and to focus angry passions upon the culprit. He does so because the Cubeo do not tolerate a judicious and cold-blooded administration of punishment. Their view is that malicious acts are committed in anger. Such acts provoke anger in return, in the course of which the culprit is suitably punished. Thus, a wrong-doer always runs away. Even if he should regard himself as innocent of the charge, when he learns that charges are being discussed he deems it prudent to leave. He need not be gone very long — perhaps just a few months. When he returns the anger against him has died down and there will be no basis for action. In cases where a sibman is being provocatively uncooperative and the senior households, to-gether with the headman, agree that he should be made to leave, they wait for a drinking party when someone, or the headman him-self, picks a quarrel with the culprit. In the heat of the quarrel the unwelcome sibman is asked to leave. The traditional drinking party seems to serve as the most appropriate setting for the airing and settling of grievances and of disputes.

Fighting is the most common social disturbance and is inevitable during a drinking party. A quarrel between two men draws in others, usually close kin; each man entering the fray loudly proclaims his reason for joining, justifying by anger his right to take part. Mem-bers of the same household always have justifiable cause for anger in assisting one another. More distant kin must cite a personal mo-tive. They can claim a past insult. A host or headman is privileged to intervene to stop a fight but will do so reluctantly. In a Cubeo quarrel the detached bystander is not welcome. Women are usually strongly disturbed by fighting. They dread that someone will get hurt and when a fracas becomes bloody they loudly demand that the headman put a stop to it. If he ignores them, pretending to be drowsy with drink, they abuse him and say he is not fit to be a headman. A headman is drawn to anger and to participation in a fray if a cere-monial friend has joined a fight without asking his permission. Ceremonial friends are as one and should share the same quarrels. Fighting at a drinking party, although actually disliked by the Cubeo, is not a punishable offense, since the angry parties have had full op-portunity to retaliate. When the fight is over the issue is usually closed, unless new threats and insults are uttered. Those will be remembered at the next drinking party and serve to start a new fight.

Retaliation for murder is the responsibility only of the members of the victim's own household and lineage. Sibmates are under no obligation to avenge a murder unless, they reason publicly, the murderer, having killed one sibmate, is surely planning to kill others. However, such reasoning is more appropriate in cases of sorcery than in cases of direct assault.

Among the *Hehénewa*, I was told, a man was beating his wife when his own brother, who had no apparent cause to do so, intervened. This led to a quarrel. While they were quarreling they heard a monkey howl, always an omen of the impending death of a kinsman. In alarm, each took his gun and together they went to the river to shoot the monkey. There the wife-beater shot and killed his brother, claiming that it was an accident. However, he decided he had better leave. Later that day, when a third brother learned what had happened, he set out to find and kill his fugitive brother. The police, however, learned of the shooting and induced him to find the killer and turn him over to them. This he did. The culprit spent some months in jail and was released. By that time anger had subsided and the brothers were reconciled.

Should a man kill his wife only her kin will avenge her. There is no one to avenge or punish a father who kills his children. The only example of such crimes that I have is of a madman, but it does illustrate the point. According to the account given me, this man, crazed by hunger, killed and ate his children. He then attacked his wife, cut off one of her breasts, roasted it in the fire, and ate it. No one interfered "because it was his own wife and children." The man then cut a piece from his own thigh. The people watching said, "Let him do this. It is a good thing that he should die." They watched as he then cut his throat and died.

I also learned of another example of unavenged death. An old *Bahúkiwa* man had died and the inquest named a man of a related sib as the sorcerer responsible for the death. The sibmen threatened vengeance. Some days later the alleged sorcerer innocently came to pay his respects to the dead. He was coolly received, but no hand was raised against him. When I asked about it I was told that no one felt close enough to the old man to want to avenge him. The widow was still angry, but women are not avengers even by means of sorcery.

Theft to the Cubeo means stealing food from a garden. Thieves pull up manioc tubers in the dead of night and they steal *mihí*. Both offenses are regarded as serious and incomprehensible. The theft of *mihí* is all the more culpable because it is a sacred drug. Such theft is correctly interpreted by the Cubeo as malice and is attributed only to men. If caught in the act the thief, even if a sibmate, is severely beaten or killed. Theft of objects is simply not acknowledged.

Technical incest, that is, incest outside the nuclear household, does occur and is not necessarily regarded seriously. A man told me that his sib sister, having become a widow, returned home. An ardent woman, she made sexual advances to him. He then told the headman that his sib sister had seduced him. The headman scolded the woman and hastily arranged for her marriage to an elderly *Tatúyo*. In the case of close incest, that is, within the extended family, the offenders are driven out of the sib. I learned of no cases.

Adultery is a common offense and is not very serious unless compounded by fears of sorcery. Only the man will be suspected of sorcery, never the woman. Since it is the women who are commonly regarded as the seducers and the men as innocent victims, the consequences of adultery are apt to be little more than a heated quarrel. An adulterous woman may receive a thrashing either from the husband or from her parents-in-law. In charges of adultery a headman, concerned first with harmony in the sib, seeks to placate feelings by emphasizing the culpability of the woman. The following example illustrates this. At a drinking party among the *Bahúkiwa*, when intoxication was at its peak some hours before dawn, the headman suddenly began to berate a man of the sib for adultery, accusing him of having seduced the young wife of his (the headman's) son. The son himself did not enter into the controversy, but he explained quietly to those about him that his wife was too passionate. Whereupon the headman shifted his attention to the young woman and began to scold her for wearing love charms in her hair and for enticing men. Then, his anger rising, he slapped the girl sharply in the face. The accused sibman, now ignored, moved away unconcerned. The young wife, for her part, showed no distress at being slapped. A few minutes later she was as flirtatious as ever, this time with another man. The headman, still wrathful, delivered a lecture on the proprieties of married life, remarking that it is not fit for a wife to request coitus; she must wait for her husband. The next day a younger unmarried daughter of the headman was assigned to chaperon the errant wife, a task she accomplished with suitable diligence.

The Cubeo regard a woman as unruly and are almost prepared to accept her adultery as inevitable. Nevertheless, an adulteress is reviled as "a woman without shame." A husband's chagrin and anger at his wife's adultery are softened somewhat by tales of *Kúwai*'s difficulties with adulterous wives. In one tale, however, *Kúwai* crushes his wife against a tree after she has copulated with a snake in her manioc garden.

Strongest feelings and strongest actions are provoked by sorcery. Most illness and death is attributed to the evil designs of medicine men, or laymen who command the arts of sorcery or of administering mysterious poisons. The Cubeo fear of sorcery and of "poisoning" is acute. They are aroused not only by the illness or death of a sib-mate or of a sibmate's wife, but they anticipate that he who has in-jured or killed one is determined to kill them all. They vow a violent death to sorcerers either by direct action or by retaliatory sorcery. In all the cases I heard of, the accused sorcerer left in time and when he returned anger against him had evaporated. Countersorcery was the most common form of retaliation. There are also men who allegedly wander about at night killing or troubling people at random. When caught, such men are said to be torn to shreds with fishhooks and then abandoned to die of their wounds.

Fig. 7. *Bahúkiwa* headman.

To determine the guilty sorcerer an inquest is held around the hammock of the ill person, or of the deceased, as the case may be. All residents of the maloca gather and wait for the members of the victim's household to make the first charge. The charge is made and evidence is cited in terms of motive and of opportunity. The charge is either corroborated or refuted by any adult in the house, other names are mentioned, and the evidence is sifted. The entire discussion is conducted in a loud and angry tone of voice, and arms are brandished menacingly. Again, we are dealing with the principle that a serious accusation can be made only in anger. The role of the medicine man in the inquest is usually limited to stating his diagnosis of sorcery. He may offer a clue that the sorcerer is a man from afar or nearby but rarely does he name the culprit. The headman is usually the last to enter the discussion. He reviews all the evidence and presents his own verdict, which usually is, but need not be, accepted. After guilt has been established in this way, they decide how to act. It is not considered necessary to ask the accused if he can refute the charges.

WARFARE (bwaíno)

People of intermarrying phratries often used to fight with one another. It was less likely, however, for sibs that had recently exchanged wives to fight. Not too many years ago the *Djurémawa* from Querarí killed Hühü, an old *Bahúkiwa* who was then living at Guaracú. The headman assembled ten men, who went to the Querarí, attacked a house of the *Djurémawa*, killed the occupants, and burned it down. The *Djurémawa*, it was explained, were on a plundering raid. When they killed Hühü and others in his house they carried off the young girls and even the chicha calabashes. One old man escaped to tell what had happened.

Small-scale raids of this sort were apparently common throughout the Vaupés. Most attacks were to seize women, and some were for revenge. Sibs of opposite phratries feuded, and on one occasion a *Hehénewa* sib fought an unsuccessful war for mastery of the Cuduiarí; but the main fear of attack came from alien tribes, Cariban, Arawakan, and, in particular, Tucanoan Desanas. The Desanas raided the Cuduiarí annually during the dry season, when they could move overland and escape detection. During every dry season war alarms spread along the river and the communities are on the alert. I witnessed one such alert. The dogs had given the alarm toward evening and since Desanas had been reported, a defense was prepared. The defense leader was the headman's son. An earlier alarm had already brought the Independents to the main house and a boy had been sent to call in the Satellites and to warn the neighboring sibs. The headman's son, after a hasty consultation with the other young adults, decided upon a psychological defense. He fetched a police officer's discarded white tunic with brass buttons and shoulder straps that he had been cherishing, put it on over his bare body, and strode out to frighten the enemey. The women and children were assembled in the maloca with one man as their guard. Other men fanned out through the manioc gardens and into the surrounding brush to search out the enemy. One stray shot was fired by a defender. The house was kept under guard for several nights thereafter and then the danger was declared past.

An attack by the Cariban Umaua (*Maúnwa*) that occurred three generations ago is still vividly recalled. The *Bahúkiwa*, warned that the enemy was ascending the Cuduiarí by canoe, prepared an ambush. They dammed the river with the bark sheeting of house walls and waited to assail the enemy with bow and arrow. But the enemy were armed with rifles and they killed a great many of the *Bahúkiwa*.

When the attackers first came, the Indians on the Cuduiarí did not know whether they were men or women, because they wore their hair long and were dressed in long shirts. The Umaua attacks were so fierce that for several years the Indians were forced to abandon the Cuduiarí altogether. Some gave up farming and lived on the savannah, foraging fruits and nuts and eating tree bark. When they finally returned to the Cuduiarí, the manioc plantations were all gone and they had to resume manioc cultivations from seeds they had preserved. The other Indians of the Cuduiarí gathered on the Vaupés under the direction of a *Hehénewa* war leader, who told them that the white man would save them from their enemies. He made a clay image called a *tupana* (the Tupían and lingua franca for a deity). They danced and sang for two months, until a Colombian came. The idea of the *tupana* came, they say, from a Brazilian caboclo. When the Colombian arrived, he told them that he had heard their singing in Bogotá and had come to rescue them. They then returned to their former homes on the Cuduiarí.

In past years raids were more frequent and determined.[3] The Cubeo fought with bow and arrow and protected themselves with body-length shields of stiffened animal hide, deer, jaguar, or tapir. The

---

[3] Tribes with whom the Indians of the Cuduiarí claim to have fought include the Cariban Umaua, all the formerly Arawakan sibs of the Querarí River, tribes of the Isana River, and the *Hehénewa*, after they had arrived from the Papurý.

shields rested on the ground and the men fired their arrows from behind them.

At a victory dance the men wore the smoked genitals of the killed warriors over their own genitals as an ornamental trophy. After the dance the women were offered the penises to eat for fertility. Except for the intestines, deemed not fit to eat, the enemies were consumed at a sib feast and drinking party. The head, limbs, liver, and heart were spit roasted, the rest of the meat was boiled.

Development of the Individual

The development of individual character is always relevant to an understanding of social organization. In the case of Cubeo social organization, founded, as it is, upon the lifelong continuity of the sibling group of males, the psychological factors are of particular importance. The following discussion will attempt to show the relationship between some of the experiences of a Cubeo from infancy to adulthood and some of the formal principles of Cubeo social organization. By and large, Cubeo social organization must conform to the direct psychological dispositions of its members for the commanding reason that the people have a low tolerance for psychic discomfort. The sib, as we have noted, is readily split; this means, in psychological terms, that those who find any cause for dissatisfaction with life within the community are quick to leave. The community, therefore, is constantly being drained of its malcontents. Those who remain are, in a manner of speaking, in harmony with one another. This harmony, it should be said at once, is not that of homogeneity. It is based rather upon individual complementarities, of extraversion-introversion, active-passive, and leader-follower, as in any community. The harmony is between the requirements of adult life and the experiences of childhood.

The Cubeo use the following age-grade terms. The nursing infant from birth until it learns to crawl is called *abohoidjó* (male) or *abohokó* (female); a crawling infant is *tcumí* (male or female, although *tcúmiko* is possible for the female); the walking child who still needs help is *tcumíhinkü* (male) or *tcumíhinko* (female); the youngster until puberty is *hwainyó* (male) or *hwainkó* (female); the adult male is *ümü* (male) or *nomyó* (female), and finally, the old people are *bekü* (male) or *bekó* (female).

BIRTH AND INFANCY

The Cubeo believe it is the spermatic fluid (*hürü*) that causes conception. They regard the womb as a ground in which the fetus grows, or is cultivated as seeds are planted in the earth. Since men and women do not discuss together the biology of conception and of pregnancy, their views differ. Men I spoke to dated conception from the time when the abdomen begins to swell, while women dated it from the cessation of menstruation. Both sexes believe that continued coitus after conception will add to the number of children that will grow in the womb. Stories are told of people who did not heed this so that the woman burst from an accumulation of fetuses. Coitus is stopped, however, by the male reckoning.

It is a common view of men that women are not eager to bear children. Women, they say, know how to bring about abortion and frequently resort to infanticide. They explain that women are sexually too ardent and rather than forgo coitus during the long nursing period they would rather not have a child at all. Moreover, a woman who has not been enjoying sexual intercourse with her husband will abort or kill her offspring. If she chooses infanticide, however, she spares the boy. Women do concede knowledge and use of abortifacients and they acknowledge that others of their sex practice infanticide. They agree that a woman who does not love her husband punishes him by denying him a child. Thus, the Cubeo are disinclined to believe in barrenness or in sterility, attributing infertility to female design. A man, therefore, has cause to abandon a wife who bears him no children. One man told that he had abandoned his wife for not bearing children. Later they became reconciled; his wife had a change of heart and began to bear children.

Male infanticide, I was assured, was rare, for even the most disaffected or self-indulgent woman would not have the heart to kill a male child. Both men and women agreed that a girl was less important. The unwanted child is buried alive, it is said, at the very spot where it was born.

The likelihood is very strong, then, that a child is born to a family that desires it, and in which husband and wife are happy with each other. Parturition takes place in the woman's manioc garden. A woman is active until the moment her labor pains begin. I have seen a pregnant woman leave for her manioc garden behaving as though it were an ordinary gardening day, and return later in the afternoon with a newborn baby. A man is forbidden to be present at the birth of his wife's first child. At her first childbirth a woman is attended by her mother-in-law. In subsequent parturitions she may be unaccompanied, but if she does not feel too strong she invites her mother-in-law or any other woman to accompany her. A woman about to give birth must alert her husband so that he will not leave the house or do anything strenuous that would interfere magically with the delivery and the safety of the infant. The Cubeo give no particular reason for having the child born in the manioc garden. They reveal only a general apprehension that if the child were born in the maloca something would go wrong. Not all children are born in the manioc garden. In bad weather, or at night, a woman settles for the rear plaza as a birth site. Occasionally outside birth is too dangerous and the woman then retires behind screens at the rear of the maloca. The point the Indians insist on is that a child must not be born within the domain of the men. The infant must be brought from the woman's domain and installed by proper ceremony in the male domain. There is a parallel here, I believe, in the bringing in of a wife from her community to that of her husband.

Difficulties in childbirth are attributed to demonic agencies and require the assistance of a medicine man. Human sorcery does not affect childbirth. The common supernatural enemy of the woman in labor is the boa constrictor. When a woman dies in childbirth it may be explained that she had copulated in her garden at one time with a boa. The boa then comes to fetch his child. If he sees that it is a human child after all, he is angered and carries away the mother.

Childbirth (*pwäntadjú*: making a person) is a dangerous period. First the mother and then the infant are subject to supernatural perils that must be warded off. Little can be done, the Cubeo believe, to protect a woman in childbirth. The magical safeguards for the child, however, are elaborate. Primary responsibility for the safety of the newborn infant rests with the parents — with the father, in particular, since it is he who has "made" the child. Some of the precautions begin well before birth. Extra coitus, we have observed, adds to the number of children. Twins, for example, are regarded as a misfortune. Some said both twins are put to death and others said only one, the last to emerge being the one to be killed. Twins may also be born if the father, during his wife's pregnancy, has eaten plantains. If at this time he should greedily break off a bit of manioc cake when it is still on the oven, the child will be born deformed. Harelip, for example, is attributed to this delinquency in eating. The pregnant woman, on the other hand, endangers her child by generosity with body paint. Women commonly give one another genipa paint. If a pregnant woman should give genipa paint to another, her child will be born without the blue marking at the base of its spine. A child without such a marking, which is called *vei* — the term for the genipa pigment — will die very soon.

When the mother has brought the newborn infant to the maloca on a manioc tray lined with cloth (in the past with soft bark fibers) she proceeds immediately to bathe it in warm water, washing its body clean. She then paints the infant's face with red spots to make it resemble a jaguar child, and the rest of its body with the same red pigment. The spots will protect the infant against the jaguar, while the red body pigment, which is common ceremonial adornment, gives the infant human status at once. Finally, she ties cord bands on the baby's wrists so that its arms will grow heavy. Having done these things the mother presents the child to its grandmother, her mother-in-law, and goes to her hammock.

For the next three days, husband and wife spend most of their time in their respective hammocks. They move about as little as possible, leaving the house only for excretion, and avoid going near the river. They drink little water, eat only stale manioc bread and, if they wish, ants. They talk to no one but are looked after by others in the house, who bring water, keep the fire going, bring them their dry food. If the woman blows at the fire to stir it up she will develop a terrible temper. The grandmother has charge of the infant, giving it up only for nursing. Almost anything the parents might do at this time would be harmful to the infant. If either stubbed a toe it would damage the infant's toe; peppers would burn the infant's insides; it would choke on a fishbone; and so the parents must avoid these foods. This period of three days is an isolation period for the parents. Their other children, if any, are taken into another household. When Koch-Grünberg was among the Cubeo he noticed that the couple was actually hidden behind screens. Among the *Bahúkiwa* the isolation was less complete. Informants had told me that the period of isolation, which is known simply as "resting," lasted ten days. However, the several instances that I observed lasted only three days, perhaps a concession to modernity.[1] But Father Giacone

[1] One informant explained that the restrictions last until the infant's fetal skin comes off, that is, three or four days.

has reported a similar three-day isolation period among the Tucano Indians.

The isolation period concludes with three major magical rites. The purpose of the first is to render all foods safe for the parents and infant, the second is to render the river safe for the parents and infant. The river anaconda and other water creatures, the Cubeo say, are enraged at the birth of a child and must be made to leave. The third is to remove the child's fetal skin (*kürüdjü*) by painting its body with genipa. The fetal skin, the Cubeo say, is not a human skin; if it is not removed the child cannot grow.

The arrival of an infant to the maloca is a period of grave crisis. It is the principal responsibility of the men of the maloca to dispel the dangers. The behavior of the father comes under the designation, perhaps, of the *couvade* — the practice of the man taking to his bed when his wife is giving birth. Among the Cubeo, however, this is no magical participation in the birth of the child. It is rather part of the rites or the responsibilities of the patrilocal community toward the welfare of a newcomer. The father's brothers bring in each of the foodstuffs that must be blown with tobacco smoke and the dangers chanted away. The headman, or a shaman if one is in residence, is responsible for blowing over the river with tobacco smoke and chanting away its dangers with appropriate spells. The grandmother paints the infant with genipa. The mother's magical responsibilities, apart from the movement and food taboos, is to look after the umbilical cord until it dries and falls off. She coats the stump with wood charcoal to keep it from bleeding. When it falls off she carries it to the spot where the birth took place and buries it there. As already mentioned, both parents must refrain from sexual intercourse or the child will develop a wasting sickness and die. Sexual continence continues until the infant can take solid nourishment as a steady part of its diet, a period of about a year. Male adultery during this period, the Cubeo insist, is equally dangerous to the nursing infant.

Every food is a source of danger to the infant and to the parents so that a specific spell must be recited to decontaminate each item. All fish as a class are regarded as bearing the common menace of a lodged bone in the throat, but I did not collect a general spell for fish. Each species must be addressed by name and its specific qualities mentioned. Some have small bones that lodge in the gums. Some have spiny backs or heavy scales. Whether a fish has a particularly troublesome feature or not, as a food it must be mentioned. The spells are highly standardized and vary only by name of fish and its distinguishing characteristic. In the charm it is the children of the fish that are mentioned. For example, a small fish that has many small bones, the *dóthe*, is addressed, "Son of the *dóthe* have no spines. Do not cause harm to our offspring. Allow [yourself] to be eaten."

In the case of the aracú, the most common fish in the diet, the grandfather who is reciting the spells takes up a fish and cuts off its tail. If he did not do this, the tail when eaten would grow into a full-sized fish in the stomach and kill the child. After each spell has been recited the grandfather blows tobacco smoke, wafting his breath by an outward motion of the hand. The magical mechanism, as it was explained to me, is that the recitation invokes the fish and the blowing (*pupŭdjü*) has the effect of dispelling the danger.

Capsicum is spelled and blown so that its odor, which has the power to dispel ghosts and spirits, will not harm the child. Manioc has a disturbing odor when raw. This odor will be harmful and the manioc itself will not nourish if the spell is not recited. The child will remain thin. Eating unspelled manioc cake will also cause the child's skin to become as hard and coarse as the bark of a tree. Each variety of manioc, however, must be mentioned by name.

For birds, however, the small white eagle is invoked because this bird, the *towáve*, eats all birds that the Cubeo eat. The spell states that as the "odor of burned birds" does not harm the *towáve* so it will not harm the human young. Similarly, for animals the young of the jaguar are invoked in behalf of all the game they eat. However, whereas the *towáve* is addressed generally in behalf of all birds, the spell for the jaguar must mention each of the animals he eats by name. Again, the danger to be avoided is in each case that of the odor of cooking.

The spell that is chanted as the river is "blown" refers to the anacondas, asking them not to notice the people who are bathing. The cigarette smoke as it is wafted over the river is told to form a heavy coating as of miriti fibers so that nothing that is below water can come to the surface.

The reference of these spells seems ambiguous for the Cubeo. It is clear, of course, that what is sought is protection for the newborn infant. Since the infant has as yet no name and must be referred to only by the general designation *pwénte hyédokü* (offspring person), the spells, my informant explained, have beneficial effects for all offspring of the sib.

The man who "blows" the river coats his hands and feet with genipa so that he seems to be wearing gloves and stockings. The genipa has magical power to dispel water spirits. He carries a handful of burning faggots from the hearth of the natal household while smoking a bark-rolled cigarette. He steps into the river, an act believed to be dangerous for him despite the magical precautions, scoops up water, rinses his mouth, and spits it out. Then he blows the cigarette smoke and recites his spells. As a last act he throws the burning faggots into the water "to drive away all the dangers."

For the rest of the month the father may not tie, cut, or press anything, such as sugar cane. Cutting and tying would prevent the child from urinating and defecating, pressing sugar cane would crush the child to death. One man told that he had forgotten this injunction and had tied together a bundle of sugar cane. When he returned home his infant was ill and died on the same day. Before each of these activities is resumed an appropriate spell accompanied by cigarette smoke is chanted.

Once the river has been "blown" the father may fish and paddle his canoe, but for five days thereafter he may not kill a fish by clubbing or he will injure the infant's head. He may not scrape scales from a fish or the navel stump of the infant will swell. He may not drink chicha for five days or the infant will suffer from diarrhea. Chicha drinking is the least dangerous act. Should the father get drunk on chicha before the chicha has been properly spelled the infant will get drunk. On the other hand, when he sobers so will the child.

For the first year of its life the infant has no name (*amyá*) and is not fully a member of the sib. I was told merely that if it were given a name too soon it would die. After the name is bestowed, the child comes under the influence of the Ancients and their growth magic. To appreciate the significance of growth magic it is necessary to understand the special relish the Cubeo have for body size, how much they appreciate heavy arms and bulging calves. Size is a virtue in itself. Thus it is also interesting to note that the term for body is *bahú* and the term for the self, the person, is also built on this stem, *bahúmikü* (or *ko*).

The naming ceremony (*amíndone híno*: giving a name) is conducted by the paternal grandfather, whose privilege it is to give the name. Seated on a bench at the forward and ceremonial end of the house, with his son at his side holding the infant, the grandfather repeatedly recites a chant over a small calabash of milk. The father accompanies him. The milk has been drawn from the child's mother's breast but is referred to as milk from the father's sister, to emphasize the point that it is the child's own sib that will make it grow. The chant itself, as well as the blowing, are forms of growth magic. Each recitation begins with sustained loud whistles followed by the cries *hi i i i i*. At the conclusion of each recitation the grandfather blows into the milk, imparting to it his breath (*umé*), which is also his spirit. After several recitations a father's brother brings in *mihi*, in the proper ceremonial manner, tongue lolling and knees bent as though staggering under a great weight. All three drink the bitter brew and the recitation goes on. A naming ceremony I observed among the *Hehénewa* lasted two hours, beginning an hour before noon. It took place on the day of a mourning ceremony but before guests had arrived. The choice of the morning hours, I believe, is to establish the naming as strictly an in-sib affair. In the late afternoon there is a drinking party attended by all the sibs. In the *Hehénewa* case the mourning ceremony took the place of the drinking party. The ceremony concludes with bestowing the name, which is stated simply, "I give you the name ———, which was the name of ———." Then the grandfather blows into a small calabash of genipa with which the infant will be painted and into the calabash of milk. The child is induced to drink the milk. The grandfather now asks the child, "What name do you want?" Its father answers for it and the grandfather acknowledges it. The old man dips his index finger into the calabash of milk and presses it against the infant's heart "to make it grow." Then he asks the child, "What is your name?" The father answers for it. Finally, the old man touches the bridge of the child's nose and the ceremony is over. The bridge of the nose where it joins the forehead is the spot from which the soul will escape at death. By touching it the grandfather has left an opening for the soul to escape at the proper time.

Among the *Bahúkiwa* I had no opportunity to observe a naming ceremony, so the ceremony and the chants had to be described to me by informants. The ceremony as described and as I observed it among the *Hehénewa* was close to identical, but the *Bahúkiwa* chant and the *Hehénewa* chant differ, the latter having more clearly defined references to sib ancestors while the former is more definitely and directly a form of growth magic. In the *Bahúkiwa* chant there is only one reference to an ancestor and that is to a *Hehénewa* ancestor, *Uráhana* (Big one). My informants claimed they could not explain why they used a *Hehénewa* ancestor other than by the obvious reason that they had a right to claim an ancestor of the phratry. It may be, too, that the name, with its connotation of growth, has an irresistible appeal for the *Bahúkiwa*. The *Bahúkiwa* text given by informants is below, followed by the *Hehénewa*.

> People of our soil
> The milk that is from this place that causes to grow
> People who are our offspring

They are given milk
Milk of our soil
Milk that causes to grow
People who are being grown
People of our soil
People who are our younger sisters
Milk of the calabash
Milk that makes one grow quickly
Milk of our soil
People of our soil
People who are our younger brothers
The first one to grow fat
He [also] will grow fat
Milk that is nourishing
Milk that is nourishing that will make [him] fat
People of our soil
Uráhana who was the first to grow fat
Milk that is nourishing
He will grow fat
Milk that is liquid
Milk that is nourishing
The manioc gruel that is nourishing
Milk of our land
People of our land
Uráhana was the first one
The manioc gruel that he ate
The milk that was given to him.

Milk of our soil
That our offspring may grow
That we may all grow
Milk of the calabash
The offspring of *Uráhana* [2]
The calabash of *Djurédo*
When she [*Djurédo*] saw the birth
Milk to make it grow, she gave it
Milk of the calabash it drank
A child was being born to *Uráhana*
The offspring of *Uráhana*
The calabash of *Djurédo*
When she [*Djurédo*] saw the birth
Milk to make it grow, she gave it
Milk of our soil
She saw him grow
The son of *Hihédü*
Her fat offspring
Milk of our soil
She saw them grow

---

[2] The first child was born to *Hehénewa* Ancients *Uráhana* and his wife *Hihédü*. *Djurédo* was the sister of *Uráhana* and she gave the child milk drawn from her own breast into a calabash.

> Milk of the calabash
> Children of our soil
> She saw them grow
> Son of *Hihédü*
> Grew big and fat
> Son of *Uráhana*
> Grew big and fat
> This milk of the calabash
> He drank and grew
> She saw it.

Warm by nature and, at the time, with no rivals for her affection, a Cubeo mother bestows a great deal of tender care upon her nursing infant. The child is rarely out of her sight and is in almost constant contact with her body, slung in a bark-cloth band across her left hip in such a way that it has easy access to her breast. In the manioc garden the child lies in a cloth-lined tray covered with a bit of cloth against the sun and insects. In the house it rests in the same tray or perhaps in a nearby hammock as the mother works. The baby spends much of the night in its mother's arms cradled between her breasts. A father playing with his child also provides it with body contact. There may well be a connection between the infant's experience with body contact and the pleasure young people derive from it.

Infants are bathed often and in circumstances that are pleasurable. Whether a woman bathes her baby from a water basin in the house or at the river she finds it a welcome interruption from arduous and monotonous chores, and she communicates her pleasure to the infant. Women are gayest when they bathe in a group in the early afternoon after work in the manioc garden. A woman washes her skirt, the manioc roots, and her baby. River bathing is the Cubeo child's first direct contact with the conviviality of group activity.

An infant is not allowed to cry for long. It nurses on demand and if it whimpers is immediately picked up, fondled, and soothed. I once saw a woman carefully crossing a small stream over a narrow log, with a basket of firewood balanced on her head, a machete in her right hand, and an infant slung on her hip. The infant reached for her breast; the mother paused, and still concerned with keeping her balance, adjusted the sling so that the infant could nurse. It is virtually impossible to frighten an infant that is on its mother's hip. Nursing is accompanied by some teasing. A young mother playfully squirts milk over the infant's face or blows cigarette smoke at it to make it angry. Then she comforts it. When an infant begins to play with its genitals, the mother encourages it. She strokes a male infant's genitals "to give him pleasure." The Cubeo are also fond of the young of animals and treat them with intelligent solicitude. One man built a long platform in his house so that his dogs would not have to sleep on the ground. Men, having shot some monkeys, found an infant clinging to its mother's dead body. They massaged the monkey's breast, saying, "The baby should have the last drop of its mother's milk."

Toilet training is casual. No one who carries a child about shows annoyance or disgust at being soiled. The Cubeo are reticent about excretory functions but they do not teach by chiding. They have no fixed ideas as to when a child should be toilet trained. The only injunctions a crawling baby is likely to hear are warnings against injury, if it is too near the fire or the liquid starch with its poisonous content of prussic acid. Still, it is rare for a walking child to urinate or defecate in the house.

Walking and talking are actively encouraged. To help the child walk the father provides a harness (*taro*) through which the child's legs pass, allowing it to sit, stand, or walk. The harness is often suspended from a beam and serves as a tether for the child. Mother and father stimulate the child to talk by fluttering its lips. Lip fluttering is a game that persists into late childhood. Cubeo parents dread passivity in a child. They want to see it stirring about and restless. It is for this reason that the mother teases her infant, stirring it to anger or gaiety. The story is told that *Kúwai* once observed a passive child. He said, "The child must be made to move about," and so created the bothersome pium flies.

The crawling baby is still in its mother's charge. When it has begun to walk and to take solid nourishment, and its parents have resumed sexual relations, it is transferred to the care of an older sister. Every little girl from the age of six on is burdened with a walking baby that rides her left hip as it did its mother's. At this age, when it is learning to walk, many people look after the child. Its paternal grandmother becomes a principal guardian and looks after the child's feeding. After a new baby is born the separation of the young walking child from its mother becomes almost complete. A woman discourages nursing by coating her nipples with a bitter substance even though a boy has casual and playful access to his mother's breast until about the age of six.

CHILDHOOD

In the life of a boy there is an interval of some four years when he no longer receives the same close attention from his mother and has

Fig. 8. *Bahúkiwa* mother and child.

not yet joined the male play pack. By the time he is old enough for active play he has been well weaned from dependence upon the mother. In the case of a girl, this "dead" interval is one in which she waits to be useful to her mother. I saw no temper tantrums. Children of this age seem rather passive and steadfastly attached to the little sister.

For the boy, growth means a gain in autonomy, for the girl it means closer ties to the mother but with ever increased chores. The boy is the favorite of his mother; the girl, who is to become a drudge, receives more severe attention from a disciplinarian mother.

What I have called the play pack, the grouping of boys from the age of six to past adolescence, is the major educational institution of the sib. It is in a sense an age grade whose members remain closely associated throughout their lives in most cases. The distinctive feature of the Cubeo play pack is that it is an autonomous body subject to virtually no regulation or supervision. A boy occasionally joins his father, but his primary linkage is to the "pack." The pack forms its own leadership, forages for food, plays in the river, roams the bush, attaches itself from time to time to the collective activities of the men, practices songs and dances in anticipation of ceremonies, and spies and reports on lovers. The pack leader assumes responsibility for proper behavior, scolding boys for wayward sexual behavior, that is, breaching the incest rules, and lending assistance and encouragement with skills. The boys are never mischievous and are never scolded or disciplined by adults. A youngster does not actually understand anger directed against him. Only once did I see a father strike his young son in a fit of temper. The boy neither flinched nor cowered. He merely stared at his father as though waiting for an explanation. The man rapidly regained his poise, laughed, and pretended he had struck the boy playfully. On another occasion, a little girl tipped over a large tray of manioc mash so that it was totally spoiled. Although the accident cost hours of work it provoked only amused laughter. One might add here that even the depredations of a pet monkey, some of which were quite costly, were met only with amusement.

The pack is not sealed off from adult activities, but its relationship to adult work is voluntary. The Cubeo distinguish sharply between play that is appropriate to young boys and work and ceremonial life that is appropriate to adult males. Thus, whatever work the play pack chooses to help with is welcomed, but when the boys become bored with a task and leave it there is no ground for complaint against them. The young unmarried men who have left the play pack are a link between the pack and the circle of adults. The older men take no notice of the pack as a group at all. After dark each boy returns to his own household.

The life of the boy is largely collective, that of the girl is individualized. She is bound, so to speak, to the household hearth, and her social or play life corresponds rather closely to that of her mother. Girls have no independent games of their own. They assemble with their infant charges for gossip, looking rather sedate as they admire one another's ornaments. They are not free to mix with the boys unless invited to take part in games. Such games as they join often have a mythological reference and may be interpreted, I think, as children's ceremonies.

The Northwest Amazon is rather rich in children's games and toys. Among the *Bahúkiwa* a popular children's game is that of the *abúhuwa*, the forest ogres or demons, and the tem tem bird, the *taíntürü*. Boys and girls, including the smallest toddlers, form a circle around a child, who is always a grown boy. The circle is of the *abúhuwa*, who have surrounded the *taíntürü*. When the game starts the "bird" is crouched in the center, his head resting on his knees, and the circle is dancing around him. From time to time a boy enters the circle to tap the "bird" on the head and to pinch his flesh to determine if he is grown enough to be eaten. Then the children stop circling and several raise the *taíntürü* to his feet, who announces that he is now awake by stopping his ears with his fingers and calling out *hru hru hru*. The *abúhuwa* link hands and again dance around him in a circle. The "bird" must now make an effort to break out. He can easily break out by charging at a weak link. But this he will not do because it would be disheartening to a very little child, who must be part of the game but not a spoiler of the game. As he hurls himself at the line the "bird" hears two kinds of encouragement. One group calls to the line *paré paré* (strength! strength!), encouraging it to hold, another calls at the boy *temúdjo temúdjo* (break through! break through! [as an arrow from a bow]). When the boy breaks through he is called back to the circle where he again frees himself, this time by verbal means. Standing in the center he turns suddenly upon a child in the line and points to part of the child's body. The child must immediately reply, "The [naming the part] of the *abúhukü*." What usually confuses the child is the necessity of saying "of the *abúhukü*." When a number of children have failed to answer properly the child who is the *taíntürü* breaks through the line once more and a new "bird" is chosen.

This game is played only on cool, pleasant evenings and seems to be a child's ceremony, for it is the acting out of a mythical incident that has great appeal to the children. The children explained the game, or ceremony, to me as follows. Some children were left orphaned by the death of their father and they lived alone with their mother, who had very little food to give them. When they asked their mother for food one day and she replied that she had nothing for them they ran out of the house. Immediately a great hole formed in the center of the house. The children sat outside on the branch of a tree and sang *hmm hmm hmm*. The next morning the children returned to the house and again asked for food. Now the mother gave them some stale cassava crumbs. They ate and returned to their tree branch. Now they began to grow feathers, and after four days they had become *taíntürü* birds. They returned to the house and lived in the newly formed hole while the eldest brother flew off each day to fetch food for them. It is he who is captured by the *abúhuwa* but manages to escape so that he can return and look after his younger brothers and sisters. The *abúhuwa* customarily attack and seize children who are neglected or have been abandoned by their parents. They are dangerous, but they are also slow-witted and so can be eluded. Adults, it should be said, pay no attention to this or any other kind of children's game.

There is another game in which a little girl constructs a bower of palm leaves around herself and waits to be flushed out by a boy hunter. As for toys, the boys spin tops of fruits, they make cat's cradles, they walk on stilts, and they make a plaited snake that catches a finger and tightens when stretched. Among the *Hehénewa* Koch-Grünberg observed a ball game played with corn-husk balls (1909, II, 226 ff.). This game, played by older men, I did not observe among the *Bahúkiwa*.

PUBERTY

The Cubeo do not recognize an abrupt transition from childhood to adulthood in the case of boys. Male maturity is an individual matter to them, although past the age of 15 a boy will almost surely be drawn out of the pack into the adult world. Boys, however, are subject to growth magic from the time they enter the play pack until they leave it. An account of these rites is reserved for a later chapter. The ordeal of the stinging ants, a feature of puberty rites elsewhere in the region, occurs among the Cubeo during one of these rites.

Girls undergo digital defloration at the age of eight, I was told. An old man of the sib who is no longer virile is charged with this task. He is said to stretch the young girl's vagina until he can insert three fingers. He then announces, "You are a woman." The Cubeo say that if a girl should reach her first menstruation with her hymen intact coitus will ever after be painful for her and she will have difficulties during parturition. Digital defloration is a secret act; officially, the Cubeo credit the moon with the act. The moon copulates at night with a young girl and brings on her first menstruation. Thus, a prepubescent girl is referred to as *paínwe bebíko* (one who has not yet copulated with the moon).

The pubescent girl (*pupúni*: one who is blown)[3] is said to be secluded for ten days behind screens at the rear of the house, taking nothing but cassava and water. She leaves the house to excrete, through a secret doorway in the side wall of the maloca so that she will not be seen by a man. She uses a scratching stick on her head or else her hair will turn white. Some said her hair would fall out. To develop a tender facial complexion she washes with a leaf that creates a lather and she covers her face with rubber latex and painfully pulls it off. She also pushes dried peppers up her nostrils until her skin burns red with irritation. The pain of this facial treatment is a parallel to the ordeal of the ants and the whipping endured by the boys, but the justification is different. A mother says to her daughter, "You have been accustomed to disobey me. Now let me see how much pain you can stand."

At the end of the ten days her mother paints her body with genipa and she goes to the river to bathe. In the evening a drinking party is held in the girl's honor and her mother pushes her forward to take part in the dances. The period of seclusion is an affair of the women and the men behave as though nothing unusual were going on.

When a *Bahúkiwa* girl came of age during my stay among them she was sent to the house of her paternal grandmother nearby for proper seclusion. I was not allowed to go near the house and I did not see the girl until she had emerged again for the drinking party. Her hair had been cut short. I may have missed many details. Father Giacone, for example, reports that among the neighboring Tucano the shaman officiated at a girl's puberty isolation. He cut her hair short, burned the cuttings in a ritual manner, and then sent the girl to dispose of the ashes in the river.

After her first menstruation a girl is eligible for marriage but the change in her life is otherwise minor. She wears love charms and takes more care of her personal appearance. She is still attached to her mother's household.

[3] She is also known as *nomínyaivi* (becoming a woman).

The Cubeo have no dread of menstruation and menstrual taboos are relatively minor. A man will not copulate with a menstruating woman because he believes it will make him lazy. On the other hand, if there is a sick person in the house a menstruant will move and live in a shelter nearby, or else the ill person cannot recover. For her part the menstruant must avoid the river, or she will be killed by the water anaconda. She may not enter a canoe for fear that the headman of the fish will destroy the canoe.

Menstrual blood (*hivé*) is not human blood, but is believed to be blood of the moon. The moon, according to the Cubeo, is an ardent hunter who comes down to earth to copulate with unmarried girls and with women who are not pregnant. No one conceives by the moon. The moon is said to deflorate the woman, causing her to bleed. The hymen, according to this belief, grows back and the moon repeats his sexual connection each month. When a woman has erotic dreams she knows that the moon will come to her.

SEX LIFE

Under Cubeo rules of phratric exogamy the young people of a community may reach the age of marriage without having had sexual relations with an eligible marriage partner. The young people are limited to clandestine incestuous affairs and to public homosexual play. It was difficult to get information on the sex life of the unmarried, although I was aware of affairs between sib brother and sister. One informant told me that it was not improper for brother and sister to indulge in external coitus. According to this man, it was intromission that constituted incest. True coitus between sib brother and sister is not regarded lightly. Offenders may be put to death, and their souls after death, it is said, will be animals that will not associate with people. I never witnessed any gesture of sexual intimacy between a grown boy and girl of the same sib or phratry. Young children who indulge in heterosexual play are shamed by the older boys for ignoring the proprieties of privacy.

As for homosexual play, girls stroke one another's nipples to produce erection, and boys sometimes indulge in mutual masturbation. This kind of play is public and involves no shame. I have already mentioned the Cubeo enjoyment of body contact. In the younger people it is a mild form of homosexual eroticism. True homosexuality, however, seems to be rare. I learned of no case of persistent male homosexuality, and only one case of a woman. This woman developed strong male characteristics and eventually, it is said, she grew a penis.

The Cubeo women are sexually forward, a trait that seems to be common in the Amazon Basin. Women become more licentious with age. Older women, those around the menopausal age, urge men to have coitus with them, remarking jokingly, "We are more satisfying than young girls because we have more sexual power [appetite]." Adultery, as I have already observed, seems common, and it is ordinarily assumed or charged that it is the woman who seduced the man. A married woman shows sexual interest in a man by grasping his genitals or by conveying his hand to hers. Unmarried women are less direct. Such women, however, are scornfully called *aménko* (shameless woman). I was surprised to hear an angry woman address her openly flirtatious daughter-in-law as *yavímiko* (bitch). Although flirtatiously forward, women prefer to be vigorously subdued before accepting coitus.

The alligator or cayman is the Cubeo symbol of male lechery. According to one folk tale, the cayman was once a man. The wife of *Kúwai*, who was the daughter of *Munyúnbekúku* (an Ancient), was sleeping in her hammock. *Kúwai* sent Cayman into the house to fetch a light for a cigarette. Cayman wanted to copulate with the wife of *Kúwai*. She would not let him. He mounted her, nevertheless, and she ate up the entire front of his stomach, as well as his penis. When *Kúwai* saw this he said to Cayman, "I warned you this would happen." Then *Kúwai* took a square mat and with it mended the front of Cayman. Then he threw Cayman into the water with the remark, "You shall always be eaten."

In view of the reputation for licentiousness that the Cubeo women have, it is interesting that they attribute the growth of pubic hair on a woman to frequency of coitus. At the same time, pubic hair on a woman is regarded as unsightly. Women, accordingly, go to much trouble and pain to depilate the pubic region. Older women allow the hair to grow. In jest an old woman may say to a man, "You may take my pubic hair and smoke it in a cigarette."[4] The sexual allusion is well understood.

Cubeo mythology identifies copulation with female pubic hair. *Kúwai*, the culture hero, was the first to plant a hair from his head upon the *mons* of his wife. He then copulated with her for the first time, asking a small boy to watch and learn how it is done.

In the recent past, Cubeo women wore no pubic covering, but men always did. Now that women have become accustomed to skirts, depilation is no longer important. It persists, nevertheless.

---

[4] The Cubeo associate hair and tobacco. Hair is *pwá*, and armpit hair is *pwá butcí* (literally, hair tobacco).

Certain indications, such as elaboration of potency magic within the ancestor cult, the frequency of adultery between young wives and older married men, and the common male complaint that their wives are too ardent, all point to some male sexual difficulties at least in the early stages of marriage. The women, who have their private erotic relationship with *avyá*, the moon, regard this luminary as an inspector of connubial coitus. He comes to observe, the women say, how much sexual power their husbands have. The moon, however, is only an observer, for male potency is the province of the ancestors and is not affected by any other magic. Women have love magic which they use often, but only to draw the attention of a man. It is interesting that while women ply men with love magic a man uses such magic only once, when he is seeking a bride. Once he is married he may prefer to apply an antiaphrodisiac to his wife. The suggestion then is of masculine potency disturbances. We may attribute these disturbances to the rules of community exogamy and their accompanying outlets in homosexual play, in masturbation, and in near incest. Since homosexual play and masturbation involve neither shame nor apparent guilt, their psychological effects are probably not lasting. Near incest, on the other hand, is censored and is kept secret, insofar as that is possible in a small community, and may, therefore, be a serious source of guilt and of more serious sexual maladjustment. Adultery does not seem to offer a convenient sexual outlet for the younger unmarried men, first because the young wives prefer an affair with an older married man, and second because very few young men would dare to risk the public disapproval of such an act. An older man will face his outraged sibmates, not to mention the outraged husband, with some *savoir-faire*. If necessary he will leave the sib and start an independent community elsewhere. But no young man will willingly break the bonds of male sib solidarity. He must fall back, therefore, upon the more troublesome sexual outlets.

Presumably what are problems of sexual adjustment for the boys are problems for the girls as well, but perhaps of lesser significance. Many girls have enjoyed satisfying sexual relationships with whites in the region, and even in near incest affairs the psychological problem for the girl would seem to be reduced because it is the male who is the guardian of sib morality and not the girl.

POSITION OF THE AGED

Among the Tucano, Father Giacone observed (1949, p. 25), the aged were miserably neglected. This in a sense is true of the Cubeo as well. The fixed relationships of mutual obligation are, as has been seen, between husband and wife, between parents and dependent children, between unmarried brother and sister, and between cere-monial friends. These relationships either do not apply to the aged, or, if they do, they may not be of great value to them. Generally speaking, the aged can depend upon those who are younger and vigorous only for the generalized sib benefits of sustenance and com-panionship. The deprivation of the aged is in what one might mis-takenly call "the nonessentials." There is no one to buy an old lady a new petticoat or to get for an old man commercial tobacco. The aged do not protest such neglect because they acknowledge their lack of claim. Nonetheless, they feel their neglect and loss of status keenly enough. When I was among the *Bahúkiwa*, an aged lady employed all her senile charms to wheedle from me a new petticoat. Her hus-band, a very proud old man, deigned to accept only an occasional cigarette. From time to time he brought me fish and the old lady fetched me some of her small garden produce to reciprocate my favors.

The old must look after themselves. The very old *Bahúkiwa* couple maintained a semblance of an Independent household. The old woman, unable to carry a load of manioc, no longer gardened, but she fetched firewood and looked after children. She cooked for her husband. Her daughter-in-law provided her with manioc cake. The old man was still a good fisherman, contributing to the maloca. Besides, he was a consultant on many matters, particularly on trees to be used in manufactures.

The focus of Cubeo culture is upon the vigorous household heads. The aged simply fall out of things. They are entitled to no particular respect, nor have they cause to be feared as spirits-to-be, for the Cubeo are interested only in their first ancestors and not in the spirits of the more recent dead.

DEATH

Death may be attributed by the Cubeo to natural causes such as accidents, violence, old age, but if it is the result of illness, it must be laid to some agency that has willed it. The most common agency is human. Whether the agency is human or supernatural the reaction to death is patterned on grief, anger, and fear. The Cubeo reaction to death is to give full rein to grief and anger and to short-circuit as quickly as possible the forebodings that what has happened to one may happen to all. The only deaths I heard about or witnessed were all attributed to human sorcery so that I have no information on the Cubeo response to natural death or to death attributed to spirits. Mourning is extensive but does not impose unusually onerous duties or restrictions upon the survivors. Mourning goes through three phases. In the first, from the moment of death to burial, which follows quickly, the immediate kin and all sibmates yield to their spontaneous emotions, but up to a point, for the ritualization of emotion sets in quickly. In the second, which is the period from burial to the great mourning ceremony, the nearest female kin of the household — wife, mother, sister — accept the burden of mourning. Finally, in the third phase, the entire living cosmos of the Cubeo — people, Ancients, birds, beasts, fish, insects, and demons — join in the mourning. This third phase, an intricate ceremony, is described in a separate chapter. The dead, as already indicated, are buried beneath the dance floor of the house, emphasizing, it seems to me, the importance the Cubeo place on the house itself rather than upon mere locality.

I was present at the last hours of old João, a *Bahúkiwa* and *baküdyó* of the headman. He had been ill for several weeks, the medicine men had given up on him, and his death was, therefore, not unexpected. The Cubeo are not solicitous of the dying. Once its inevitability has been accepted death is awaited almost with indifference. Father Giacone (1949, p. 29), speaking for the neighboring Tucano, also observed that once the illness appears to be fatal the patient is given up for lost. Such patients, he adds, will be buried alive. When death seemed near — the old man was breathing with difficulty with a dry rasp — his wife took up the death watch at his hammock. At the moment of death her loud wailing awakened the house and all rushed to surround the hammock except the headman and his wife. Since it is the duty of the headman to preside over the inquest that follows upon the first outburst of grief he must plan upon a properly timed arrival. A shaman of another sib who was in the house also did not intrude upon the mourners, both in his role as shaman and as a sib outsider.

The old woman, truly grief-stricken, had embraced her dead husband's body in the hammock and rocked over it, moaning and wailing. She withdrew, however, when the younger brother of João arrived. He felt for the heartbeat and then covered the old man's face with some rags that had been the sick man's blanket. The women had all gathered to one side of the hammock and they wept continuously, chorusing the loud and emphatic wailing of the widow. The brother fetched his shotgun, moving slowly and grimly. He loaded it with a wad and turned to face the corpse. Each man now went with the same slow deliberateness to fetch his gun. The armed men formed a tight circle about the hammock, the widow in their midst pressed against it. Brandishing the weapon, the brother began the funeral declamation, a statement of grief and then anger and the threat of retaliation against the enemy. Each male mourner delivered his own address, always declaring his kinship relationship to the old man. The women accompanied the hoarse shouts of masculine anger with their own counterpoint of grief. After the last man had spoken they all fired their guns into the air together. The widow then withdrew to her hammock and lay silently while the men gathered about the hammock, caressed the corpse, and wept, accompanied in their grief by the women.

When this first wave of mourning, which lasted some two hours, had subsided, the headman's wife arrived, took her place at the head of the hammock, and delivered a long funeral oration that began in anger and ended in tears. As she finished it seemed that the grief had subsided; people stirred about more. Informally, and apparently spontaneously, the inquest began; names were mentioned and evidence cited. Women added their observations to those of the men, each citation being delivered in a loud and angry voice. The headman broke in on this, an hour after his wife had finished speaking. Armed with a gun he, too, approached the head of the hammock and delivered his funeral oration, concluding like the others with grief. During the angry part of his oration he summarized the suspicions and submitted his own. When the headman concluded, all the mourners drifted off and, since it was the middle of the night, all went to sleep. The respite was brief, and well before dawn mourning began again; mourners, men and women, approached the corpse (*yaiyü*) in the hammock, caressed it, and wept.

Preparations for burial began promptly at sunrise. Four men of the sib dug the grave (*tobékatcino*: hole underneath) four feet deep in an east-west direction to the left of the dance floor at the forward end of the house. They measured the corpse to get dimensions of the grave. When the grave had been dug halfway down one of the men lighted a cigarette and, bending over the sides but not entering the grave itself, blew cigarette smoke into each of its four corners, "so that the dead would always have tobacco."

It took several hours to dig out the grave with machetes. While this was being done, others were preparing a canoe as the old man's coffin. A man is buried in his own canoe as a rule. However, the canoe of João was an excellent one, whereas one of the men had only recently split a new canoe while spreading it. It was decided to substitute the split canoe. The canoe was cut in half, one end serving as the bottom and the other as the top of the coffin.[5] When the canoe was ready, the headman and three sib elders untied the hammock in which the dead man was lying and brought the corpse, bound in the hammock, to the canoe half that lay alongside the grave. The Cubeo prefer not to handle a corpse, except to caress it as a gesture of grief and affection. The corpse is wrapped in its hammock in the same way in which household effects are wrapped in it for transportation. The corpse lying in the hammock had naturally assumed a moder- ately flexed position, the knees drawn up and the hands folded across the abdomen. They laid it carefully in the canoe, face down. A woman of the sib brought a gourd dish that had a hole drilled in it and placed it over the old man's head. The dish is for use in the after- life and the hole is for breathing. A young man brought up the sib's *behórü*, dance staff and pennant of all social ceremonial. He broke it in two and laid the pieces alongside the corpse. From what I had been told about burial practices I had expected that all the personal effects of the old man would be buried with him. When I asked they shrugged and said, "He won't need them." Koch-Grünberg, among the *Hehénewa*, reported, on the other hand, that a man is buried with his dance feathers, which are laid upon his breast. His bow and arrows, fishing gear, and other possessions are burned upon the grave. A woman's trays and dishes are burned and her pots broken up and thrown into the woods. These things must be disposed of, he observed, to prevent the dead from coming back. Presumably burial practices have changed to some degree. When I was among the *He- hénewa* they were not burying a man's ceremonial feathers with him, but used them in the mourning ceremony as a representation of the deceased.

The entire community had gathered to watch the preparations for burial. Men and women wept, except those men who were handling the burial. The widow punctuated the weeping with her own loud wails. The top of the canoe was lashed into place and the canoe was lowered by ropes into the grave by four men. All the men of the sib crowded over the grave and reached into it to touch the canoe, weep- ing unrestrainedly.

Through all of the first stage of mourning the children had taken

---

[5] An alternative method of burial is in a large pottery jar. Urn burial is pre- ferred for women and children, who may not have a canoe. In their tales the Cubeo do not mention canoe burial at all. They speak of the body as put in a large urn in a sitting position.

no part. They stood aside and watched, but none wept. But as the last action, before the grave was to be covered over, the men and the older married women seized each boy and brought him forcefully to the grave, pushing him down to his knees and forcing him to touch the coffin. The grave was covered, the earth smoothed, and excess earth removed to leave no hump on the dance floor. Weeping continued for half an hour after the earth had been leveled. Then, abruptly, all mourning ceased and people resumed their customary activities. By noon the children were romping over the burial place.

In the second phase of mourning, which pertains to the widow (*nomyópeko*) alone, all sib, subsib, and phratry mates arrive to grieve. Sib and subsib mates have an obligation to be the first mourners. Phratry mates who are passing by are obligated to pause and mourn. During this period of mourning the widow greets each arrival and escorts him or her to the burial place, where they both crouch, facing one another, arms about each other's shoulders, heads lowered, and weep. This weeping is ritualized. It begins abruptly and ends abruptly. This abruptness has impressed other observers as a mark of insincerity of grief. This is not the case at all, for mourning must, in Cubeo religious doctrine, become ritualized. One might say, however, that depth of grief and the expression of it need not be related too closely. As we have seen in several other contexts the Cubeo seek to identify an action with its appropriate emotion. Polite and restrained expressions of grief, as in Anglo-Saxon society, are inappropriate. The statement of grief must be a strong one. But as with any statement, it has a beginning and it has an end.

Apart from her obligation to escort visiting mourners to her husband's grave, the widow has no other formal obligations of mourning. She may remarry after one year, although the prospects for her remarriage are actually poor. Even though the Cubeo sense a shortage of marriageable women, they seem to be afraid to marry a woman whose husband has died.

The Cubeo narrate the myth that once death was not permanent. A woman had died and later returned to her husband. She pleaded vainly with him to accept her back. If he had taken his wife back, the people say, all the dead would then have been able to return to life.

FUNERAL ORATION BY A SON

Quickly he died. An evil person, a thoughtless person, poisoned us. And so he died. He who was one of us. He [the murderer] did not care to behold us and so he did it. He [the deceased] did not live through the day. He, the evil one, will also die. He who has the poison, he shall go behind [he shall be abandoned]. His flesh will not be firm, he will rot away. He shall not shorten the days of my life. This one here [the deceased], he has departed. We shall endure. That thoughtless person, he did it. That poison had no power to make us sick, but he died. We do not have such poison. Such is not with us. He is the one who died. He did not live long enough to go and walk with us. Now we do not have a companion. As he died, so we, too, are going to die in this evil land. Let us bury him in our house, under the earth. Let us cover him. He has poisoned us and so we have lost one of us. And so my father has died. Where shall I see my father? He is buried. He has gone. He is ended on this day. He made me a man, he left me as a male descendant. I am still here. My father, my father. It is as if I, too, had died. I, too, can go. I know how. I am a man. When I shall see him [the murderer] I shall confront him. He and I shall meet. He who poisoned my father. It is I who live here. He did not care to behold my father and so he did it. My father raised me here. In my own land, in my father's house I will continue to live. He died, but I am not dead. I am still here. My father reared me as a man. I am going to kill him who poisoned my father. He who did this. I will do the same thing to him. [He fires his gun.]

FUNERAL ORATION BY A WIDOW

My husband has died. That evil person who did this to me, he, too, will die. We here shall not survive. He whom I wed at this place, my husband. Where shall I see him? They have buried him who was mine. He is gone now. It is finished. It is only today that he began to live here. They schemed, those who are of another place. They schemed about this, and so my own, my husband, has died. He died while with me. Now I remain a widow. Your father has died. Come and bury him. Your father said he had raised men as descendants of ours. My children, you are our men. They who did it did not care to behold your father and so now we are no more.

FUNERAL REMARKS OF A PHRATRY VISITOR

Over there where I live, I heard about it so I came to your house. Is it true you have lost your father? Where did you bury him? I heard about it over there where I live, so I came to your house. It is my privilege to shed tears for your father. Do not scheme revenge. He who killed him will also die. You and I, we have lost one of our own. We shall all die.

REPLY BY A SON

All right! Come in. I allowed my father — we allowed my father to die. In the same way that he died, we shall die. You have come from over there to shed tears. We are already finished, because we have lost one of ours. I allowed my father to die. As you have just spoken to me and asked, it is here that my father is buried. He did not last through the day. That evil one, he did not wish to behold us. He poisoned my father and that is why he died. Look over here [drawing the guest over to the grave]. Here is where he is. Here is where he is residing. Behold my father's house. My father has died. He is no longer alive. Badly he went.

8

The Ancestor Cult

The ancestors of the sibs, the *Bekûpwänwa* (*bekû*: old man; *pwânwa*: people), literally, the Ancients, form the center of what may properly be called a cult.[1] The ancestral cult is neither elaborate nor well integrated. What it includes are a number of rites in which the ancestors, or Ancients, are invoked. In some cases the invocation of the Ancients has no special magical significance, as when the origin myths are recited at major drinking parties, or again when the ancestral couple *Xudjiko* and *Xudjikü* come to mourn for the sib dead. The first occasion is simply a remembrance by the sib of their ancestors, and the second is a reciprocal remembering and honoring of their sib by the ancestors. The relationship in both instances is mainly social. On the other hand, when an infant receives a sib name, when cohabiting couples bathe in the river, when youths bathe before dawn and sound the trumpets that embody the Ancients, and finally, when the young boys as well as the mature are whipped by the Ancients, the relationship is then fundamentally magical. On these occasions the Ancients bestow upon their sibmen the specific benefits of bodily growth, vigor, potency, and fertility.

The Cubeo do not assemble all of these rites and cite them as a connected series. The term *Bekûpwänwa*, in fact, is used to refer only to the Ancients when the origin myth is recited and to the bathing and whipping in the presence of the flutes and trumpets that embody

---

[1] The ancestors are also known as *Bekûdowa* (Old ones), a term that has the connotation of a grouping comparable to that of a sib.

the Ancients. In the naming and in the mourning ceremonies specific ancestors are invoked by name and by specific kinship reference, as the mother or the grandmother of the sib. In the case of postcoital connubial bathing the ancestors are not invoked either by name or by spell; the bathers merely participate in their magical presence in the river. Some cult activities are secret, others are not. The rule of secrecy applies to the flutes and trumpets. These bear the names of ancestors and may not be seen by women. However, whenever these instruments appear, a specific ceremonial role is assigned to the women. In the whipping rites, which are also initiation rites for boys, the women receive gifts of fruits and berries in the name of the Ancients. In the mourning rites the ancestor trumpets sound their notes of grief, to which the women respond with wailing of their own. That is, when the Ancients enter the maloca they naturally establish a relationship with the women of the house. On the other hand, when the Ancients' blessings are invoked, but without the ancestral presence, the women have no part in the proceedings. The women are ignored during the naming ceremony and during the recitation of the sib mythology. Basically, the ancestral cult belongs to the men. When the boys are shown the hiding place of the flutes and trumpets and are taught their names they are being initiated into a male cult and are drawn fully, thereby, into their roles as sibmen. The social function of the initiation is twofold: to complete the separation of the boy from his mother and align him with his father and his father's brothers, and to draw him from the immaturity of the play pack into the mature company of men. We may speak of these rites, therefore, as *rites de passage* as well, bearing in mind, however, that the passage is a long and gradual one. The Cubeo emphasis with respect to the development of the male is not that he suddenly crosses a dividing line from boyhood to manhood but that he grows. The magic of the initiation ceremony is a magic of growth. Growth magic, it will be recalled, occurs at three stages in a boy's development: at birth, after a year when he receives his name, and then for a series of years after he has entered the play pack.

For a fuller understanding of the Cubeo cult of *Bekǘpwänwa* one would need to know more about corresponding ceremonies among neighboring tribes. Curiously, no other ancestral cult has been reported for the entire Northwest Amazon. Koch-Grünberg, whose knowledge of the tribes of the region extended over many years, did not mention any ancestral doctrines even though he had lived for several months with the *Hehénewa* on the Cuduiarí. But like others who have studied this region his investigations were surely led astray by that ubiquitous and meaningless term *yurupari*, lingua franca and Tupían for "devil," "spirits," "sacred," "mystery," and the like.[2] The Indians have learned to satisfy all foreign curiosity about their sacred practices by uttering the impressive word *yurupari*. All rites involving the use of the sacred and taboo-to-women, trumpets and flutes, have been invariably described in the literature as *yurupari*. We cannot assume, however, that because these instruments are ancestral embodiments among the Cubeo that they are so among all other tribes who use them. One of the striking characteristics of the entire Amazon drainage is the ready way in which form and content separate and recombine in new ways. It has been reported that among the Arawakan tribes in the region the flutes and trumpets represent the spirit of *Kówai (Kúwai)*, the tribal culture hero (Koch-Grünberg, 1909, I, 187). On the Orinoco, von Humboldt (1852, II, 363) found a cult of sacred trumpets associated with the fertility of fruits and berries. The plant fertility aspect of the instruments is well-nigh universal in the region, suggesting that this may have been the oldest association. Among the Cubeo, too, the whipping ceremonies are quite explicitly associated with the harvest of fruits and berries during the short summer season. Among the neighboring Tucano Indians, where sacred horns are used in the initiation of young boys, the instruments all have animal names, such as armadillo, paca, and agouti, as well as a little bird. They are reported to be known as tamed animals, but there is no reference in this report to an ancestral cult (Ypiringa Monteiro, 1960).

As for the Cubeo ancestral features, it may be reasonable to suppose we are dealing with an Andean culture trait that has diffused eastward into the rain forest. Ancestors are prominent in the religions of the Chibchan-speaking Cágaba (Park, 1946), in northern Colombia, and, southwest of the Cubeo, among the Witoto Indians (Preuss, 1921–23; Whiffen, 1915; Steward, 1948), with whom the Cubeo show remarkably close affiliation. Among the Cubeo, we may speculate, a fusion has occurred between an early ancestral cult and a series of other culture elements such as harvest festivals, cultic whipping, male puberty rites, and a secret men's cult in which spirits taboo to women are represented by musical instruments. As will be seen in a later chapter, a similar fusion seems to have occurred among elements making up the complex mourning ceremonies.

Among the *Bahúkiwa* there are five pairs of musical instruments

---

[2] Actually Koch-Grünberg (1915–16) does give a native term for "*yurupari* dance" (*bekeboikelehapuive*, which has the meaning of "festival of the Ancients"), but he apparently attached no significance to the term.

that are specifically identified as the *Bekúpwänwa,* and that are used in the whipping and initiation ceremonies as well as in ritual bathing.

1. *Emíhehika* (also known as *haraíbipobü*: whipping staff) is a wide-mouth trumpet of bark wound within a framework of splints. It has a short palm-tube mouthpiece set into a ceramic plate that is mounted firmly to the upper end of the bark. This trumpet is some 30 inches long.

2. *Kwühünku* (also known as *Uménahonkü*) is also a wide-mouth bark trumpet that is over five feet long and is played with one end resting on the ground.

3. *Bwü* (Agouti) is a long flute of a black palm, also with a mouthpiece set in a clay mount and with two external reeds bound around an opening toward the top. It is about four feet long.

4. *Onpwénda* is a flute similar to *Bwü* except that it has no separate mouthpiece and is only some 30 inches long.

5. *Onpwénda küdjüwe* is identical with *Onpwénda* and is the length of a man's forearm. It is the shortest of the flutes.

Bwü and *Onpwénda küdjüwe* are said to be the strongest and fiercest of the ancestors and are esteemed for the vigor with which they whip. They are referred to as *parihihekü* (very powerful beings). *Bwü* is, of course, the founding ancestor of the *Bahúkiwa.*

Among the *Hehénewa* of the Cuduiarí the largest bark-wound trumpet is also called *Uménahonkü.* Koch-Grünberg translated this name correctly as "Dragonfly." The name, however, is that of a first ancestor of the *Hehénewa.*

The whipping rites, the Cubeo say, go back to the "first people," who were taught what to do by *Kúwai.* At the beginning, however, it was women who played the flutes and trumpets. They spent so much time on play that they did nothing else. *Kúwai* corrected this. He took the instruments from the women and gave them to the men, warning them never to allow the women to get them back.[3] This is the story that is cited to explain why the instruments are taboo to

---

[3] A variant account states that the *Bekúpwänwa* had belonged to the women and that the men were afraid of them. The women came out of the forest bearing the instruments and the men ran away in fear. Then *Dekókü* (Ghost person) learned about this and said, "Women have no right to this." He came down to witness the ceremony of the women. He saw only women and he said to them, "You are women, you have no right to this. Now I am going to take this away from you." He brought the instruments to the men and laid them on their forearms. When the women had the *Bekúpwänwa* they danced all the time and never worked. After the men had received the instruments they allowed one old woman to see them. She turned insane and they had to kill her. Since then women have not been allowed to see the *Bekúpwänwa.*

women. The men cautioned me not to speak of the *Beküpwänwa* to the women for fear they would be driven mad. A woman who hears about the Ancients will wander about singing their songs until she dies of her madness. If a woman actually sees the instruments, it is felt that she should be put to death by sorcery so that the secret will be kept from the other women.

The *Beküpwänwa* come annually in the summer when a species of palm berry (*konhá*) and certain other fruits and berries are ripe. Of their coming it is said, "They come to whip the boys to make them grow." At the same time, it is explained that if the people did not dance with the flutes and trumpets the berries and fruits would not grow. The *Bahúkiwa* would not assert a magical connection, however, between the two kinds of growth, yet the association would seem to be an obvious one.

As an age grade, youths are known as *hwainyó*, but as boys who need whipping for growth they are known as *bahúdjo*, which may be rendered as "bodying." A boy's first whipping occurs when he is no more than eight years old and continues until he leaves the play pack at about 15. Thereafter, as a man he continues to be whipped but under different auspices. As a man he accepts whipping voluntarily. As a boy it is imposed upon him by his elders.

I observed two initiation ceremonies, one among the *Bahúkiwa* and one among its subsib, the *Bahúküdjauwü*.

The *Bahúkiwa* rites were conducted entirely by the younger men of the sib, not by the real elders as I had been led to believe. These younger men were in their prime of physical vigor. One was not yet married but he was very strong, energetic, and exceptionally capable in all respects. They were the men whom the play pack admired and emulated, to whom they attached themselves, and to whom they owed no special respect. The initiators were the fathers and the fathers' brothers with whom the boys could most readily feel at ease.

I was not invited to accompany the small band as they left the maloca in the early morning, the men in high spirits, the boys subdued, although they had been told only that they were going to pick berries. This was sheer euphemism since there are no secrets from the play pack. The gaiety of the initiators is characteristic. Only the women are expected to be afraid and one suspects that much of this is mock fright. Among the initiates was a boy of an in-law sib. But as a resident, a member of the play pack whose mother, the headman's sister, had standing as a household head of the sib, his initiation seemed natural enough to the *Bahúkiwa*. It is not an exclusive sib cult.

The ancestor instruments lay nearby in a secret place on the river bank, upstream from the maloca, dressed in ceremonial dance feathers (*mápena*) because, as the Indians said, "our ancestors love to dance." (When the trumpets are removed the *mápena* is laid aside). The party first fetched the instruments so that the ancestors might accompany them on berry picking. Intermittently during the morning those of us at the maloca could hear the horns, at times sounding near and then trailing into the distance. The party returned in the late afternoon. The women at their chores near the river bank paused to listen to the low, mournful notes of the oncoming horns. A shot from the canoe was a warning signal that sent the women running for the house, laughing and shrieking at one another to hurry.

The canoe came into sight, low in the water with its heavy burden of berries neatly packaged in baskets of loosely plaited palm fronds. The youngsters were paddling and their escorts played the horns, swinging them from side to side to sound in all directions. Now the women, who had gathered at the rear door of the maloca, ran off together to the manioc gardens, their traditional sanctuary, those in the lead calling to the laggards to hurry.

The river was low and the canoe could not be seen except from the very edge of the high bank. No one, except the ethnographer, came to look. The party unloaded the berries. They bathed, and having bound fresh sprays of fragrant leaves over their buttocks, ascended the steep path. At the top of the bank the men formed themselves two abreast and marched upon the house sounding the horns, the youngsters trailing after them. Only three pairs of the traditional five were used, *Bwü, Onpwénda kúdjüwe*, and *Onpwénda*.

The men sounding the horns, as embodiments of the ancestors, assumed a stern and almost menacing manner. This unaccustomed countenance seemed to frighten the boys and they were visibly nervous. The men were not at this moment concerned with the boys, but with bringing the ancestors and their powers into the house. They marched upon the house in the familiar dance step of a long measure and a pause, two long measures and a pause, and then three quick steps. At the pause, the six players swayed and swung their instruments in a high wide arc before them, the two *Bwü* horns in the lead, followed by *Onpwénda kúdjüwe* and *Onpwénda*.

The ancestors did not enter the house immediately but paused at the front plaza. No man came out of the house, not because it was taboo but as a courtesy. When the ancestors paused, the youngsters went back to the canoe landing to bring up the berries. When the boys left, the ancestors sounding the trumpets circled the maloca counterclockwise, going from the front door to the rear door. When they returned to the front plaza again, men of the subsib who had arrived as guests came out of the house, and taking over the horns, they circled the outside of the house, sounding the instruments to all corners of the clearing. They re-entered the house and a new group, men from a related sib, came out and took the horns from them. As each group completed its circuit of the house it re-entered and was given pupunha chicha.

All the men had had their turn with the ancestor horns when the boys trudged up the path in single file, each holding out before him a tray piled high with berries. Young boys normally provide fruits and berries for the community, as part of playful foraging in the forest. Women sometimes bring in fruit, but in the main such gathering is left to the boys. I assume therefore that the boys at the initiation are ritualizing a traditional role. They bring fruit to the maloca, not to the ancestors, who are *givers* of benefit and not receivers. By the same token, the offering of the youngsters is at this point ritually recognized. The boys set the trays down on the dance floor of the house. Then the men of the house returned to the canoe landing to bring up the heavy bundles of *konhá*. The seven initiates in the meantime were asked to occupy the long guest bench near the door. When the men had deposited the last bundle of *konhá* they gave to each boy a calabash of pupunha chicha as though he were being received as a guest, and they passed among the boys the ceremonial cigar, as another acknowledgment of honored adult status.

When the youngsters had consumed their portions of chicha and had puffed self-consciously at the cigars, they helped the men unpack the *konhá*, arranging all the berries into eight trays and setting them along the rear of the house, the women's quarter. While the trays were being set out, a solitary dancer sounded *Bwü* throughout the house.

When the berries were in place the *Bwü* dancer put aside the horn and began to prepare a switch (*harámu*) that he had picked at the water's edge.[4] The switch is from a bush that grows quickly, and is wound with sturdy kumari twine. The boys withdrew to the guest bench where they huddled nervously, watching the switch being pre-

---

[4] Some sibs have a more or less permanent switch that is beautifully plaited and tipped with seed beads. Whipping is called *haraíhume* (*haraí*: to strike; *humé*: bitter, unpleasant).

pared. Other men picked up the horns and danced. The whipping could not begin before dark and it was evident that the man preparing the switch was working slowly so as not to finish too soon. The deliberation of his movements added to the apprehension of the boys. As the last rays of light in the doorway faded, the boys suddenly leaped from the bench and bolted out of the house. The man who was preparing the whip ran to the doorway and shouted at them to come back. All but one returned. The boy who did not return was a fatherless orphan and a maverick who did not share foraged food with his age mates.

The boys took their seats again and the men resumed dancing with the ancestor horns. They danced until the house was pitch black. A taper was lighted and *Bwü*, represented by the senior member of the initiating group, stepped forward. He dragged the first boy to

Fig. 9. *Bahúkiwa* boy.

be whipped violently to the center of the dance floor. He chose an eight-year-old boy, his own son. Normally the most amiable of men, he glowered at the boy, and in a harsh voice commanded him to stand straight, his legs together and his arms above his head. The little boy solemnly obeyed. The father faced his son, poised his whip for the first blow, and waited while the dancers circled them once, sounding the ancestor horns. When the dancers had completed one turn, the man inserted the switch in the far end of the horn and stirred it about to "draw from it the power of *Bwü*." He then struck the boy across the loins with such force that the child ran screaming down the corridor toward the door. His father ran after him and without a word dragged him back. The first blow across the loins left a bloody scar on the boy's abdomen and was to impart sexual vigor, which resides inside the horn. The boy's paternal uncle stepped forward and rolled the second *Bwü* horn along the child's back, starting at the calves and rolling it up to the head. This was to impart growth of stature, that resides on the outside of the horn. The boy had now regained his composure, and his father brought him a calabash of chicha. His father whipped him a second time, in the same way, and this time the boy controlled his fright, emitting only a gasp of pain as the whip lashed across his abdomen, raising a second welt. Again the uncle rolled the horn up the back. His father gave him a second calabash of chicha and the boy returned to his place on the bench, where he displayed his scars to his companions, composed and grinning from ear to ear.

Next to be initiated was the son of the headman's sister, the boy who was not of the sib. The same man did the whipping, using not *Bwü* but *Onpwénda*, the least powerful of the three ancestors they were invoking. I concluded that a father would naturally initiate his own son with the most powerful and the very first of the ancestors, while saving the least potent for his cross nephew. When I mentioned this to the man he assured me I was wrong, explaining that it made no difference who was whipped with which ancestor since their blessings went not to any one person, but to all being initiated as well as to the sib as a whole. The important thing, he said, was not to neglect an ancestor who had been brought to the house. I am inclined to accept this explanation with some skepticism, because the Indians always deny inequality as a matter of courtesy, but they recognize it nonetheless. When informants discussed *Bahúkiwa* ancestors in general terms they all agreed that it was best to be whipped by *Bwü* because "he is the strongest."

This boy was exceedingly apprehensive. Before the first blow could be struck he had bolted and had to be literally dragged back. The first blow reduced him to such a state of trembling and hysterical sobbing that I thought he would collapse. He could not swallow the chicha. The men paid no attention to the boy's terror and when he returned finally to the bench, still sobbing, his companions ignored him.[5] The first boy was by this time enjoying himself immensely.

The third initiate was the son of the headman, a boy who was the leader of his play pack. This lad strode confidently forward and raised his arms above his head without command. He faced his age mates, smiled at them, and took the blows without flinching. The next boy faced the ordeal with equal composure. The men waited for the orphan boy to return. When he did not they sent the youngsters to bring him. but they returned very quickly to say that he had run away.

There now remained two very young boys to be whipped. These were treated in a sense as junior initiates, old enough to know the secrets of the *Bekŭpwänwa* but too tender to be whipped very hard. The senior initiator who had begun to whip with *Bwü* was said to have a very hard blow, because of having absorbed the strength of *Bwü* in his arm. He therefore turned the whipping over to his younger brother, who used *Onpwénda*. This man, who was unmarried and therefore closer in spirit to the age group being initiated, assumed a jesting manner. He dragged a little boy forcefully to the center but in a playful manner. He measured his blow carefully, heavy enough for the child to know he had been through the ordeal but without raising a welt. The two blows were spaced farther away from the genital region because the children were too young to receive sexual power from the ancestors yet. The gentle blows meant that growth would still be gradual. At puberty, I was told, a boy receives the full hard blows of *Bwü*. However, since some precocity is welcomed, the full blows, as on this occasion, may precede puberty by some years.

After all the youngsters had been whipped and were seated together on the guest bench drinking chicha, the ancestors, who had been dancing inside the house, now danced about them several times in a close circle, finally leaving in single file through the door. They circled the house on the outside and returned to the front plaza. When they stopped playing, the youngsters rose from their bench and went outside to watch as the men hid the horns in a clump of bushes nearby. Then all cut swatches of leaves and ran through the

---

[5] It is hardly a disgrace for a young boy to weep. When young adults, young married men, are injured in a drunken brawl, they will also weep freely.

house, sweeping every bit of ground to remove the traces of the ancestors. They bent low and uttered low cries of *hi hi hi iii iii*, the same sound used when *mihí* is brought in. This is a sound that spirits understand.

When the last traces of the ancestors had been swept out, the men called to the women to return. The return of the women restores the house to its normal condition. Before that it is a man's house, a cult house and not a true domicile. This change was marked by having the guests, who had already taken part in the earlier ceremonies, leave, go down to the landing place, march up the path, and be received at the front door in the usual reception line. What seemed to be the beginning of an ordinary drinking party then followed. However, later that night the women were told to move to the rear and to sit facing the rear door. The torches were put out and some old men fetched the hidden horns to play them in the forward men's section. They danced out again and hid the instruments. When the playing stopped, the women rose, lighted the torches again, and took possession of the *konhá* berries. The headman's wife, in her traditional role, supervised and assisted in the preparation of a *konhá* porridge, and the remainder of the berries were distributed to all the adult women. The porridge was prepared quickly and calabashes of it were sent down to the forward end of the house for the men.

Now the mothers turned to their sons to inspect the welts raised by the whippings. But the boys turned away and the mothers knew enough not to persist. The ceremony was over.

This was a truncated ceremony. Normally, the elders who have danced into the house with the ancestor horns after the lights have been put out dance among the women, while other men thrash the women with switches. Then the adult men take turns in whipping one another. None of this was done, they said, because most of the guests they had invited had not come, and feeling dispirited they cut the ceremony short.

However, I had the opportunity of attending another whipping ceremony at the maloca of a subsib. This one was well attended and the atmosphere was properly charged with excitement, helped by a great quantity of chicha and *mihí*. Yet here too the whippings were confined to the young boys and the women were unmolested. At one point, however, the ancestors danced outside the house, and two boys guarded the door while youngsters pelted the front door with berries. This was done not to frighten the women within but to give them a more vivid sense of the "presence" of the ancestors. This was repeated three times. The ceremony concluded with a chant of the origin traditions.

The men say that in the "old days" whippings were terrifying. One man narrated that when he was a boy he was held by two men in a horizontal position face down. One man held his ankles and another gripped him under the armpits. A third man whipped him at the loins. As each blow struck he was allowed to drop to the ground. This was done three times and not only twice as now. The man added, however, that he was fortunate, because the man holding his armpits was his father, who did not allow him to drop but only dipped him downward. "I have always loved my father for that," he said. Another man said that when he was a boy one man held him by the ankles with his face a few inches from the ground and he was whipped from this position but was not allowed to drop. The point of these two methods, the men said, was that the boy was stretched so that he would grow. Nowadays the boy merely stretches his arms overhead. After the young have been whipped the senior initiator challenges any man to come forward and whip him to test his fortitude. They use a special whip tipped with shell beads. In the course of the night they take turns in whipping one another. Men who think they might involuntarily flinch do not step forward so as not to discredit themselves before the ancestors.

I never observed the ordeal of the stinging ants, common in the region. Informants said that they sometimes asked a boy to put his arm into a calabash of red stinging ants and to allow the creatures to crawl up his arm and sting him. This, they explained, was merely a test of fortitude and had nothing to do with powers acquired from the ancestors.

Growth magic imparted by the Ancients continues all through adolescence up to the time of marriage. I have already mentioned bathing with the ancestor horns. Such bathing is most effective during the summer season, and lapses during the winter. A supplementary form of growth magic that is not connected with the Ancients is to soap oneself with the suds from certain plants. Certain emetics also favor growth. A youth who has begun to use growth magic seriously shows almost immediately a marked change in personal qualities. Even if he has not yet broken away from the play pack his bearing has become more manly. He spends more time at fishing and he begins to join hunting parties. He adopts the more somber masculine countenance and walks with a more energetic tread. In one particular case of a boy who had seemed rather backward the transformation was abrupt.

9

The Drinking Party

The drinking party (*unkúndye*: chicha, or *unkwínemu*: drinking affair) is the mode of exchange that, generally speaking, governs the relationships among the sibs of the same phratry. Sibs, as I have already noted, do not feast one another, an observation that Koch-Grünberg also made. A sib has its internal drinking parties during which one household head serves chicha to the rest; but the serious and regular drinking parties are those that are held for the purpose of entertaining the sibs of the phratry. I could not determine definitely the pattern of intersib drinking parties, but I believe that an important principle is one of social rank. Higher-ranking downstream settlements prepare chicha more often than do lower-ranking sibs. This accords with the aforementioned Cubeo doctrine that leadership comes from giving and subordination comes from receiving. Drinking party invitations, however, must also be reciprocated, so that over a long enough period of time each sib will have entertained all the others. Since sibs are under no formal obligation to honor a drinking party invitation, the result is that most drinking parties bring together only near sibs who are obligated to attend for personal reasons. Nevertheless, each full-fledged sib plans at least one event during the year when it will have entertained most if not all of its fellow sibs. Attendance at an intersib drinking party is normally by an entire sib although there is flexibility in this.

The drinking parties are of prime importance in unifying the sibs of a phratry. Their frequency and their attendance attest to the state

of social health of the sibs. They follow, in fact, a cycle of active entertaining leading eventually to drunken brawls and quarrels with
allegations of sorcery and so to an era of bad feeling when only very
close sibs entertain one another at parties where the drinkers are
subdued and dismal. The cycle of euphoria-depression in the drink
ing parties reflects rather accurately the shifting state of social rela
tions among sibmates and phratry mates.

The *unkúndye* is to be distinguished from other ceremonial occa
sions that are accompanied by drinking, such as initiation rites,
mourning, and naming a child. It is more of a secular affair. It may
commemorate an event, such as completion of a house or the end of
a pubescent girl's brief isolation period. In the main, it has its own
justification and its own compulsion. The justification is to bring the
sibs together so that they may drink, dance, sing, gossip, and narrate
publicly their origin traditions. Since attendance is generally limited
to sibs of the phratry, the *unkúndye*, with all its erotic provoca-
tiveness, is hardly for courtship. It does stimulate and encourage
adultery, however. The compulsion is to demonstrate economic capability. A sib should be able to provide all its phratry mates with more
chicha than they can possibly consume. It should have a house large
enough to encompass the entire phratry, and its young people should
be vigorous enough to dance virtually without rest from late afternoon on one day until after dawn on the next. The rule of the
unkúndye is that it must go on until the last drop of chicha has been
consumed. The pride of the hosts is that with all the guests' efforts to
drink heartily they could just not make it. Thus, while the *unkúndye*
is a social binder, there is enough conflict in it to provoke serious resentment, quarrels, and temporary disruption of phratric unity.

The hosts of an *unkúndye* have two very evident anxieties as they
go about their preparations. One is that they will have enough chicha. This they can control, for they have planned their cultivations to
allow for at least 15 per cent of total manioc production to go into
chicha. And they work hard at preparing the brew; an entire community will work happily all through the night, reducing the manioc
to a mash and masticating it all mouthful by mouthful to give fermentation a speedy start. What they cannot control is attendance.
The *unkúndye* is also a test of a sib's standing within the phratry. If
it is well esteemed it will attract many guests. When I stayed with the
Bahúkiwa they held a drinking party almost weekly, counting upon
me as the novel attraction that would assure good attendance. As already mentioned they were then in an "up" phase, having moved to
the main stream from the *caño*, and they basked for a time in an orgy

of drinking parties that drew guests from every sib. For the *Bahúkiwa* this was a considerable social triumph since, being relatively low-ranking, they would ordinarily have had more modest social ambitions. Eventually this activity tapered off, and by the time I left the drinking parties had become very small and subdued.

Social rivalry is only an undercurrent of the drinking party, for nothing is more reprehensible than open boasting. A sib must also be careful not to overdo, for then people will regard it as too presumptuous and will not attend. At the conclusion of the most successful of the parties given by the *Bahúkiwa*, when the headman was beaming at the sight of the immense and disorderly throng drinking and dancing in his still-uncompleted house, the guests were already saying that he was overdoing matters. Some told me that they suspected the headman of wanting to become leader over the river. The anxiety of the host as to whether his guests will come is matched by that of the sib that fears it may be ignored when the invitations go out. The normal expectation is that all will be invited and that all will come. At the same time, the drinking party is thought of as a display of friendship and trust, so that if there is any cause for rancor between sibs they will not attend one another's parties. Thus, when sibs that have been invited do not attend and sibs that should be are not invited, speculation is provoked as to why. Some speculation can take an angry and morbid turn.

In its predominantly positive aspects the *unkúndye* has a tonic effect upon the life of almost the entire river. It is particularly bracing to the host sib. An intersib drinking party is given both in the name of the sib and in the names of individual sponsors. The instigator and chief sponsor of a party is, of course, the headman. He will invite cosponsors, usually but not exclusively the male heads of the individual households, so that he can count on the full cooperation of all. The week or so of active preparations demanded by a good-sized *unkúndye* is, in spite of heavy and often round-the-clock labor, a very happy time. The Cubeo regard collective effort that is carried out in good spirits as a great happiness. The preparations for the *unkúndye* mark one of the very few occasions when men, women, and children are all working together. Males normally avoid contact with manioc that is being prepared as food. But they do handle many stages of manioc being prepared as chicha. Even so, to handle manioc in any form a male must adopt an appropriate attitude of levity; it should appear that what he is doing is a game. The women thus are surrounded by rollicking men and are readily infected by their gay mood.

In preparing chicha, the manioc is allowed to soften for four days. It is left in the maloca covered with leaves until it has turned a dark green color and has lost much of its moisture. Then it is grated, pounded through a sieve, and put through the tipiti press. The dry lumps are toasted lightly on the manioc oven and stirred into a fine grain. Small manioc cakes are prepared from these grains. The cakes are thoroughly masticated and the saliva-drenched balls are mixed with water. After fermentation has begun, a quantity of sugar cane extract is added, and this mixture is left to ferment for several days. Masticated pupunha mash may be substituted for the manioc. A mixture of pupunha mash with sugar cane extract makes a potent and very laxative drink. Many communities add maize as well as a variety of root plants to a basic manioc mash.

This period of preparation is one in which the house is spruced up and personal possessions and ornaments are inspected, compared, and readied for wear and display. Nowadays women regard their long cloth skirts as gala wear. If it is to be an important drinking party a woman hopes to have a new skirt that she has never worn before. All the elaborate male ornamentation of feather headdresses, necklaces, girdles, and pendants are fetched out and tried on. Musical instruments — Panpipes, long flageolets, whistles — are tuned and repaired. Songs are practiced and dance steps tried out. A nightly respite from the labors of manioc preparation is the amusement of watching the children play at dancing the adult dances, singing the dance songs, tasting the freshly prepared batches of chicha, taking coca, smoking, and listening to the old men chant snatches of the origin traditions. The mood is such that the minor rancors of community life are smoothed out. The headman takes advantage of this mood to bring the Satellites back as permanent residents of the community. The Satellites are normally invited to be cosponsors of a sib affair, bringing a contribution not of manioc but of sugar cane, or pupunha when that fruit is in season. The headman believes that when the estranged sibmates see how happy all are they will want to come back. There is no doubt that a Satellite is strongly drawn to the festive spirit of the main maloca. But he always has the time during the hangover of the morning after to consider whether it is worth returning.

The headman makes the first proposal for a drinking party and discusses the date and its scale with the male household heads. Cosponsorship means that a household head undertakes to prepare a notable amount of chicha that can be shown to the guests. When the invitations go out, the names of the cosponsors are given, and when the guests arrive they are asked to drink from the chicha prepared by each cosponsor. Those who do not choose to be cosponsors help in inconspicuous ways. There is honor in being a cosponsor but no competition for the privilege either. A household head feels free to decide when he desires cosponsorship. Those who have the most manioc to spare accept cosponsorship most freely. Major drinking parties are always sponsored by the headman, but smaller parties that bring together only close sibs may be offered in the name of a household head who wants the honor. The headman paternalistically defers to this. Some drinking parties are announced as being sponsored by a group of brothers. Of course if there is a special occasion the household head most closely concerned is expected to be a main sponsor. Women do not sponsor or cosponsor drinking parties except for the father's sister, who as widow or divorcée living in her own sib has the status of a household head. The Cubeo use drinking party sponsorship as a means of dealing with the minor frictions of community life, for cosponsors, by the symbolic act of doing something together, have reaffirmed their closeness. On a larger scale, attendance at drinking parties serves the same function.

The guest list provokes much discussion and entails in a sense a review of the sib's relations with its fellow sibs. An invitation may help achieve a reconciliation or it might yield only a humiliating rebuff. Invitations will be delivered in person, by the headman and by all cosponsors, the headman undertaking the downstream higher-status sibs, the others the upstream lower-ranking sibs. The proper time to deliver an invitation is six days before the event. The host delivers the invitation in a chanting tone during which he does not look at the guest but over his shoulder, and the guest replies in the same manner. The host holds up his hands, palms out and thumbs together. When the thumb of the right hand meets the thumb of the left hand it means there will be drinking. Holding two thumbs together is also a jesting sign, meaning, "Now we are going to drink." The four fingers of the right hand mean days of work, and the right-hand thumb means a day of very heavy preparation. The invitation means, then, "We are going to be very active for five days. On the sixth we shall drink."

One principle of Cubeo social structure is that whatever is accomplished on a multisib scale must have its counterpart on the smaller community scale in which household stands for sib. Thus, the five preparatory days are all small drinking parties within the sib so calibrated by degree of festivity — drinking, taking coca, singing, smoking — that each day the festive atmosphere is heightened, so that when the guests arrive the hosts have been honed and keyed up for the day almost like fighters who have been in training. The guests who come to a drinking party see their host sib in its prime condition. The allusion to a fighter training for a match is not out of place here because the gathering of the sibs is dramatized by the Cubeo not as old friends coming together but rather as jealous, aggressive, and fiercely independent segments who have resolved to be friends.

On the morning of the drinking party the *behórü* dancing staff is planted into the ground before the house as a pennant indicating that a party is to take place. It symbolizes dancing and gaiety. The young men, helped by the boys, decorate the staff with its colored feathers. When they have dressed the *behórü* they go to the river to bathe, returning clean and fragrant with sprays of leafy twigs thrust through the belt at the rear. Bathing in this context is bodily cleanliness but also ritual contact with the river.

The drinking party itself proceeds according to fixed stages. The first is the reception of guests. This follows a distinctive protocol. Guests arrive by sib and are received by sib. Having reached the landing beach and drawn up their canoes, a group pauses to make itself more presentable, washing face and hands, adjusting garments, tidying the children, and freshening body paint and ornamentation. The guests then walk slowly and with dignity up the path to the house, the older men in the lead and the women and children making up the rear. The women carry the burden of hammocks, food, and utensils, the men carry the ceremonial regalia, boxes of feather headdresses, dancing staffs, Panpipes. They are not greeted until they reach the house. There, inside the great front doorway of the house, stand the men of the maloca, one behind the other in order of seniority, the headman at their head. Long, low benches have been set inside the doorway for the seating of the male guests. Guests are received by sib in order of seniority, but the order of reception of sibs is fixed only by the time of arrival. Men greet men and women greet women. Persons of adult status only are greeted. The greetings are stereotyped and formal, delivered in the characteristic chant and with averted eyes that marks the speech between persons sharing a respect relationship. The guests' reply must echo the phrases of the host. "You have come" is echoed, "I have come." At very solemn occasions when the ritual separation of men and women is to be emphasized with particular rigor, the women are received at the rear (women's) entrance by host wives. On ordinary occasions the women may come through the front door after all the men are in. They, too, are received in a ceremonious greeting, but an abbreviated one. Each guest passes down the full line of the hosts, repeating with each one the standard greetings. Cosponsors of the *unkúndye* are always in the receiving line, with their wives in the parallel line, whereas household heads who have not cosponsored have the option of greeting the guests formally or informally. It would seem that if there were a large attendance the reception would take up a good part of the evening. In practice there is a tendency to curtail the formalities once the drinking has begun, unless the circumstances are particularly sacred. The first guests are received when the sun has set two-thirds of the way to the horizon, or at four o'clock in the afternoon. As soon as the first man has passed through the receiving line he is escorted to a bench by a young man of the house and handed a calabash of chicha. By nightfall the guests who have been drinking for a while have become more restless and more boisterous, and the greetings on the receiving line have become more curt and less formal. Younger guests slip by without being greeted and younger hosts slip out of line to take part in the drinking. In this way it often happens that the late arrivals are greeted with little more than a casual handshake by a slightly tipsy and gay host.

This seemingly spontaneous deterioration of a pattern of greeting follows, in fact, a characteristic Cubeo ceremonial procedure, which is that every sacred event begins in a slow, solemn, and stately manner and proceeds stage by stage through a steady mounting of tempo until an orgasmic peak is reached, which is then followed by subsidence. I use a sexual figure of speech here because in the prolonged and elaborate mourning ritual which represents Cubeo ritual activity at its most complete, the entire proceedings unquestionably follow the sexual rhythm from courtship to coitus.

The women who have come as guests sit in a bunch at the left side of the maloca near the front door. The men sit on two long benches in a V formation opposite the women and also near the door. At the rear of the house sits the first group of dancers, men of the house. After a while the guests begin to move deeper into the house, where each woman visitor stakes out a space along a side wall for her effects and her children. Men form separate clusters. The older men, whose behavior is consistently more restrained, are the last to leave the forward benches. When the women have gone back into the house these elders occupy all the benches and, facing each other in two rows, smoke cigars in a ceremonial manner, waving the smoking cheroot before their faces and nodding pleasantly to one another. The cigars are held in a carved forked holder with a pointed stem that can be stuck into the ground before each smoker.

An ordinary drinking party lasts from late afternoon until dawn of the following day. During this time only children will be fed or will sleep. With hammocks and cooking utensils out of the way the maloca yields up its everyday character and is exclusively a dance hall, in a sense a ceremonial center.

At the height of the festivities sibs are all intermixed. But this mixing happens slowly. Earlier in the evening sibmates have bunched together. One has the impression that one of the "functions" of the drinking party is to break down, temporarily at least, the excessive autonomy of the individual sibs. At big drinking parties the men of the visiting sib arrive armed with loaded shotguns, as in the past they came armed with lances. The armament symbolizes the autonomy and the latent hostility of the separate sibs. When the men are armed, the transition from separateness to mixing is more dramatic because then the sight of bunches of armed men crouched with their rifles between their knees conveys, as it is intended to, an atmosphere of menace. At the end they have put their arms away for the fellowship of drink and dancing. Women, however, are fearful that after the men have begun their usual drunken brawling they will use their weapons. I never saw this happen although several women assured me that drunken shootings were common enough.

The chicha is kept at the rear of the house in great pottery jars, in great drumlike wooden tubs as big as canoes, and in canoes that have been scrubbed clean for this purpose. The quantity that is always prepared is intended to be prodigious. It will call for very active drinking on the part of all, men, women, and in a playful way by children, for the last of it to be consumed by dawn. The saying is: "No one leaves until the chicha is all gone," and the male guests gayly promise to drink "until we vomit." The hosts ply the guests mercilessly with chicha, hunting them down in the dark corners of the house, waiting for them to leave a dance formation, good-naturedly pushing them if they are asleep or more likely pretending to be asleep. After a time, the groan of a guest who sees the pursuing calabash thrust at him again is genuine enough. Women will serve chicha but it is properly a man's chore. Only the men are aggressive servers.

Among neighboring Tucanoan-speaking as well as Arawakan tribes chicha is served ceremoniously, the bearers of the calabashes dancing toward the guests in single file, crouching, knees raised high to chest. They weave in a snake dance and utter monosyllables such as *ma ma ma* or *tsa ha ha ha*, and conclude with a piercing *he he he*. The Cubeo do this when they serve the sacred drug *mihi* but I never saw them serve chicha in this manner. The Cubeo offer the calabash with a jest: "Drink quickly so that you may be drunk soon." The aim of the drinking party is to achieve an intense state of excitement and to maintain that until overcome by sheer fatigue and sleep. Tobacco, coca, and *mihí* supplement drinking to intensify and hasten the reaction. When *mihí* is taken, producing color visions and finally a blackout, the Indians say, "Now we shall get drunk quickly." *Mihí* is associated with *miwa* (birds), which are the patrons of ec-static intoxication.[1] Drunkenness is not to be avoided. If a little boy gets drunk his father is proud of his precociousness. Women, however, are not expected to get drunk and they rarely do.

Mihí is not taken at every drinking party but only at those that are considered very important. At the mourning festival (*óyne*) a great quantity is consumed. The narcotic plants (*Banisteriopsis caapi* and others) from which *mihí* is prepared are cultivated by the men only and they alone drink it. The Cubeo regard it as a sacred drug, and from all indications it is so regarded throughout the Western Amazon region where it is used. Along the Orinoco the Indians chew the skin, but all along the Vaupés an infusion is prepared by boiling the leaves, bark, and roots to form a greenish-brown "soup" that is strongly bitter. The Cubeo prepare several varieties that are graded according to potency. Upon truly solemn occasions they begin with a mild infusion from the leaf of a variety that is taken exactly at midday, and conclude with a very strong variety just before sunset. This sequence of *mihí* transports a man from vague and mild visions of whiteness to intense hallucinatory experiences, bursts of violence, and finally loss of consciousness. *Mihí* almost invariably causes vomiting, and for that reason alone each man must take many servings. For each type of *mihí* there are four servings taken from a small gourd dipper. The first service is of two dippers, the second of one, and the third and fourth of two each. At the beginning, the Indians say, the vision becomes blurred, things begin to look white, and one begins to lose the faculty of speech. The white vision turns to red. One Indian described it as a room spinning with red feathers. This passes and one begins to see people in the bright coloring of the jaguar. When the final strong forms of *mihí* are taken the hallucina-tions begin to assume a disturbing and fearful form. One becomes aware of violent people milling about, shouting, weeping, threaten-ing to kill. One is seized with the fear that he no longer has a home. The house posts and trees come alive and take the form of people.

---

[1] There is also a bird called *mihíkü*.

There is a strong sensation that an animal is biting one's buttocks, a feeling of the feet being tied. The earth spins and the ground rises to the head. There are moments of euphoria as well, when one hears music, the sound of people singing, and the sound of flowing water. The Cubeo do not take *mihi* for the pleasure of its hallucinations but for the intensity of the total experience, for the wide range of sensation. I spoke to no one who pretended to enjoy it.

A sacred drug, *mihi* is handled in a ritualistic manner and is served from a distinctive pottery jug that is never washed. When the hosts — always a pair, one man holding the jug and the other the serving dish — offer *mihi* the following stylized exchange takes place. The guests exclaim, "*ho ho ho ho ho o o o,* here it comes." The host asks, "How are you?" and the guest replies, "I am well. I have come well." The host stirs the *mihi,* saying to it, "Stir! Look, it is bitter. It tastes bitter. Our Ancients also drank it." The guest replies, "Let me take it. Let me see if I can drink it in the same way as our Ancients did. I am going to drink." He drinks it down and is offered a mandatory second drink. The host says, "Look. Here it is, drink again." The guest now replies, "I am going to drink so as to see [a vision]." A guest whose father is dead will say upon receiving the *mihi,* "My father, when he was alive, drank like this, so he told me. He sought me out that I might drink. My father never got drunk when he drank it."

When each guest has had his two portions of *mihi* the hosts drink off two portions and then serve one portion to each guest again. The guests murmur *ba ha a a a,* meaning "well done." When the last portion is given, the host announces, "We have finished drinking," and each guest replies, "I am pleased." At this the host announces he is sitting down to have a vision, and he retires. Suddenly he leaps up at the guests in the characteristic *mihi* dance and with the sucking sound. He intends to frighten them and shouts *wetcówe* (vomit!), and the guests reply, "Bring it on. We wish to vomit."

Drinking, smoking, chewing coca powder, and taking the infusion of *mihi* are all acts with strong symbolism of sharing a group experience. Out of bravado a man may down an entire calabash of chicha. More often he will pass it to a neighbor, who will also take a few swallows and pass the calabash along. The drinker will also have taken chicha from the quantity prepared by each cosponsor. The cigarette is passed from mouth to mouth. The host provides tobacco, which he passes among his guests from a bark-cloth pouch, and a bark wrapper, which is tied to the house posts. Guests may smoke their own tobacco but will always use the wrapper that is provided. Men pass cigarettes to one another after a puff or two. A man will ordinarily pass a cigarette to his own wife only, for the giving of a cigarette to a woman has a potentially erotic significance. When a woman receives the cigarette she passes it among her children until finally the suckling baby has had a smoke. She then returns it to her husband. The custom of sharing the cigarette has been widely observed along the Vaupés and its tributaries. The Indians accept it as a mark of friendship and of trust. Ceremonious smoking of cigars held in forked holders accompanies the dignified conversations of the sib elders and is mandatory when these old men get together to chant the sib origin traditions. Several cigars are lighted and are passed around. There is no way of sharing coca, but *mihí*, as we have noted, is "danced in" by the sons of the hosts, and the little ornamented beaker in which it is kept is passed around.

Dancing begins when the assembly is warmed up with drink. At an *unkúndye*, dancing, being secular, is for the young, the adolescents and unmarried and the younger married men and women. In the most common dance three or four young men line up abreast, left arm across a companion's shoulder, with the long dance flageolet, that sounds the song of the butterfly, in the right hand. An orchestra of Panpipes, seated to one side, sets the rhythm to which the dancers move and sound the flageolets. Starting at the rear of the house they move down the long dance corridor to a beat that starts as one slow step, a pause, two shorter steps, a pause, and then three rapid, almost running, steps, the inevitable Cubeo procedure of placing all ritual in the metric structure of *adagio* to *presto*. They reach the front of the house, their bodies swaying forward and back as they come down the corridor and gracefully swinging from side to side as they prepare to pivot, swinging the flageolets up and around in unison. The first dancers are usually of the host sib and are brothers. During the early stages of the dance, as each of the visiting sibs puts its dancers on the floor, the formation is of brothers. It is not until much later during the night that drink and excitement have dissolved the fraternal bonds and allowed for the indiscriminate formation of dance teams. As the dancers move down the corridor the unmarried girls begin to stir; they giggle, nudge one another, sway forward with the desire to get up and join. But they are shy. They seek encouragement from one another. Often an older woman, a girl's mother, whispers sharply, "Go on, dance." Then two or three girls get up from the side lines and run behind the dancers, pacing themselves so as to slip under the yokes of the men's arms in the precise beat.

Koch-Grünberg has observed this dance among neighboring Tucanoans as well as among Arawakan-speaking tribes. He observed it as a courting dance, boys and girls leaving the house after a dance and disappearing into the surrounding darkness (1909, I, 293, II 272). There is no mistaking the erotic undertones of this dance among the Cubeo. But it cannot ordinarily be a courting dance since the participants are normally sibmates and phratry mates if unmarried. The first girls to join the dancers are, in fact, their sisters. But as the evening wears on, the erotic character of the dance emerges in a dangerous form. An unmarried girl too often chooses to thrust herself beneath the arms of her sister's husband, a married woman "chooses" a husband's brother. What is ordinary courtship in tribes that bring together potential marriage mates at their drinking parties is largely adultery or the threat of adultery among the Cubeo, who entertain within the exogamous circle. I suspect that in the case of the Cubeo, simple courtship dances have become embroiled in a changing social order that has gradually built up a phratric system out of independent exogamous local groups. In the process the dance has lost its innocence.

The dancing has a deceptively decorous appearance. As the girls insert themselves between two male dancers, under the arm of one, the men never pause, turn their heads, or change expression. The girl puts her right arm lightly around her partner's waist. She holds her left hand before her, at her skirt. Crouched beneath the yoke

Fig. 10. *Hehénewa* men in full dancing costume.

she looks uncomfortable and solemn. The girls accompany the men for a few turns and then as unobtrusively as they entered the dance formation they leave it, disengaging their heads, backing away, and running quickly back to their places among the women. They are replaced by another group. Much later in the evening an observer is startled to discover heated and even violent disputes erupting all over the house as a result of these innocent-appearing dances.

There is another dance in which the sexes are actually paired. The man plays either a Panpipe or a long flageolet and drops his left arm over the woman's shoulder while she encircles his waist lightly with her arm. This dance formation starts as a circle which, after making several turns, breaks up into couples who dance down the corridor one behind the other. During the circle dance a woman emits a long piercing shriek. I was given no explanation for this other than the vague comment, "Women feel like doing this."

Perhaps it is not overinterpreting too much to suggest that the form of the dance parallels some basic principles of Cubeo social structure: the unity of the fraternal sibling group; women as ancillary, fitting themselves in between thé brothers, coming and going; the segmentary nature of the sibs; the feeling for obliterating what is after all an indelible mark of sib apartness. As for the erotic connotations of the dance, one may perhaps speculate on the phallic character of the flageolet. This instrument, by the way, is so long that when the dancer holds it before him the bottom is only bare inches from the ground. If he is careless as he dances and allows it to strike the ground he may lose his teeth. The dance starts with the instrument held down close to the earth. When the dancer has reached the forward end of the house he arcs the instrument high over his head. The flageolet resembles, but is not to be confused with, one of the ancestor trumpets that is brought out during ancestral cult celebrations. Then the deep sound of the flageolet stands for the deep and sacred voices of the ancestors, that bring to the men physical force, sexual potency, and bodily growth. The Cubeo make the obvious association between the deep tones and the solemn, and the high tones and the frivolous. In ensemble playing they also recognize one of the instruments as a leader and the others of the same group as followers. In the drinking party dances, flutes and Panpipes complement each other; the flutes are butterflies and the large Panpipes are vultures. Solemnity is always associated with the acquisition of powers. The movement of the dance is, as we have already noted, from slow to rapid. The last step before the dancers leave the floor is very rapid, almost a run, and the dancers in their excitement

shout *hi i i i* and are answered by the audience. The men start dancing alone and finish dancing alone. Dancers of the host sib begin
their dance in the house and may sally out onto the plaza, an extension of the house, and then dance back in. Guests, on the other hand,
begin their dance formation on the plaza, move into the house, and
conclude on the plaza.

The Cubeo regard women as disruptive elements at a drinking
party. They have cause to do so, since it is the women who are encouraged by the character of the dancing to make the overtures of
flirtatiousness. Women choose their partners and men maintain an
air of innocence. A woman's sexual forwardness goes beyond that.
Young girls and many married women wear love charms in their hair
at a drinking party. This is nothing more than a colorful blossom
that declares that a woman would like to attract the interest of a
man. The Indians themselves are not quite sure whether the blossom,
which they call *chondú* (*pedídya* in Cubeo) has inherent qualities
as a love charm — a serious woman has truly powerful love charms
that she uses secretly — or is merely provocative symbolically. In any
case a man cannot be blamed if *chondú* provokes him. The use of
chondú adds intensity to the atmosphere of a drinking party as effectively as do chicha, coca, tobacco, *mihí*, and dancing. Whether or not
chondú is an official ingredient it is hard to say. The men speak of
it as a feminine provocation. Yet if one looks at the drinking party
in its inevitable progression from calm to frenzy it seems that,
whether it is an official ingredient or not, it fits. Just as the counterpoint of male and female is part of everyday community life, so the
more intensely experienced counterpoint of male and female is ex-
ploited for its frenzy-producing quality.

A married woman should not wear *chondú*, but a man cannot stop
his wife from displaying her interest in other men. He then ex-
cuses her by saying she does it only to look pretty and keeps a wary
eye on his brother sib and phratry mates. For the unmarried girls
chondú is formal wear, even though the only man whose eye it might
catch is likely to be a sister's husband or a forbidden phratry mate.
Curiously, unmarried girls are often even more provocative by not
wearing *chondú*. This is arrogance that says, "I am not interested
in the men here." A married woman may wear *chondú* only to tease
her husband in a lighthearted way. Understanding this he is even
delighted. She may do so, on the other hand, to irritate him. The
rule of sober everyday life is to avoid quarrels and issues. The drinking party roils up feelings to the point where what has been latent
erupts forcefully into the open. If emotional catharsis is a "function"

of the *unkúndye* then it should be said that it is the women who supply the charge that explodes the emotions and issues into the open.

Because they are so much in the background during everyday life, compartmentalized in the manioc garden as in the house itself, women are strongly stimulated by the social heterogeneity of the *unkúndye* as by the inherent excitement of drinking, dancing, noise, and close body contact. The women's responsiveness seems to be spontaneous from the very beginning of the drinking party, whereas the men groom their emotions by stages, until at the end they are responding with a spontaneity of their own. The spontaneous emotional excitement of the women feeds into the emotional pool, so to speak, of the whole *unkúndye*. During the great mourning festival with its ritual eroticism this counterplay of men and their formal ceremoniousness and women and their emotional spontaneity leads finally to a unified response that is ceremony deeply charged with feeling. At the mourning ceremony this juxtaposition of male and female roles is very evident. And it is because of my observation of the mourning ceremonies that I have been led to see each drinking party in a similar fashion. In short, for the men the drinking party is collective and ritualistic; for the women it is individual and personal. In the end, these two roles are fused so that the aim of strong feeling within a formal setting is achieved. Perhaps it would be better to say overachieved, since the jealous quarrels that women provoke are sometimes serious, splitting sibs from one another and antagonizing close sibmates.

Every drinking party that I ever attended ended in a quarrel. All quarrels were sexual, either provoked directly by jealousy or by disparaging remarks about a man's virility. The quarrels may lead to minor violence and may have no consequences. Sometimes, however, they stir up unexpectedly deep layers of feeling. A fresh affront recalls earlier offenses. These are aired. Before long the disputants have brought out a tangle of charges and countercharges revealing long smoldering issues. Men start a quarrel over an accusation of adultery. One man then comments that the father of the other had once said that he would not mind if his, the complainant's, sib were to die out. It is a remark of this nature that suddenly and chillingly transforms a simple quarrel into a later suspicion and then open accusation of sorcery, should someone sicken on either side.

The quarreling of men sounds more violent than it really is. If they are content to merely pummel one another with their fists there is little interference except that the women fret anxiously. Should they reach for dangerous weapons they are restrained and content themselves with an exchange of vituperation. Brothers will defend one another, as well as sibmates, so that a quarrel is difficult to isolate. The men listen to the vituperation and, far from regarding what is said as meaningless drunken chatter, draw implications that may involve them. What began as a quarrel between only two men over one man's wife can become a maloca-wide brawl. Then the sibs taunt one another, each reviling the other's weaknesses and calling attention to its own strength. It may all come to nothing. A diplomatic elder calms tempers; the headmen remember their obligations to preserve the peace at drinking parties. Some disputants have enough sense of humor to laugh. It can all blow over quickly and will then have served as another way in which feelings are lightened, provided the sinister specter of sorcery has not been drawn in.

The following is an example of a quarrel at a drinking party. A man began to beat his wife because she was dancing too often with the same man. The latter remonstrated and soon he and the angry husband came to blows. The bystanders remarked that the husband's jealousy was unwarranted. Encouraged by these remarks, the woman's father got angry and attacked his son-in-law with his fists. The son-in-law did not defend himself, whereupon the old man calmed down and proceeded to explain to those present that his daughter's conduct was altogether proper. At this point the wife became enraged, and flinging herself upon her now pacified husband, pummeled him soundly on the back with her fists. Since he did not strike back her fury subsided and this incident blew over.

However, another young man who had been witnessing this violent flurry began in a tearful voice to inform his audience that his wife was having an affair with a phratry mate of his. He named the woman's lover, who was present, but for the moment said nothing. The accused's father, however, jumped quickly to his son's defense, shouting that the charges against his son were false. The jealous husband turned upon the old man and shouted at him angrily, "You are already an old man. It is time you were dead!" At this, the accused man rushed forward, livid with fury. In a hoarse voice he shouted to the assembly, "Did you hear? He is planning to kill my father." But the jealous husband was already beyond calming down. Instead he shouted back that the sib of the accused adulterer was weak and few in numbers, whereas his own sib was strong. With these ominous remarks this incident closed, for the time being. All felt that the outraged husband had gone too far. No further remarks were exchanged, but the two sibs did not invite one another to their drinking parties for the remainder of the season.

Sorcery is the great fear. All illness is attributed to sorcery and so are deaths that cannot be readily accounted for. When the drinking party is over and someone has become ill, the quarrels will be recalled and a phratry brother will be charged with sorcery. If the shaman bears out the allegation, the sib of the accused will not be invited to the drinking party of the afflicted sib. In the course of a ten-month stay on the Cuduiarí I have seen drinking parties go through a cycle from full participation by most of the sibs to dismal solitary affairs where subdued members of the sib drank with one another and a few friendly phratry mates from closely adjacent sibs. When the fear of sorcery begins to grow, accusations may strike within the sib and split it down the middle. Gradually confidence is restored, headmen begin to think again of large *unkúndye*, and step by step the scale of attendance mounts.

10

The Mourning Ceremony

Mourning for the recent dead provides the setting for the most complex and most important of Cubeo ceremonies. These ceremonies, known collectively as *óyne* (weeping),[1] usually take place as late as a year after death, preferably during the dry season when the pupunha palm is ripe. I attended two mourning ceremonies, one among a *Bahúkiwa* subsib and one, a very elaborate affair, among the *Hehénewa*. The last I witnessed from the very beginning.

The *óyne* consists of two parts: a long, three-day section, followed about a month later by a one-day concluding ceremony at which the spirit of the dead is finally evicted from the community.[2] During the first part, masked dancers impersonate many of the familiar beasts, birds, insects, and fish, as well as the mischievous spirits of the Cubeo world. These spirit beings come to mourn, but mainly to turn the people from grief. On this occasion the tribal "grandmother" and her consort, in the form of two great bark trumpets, also arrive to mourn.

Koch-Grünberg, reporting on the same group of *Hehénewa*, says that the trumpets are called *Uménahonkü* (Dragonfly) (1909, II, 151). He was not aware that the name referred to a *Hehénewa* Ancient. There are several possibilities to be considered in accounting

---

[1] Also *oíwinu* (weeping affair).

[2] There are also abbreviated one-day ceremonies for women, children, and men of small extended joint families. The three-day ceremony is most appropriate for a headman.

for this contradiction. One is that different Ancients are represented at different times. This possibility, though, is one that was never mentioned to me. The origin myth of mourning, it should be noted, refers to *Xudjiko* only. The other is the possibility of error, since Koch-Grünberg also labeled a trumpet used in initiation ceremonies as *Uménahonkü*. *Oýne* and initiation trumpets are never the same.

The dances, rituals, and dramatic representations of these first three days range over a variety of themes, but all have the common purpose of transforming grief and anger to joy. In keeping with the characteristic pattern of Cubeo ritual that begins slowly and solemnly and ends in frenzied disorder, the first phases of the *oýne* also start from the dark mood of grief and anger and end in a sexual orgy. This first part of the *oýne*, in which the emphasis is upon transformation of feeling, is largely dramatic. The second part of the *oýne*, that lasts from late afternoon until the dawn of the following day, carries forward the theme of emotional transformation, ending in fact in true sexual license, when men are privileged to copulate with their sib and phratry brothers' wives. Its main themes, however, are religious and magical, including the aforementioned expulsion of the spirit of the dead as well as the magical absorption of the substance of the deceased into the body of the sib. The latter is presumably accomplished by pounding the exhumed limb bones of the deceased into a powder and mixing them with chicha, which the men of the sib drink.

The women are weepers and have, in the main, a passive ritual role. They huddle together with their nursing infants in the rear half of the house that for the occasion has been partitioned with a six-foot-high fence of poles and leaves set so as to form at the center an overlapping slit opening. The women are not allowed to see what is going on in the male section, while the slit opening allows the men to dance freely in and out of the women's section. Stimulated by masculine-initiated activity, the women burst into fits of ritualized weeping, their only active ritual role. Their proper role is to be acted upon, and to be brought to a point of ritualized sexual excitement so that they can be engaged in ritual and simulated coitus.

The masked dancers represent the nonhuman world of beings, the beneficent and malevolent, the threatening and the ludicrous, as well as the neutral creatures. Their songs (*kwimaiwü*) are mournful and indicate grief for the deceased, but their dances and dramatic representations are of their own world. Each mask generally has its own song and characteristic dance, although the connection between mask, dance, and song is not rigidly kept. As the ceremony reaches its inevitable crescendo of excitement and disorder, dances and songs are interchanged.

In the course of the ceremonies, the relationship between the nonhuman world of the masked representations and the people, represented by the women, becomes increasingly more intimate, culminating, as we have already noted, in the total intimacy of coitus. The spirit of Cubeo ceremonialism is generally Dionysian. In religious excitement the Cubeo achieve a desired and temporary dissolution of the segmentation and conceptual separatenesses in normal social and religious life.

Koch-Grünberg (1906a), who observed part of an *óyne* in 1903 among the *Hehénewa*, saw in the masked dances two themes, an appeasement of evil spirits and fertility rites. My own information does not agree entirely with this interpretation. It is a fact that several of the masked dancers represent malevolent beings; the jaguar, that is the embodiment of the dreaded sorcerer, the butterfly, that symbolizes the act of sorcery, and the *abúhuwa* or forest monsters, that devour human victims. In addition the masked dancers represent the dung beetle and the vulture, eaters of offal and carrion. These creatures represent to the Cubeo the facts of death. Except for the *abúhuwa*, who are not taken too seriously, the most common agency of death is to the Cubeo a particular human enemy. Evil sorcery can be warded off by particular magical means. The masked dances, however, are not magical means for warding off danger. They are, rather, dramatic rituals whose purpose is to generate a frame of mind in which the fact of death is confronted and made to appear natural and tolerable. By coming to the house as guests, to dance, to sing, to drink chicha, and to "copulate" with women, the masked creatures are made to appear, finally, as a friendly part of the Cubeo world. The malevolent creatures are not singled out, but appear in the context of the whole ensemble of masked dancers.

As for the fertility theme, this has been a cherished cliché of earlier anthropology that promptly labeled any ritualization of sex as "fertility rites." The situation is more complex. The dancers do indeed represent male potency, but the simulated coitus emphasizes rather the carnal aspect of sex, for it is the older women, possessing the privilege of obscenity, whom the masked dancers "attack sexually."

THE MASKS

The dance masks of the Cubeo are made of a white bark cloth called *táwü* (tree bark), which is also the name by which the masks are generically known. Koch-Grünberg (1906a) has argued that they are sacred, citing as evidence that after the ceremonies the masks are burned. Many masks, however, are spared at the insistence of children who wish to play with them, and some masks are spared and used as storage sacks. Sanctity, I would say, is attached to individual masks, and is the sanctity of the being represented and not of the mask itself. Women, it is true, do not handle the masks, not out of taboo but rather out of the feeling that the masks are in the masculine domain. The masks represent spirits who are called generically *takahédekokü* (bark-cloth spirits). These spirits are visible only to the shaman.[3] All masks have a common basic shape, a large triangular sack that fits over the head and covers the body to the knees. Armpits are always cut out, and sleeves that come below the elbow are sewn in. The bottom of the skirt is stiffened with a circular hoop, and sleeves and skirt are hung with bark fringes. The masks have a head section, a middle section, and a bottom part. The head section is ordinarily painted with a face design that has eyes and a nose but not necessarily a mouth. Two eye holes and a nose hole are sometimes torn through for the wearer's convenience and do not correspond to the painted design. In some masks the head section is soft and in others it is surmounted by a calabash, painted brown or black, depicting a skull top; or the calabash itself has a face design painted on it and depicts, therefore, the face. The middle section is divided into several panels, half of them at the front and half at the rear. Each panel is painted in a geometric pattern that depicts the characteristic body features of the being that is to be represented. Fish, for example, have scale designs, and birds and flying insects wing designs. These designs are painted with great care by men who are particularly proficient. They follow traditional forms rather casually, however, each artist giving his own interpretation. The Cubeo do not quibble about the details of design. The fact is that no one can identify a particular representation with certainty without knowing who has made it. Only some of the masks, such as Jaguar, Butterfly, and *Abúhuwa*, are distinctive enough to be immediately recognizable. These masks, incidentally, also seem to be the most important.

The use of ceremonial masks is common enough in South America, as Professor Alfred Métraux (1948) has observed, but we have as yet little information as to their meaning, nor do we know their full distribution. What is certain, though, is that masked cults have

---

[3] Koch-Grünberg (1906a) has observed that while the animal represented may be harmless, the spirit itself is magically powerful.

different significances in different tribes. The Central Amazon is one center of distribution of ceremonial masks and the Northwest Amazon region is another. In the former region, masks are not of bark cloth but of palm leaves that cover the entire body. The headpieces with human features are cylindrical and of wood. According to Cubeo tradition, they, too, once used palm-leaf masks before being taught by *Kúwai* to prepare bark cloth. Karl von den Steinen, who collected many dance masks from the Xingú River region, never saw them used and guessed that they were mainly ornamental. As among the Cubeo, the Xingú region masks represent animals, beasts, and fish (Steinen, 1894). Along the Araguaia, a tributary of the Amazon, ceremonial masks seem to be part of a secret men's cult and, of particular interest to a Cubeo comparison, they are also used in funeral rites (Krause, 1910, p. 109; Lehmann, 1911). In both parts of the Central Amazon, the Xingú and the Araguaia, the dance songs that are associated with the masks are similar to those of the Cubeo and may have been brought there by Arawakan-speaking peoples who still live there. In the Vaupés River region all the Arawakan tribes share the masked dance cult with Tucanoans. However, among Tucanoan tribes, Uanana and Desana do not have them (Koch-Grünberg, 1909, II, 64).

To the west of the Cubeo, in northeast Peru for example, masked dances are, surprisingly, not found among the Tucanoan-speaking peoples but rather among the Witotoans, such as the so-called Witoto proper, the Bora, and the Muinave. In this same region the Yagua, the Okaina, and the Tucuna, all of whom speak as yet unidentified languages, also have bark-cloth masks (Tessmann, 1930). The nature of their masked dances is similar enough to those of the Cubeo to leave very little doubt that they are historically connected. The masks of these tribes represent animals and demons, as among the Cubeo, and are similarly decorated. However, nowhere in this region are bark-cloth masks used in connection with mourning rites. The Tucuna use masks in girls' puberty rites, while among the Bora masked dances accompany the harvest festival of the pupunha palm. This is a point of historical interest, since the Cubeo mourning ceremony is held during the season when the pupunha palm is ripened and has other "harvest rite" motifs. Because information on masked dances in the Amazon area is so limited, no firm conjecture can be made as to their place of origin. It would seem, though, that the Cubeo have taken ceremonies that in other tribes pertain to harvest festivals, secret men's cults, or girls' first menstrual rites, and have adapted them to funeral rites. Simi-

larly, they have adapted harvest and demon cult ceremonies to ancestral cult rites. Evidences of religious syncretism are important in
interpreting a complex ceremony. Thus, the fact that the mourning
rites commonly begin during the pupunha season and the fact that
at one point in the ceremonies the men pelt the roof of the house
with pupunha fruit to "frighten the women" must be evaluated in
the light of the possibility that we are dealing with a portion of a
foreign ceremony, incorporated in the structure of the *óyne*. Cubeo
ancestral or initiative rites also include "harvest festival" elements.
But in these, as in the *óyne*, the harvest theme is a minor one.

MASK REPRESENTATIONS

Dr. Koch-Grünberg, in his travels through the Vaupés region, collected some 50 different mask representations. My own observations
along the Cuduiarí covered 30. Altogether, there is now a combined
list of 62.[4] Since the masks are intended to portray *all* the living
creatures of the Cubeo world the number of masks is potentially vast.
No one ceremony uses them all. There are, however, key characters
that are most commonly represented. These are Jaguar, Dung beetle,
Carrion vulture, Butterfly, Aracú fishes, Eagle, Sloth, Parrot, Dragonfly, Minnows (who are not masked but are an important element in
the ceremonial dramatization), *Pyénkü* (a small black fish), Frogs,
and a variety of cannibalistic ogres or forest demons, the *Abúhuwa*.
Informants would not say which of the masked representations was
most important, presumably because invidiousness is, to the Cubeo,
in poor taste. Judging, however, by their prominence, I would say
that Jaguar, Butterfly, *Abúhuwa*, Dung beetles, Carrion vulture, and
Aracú fishes were most important, more or less in that order. Except
for the aracú, the esteemed fish of the region, these creatures all have
an association with death. The jaguar is, of course, the dreaded sorcerer. The sorcerer is called *yaví* (jaguar) and the Cubeo regard any
jaguar as likely to be either a sorcerer or a sorcerer's dog. The morpho
butterfly with its beautiful blue wings is a creature of sorcerers and of
evil. The information Koch-Grünberg received was that the morpho
butterfly (*tatárako*) lives at Yuruparí *cachoeira* on the Vaupés, where
he brews malaria in a calabash and strews it over the land (1909, II,
181). I did not hear this account, but I was told that when a sorcerer
is cooking a brew that will kill a victim at a distance the morpho
butterfly appears and encircles the pot. Finally, it falls in and is con-

---

[4] See the end of this chapter.

sumed and at that moment the victim dies. The Arawakan tribes in the region call him *Makálu* and regard him as the chief of the masked dancers. The *abúhuwa*, of which there are several types, are grotesque forest ogres, a menace to the hunter whom they lead astray, tease, or kill, and the bogy man of the children. It was not my impression that the *abúhuwa* were deeply feared. They represent, rather, a caricature of human fears. The dung beetles (*keratamówa*) are literally devourers and cleansers of decay. They are, as Koch-Grünberg observed, good spirits and guardians against dangers. The carrion vulture (*kavá*) is simply a literal representation. The aracú represent the ordinary world that is neither good nor bad.

The masked dances (*wahómu*: bark-cloth tree) are mimetic, each illustrating some distinctive gesture or movement of the being represented. The songs, on the other hand, are not readily translatable, but many do mention the name of the being. As for the masks themselves, they are recognizable either specifically or at least by class by such distinctive design motifs as wings, fish scales, feathers, and jaguar spots, as well as by characteristic features of over-all design. The intent is clearly to represent the being with some directness.

The jaguar masks have a design of yellow spots outlined in black and in red that covers the entire surface including the facepiece. In some masks the spots are distributed evenly and in others they are divided into fields. The jaguar sleeves are made of a coarse brown bark cloth that seems to be associated in the Cubeo mind, judging by how they use it, with more violent feelings, a point I shall deal with later. The jaguar dancers carry a jug whistle upon which they produce the deep *hoo hoo hoo* sound of the angry beast. The whistle is a short length of ambauva palm set into a pottery dish made expressly for the purpose. The pot is enveloped in brown bark thongs that cross the opening, where they are fastened to the whistle, thus allowing the instrument to be held with one hand. The entire pot is hung with bark fringes. The dancers move as a pair, sometimes holding hands and sometimes separately. As all dancers do, the Jaguars begin with a slow, stately walk, and then move into their characteristic movement. Legs held close, they spring forward and then back, sounding their booming *hoo*'s during the walking intervals. They follow a circular movement in either direction. The Jaguars have an important role in stirring the assembly, particularly the women, to the desired state of frenzy. They are almost always on the floor. They begin wild and are capable of increasingly more violent actions. The Jaguars are always men in their physical prime. At some time during the ceremonies all the mature and vigorous men will have danced the Jaguar. During the early part of the *óyne*, when proceedings are still orderly, the Jaguars and the Butterflies form an appropriate ensemble, the latter dancing in front of the Jaguars. Later a calculated disorder takes place. At this time the Jaguars tear the bark fastenings from their jug whistles and distribute the tough brown material to all the men to chew on so they may become "as strong and fierce as the jaguar." The jaguar song I collected is different from that recorded by Koch-Grünberg, but variations are common. Thus, when Koch-Grünberg saw the Jaguars among the *Hehénewa* they were not using jug whistles, while the Arawakan tribes were. The song I recorded was:

> *yavirárü   yaviráki*   [repeated]
> *yavirárü   manika*
> *yavirárü   ya*
> *ho ho ho   o ho.*

Like all mourning songs it had a slow rhythm and a hauntingly mournful tune. The Cubeo offered no translation. *Yaviráki* means "big jaguar," and *manika* may mean "children."[5] Koch-Grünberg collected a similar jaguar song among the Arawakans on the Aiarí River, whereas the song he recorded among the Cubeo is curiously quite different and does not even include the descriptive name *yavi*. There is good reason to suspect that these songs are widely exchanged.

The mask of Butterfly (*Tatárako*) is marked by triangular wing designs. The headpiece, moreover, has attached to it winglike structures made of bark cloth stretched over a frame of splints. The headpiece, which, like the Jaguar, has no facial markings, is built up around basket work to give it a bulbous appearance and to identify it with caterpillars, beetle larvae, and the sloth. A mask photographed by Koch-Grünberg has, in addition, an antennae-like strip arching forward over the face. The Butterflies also dance in pairs, often holding hands. Each holds a calabash in one hand and a stick in the other with which he strikes the calabash violently. This gesture imitates that of the sorcerer striking the pot into which the butterfly will fall. Their characteristic step is to run forward quickly and then take several slow steps back like the flight of the butterfly. Sometimes they drop to their knees to imitate the creatures resting. The song I recorded had the refrain *kaviré kaviré* and is not the same as that recorded by Koch-Grünberg on the Aiarí.

Koch-Grünberg observed nine types of demons or ogres, including

---

[5] The Cubeo term for children is actually *manáwa*. The term *manika* may be a song transformation. However, this translation is very uncertain.

a dwarf pair, several pairs of giants, a great owl demon, and two kinds of *abúhuwa*. I saw three *Abúhuwa*. The *Abúhuwa* are made to appear grotesque. Their masks are of coarse brown bark cloth and, unlike any other dancer, they sometimes wear bark-cloth trousers. One Indian said to me rather maliciously, "They are like the white man." One of the *Abúhuwa* not wearing trousers had large flapping breasts of bark cloth and was a "wife." The headpiece has a calabash to form a face painted with human features. The masks are intended to be as grotesque as possible. Since the *Abúhuwa* act clownishly, they induce in the spectators only mock alarm. The *Abúhuwa* have no song of their own and no fixed dance. They are free to improvise. There are two kinds of improvisation: wild when young men impersonate them, and listless and lolling when acted by old men. While the Jaguars act to build up a sense of violence, the *Abúhuwa* work to create disorder. Thus, no masked dancers will enter the women's quarter through the rear or women's door except the *Abúhuwa*. They burst in through the rear door, hopping in short strides as though they were on pogo sticks. They interfere with dances and perform a number of amusing skits.

The Dung beetles (*Keratamówa*) are a pair. The masks have a white facepiece with a pair of eyes, or sometimes with no features at all. The body design includes the wide bars of the insect's body flanked by lozenge designs on each side. The headpiece is surmounted by a short hourglass-shaped tube of splints and bark cloth. They dance holding hands. Each holds a short stick. In a dance Koch-Grünberg saw, they pushed along another stick on the ground in imitation, he noted, of their work as cleaners. I saw them holding their short sticks before them like wands. Their dance is a slow movement, forward and back. The songs recorded by me and by Koch-Grünberg are not the same.

The Carrion vulture (*Kavá*) wears a mask with human features, although Koch-Grünberg saw one that he described as "naturalistic." The main design consists of very large lozenges (to depict the large feathers of the bird) flanked by horizontal bars suggesting outspread wings. The Carrion vulture carries a short stick held against the back of his neck, its ends extending over his shoulders, where his upraised hands hold it in place. The dancers bow gracefully from the waist to suggest the bird's soaring flight.

The Aracú (*Borikakü*) are usually represented in their several varieties. The headpiece is built up to a high peak made of splints covered with bark cloth in an hourglass design. The Aracú dance slowly, in pairs, and hold hands. Each carries a ten-foot pole bearing, like a pennant, bark-fringe streamers. The *Boríkakü* usually dances with *Mávayo*, its compatriot, the red-mouthed aracú. In a joint dance they carry a rope ladder (*towándo*) made of three parallel strands of rope into which wooden rungs are set. Attaching the ladder to a roof beam, they climb and descend.

THE MINNOWS

Although the Minnows (*Emíwa*) wear no masks they are definitely part of the dance ensemble; they have a dance step, a song, and a dramatic role. The Minnows are the youngsters and form a school of fish that presumably stands for the youngsters' play pack.[6] They are a boisterous element, moving in and out among the masked dancers. Lacking masks and, accordingly, formal ceremonial status they play a counterpoint of sheer spontaneity to the more solemn dances of the masks. While the role clearly belongs to youngsters, boys are not limited to it. Prepubescent boys do, indeed, wear masks. Those I saw were Butterflies and I was told that a youngster may dance any role but *Yaví*, the Jaguar. The Minnows play on curious shrill whistles. The whistles resemble a short three-tube Panpipe and are mounted at the end of a stick about a yard in length that is hung with three streamers of bark cloth. The dancers wear ankle rattles and dance in a spiral formation, taking two accented steps forward and then two oblique steps back. They hold their whistle sticks pointing up. They have no particular formation, dancing sometimes abreast, sometimes in line, and, alternately, in disorder. The Minnows do all their dancing among the women, who dote on them and ply them with chicha.

XUDJÍKO AND *XUDJÍKÜ*

The "grandmother" and her consort are, for the Cubeo, the truly solemn and sacred element of the *óyne*. Represented by giant 15-foot-long trumpets of wound bark that are bound as twins to a single frame, they are taboo to all the women, as are all ancestral horns. The trumpets are capable only of deep, mournful notes and represent ancestral mourning. It is the grandmother, however, who has come to mourn and not the grandparents. The reason for this is that it is a woman's role to be an official weeper. Men may and do

---

[6] It will be recalled that in the story of *Kúwai* and the anaconda, the penis of the anaconda is transformed into four minnows that are given to the adulterous wife to eat.

weep at an *óyne* but only as partners of women, whom they join in the formal weeping embrace. The ancestral role of *Xudjiko* and her consort is different from that of the ancestor trumpets used in the initiation ceremonies. Some of the latter are regarded by the Cubeo as sib or as phratry ancestors and are incorporated in the genealogies. *Xudjiko*, on the other hand, is a tribal ancestress and, so far as I could determine, is not a part of any genealogy. *Xudjiko* and *Xudjikü* are constructed for the occasion and are secreted along the river, to arrive at the proper time by canoe. A special place over the grave, in the forward side of the house at the left, is prepared for the twin trumpets, and they are almost constantly played by two men seated side by side on low stools.

THE SIB UNITS

The last group of dramatic characters are the sib units. An *óyne* is normally a phratric affair, each sib attending as a unit to express condolences, to mourn, and to vow vengeance against the enemy. Since the suspicion of sorcery may fall upon any man, even within the nuclear family, the sibmen are in effect required to declare their innocence by the strength of professed grief and anger. Sibmen also appear as masked dancers, but in that guise they have no sib identity. As sibmen they play a role of great solemnity, behaving with meticulous decorum, grim-faced and unsmiling, carrying weapons as signs of male wrath and power. They maintain this demeanor undeviatingly since they perform their necessary ritual observances early, before the effects of chicha, narcotics, and the excitement of the dance have eroded the orderliness with which the *óyne* began.

ORGANIZATION OF THE *ÓYNE*

As a complex ceremony, interweaving many ritual elements and magical and religious themes, the *óyne* follows its intricate course with apparent spontaneity. One does not observe overt central direction; the dancers seem to know just what to do and when to do it. The hosts act as general guides only, not by instructing the guest dancers but by guiding the major phases of the ceremony. In this way they manage to achieve the desired atmosphere of emotional spontaneity. For all its complexity, the *óyne* is well adapted to the segmentary social structure of the Cubeo. It is a phratric ceremony in which each sib acts as a unit in ritual acts and in the dances during the early stages. In the later stages, after the drink, the narcotics, and the general excitement have taken effect, the sib units disintegrate, so to speak, and the entire gathering becomes one generalized melee of phratry mates. The Cubeo do not call attention to the symbolic significance of the merger of sib identities; but that a mixing of the sibs is a desired result seems evident enough to an observer. For as long as the sibs maintain their separateness the mood of the *óyne* is solemn and decorous. The point of mixing is also the point of desired disorder. As a unit each guest sib is responsible for preparing a number of masks (as well as other ceremonial objects) and for representing them in song and dance. To my knowledge a sib has no fixed prerogative to a particular mask or group of masks. It is free to make any it chooses. Presumably there are preferences, although when the host issues the invitations to the *óyne*, he or his messenger negotiates the masks that each sib is to prepare. If the purpose of the negotiation is to ensure that all the mask beings will be represented, that purpose is not always fulfilled. However, if a mask is not present, the spirit being it represents can still be enacted by the appropriate song and dance, for while the Cubeo do believe that a mask has a particular character they are not dogmatic about it. Masks and spirit beings are interchangeable.

The masked dances follow neither a precisely fixed sequence nor a precisely patterned ensemble, although they do follow a general order that is familiar to all. Since the principal sequence is one of mounting emotional intensity, it follows a natural course as the ceremony proceeds. The dance groups respond to one another. An ensemble is formed more or less spontaneously as one group of dancers stimulates others to join it. In the same way, the emotional level set by one group of dancers influences all others who follow.

MYTHOLOGICAL BASIS OF THE ÓYNE

The Cubeo tradition of the *óyne* is as follows. There was a time when people did not die and there were then very many people. One morning a boy followed his sister into her manioc garden and copulated with her. In the afternoon the girl returned home and told what her brother had done. The people beat the boy and drove him out. He wandered about in the forest for three months feeling ashamed. He could find nothing to eat and so he returned home very thin. He entered the maloca and, speaking to no one, lay down in his hammock and died. His own people did not mourn him but said,

"*Dekókü*[7] has punished you." Then other people came and wrapped the boy in his hammock, put him into a large jar, and buried him in the house. No one wept. After three days an old man began to think what people should do about death. They decided to have an *óyne*. They made dance masks. At first they did not know how to make bark cloth so they made masks of leaves. *Kúwai* came and told them this was not good. In one day *Kúwai* made all the bark-cloth masks for the people. They did not know how to paint the masks and *Kúwai* showed them how. They gathered red pigment and carbon soot, and by midday the masks were all finished. *Kúwai* climbed the duka tree. At the top he cut off the bark and brought it down to make the fringes for the skirt and sleeves. The people then divided the maloca into a men's and women's part. In the men's part an old woman sat down to sing. But soon the real *Xudjiko* came along singing and the people were frightened. But *Kúwai* said, "Don't be afraid. This old woman is *Xudjiko*, who has come to help you weep." The old lady ran away and *Xudjiko* took her place. Then *Kúwai* said, "When other people die do the same thing. Weep for a short time only." He told them to dance and sing. When they had finished *Xudjiko* went away. She no longer comes. Instead they make a horn.

Xudjiko and her consort live at Uaracapurí, the source of the Cubeo. They were the first of the Ancients to die and they were the first to make the bark-cloth masks. The headpieces of the masks are set with feathers; the most prominent vertical feather is said to represent *Xudjíkü* and the most prominent horizontal feather is said to represent *Xudjíko*.[8]

RITUAL THEMES IN THE *ÓYNE*

The five main sets of characters in the *óyne* each represent then one major ritual theme: the women represent weeping; the masks, the concern of the living world for the deceased as well as for the living; the minnows, the boisterous character of young men;

---

[7] The term means "ghost" or "spirit" but it has here the connotation of "Great Spirit." However, since I did not learn of a Cubeo belief in a Great Spirit the allusion is puzzling, and is to be considered as unexplained.

[8] The apparent inconsistency between this account and the previous one referring to *Kúwai* illustrates two strands in Cubeo mythical thought. One strand, nonancestral, focuses on *Kúwai*, a figure of the Arawakan tribes. The other strand is ancestral and is, perhaps, truly Tucanoan. The Cubeo do not reconcile both strands. The question of which version is produced depends on the context, which may be either general or ancestral.

Xudjiko and her consort, the mourning by the primordial ancestors; and the sib units, the solidarity of the phratry in expressing both grief and anger. The dramatizations and mimetic dances present a variety of minor themes, such as menace and hilarity. If one looks at the *óyne* as a whole, however, and follows the sequence of events from their slow and solemn beginning to their conclusion in a simulated sexual orgy and then in a real one, a single main theme emerges, and that is the sexual interplay between men and women. By contrast to the sexual emphasis, the ritual of dealing with the spirit of the deceased seems almost minor and anticlimactic. It is only at the very end, when most guests have departed, that the ghost is dispatched. The climax of the first part of the *óyne* is ritual coitus, just as the climax of the second part is sexual license. We can therefore describe the *óyne* in terms of ritualized sexual sequence.

Fig. 11. Mourning ceremony, women's entrance.

The sexual play between men and women begins when the first visiting women arrive and try to pass through the rear entrance of the maloca. The rear door has been removed and the opening barred by poles set in an × over which the women must climb. The Dung beetles, armed with wooden staffs, "guard" the entrance by thrusting at the women as they climb in. The women are burdened with great baskets containing household utensils. Many carry a nursing baby in a sling across the hip, with a walking child clutching the skirt. A woman can make no dignified entrance. Prodded by the Dung beetles she tumbles into the house, clutching her infant, her skirts flying, her utensils scattered. She laughs with excitement, recognizing her fall as a burlesque of the rough play that initiates sexual courtship. At this moment the men are being solemnly and decorously received at the front door. However, after having been tumbled into the house the women reassemble outside, the bars are removed, and they, too, are received in the conventional manner by the host women. They then settle themselves along the left wall of the women's section.

The second molestation of the women comes at nightfall, when little boys rush in among them with a bark *dúpu* (a lizard which supposedly makes the women squeamish) suspended along a sturdy rope. They invite the little girls to join them in a tug of war. The little girls act shy so the boys first play of tug of war among themselves, arranging to fall among the girls. Emboldened, the girls seize the *dúpu* and join the tug of war. Another group of boys also bearing a *dúpu* enters and engages more girls in a tug of war. The purpose of the *dúpu* is to generate excitement among the women. The boys fall upon the little girls, who shriek with laughter and mock alarm while their mothers dodge the thrashing bodies artfully.

The youngsters are followed by an older group of Minnows, not masked, who swarm in noisily, stomping and whistling, dancing close among the women and jostling them. Finally, all the masked dancers, the adult males, enter. The air clouds with dust, and the women's section resounds to the shrieks of laughter, to song, and to the thump of dancing feet and the dry clatter of rattles. Young boys who are sent to sprinkle the floor with moist chicha mash, to settle the dust, pelt one another, and "accidentally" the women, with balls of mash. Throwing chicha mash is, for the Cubeo, a common form of flirtation. Ordinarily the woman throws at a lover. Children do not ordinarily play this game. Thus, the incongruity of being hit with mash thrown by little boys amuses the women enormously. It is the guest women who are flirtatiously singled out at this time. The host

women stand apart on their side of the house and serve chicha to
the Minnows.

The males leave and the excitement of the women subsides.
Through the night, however, the men come to dance among the
women. The fence that divides the house into a male and female
half is also an emotional dividing line. Dances form on the male
side, where they are solemn and subdued. When they pass to the
women's side, the dancers are excited. When they go back they re-
vert to calm. It is tempting to interpret the movement of the masked
dancers — who look phallic — through the overlapping slit in the
wall as symbolizing coitus, particularly since with almost each passage
the level of excitement is heightened.

The excitement of the Minnows is allowed to subside in a calm
interval. *Mávayo* (the red-mouthed aracú), and *U* (sloth) do a slow
dance, holding long poles with a crook at one end which they sus-
pend from a roof beam and upon which they swing. The Sloth always falls. He lies on the ground kicking a leg and making feeble
gestures of arising, only to fall again. But *Mávayo* is slow and grace-
ful and swings gently on his pole. The Sloth arises, and the dancers
cross poles and gracefully dance out.

They are all followed by the Minnows. Each Minnow now carries
a long pole that is joined to all the others by a string from which
dangles a carved wooden bird. They do a circle dance with the bird
in the center. As they circle, stamping strongly to accent the beat on
the right foot, they jostle the women, moving in upon them to en-
close them in the circle. The Jaguars now rush in, wilder than ever,
leaping about among the women and falling upon them. They are
followed by the boys with the *dúpu* on its string. The boys ensnare
the young girls in the *dúpu* string. Now two masked dancers come
in with long flaming broomsticks. They dash about among the
women, swinging the flaming fibers among them. The women scatter
in noisy panic, kicking over baskets and dishes. The attack by flame
excites the Jaguars as well, and they whirl around among the women
in sheer frenzy. As they flee this new menace, the women say, "The
jaguars are angry. They will soon attack people." The Jaguars, however, are no menace to the men. One climbs on top of the partition
and blows noisily into his jug horn, and another climbs a roof beam
overlooking the women, both in a simulated attack upon them.

The Jaguars withdraw, and the next entrance is again a quiet
one. Two Spiders, slowly and gracefully holding a long string from
the middle of which hangs a feather, dance toward one another,
winding up the string until they are face to face at the feather and

then unwinding it. They repeat this over and over, joining and part-ing. Watching this, the women regain their composure.

When the Spiders leave, the wives of the mourning sib are led into the men's side. Here, in pitch blackness, they sit in a circle around the ceremonial regalia of the deceased and weep. The men are no longer in masks; the masks are on poles and shield the women from the *Xudjíko* horns, whose low, mournful notes, that sound like a bull-roarer, accompany the weeping.

This most solemn interlude is followed by an entrance of all the men. Previously the masks had danced only with their own kind. After midnight all the masks form one line. Each man carries a lighted taper. They circle the house several times, singing the same song. They re-enter by the front door and pass immediately through the slit to the women's side, still bearing their flaming torches. A number of the dancers suddenly move forward, and seizing the chief female mourner by the hair, arms, and legs, drag her violently across the floor from side to side. They do the same to other female mourners but with less violence. The themes of sexuality and of hos-tility are intertwined in the *óyne* the way they are in daily life. Sex is always associated with the out-group. The parallel seems very clear between the ritual of "marriage by capture" and the ritualization of sex and aggressiveness in the *óyne*.

From this moment the dancers are constantly among the women. Throughout the entire second day, dancers move in and out — one group leaving as another enters. Masked dancers fall upon the women, roll over them on the ground, or jostle them. The men say, "We are looking for *Míavi* [Eagle]." The jostling, which seemingly excites the women, is, however, largely formalized. No dancer touches a woman with his hands, and he makes the jostling appear to be accidental. The young boys, however, who are sexually aroused by this play, take advantage of the confusion and of the women's excite-ment to fall among them and to clutch at their breasts and thighs.

The third day begins with a series of comic enactments for the benefit of the women. In one, the *Abúhuwa* carry a basket of bark-cloth balls called *wakúiu*, which they throw to one another, among the women, and then dive after. This violent buffoonery is counter-pointed by a solemn dance of men, not in masks, who hold a long pole before them and move down the corridor in a slow tread sing-ing the mournful refrain *kamiré, kamiré*. These dancers leave, and another *Abúhukü* comes forward. He carries a bark-cloth coconut (*dudúki*). He pantomimes futile efforts to break it, studying it closely and tapping it against his head. He throws it on the ground among the women and dives clumsily after it, rolling among the women and over them. He recovers it and tries to crack it in his mouth, but of course he is wearing a mask, and finally he examines it with a marvelously executed air of puzzlement and dejection. The women have been so dazed by now that the comic virtuosity of this "clown" does not draw the expected laughs. The *Abúhukü* leaves and there is a respite. The women stir about and look after their children, and it seems as though the emotional gradient, having been broken in its upward ascent, has dropped to the most ordinary level.

But this quiet interlude is short. At midmorning all the masked dancers storm noisily among the women in a dance called the *hwananíwa* (wild peccary). They throw themselves upon the women, forcing them to the ground and to the copulatory position. Three or four men cover a woman. The dancers rise again to dance in sheer frenzy, careening about the room, shrieking and falling again upon another woman. But even though their excitement seems more feverish than ever, the men still do not lay a hand upon a woman. They choose for their attentions only the older women. The older women among the Cubeo are licentious, and they behave at this time as though they have become sexually aroused. They laugh and shriek and reach for a man's thighs. The daughters observe this spectacle of their mother's sexual excitement with evident dismay and great interest. The mothers shrilly command their daughters to run away and so escape sexual molestation. At the command to run they begin to leave, but they come back to watch. Again, the very young boys who share this masculine license are carried away by sexual excitation and lustfully attack the women, the wives of their phratry mates. The women "fight them off" with the standard courting resistance and succeed in inflaming them all the more. Not all the masked dancers join this revelry in the same spirit. Some men, the older ones in particular, are restrained, treating the dance symbolically, and some are simply shy and only brush lightly against the women. The point of view is that of symbolic frenzy rather than of sheer unrestraint. The mastery of this mood is surely a difficult one, because the women, who are a laity, are under no compulsion to discipline their feelings. This is presumably the Cubeo ceremonial conception — pitting masculine symbolically controlled behavior against the spontaneous emotionality of the women. This interplay between emotional form and substance, so to speak, adds spontaneity and emotional spice to the ceremony but always within the framework of form. That the youngsters should succumb to simple lust in this licentious dance is, to be sure, a spontaneous consequence of the

ceremony. But their lust and that of the women is what really provides the desired emotional level for this stage of the ceremony.

The *hwananiwa* is really a precopulatory performance. It is followed by another comic interlude in which the *Abúhuwa* return
with their repertoire of cracking a nut, killing an alligator (cayman),
and killing a jaguar. The alligator performance is a great success.
The animal, which is a symbol of masculine sexual lust (in the leg-
ends it copulates with the wife of *Kúwai* and continues to do so even
while she is devouring its abdomen), is made of coarse brown bark
cloth. This bark cloth itself has an obscene significance for the Cubeo
and is associated with violence and lack of control. The brown bark
cloth goes with the Jaguar and the *Abúhuwa* and with all the objects
used by the *Abúhuwa*. It represents the power of beasts. In the phallic dance the huge penises are also made of brown bark cloth.

The *Abúhuwa* and their helpers come in from the men's side,
carrying this bark-cloth alligator, and say, "We have killed our alligator." They proceed to cook it in a hilarious demonstration of inepti-
tude. The women, who are now at a high pitch of excitement, shriek
with glee at the antics and the men are stimulated by their appreciation. They light a fire under the pot with brown bark cloth, sending
a choking wave of acrid smoke into the house. They bustle about the
pot in a crowd, cutting up bits of the "meat" and throwing it into
the pot. One performer almost falls into the pot in his zeal. Another
tries to set fire to the "meat" in the pot. They stir and smell and
taste, mimicking the woman as cook. Then they pull out small bits,
and putting a piece daintily on a leaf, pass it to the women. The
women promptly throw the pieces at the *Abúhuwa* — the courtship
gesture of the woman throwing food at the man.

The interlude of cooking the alligator and feeding it to the women
strikes a new note in the sexual sequence. This is a domestic scene.
Men feed only the wives of the house. By throwing the "meat" at
the men the women are responding to sexual excitement in the uncontrolled sense. By killing their alligator, cooking it, and acting inept the men are symbolically subduing uncontrolled sexuality. The
men are actually acting out a feminine role, for it is women who cook
meat in a pot. This reversal of sex role is a humorous incident and it
also strikes a domestic note.

The men reinforce this domestic mood in a series of portrayals
representing hunting, killing, and eating. Each sequence becomes
less humorous. The men bring in a brown bark-cloth representation
of a jaguar slung on a pole. They sing the jaguar song. They cook
the jaguar and eat it, passing out the "meat" to the women, who,

recognizing the symbolic distinction between an alligator and a jaguar, do not throw it back at the men. Then the Jaguars kill a deer, who is represented by a masked dancer. The Jaguars dance wildly about their "victim," blowing loudly into their jugs. The victim writhes and falls agonizingly to the ground, kicking up a leg, moving an arm, and then lying inert. Other dancers, his "comrades," come to look at him. They lift his arm and it falls back. They lift his leg and it falls back. They sniff his body and murmur *ttt tttt*. Now the Carrion vultures come, with their short staffs held against the back of the neck. They dance about the victim singing the jaguar song. They buzz about the victim and bend down and kiss him. The Jaguars also kill *Pampámibo* (a frog), and the procedure is repeated.

This dramatization of the modes of violent death — the killing of the alligator, the lustful adulterer, the killing of the jaguar, the dread killer himself, and the killing of the weaker and defenseless game animals — restores the mood to one of sobriety. The dance of the Carrion vultures has a note of pathos that is not lost on the women.

When these sequences are done there is an intermission. The boys busy themselves with the fabrication of great bark-cloth penises. The phallic dance that is to follow is known as the "dance of the potent penises" and is under the jurisdiction of the young men. As they complete the penises, the boys begin a sexual play with them, thrusting at one another in a hilarious burlesque of coitus. It is all play, in a spirit of gaiety and with much noise.

During this interval of male sexual play, that takes place in the men's part of the house, the women on their side are mourning in the conventional fashion, arms about one another's neck, faces together, crouching in a mournful circle.

On this, the third day, the women's section is not entered again by the men until late in the afternoon. Then the entire corps of masked dancers dances in, each man carrying a sprig of leaves with which he beats the women, centering attention on the elderly. Some strike with such force as to make the women scream with pain. Others brush a woman's shoulder lightly. They then dance into the men's section and whip the hosts, but perfunctorily, since the real interest is in the women, from whom they should draw blood. The Jaguars enter briefly among the women. They leave and all the masked dancers — the *nowánparatowü* (potent penises) — come in. Each holds a bark-cloth phallus before him with both hands. The dancers thrust at the older women, some doing so very mildly, and others, the younger men, forcing the phalluses between a woman's legs. The women again shriek at their daughters to escape. As before, the girls dart about in confusion, running as though to escape, but returning to witness the sexual "attack" on their mothers. The shrieking women lift up the bark-fringe skirts of the men, and recognizing a dancer by the design on his thighs, shout out his name. This seems to be a spontaneous gesture, for the sexual attack as the Cubeo dramatize it is, after all, symbolic and abstract. The dancer, to be sure, is attacking a particular woman, but he does so in an impersonal manner. The woman, however, does not accept sexual interest in an impersonal manner.

The symbolic coitus is decidedly less spirited than the previous onslaughts against the women. There is less body contact and, except for a few of the more aggressive younger men, the entire interlude has the appearance of a dance and not of an orgy.

The phallic dance concludes the first sexual sequence at this ceremony. Outside the house the boys conduct a homosexual play with the bark-cloth phalluses, but this does not seem to be a part of the ceremony proper. One month later the mourning series is completed at a two-hour dance, at the end of which the masks are burned and, as the ultimate act, men take women, the wives of their phratry mates, into the bush and copulate, couples changing partners as often as they like. While there is a one-month interval between the phallic dance and the actual sexual license, the final act of copulation is still part of the sexual sequence, just as the final dances and the burning of the masks are also part of the ceremonial sequence involving masks.

The final sexual event in this ritual sequence is to be understood as somewhat more than sexual consummation. It is also an act of mass adultery, as the Indians are only too well aware. In this act, the adulterous longings of the people are given expression without any real suppression of the stormy feelings of jealousy that adultery provokes among them. The adulterous act adds still another modality of sexual passion.

The entire sexual sequence is very close to Cubeo life, even to the point of including the homosexual play of the young boys, which in Cubeo life is also only a byplay in the formal sexual life of the community. The very young girls receive only playful teasing attention by their male age mates. The younger married women — the sexually most desirable — are almost entirely ignored during the play phases of the sexual sequence. But in the final act it is they who are taken and not the older women. It is for this reason, too, that I regard the final sexual event as a provocative act of adultery, for the adultery of an older woman is not regarded quite as seriously as is the adultery of a young wife.

THE MEN'S SIDE

In the interaction between men and women we have seen the ritualization of sexual passion as a principal theme. In the events that are localized on the men's side of the house we see as a principal theme the ritualization of another range of emotion, the masculine emotions of grief and anger as well as a symbolic display of masculine sentiments of sib and phratric unity.

The *óyne* begins as an intrasib affair, and its first ritual acts are those of arrival: of the masked dancers, the beings, and the "grandmother," *Xudjíko* and her consort.

On the evening before the guests come, the men of the sib prepare the masks. The masks are mounted on poles before the house and are decorated with macaw and other feathers. Among the *Hehénewa* the men had hung the ears of the masks with the metal cylinders of cigarette lighters bought in trade for the occasion. The cylinders reminded them of *kenádox*, the quartz cylinder pendants. Decoration of the masks is timed to finish at sunset, not earlier, not later. On this night only the major masks are represented, the rest are brought by guests. The masks are arranged in pairs of the same kind, except for Aracú and Sloth, who go together. The Indians assured me that the pairing is not sexual; both are male, they said.

As darkness falls the men put on their masks and form up in pairs in a line, the Butterflies in the lead, followed by the Dung beetles, the Jaguars, and the Aracú-Sloth pair. They dance around the plaza in a circle, each singing its appropriate song but all using the same dance step — a simple one-step accenting the right foot, that bears ankle rattles. When they complete one circle, the Butterflies break away and, now in their proper dance step, approach the doorway of the house, strike the side wall violently with their rattles to announce their presence, and move back to continue dancing and singing as a pair on the plaza. Each pair, in turn, does the same, and there follows an interval in which the paired dancers move about the plaza unmindful of the others.

The first blow against the doorway by the Butterflies is a signal for the women behind their partition to begin wailing, and to continue to wail as long as they hear the dancers singing on the outside. This is an interval of some 15 minutes. Again the Butterflies strike the doorway violently. This time they run swiftly through the doorway, and within the darkness of the house they remove their masks and wait for the others to enter in the same manner. Assembled in the house, the men listen for the sound from the canoe landing that will announce the arrival of *Xudjiko* and her consort. Bearing their masks over their arms, they file out silently and form a double line along the path from the canoe landing to the plaza.

Four men bring the great trumpets by canoe. Watched by the others, they carefully lift out the trumpets noiselessly. When the trumpets are on land the watchers whisper, "Here comes our grandmother." Two bearers mount the forward ends of the trumpets on their shoulders and two in the rear are the players. The trumpets sound their first low, mournful notes, and the watchers put on their masks, form a file, and escort the "grandmother" into the house. A trumpeter accompanies with a rattle.

The "grandmother" is first set in the very center of the dance floor of the male section, and as the trumpets are played by two men, the masks circle "her," their songs blending with "her" lamentation. Again the women behind their barrier respond with their own higher-pitched and human wailing. After a brief interval the "grandmother" is moved to her permanent place at the left, where a framework to receive the trumpets has been installed. The rest of the night is devoted to the dancing of the masks and the lamentation of the "grandmother." The men take turns in sounding the trumpets. Occasionally they rest and drink chicha and smoke. They dance on the plaza, in the men's section and in the women's section. Whenever they enter the house they strike the doorway loudly and spur the women to renewed wailing. Shortly after midnight the men drape the doorway with brown bark cloth as a barrier against evil sorcery. At dawn they remove the drape and hang it over the inner partition. It will be used for making the *dúpu*, the phalluses, the alligator, and other paraphernalia.

As day breaks they prepare for a third admission, that of sibmates who will pay their respects to the dead. The oblong box of plaited palm fibers in which a man keeps his ceremonial possessions is brought out and set in the center of the dance floor. These are the ceremonial belongings of the deceased and at this time they represent him. Among the *Hehénewa*, where the deceased had been the father of the headman, the box, as well as a tray containing the full Cubeo ceremonial regalia — feathers (*mápena*), quartz cylinder pendant, jaguar-tooth and aramadillo-vertebrae girdles — were laid out.

The sons and grandsons form a circle around these representations of the dead. Each carries in his left hand either a shotgun or a heavy staff as a weapon. They pose with head bowed, both hands resting on the weapon. The chief mourner holds a rattle hung with a feather and eagle down in his right hand. He begins the formal oration, an angry declaration denouncing the unknown sorcerers who have killed his father. As he speaks, in a hoarse, changing voice, he swings the rattle in a vertical arc, pivoting on his left foot, facing one mourner and then the next. His gestures are vigorous and his pivot is crisply executed. He swings the rattle upward almost into the face of the mourner whom he is addressing. He has hardly completed the circle when each of the mourners, swinging his right arm in an arc, turns to a companion and recites a similar angry declaration. The companion to whom he turns also pivots to face him, awaiting his return to reply. This part of the ritual is executed as a ballet. The declaimer is poised with his right foot forward, waiting for his partner to pivot and face him, and not until the partner has executed his pivot does he begin his declaration. The headman, having initiated these hoarse and angry harangues, turns his attention to the ceremonial remains of the deceased. His head bowed, he gently shakes the rattle over them and utters a sad lament that he has lost a father. After an interval of angry shouting the mourners re-form the close circle, bow their heads, and weep. They pause to blow their noses, wiping their hands on the fringes of the masks that have been hung nearby.

Other members of the sib are not part of this close mourning circle. They put on their masks and dance, circling the mourners. The *Xudjiko* trumpets are silent because they are sounded only by the men of the household of the deceased, who are now part of the circle of mourners. The mourning of the men signals the women to begin again their wailing, their piercing lamentations rising clearly above every other angry and mournful sound.

This interval of mourning lasts some 15 minutes. The ceremonial property of the deceased is then removed and the men rest, drinking chicha and smoking. Dancing resumes after half an hour. At dawn the Jaguars cut off the brown bark-cloth trimmings from their jug trumpets and pass them among the men to chew. This will guard them, they say, against sorcery from their phratry mates, who will arrive as mourners late in the afternoon.

Later in the morning the men put up crossbars to "guard" the women's entrance. After this *mihi* is prepared. A sibman staggers in with a bundle of the narcotic vine. *Mihi*, as always, is carried in the ritual manner, one of its features being a representation of great weight. The bearer bends low, raising his knees high, and circles the men's section making a sucking sound with his lips. Having circled once, he proceeds to prepare the *mihi*. He prepares a quart, which is considered a great deal.

The younger men now fetch the *abúhuwa* masks, that have already been prepared except for final decorations and embellishments. A completed mask has the full sacred character and for that reason the last touches are put off until the very end. The same principle applies to *mihi*, coca, and chicha; they must be fresh or their potency will be lost. In the case of the masks, however, it is a matter of the spirits not being kept waiting. When people come to a ceremony they also complete their decorations just before entering the house, pausing at the canoe landing to do this. Hosts for their part arrange to complete their preparations almost at the moment the first guest arrives.

The first guests to arrive are the Satellites — members of the sib — who appear precisely at noon. They go first, informally, to the rear of the house, where they deliver a bundle of dried fish, a traditional Satellite food offering, to the headman of the sib. They then return to the canoe landing to prepare for a new and formal approach to the house. They carry heavy staffs or other weapons. The head of each Satellite household approaches the open doorway, strikes the side wall a resounding blow with his staff, and steps a few paces into the house, his sons behind him. Inside, the male hosts are in line in order of age seniority, the headman and chief mourner at the head. Each man holds either a staff or a loaded gun planted firmly at his side. Guests and hosts exchange formal greetings in a rapidly delivered dirge that is punctuated at intervals with a moaning sound *ee ee ee ee* followed by a whistling sound *i i i i*, as when *mihi* is brought in. The men, as is customary in formal greetings, do not look at one another but at some distant point past the other's shoulder. The guest moves down the line, spending about five minutes with each host, and the next is received in the same way. When the first arrival has passed down the line, he is given a calabash of chicha by a host, who leaves his place in line to do this. Women are greeted at the rear door by female hosts.

While the hosts safeguard themselves against sorcery by chewing the Jaguars' bark cloth, the guests wear a little pouch at the throat for the same purpose. The effort to protect against sorcery is realistic, since the Cubeo regard every drinking party, an *óyne* in particular, as a prime occasion for a sorcerer to practice his art. These safeguards also carry out the theme of anger and implied hostility that characterizes the early stages of the *óyne*.

After the formal greetings, the guests return to their canoes to complete the decorations on the masks they have brought and to apply personal body decorations.

The sibs of the phratry arrive in late afternoon. These later arrivals are greeted by the hosts wearing dance masks. When they sight their guests they sally out of the house dancing and singing in a winding line around the front plaza. The guests respond by donning their own masks and dance up the path, each pair of masked dancers singing its own song. They mingle with the hosts. All complete a circle about the dance plaza, the hosts dance into the house, and the guests continue dancing outside.

Two Butterflies from among the guests approach the open doorway. Each in turn strikes the side wall violently with his rattles. From within Sloth and *Mávayo* thrust their long poles out at them and "beat them off." The Butterflies rejoin the others. Suddenly all the dancers rush the doorway and skirmish with the spirits within. Those with staffs thrust them at the attackers or use them to ward off a thrust. Those with rattles shake them violently. The "attack" is noisy and spirited. Beaten off again, the attackers re-form their dance line and dance to the rear of the house, seeking an entry through that quarter. But here the doorway is blocked with crossbars and guarded by Dung beetles, who thrust their long lances at the "attackers." Again the attacking dancers retire and resume their dance at the front of the house. After a while they take off their masks, hanging the garments on poles that have been set for this purpose along the front walls. Now, as humans, each strikes the side wall violently with his staff and enters the house. This entry is ritualized. The men flit in swiftly and silently on tiptoe, whispering *t t t i i i*, and circle the ceremonial remains of the deceased.

The male hosts have formed themselves into an outer semicircle facing the guest dancers. They lean on their staffs and look on grimly as the dancers complete the circle; then they whistle. At this the dancers come to an abrupt halt in a semicircle facing the hosts and launch into the orations already described. The speeches are short, and the men change partners often, each moving out of position when necessary, or leaning past a companion at his side. After a few minutes the guests resume the flitting dance. They circle clockwise, whispering *iii iii iii*, and having completed one circle, dance counterclockwise and whistle. Alternating between clockwise and counterclockwise and whispering and whistling, they complete several circles led by their headman, who carries a rattle in his right hand. During this dance only the host headman remains standing and facing the dancers; the others retire to the benches set behind the dance masks and drink chicha. The guests finally stand in a circle around the ceremonial remains of the deceased. With heads bowed and leaning on their guns or staffs before them they chant a lamentation, their leader shaking his rattle slowly. They weep, the *Xudjiko* trumpets pick up the lament, and the women join in. They repeat this performance with little variation three times. After the third, they break ranks and face their hosts again in the postures of the angry harangue. Finally each guest breaks away and rushes toward the open doorway brandishing his weapon outside and shouting defiance at the sorcerer or other enemies of the phratry.

Concluding this phase of mourning, the guests leave the house so as to make still another entrance, this time to be received as men with the formal salutations at the doorway.

Guests from others sibs arrive by maloca groupings, each group of eight or ten men acting out the same ritual. Each group appears in three roles: as spirit beings who are repulsed, as generalized mourners who act out grief and anger, and finally as kinsmen, each of whom is received individually and with a kinship greeting as he makes his final entrance to the house. When they are greeted as kinsmen, the ceremonial remains of the deceased have been removed; they are welcomed at this point with a calabash of chicha and with *mihí*.

There are some minor variations in this pattern of greeting. At the *Hehénewa óyne* one group "attacked" with a barrage of pupunha thrown against the roof and the front walls. This "attack" had, however, another side to it. In part it was an attack and some of the fruit was thrown violently through the door, where the defenders threw it back at the masked attackers. But punpunha is also regarded at this time as an offering for the women of the house — just as it is during the ancestral whipping ceremony, when the house is showered with fruit by the ancestral spirits. The sound of pupunha fruit striking the roof frightens the women.

This dualism of assault and of offering is carried out in somewhat different form in the course of the ritual receptions to the house. The first instance is when the guests arrive as masked dancers or as spirit beings. They are received first in a friendly way, joining in a dance with their hosts. Then the two groups separate and engage in ritual attack and defense. In the second entrance, as generalized human beings, there are a number of alternations between aggression and friendliness and between anger and grief. Even the circle dance around the ceremonial remains of the deceased has a gentle clockwise motion symbolized by the whispered *t t t t* followed by a more

violent counterclockwise motion for which the symbol is the loud
whistle.

On the women's side a parallel form of greeting, but with a minimum of ritual, is going on at the same time. The greetings among the
women are, in many respects, a counterpoint to the greetings among
the men. I have already mentioned how the women are made to
tumble into the house so that their entrance is as ludicrous as the
entrance of the men is somber. However, having picked herself up
and having straightened out her belongings, each woman is greeted
in a file by the host women. Like the men, the women are grouped by
maloca and in order of their husbands' age seniority. Having been
greeted with the conventional handshake, the group of hostesses and
the group of guests face each other and shout angrily at one another;
these shouts are not accusations or recriminations, but expressions
of anger at the enemy who has killed the deceased. Two women who
have been facing one another in postures of anger suddenly fall to
a squatting position, each with an arm around the other's shoulder,
drop their heads, and weep. Women who are nursing babies seem

Fig. 12. Angry declamation at mourning ceremony.

able to carry through what are abrupt and violent gestures of mourning without disturbing the infant's feeding. In the midst of what seems to be an uncontrolled paroxysm of grief the mother adjusts her infant to a more comfortable position. The infants seem undisturbed. The women are wandering mourners, seeking out new partners with whom they exchange shouts until, with their voices hoarse and cracked, they crouch down together and weep.

FORMAL RITUALISTIC ELEMENTS

The dramatization of emotion is, I believe, the central theme of the *óyne*, as it is, indeed, the central theme of all Cubeo ceremonials. In the *óyne*, the dramatization of emotion is conducted most directly in the sexual interplay between men and women and in the variety of enactments, as in a pageant, of scenes of emotional significance. Dramatization is never the most direct evocation of emotion; it occurs only in the *óyne*, which of all Cubeo ceremonials demands the fullest emotional orchestration. In other ceremonies emotionality is either generalized, in the sense that one acquires a special lift from drink, narcotics, and dance, or else the emotional range is more limited, as in the ancestral cult initiation. The *óyne* provides for many modes of emotional stimulation. A secondary mode is physiological stimulation, which relies upon chicha, coca, tobacco, and *mihí*. On physiological stimulation I have only to add the note that in the *óyne* indulgence is greater and the state of frenzied excitement is sought quickly.

Chicha consumption at the *óyne* is prodigious. Months of labor go to the preparation of manioc mash, which is then allowed to ferment fully in combination with sugar cane extract. Men eat little or nothing during the three days of the *óyne*. They are nourished on chicha and blunt their hunger and fatigue with coca. The *Hehénewa* also bought *aguardiente* for guests who could not get drunk on chicha quickly enough.

The traditional Cubeo attitude toward drink and intoxication is religious, not secular. They do not drink for mere pleasure or to overcome anxiety. Secular drinking is for them distasteful, and it is rare to see an Indian drunk except at a ceremony. In the white settlement of Mitú it is the white man who is drunk and the sober Indian who watches him with amazement. Intoxication is a sacred state. In the *unkúndye*, drinking leads from passivity to quarreling. In the *óyne* the emotions unleashed by intoxication are channeled more directly.

Drinking at the *óyne* is disciplined and follows the emotional gradient of the ceremony. On the first day, which is intramural, the mood is somber and little chicha is taken. On the second day, when guests arrive and the mood is anger-grief, the drinking is still slow.

Guests receive the welcome offering of chicha after their third entrance into the maloca and thereafter they drink during all intervals between dances. Formal drinking begins two hours before sundown. The moment is signaled when the hosts brings in *mihí*, the symbol of intoxication. Only the older men take the potion. Thereafter all drinkers are free to grow excited. The elders remain restrained, however, since it is their role to license the excitement of others. They describe their own intoxication as an inner state. They feel a change in mood, they see color visions, but they do not overstep to overt excitement. That is the role assigned to the younger men.

The rate of drinking and the shift in mood gains momentum in the course of the interplay with the women. Women drink as much as men, but do not take *mihí* and do not get drunk. Their excitement is imparted to them by the men. Thus, the men drink to initiate excitement; the women drink so that they may react. When the men are not among them the women sit passively among their young, the dogs, and their household goods.

Mihí has magical power which the bearers portray dramatically. They pretend to stagger under its weight because *mihí* has power to fell a man. The people I asked did not know, however, why the bearer of *mihí* pranced with his torso bent forward and his knees kicked up high. The bearers whisper *he he he* and then whistle. These are the sounds of spirits and they are the same as the sounds made by the guests when they circle the ceremonial remains of the deceased. A bundle of *mihí* vines is laid with the ceremonial remains during this dance. From a roof beam at the exact center of the house, where it overlooks equally the male half and the female half, hangs a vulture figure. The body is an ear of corn, the head is carved of wood, and the spreading wings and tail feathers are made of old basket fragments. The bird hangs like a mobile. It is said to be "drunk" on *mihí,* and it presides over the *óyne* to give the proper spirit of intoxication. The vulture of intoxication is the patron, so to speak, of the *óyne.*[9] Mobiles of other birds are also hung about the house, as are painted images of fish. I did not learn the significance of these.

---

[9] The vulture is thought of here not so much in the sense of its being a carrion eater, but for its quality of soaring. Compare *kavá* (vulture) with *kaváno* sky).

The first phase of the *óyne* concludes on the morning of the fourth day. Despite the drinking and the exhaustion of frenzied dancing the departures are as formal as the arrivals. The hosts form their line at the doorway and the guests pass along, exchanging final expressions of grief. Men embrace one another and weep. Women weep once more with women. Before he leaves the house, each man presents the host with the masks he has brought, including all its ornaments. Among the *Hehénewa* the men mimicked the lamentations of the guests after the last one had left, and all laughed.

One month later a concluding and simpler ceremony is held. On the first evening the masks dance again and the *Xudjíko* is sounded. At dawn the masks and their ornaments, as well as all the ceremonial paraphernalia made specifically for the *óyne* including the trumpets, are burned in a great fire on the front plaza. Not all the masks are destroyed, because the children are privileged to reclaim any they wish from the flames. The burning puts an end to the jurisdiction over the house of the spirit representations and ófficially concludes the mourning.

That evening the final dance is held. The house has now been restored to a normal ceremonial state, and the dances of this evening include men and women. They dance the ordinary dances of the drinking parties and conclude with a great circle dance within the house that includes all men, women, and youngsters. This dance is known as *kompaíndüwü* (going home). The dance forms on the plaza and circles about a fire in the center of the house, moving clockwise and then reversing. The men are fully ornamented and carry stamping tubes; a woman dances between two men. They sing a refrain, *kenadjú marié kenadjú pimári*. Periodically a woman dancer screams loudly in a high-pitched voice, breaking in upon the somber melody. As this dance continues through the night, couples break away and leave for the brush behind the house. They copulate, return to the dance, and seek new sexual partners. At this point the dance has become chaotic. No overt sexuality, however, occurs within the house. These events conclude the social aspects of the *óyne*, and the following morning, after the guests have begun to depart, is devoted to dealing with the spirits of the dead. There are two events, the first of which I was regrettably barred from observing. This may have been the endocannibalism that Wallace reported in 1853 [10] and that

---

[10] "The Tarianas and Tucanos and some other tribes, about a month after the funeral, disenter the corpse, which is then much decomposed, and put it in a great pan, or oven, over the fire, till all the volatile parts are driven off with a most horrible odor, leaving only a black carbonaceous mass, which is pounded into a

Koch-Grünberg had described to him in 1903 (1909, II, 152). I observed the *Hehénewa* headman, with the older men of the sib around him, pounding bones in a mortar and adding the substance to an urn of chicha. When they saw me they angrily ordered me away. Later, informants denied knowledge of what they may have been doing. Koch-Grünberg, however, was told by the *Hehénewa* headman that the limb bones of someone who had died some 15 years earlier were cooked for about a month, reduced to ash, and then added to a special corn chicha which was then taken by all old men and women and by parents of more than three children. I did not observe the drinking of this chicha, nor did I hear of the custom during my stay among the *Bahúkiwa*.

Finally, the younger men of the sib burn dry capsicum peppers in the maloca to drive away the ghost of the recently deceased. Thereafter, the deceased is to be forgotten and his name not mentioned for at least another generation.

MASK REPRESENTATIONS IN THE *ÓYNE*

Anthropomorphic Beings or Demons

1. *Makuko*	(K-G)[a]	A bearded dwarf, represented by husband and wife. They lure hunters from their game and pantomime shooting a bark-cloth monkey with a blowgun.
2. *Kohako*	(K-G)	Husband and wife giants who carry clubs and strike down hunters with them.
3. *Hailako*	(K-G)	A giant who carries two heavy clubs, one in each hand.
4. *Palutxiko*	(K-G)	A giant.
5. *Anauako*	(K-G)	A giant.
6. *Abúhuwa*	(K-G;IG)[b]	Forest demons.
7. *Hokoaboxoko*	(K-G)	Giant tree demons.

[a] Reported by Koch-Grünberg.
[b] Personal observations by the author.

---

fine powder and mixed in several large conches (vats made of hollow trees) of caxiri; this is drunk by the assembled company till all is finished; they believe that thus the virtues of the deceased will be transmitted to the drinkers" (Wallace, 1870, p. 498).

Endocannibalism has also been reported by Coudreau, who has observed that the Tucanos and Tarianas no longer follow this practice, which he attributed only to the Cubeo. "Ce ne sont plus aujourd'hui les Tarianas et les Tucanos qui boivent la cendre de leurs morts, comme le disait Wallace. Ce sont les seuls Cobbêos. Les gens de cette peuplade enterrent leurs morts; puis, quand les chairs sont pourries, ils lavent les os, les dessèchent, les brûlent, les pilent et, dans les dabucuris, mêlent cette poudre, précieusement conservée, au cachiri avec lequel ils boivent, en s'enrivant, les cendres des leurs ancêtres dont ils s'incorporent ainsi toute l'energie. Cette étrange boisson leur procure des délices extatiques ou furieux" (Coudreau, 1886–87, II, 173).

8. *Valuliaboxoko* (K-G) A giant demon, killer of fish, who is actually the carara bird, a great devourer of fish.

Birds

9. *Murukutuko* The owl. Has a mask covering only the head.
   (*pupuli*) and (K-G) Holds a torch in one hand and a stick in the
10. *Hauhabo* (K-G) other and jumps up and down in imitation of the owl jumping from branch to branch. Regarded as an evil devourer of people.
11. *Kavá* (K-G;IG) The carrion vulture.
12. *Miavi* (K-G;IG) The eagle. The mask has a white facepiece with an hourglass frame surmounting it.
13. *Kolapilabo* (K-G) A small prey bird.
14. *Kulika* (K-G) A bird of the parrot family.
15. *Vekó* (K-G;IG) A bird of the parrot family.
16. *Kobauako* (K-G) A bird of the parrot family.
17. *Olo mo oko* (K-G) The aracua.
18. *Umanami* (K-G) The tem tem (*Tachyphonus*).
19. *Yoloueua* (K-G) Swallows.
20. *Pinikabokü* (IG) A small white bird.

Fish

21. *Borikakü* (K-G;IG) The aracú.
22. *Mávayo* (K-G;IG) The red-mouthed aracú.
23. *Avali* (K-G) A small aracú.
24. *Pyénkü* (IG) A small black fish.
25. *Ihiabolü* (K-G;IG) A small fish.
26. *Haima* (K-G) The yaudia.
27. *Batakahaima* (K-G) The black yaudia.
28. *Auaholabo* (K-G) The colored aracú.
29. *Iyudyo* (K-G) A small aracú.
30. *Emiwa* (IG) Minnows.

Insects

31. *Keratamówa* (K-G;IG) Dung beetles.
32. *Tatárako* (K-G;IG) The butterfly.
33. *Maka* (K-G) A bird-catching spider.
34. *Peká penkünkü* (IG) Beetle larvae.
35. *Budyauobo* (K-G) The leaf bug.
36. *Bobobo* (K-G) The house spider.
37. *Uménahonkü* (K-G;IG) The dragonfly.
38. *Malakaibo* (K-G) A large night butterfly.
39. *Bobako* (K-G) A small night swarmer.
40. *Kumatidiauo* (K-G) A caterpillar.
41. *Tadyiva pikoa* (K-G) A caterpillar.
42. *Kohidiveko* (IG) The cockroach.
43. *Himáuwa* (IG) Caterpillars.
44. *Utáwe* (K-G) The firefly.
45. *Henohenóri* (IG) The bee.
46. *Utcikü* (K-G;IG) The wasp.
47. *Kubuva* (K-G) Sand flies.

Mammals

48. *Yaví*   (K-G;IG)   The jaguar.
49. *Nyamáko*   (K-G;IG)   The deer.
50. *U*   (K-G;IG)   The sloth.
51. *Pamúrü*   (IG)   The armadillo.
52. *Kapáro*   (IG)   The monkey.
53. *Hwani*   (IG)   The peccary.

Reptiles and Amphibians

54. *Ala*   (K-G)   The yararaca snake.
55. *Ba ko ko ko*   (K-G)   A small frog.
56. *Umáua*   (IG)   Frogs.
57. *Pampámibo*   (IG)   Frogs (another variety).
58. *Pwénwa*   (IG)   Small frogs.
59. *Xiábü*   (IG)   The alligator.

Unidentified

60. *Pikuré*   (IG)
61. *Tonkákü*   (IG)
62. *Imihikü*   (IG)

11

Religion

The religion of the Cubeo has no gods and therefore no worship. Anthropomorphic beings are plentiful in the form of forest monsters, fish, beasts, birds, insects, not to mention the *Bekŭpwänwa* and *Kúwai* the transformer. But the Cubeo do not approach these beings and spirits in a supplicatory mood. They establish, rather, a mode of communication, of intercourse, with them, in the course of which specific results, the warding off of dangers, and the positive benefits of body growth and sib growth are expected to follow. Religious attitude must almost inevitably be modeled upon the experiences of relations among people. In Cubeo social life, as we have seen, one neither commands nor submits. People enter willingly into a relationship that will accomplish a specific end. A social relationship among the Cubeo, as we have repeatedly noted, demands a specific atmosphere of feelings, sentiments, emotions. To the Cubeo nothing of consequence can result from an act divorced from its proper mood. In precisely the same way, the Cubeo seek to establish a relationship with a supernatural being.

The Ancients, to recapitulate what has already been described in another context, join the people in drinking, dancing, smoking, and chewing coca. They come to whip the boys and men to make them grow and to give them potency and force in the initiation rites. They are bathed with in growth "magic." As *Xudjiko* and *Xudjikü* they come to mourn for the sib dead. In the mourning ceremony they are invoked by name only and do not appear. The invocation chant, however, does not compel them to make the sib child grow. The Cubeo think it absurd to suggest that the *Bekůpwänwa* might need any urging to do for the sib what needs to be done and what they are capable of doing. It is impossible for a Cubeo to say that the *Bekůpwänwa* have withheld a benefit or that they can be made to do more under some circumstances and less under others. What is required — and the Cubeo do not say that the *Bekůpwänwa* have set requirements — is that a proper mode of social intercourse be established and maintained. The spirit and the manner of social intercourse must be correct, however, although not letter perfect. The spirit in which the social intercourse is carried out is more important than the ritual act. Many Cubeo ceremonies are abridged because, as they explain, the mood was wrong. Guests who should have come did not, and in the feeling of disappointment the ceremony is cut short. An error in a chant, in a dance, in a song, or in a ritual sequence is of no importance. Failure to conform to the rules of social intercourse with the supernatural beings, such as the Ancients, may have serious consequences only if the neglect is deliberate. In any case, *Bekůpwänwa* do not punish. They only withhold. In the case of the boy who ran away from his whipping at the hands of the *Bekůpwänwa*, my informants assured me that he would not be deprived of a year's growth. Since they, the elders, were prepared to forgive the youngster his uncontrollable timorousness on this occasion, the Ancients, they knew, would do likewise.

The Ancients are not referred to as "spirits." The term for spirit is *dekóků* and has, for the Cubeo, a more alien connotation than the term *Bekůpwänwa*. The Ancients or the ancestors are referred to by name so that association with them conveys directness and immediacy. I believe that it is for the sake of maintaining a sense of immediacy and of directness with the *Bekůpwänwa* that the Cubeo do not place them in some ancestral abode in some other world. The Ancients, to be sure, are known to have been buried in the ancestral rocks from which they emerged, at the rapids of Uaracapurí and Yuruparí. But the burial place is not their place of abode. Strictly speaking they have no place of abode. The flutes and trumpets that embody them reside in a *caño* near the main stream of the sib. The Cubeo do not, however, claim that these sacred crypts are the residences of the Ancients. The ordinary dead, on the other hand, do have an abode. The point of distinction for the Cubeo is that the ordinary dead have been sent away and are no longer welcome, whereas the Ancients, who are not spirits of the dead in the ordinary sense, are always welcome.

Apart from the Ancients there is *Kúwai*, who has been referred to here as a culture hero and as a transformer. He is not, as Koch-Grünberg called him, a "god." The Cubeo and the Arawakan tribes in the area share *Kúwai*. Among the Cubeo he is a mythical being who has long since withdrawn from any relationship with people by taking up a specific abode upon the high savannah. There are no rites involving *Kúwai* today, nor are there traditions that refer to any sacred relationship between the people and *Kúwai* in the past. *Kúwai* taught the Cubeo all their useful arts — fishing, cultivation, the making of all major implements. He instructed them in copulation. Illustrative of Cubeo attitudes toward the sexes is *Kúwai*'s constant difficulties with women — all human — and, by contrast, his orderly relations with Cubeo men. It was, as the legend narrates, his disappointments and frustrations in dealing with Cubeo women that led *Kúwai* to take up what is virtually a voluntary exile. *Kúwai* as transformer altered terrain features and created some smaller rivers. His role as creator is a limited one.

Some Indians did speak of a god whom they called *himénihinkü* (my little soul). This god lives in the sky (*kaváno*) in a house with his wife. He accepts good people into his house and puts bad people in a house for dogs. There is *Uménahonkü*, an Ancient, but *himénihinkü* is evidently a Christian doctrine that has been bady understood by the Indians of the Cuduiarí, whose relations with missionaries have been very marginal at best. Those Indians who had missionary contact attributed *himénihinkü* to Christian teaching and rejected the doctrine as alien to them. They scoffed, particularly at his role as a creator of the world and of man. A fundamental feature of Cubeo religious thought is its reluctance to grant broad and extraordinary powers to any being. I shall return to this point.

Earlier writers on the Indians of the Vaupés have without exception reported "gods," "demons," or a "great spirit" called *Yurupari*. In simple fact there is no *Yurupari*. The term is jargon from the trade language of the Amazon based heavily upon Tupían and is used indiscriminately by the Indians to refer to anything that is sacred and taboo. In the Northwest Amazon region the sacred trumpets and flutes receive the designation of *yurupari* most commonly. But the people will put off any prying into their religion with *yurupari*. I never heard the *Bahúkiwa* refer to *yurupari* except when talking to some white man whose questions they did not regard seriously.

The ancestor beings represent for the Cubeo the only true beneficent "supernaturals" with whom they have relations. But we note that they are not credited with extraordinary powers. They do not move against other powers or forces. That is to say, the Cubeo know that growth, potency, and fertility are part of the ordinary scheme of things and that there is no force conspiring against such ordinary developments. The *Beküpwänwa* are not thought of as jealous, sensitive, threatening, or likely to take offense. It is noteworthy, too, that the emphasis in growth is upon the individual far more than it is upon the more abstract concept of sib. The Ancients will not guard the people against any unexpected dangers. To guard against menace, whether general or specific, there are specific measures that the sibmen themselves must take.

All other anthropomorphic beings in the Cubeo cosmos are either menacing, mischievous, or harmless. Menace from supernaturals, however, is relatively moderate, not to be minimized but lacking in dread. The only menace that truly frightens the Cubeo is that which they attribute to persons.

The *abúhuwa* are cannibalistic forest monsters, the bogy men of the children. At the mourning ceremonies they are made to appear grotesque and absurd and hence harmless. There are many stories of human encounters with *abúhuwa* as ogres. In most, the *abúhuwa* are overcome. They can be outwitted, caught, and killed.

The story is told of an old woman alone in the maloca with two young children. *Abúhuwa* entered the house and the children were able to escape by climbing up to the house beams. But the old woman was caught. An *abúhukü* rolled her between his palms until she became all soft and he sucked her out from the top of the head in the way a Cubeo child eats a banana. He hung her skin over the branch of a tree. When the others of the maloca returned they saw an *abúhuwa* family within. They set capsicum afire at the door of the house and as the *abúhuwa* sought to escape its acrid smoke, that is noxious to all unwanted spirits, they struck them down with clubs and killed them all.

Another tale is told of a hunter who, in the woods at night, was seized by the throat from behind. It was an *abúhukü*. He struggled with it and killed it with a knife. In the morning he went to see it and it had taken the form of a sloth. *Abúhuwa*, it is said, are all very hairy. Their armpit hair makes a very potent sorcery "poison." Any man who is bold enough may seize an *abúhukü* and tear his armpit hair. It is said that the ogre can be seized only when the moon is in eclipse or is red and low in the sky. The hair must be from the left armpit and can be cut only with a corn husk. It is cooked until reduced to ash, and then is mixed with water and allowed to dry to a paste in the sun. The paste is kept in a small gourd dish sealed with beeswax. When enemy *Maúnwa* attack, the paste is thrown among them, causing them to fall stupefied to the ground. It is the shaman, however, who can contend with these orgres most successfully. The *abúhuwa* are frightening to behold, the Indians say, because they have two faces, one in front and one in back. Some have sticky bodies and when they embrace an unwary victim he can no longer escape. A mother and child are favorite targets of these *abúhuwa*. The mother is killed and the child is reared as one of them. It in turn then seizes people. Female *abúhuwa* have a preference for men and the *abúhukü* tries to catch a woman.

Nyáma abúhuko (Deer ogre) is a black ogress, an evil spirit of the deer, who catches children wandering about alone. She tosses them into the air so as to break their necks and then and there eats them.

Another ogre is *Opómbibekü*, a dwarf with an enormous penis, who flies about at night, seizes little boys, and eats them.

Kómi is also an ogre, one who emerged with the first people. Eventually people caught him and burned him alive. They then noticed that whatever came near his ashes died. Sorcerers still go to fetch his ashes for their "poisons."

Snakes, the boa and anaconda in particular, are dangerous to women. The land boa rapes women in their manioc gardens so that they give birth to snakes. The water anaconda attacks menstruating women who come to the river. A menstruant is endangered by land snakes, too, but can ward them off by painting with genipa. Nothing, however, will protect her in the water. The water anaconda is a threat to a newborn child and to its father as well. This menace, however, is easily counteracted by the simple magical techniques of the old men. The dangerous anaconda is the white anaconda and not the ancestral black anaconda, which is regarded as friendly "because he knows his people." He is not venerated and is not the object of ritual although he is represented in petroglyphs on the Cuduiarí. In the old days, I was told, he was kept as a household pet but for sentimental reasons only.

The river is also the home of the *mwápwänwa* (fish people), who are anthropomorphic spirits. They are small people who live in a house beneath the river and move about at night, sometimes brushing moistly against travelers and frightening them but otherwise harmless.

The fish, who are of great importance in Cubeo ceremonials, not only in the *óyne* but in their own fish dances and fish songs by which the Cubeo celebrate great catches, are a "people." They, too, live in a house and have a chief, *Munyúnbeküku* (Old man *munyún*), a mythical fish with a mouth that has the lower jaw of the puño and an upper jaw shaped like the beak of a parrot. Should a menstruant enter a canoe he will break it to bits. The Cubeo do not say that their fish ceremenials are for the purpose of promoting success in fishing. Their view rather is that when they are happy with a catch of fish they enjoy dancing with them. Increase magic may underlie the Cubeo relationship with fish. But if it does they either no longer recognize the instrumental motive or else they refuse to acknowledge it.

As with the *Bekúpwänwa*, the Cubeo relationship with the animal world is largely one of establishing proper social relationships. In such relationships compulsion is out of place. In the animist world view of the Cubeo the entire animal world is communicant with the world of man. Some relationships, as has been noted, are dangerous, and therefore stand out in a special category. Among the dangerous relationships is that of the jaguar. Since the jaguar is identified with the shaman, it is more suitably discussed under the heading of shamanism. There are birds, such as a parrot called *bauvéko* and marúku monkeys, who are feared because they are foretellers of misfortune. For the rest, and with the exceptions noted previously, the relationship between man and the animal world is casual and friendly. On the river, as we have already observed, the Indians address birds and fish by name. Their intense interest in domesticating animals of almost every variety as household pets must also be considered as part of the effort at communication of a concrete form.

The birds, *míwa*, are friendly spirits. They emerged, it is said, from Uaracapurí with the Ancients and were originally in human form. The birds are the planters of fruits and berries and are their guardian spirits. They are appropriately at the same time the guardian spirits of intoxication, a bird with a corn-cob body and wings of a manioc tray fragment presiding in that capacity over the *óyne*.

The luminary *avyá*, who is both sun and moon, is a more distant anthropomorphic spirit.[1] The Cubeo interest is in the moon, the li-

---

[1] The doctrine of *avyá* as both sun and moon is mythological only. It does not mean that the Cubeo do not distinguish clearly between these two bodies. *Avyá* refers to the anthropomorphic being whose activities are actually in moon form; it refers also to direction. East is called by the Cubeo *avyádaino* (*avyá* [the sun] is coming). West correspondingly is expressed as "*avyá* is going." To express time, however, the sun is referred to by the particular name of *hanáwükakü*, an anthropomorphic form that has, however, no anthropomorphic connotation to my knowledge. *Hanáwü* refers to time in the abstract, while *hanáwü koríka* (sun in the center) means "midday." All specific times are given by describing the position of the sun in the sky. The word for "day" or "daylight" is *hánan* and is apparently based upon the verb root *ha* (to see). The Cubeo disclaim any anthro-

bidinous nocturnal hunter, and not in the sun. The sun, they say, is merely the moon giving heat and light during the day, "when people need it." As sun, *avyá* lacks anthropomorphic character. The interest of the Cubeo in the moon rather than in the sun seems related to their concept of nightfall as the sacred time. Almost all ceremonies are night ceremonies, whereas daylight is the time for work. Apart from his erotic role the moon is a hunter with a stone-tipped spear (*temúdjo*). Bits of the blade chip off which the finder can use as potent sorcery magic, killing his victim by poisoning. The moon is also an opener of graves of those who eat a seed the Cubeo call *óthai* and which is used as fish bait. The Cubeo tell the story of the man who hoped to steal the lamp of the moon (*djuwaíbo*) by covering it with a pottery dish. Some light showed and *avyá* secured the lamp to the back of his neck and flew off.

When there is an eclipse of the moon, the Cubeo say that the spirits of the dead are being dispersed. They also fear that the moon is dying. As the moon reddens I have witnessed them running about shouting to one another in genuine terror that the moon is dying. They believe that those who live in the direction from which the eclipse shadow is moving will die. The moon sickens of the same sorcery afflictions that beset humans, although they do not believe that one of their medicine men has the power to sicken the moon.

HUMAN SPIRITS

The soul is called *umé*, which also means "breath" and "breeze." [2] As a spirit entity the soul is referred to as *umémakü* (or *umémako*). The soul leaves the body during dreams, returning as the dreamer awakes. The *Bahúkiwa*, at least those with whom I discussed the subject, did not believe that the *umé* might fail to return and so cause death. Death and illness result, they insisted, from something entering the body. At death, the *umé* leaves the body permanently, journeying after a suitable interval to a nearby river, dwelling of the spirits. After death the *umé* has human form. It can be heard talking and can be seen by the shaman. The spirits of people who have been adulterers, uncooperative, breakers of the bonds of ritual friendship, or in any other way markedly unsocial assume an animal

---

pomorphic beliefs about the sun. Linguistic evidence suggests also that the concept of sun and of time is built around the notion of visibility. Thus, direction, having nothing to do with visibility, is based on the *avyá* form.

[2] Koch-Grünberg (1915–16) also noted *uméde* (pulse) and *uménde* (heart). I believe that the connotation of the term is revealed by the verb *umédani*, which means "to get up," "to rise."

form. "Since they did not care for people," the Cubeo say, "they cannot live among the souls of people after death." Those who have committed incest or have eaten a forbidden fish called *namúri* have souls after death in the form of the *bauvéko*, a bird that is feared greatly.

The ghost is called *dekókü* (dream man) or *pwănkü dekókü* (dream man person).[3] The distinction between *umé* and *dekókü* is not precise. That is, when the Cubeo speak of the death of a person they will say that the *umé* leaves and the souls take on human form, and add that the *umé* may return to the house and disturb people. Having begun to speak of *umé*, they follow it into its ghostly phase. On the other hand, it is when the narration begins with the spirits of the dead that they will use the term *dekókü*.

The Cubeo have no dread of the spirits of the dead. The spirits depart and live their own life under their own headman. Beliefs on the nature of the afterlife are not uniform among the Cubeo, however. The most common view is that the spirits of the dead of the same phratry live together, all in one great phratry house under a headman. Women, however, occupy a vague place in the afterlife, wives staying with their husbands. The women spirits, however, lack their full economic function, since in the afterlife spirits live by hunting and gathering but not by farming. The dead do constitute a nuisance. Shortly after death the ghost returns to the house hoping to entice a sibmate to go with him, but he is easily dispatched by burning capsicum. The grave, in the house, is no hallowed place, and shortly after the earth has been packed in place the children play over it. When people encounter a place on the river where the spirits of the dead can be heard they do not hurry on but pause to listen. The spirits of the dead will never be encountered at high noon, the zenith, so to speak, of the secular part of the day. The spirits of the dead hunt only at night. They eat butterflies, grubs, and all snakes including the founding anaconda. Significantly, they do not drink chicha. The Cubeo do not say why, but it would seem that they have visualized an afterlife that is lacking in the essences of life, that is to say, the ingredients that the Cubeo associate with vital intensity. The spirits of the dead also lack manioc. There is some debate among the Indians as to whether the dead live in a house; they lack ceremonial life and sib autonomy. Literally, then, the Cubeo visualize a shadow existence after death.

The spirits of the dead remain bound to the phratric system. All

---

[3] *Dekó* is the stem in the verb "to cause to disappear."

the dead of the sibs of a river are joined together. While the individual spirit has his sib identity, the sibs do not exist in the afterlife as social entities. The *habókü* of the dead is *Mavitcikori*, grandson of *Djurédo*, an Ancient of the *Órobawa* and of other high-ranking sibs such as the *Hehénewa*, who was the first headman at Uaracapurí. However, the Cubeo have no great interest in speculating about the life of the spirits of the dead, since, except for the Ancients, they have no formal relationship with them. With the dead, the point is to break the bonds, and for this reason alone Cubeo speculation about the spirits of the dead is at best a moderate one. I have already related the story of the woman who, having died and been buried, returned to her husband and pleaded with him to take her back. It is said that if the husband had accepted her she would really have come to life, but that because he drove her away people who die remain dead.

In Freudian theory, fear of the dead is a projection of ambivalent feelings toward the living. From this point of view one would have to assume, most incorrectly, that the Cubeo are markedly lacking in the ambivalences of love and hate. The Cubeo attitude of neutrality toward the spirits of the dead is due rather to the fact that they attribute almost all misfortune to active human agency. If one is to look for evidences of ambivalence in Cubeo feelings toward kin the proper source is in the imputation of sorcery and not in the attitudes toward ghosts.

THE CONCEPT OF POWER

An important concern of all instrumental, as distinct from ethical, religions is power, the grasp of power and its control and manipulation. Power, to be sure, is valued for its direct application to common human interests in food, safety, and the overcoming of enemies, to name but a few, but it would be rash to underestimate the sheer attractiveness of power acquired and power used for its own sake. In Cubeo religious thought, too, power is both instrumental and compelling in its own right. In keeping with the moderate role of power in social and political life, however, the power theme in religion is a muted one. The Cubeo do not attribute to anyone, man or supernatural being, grandiose powers. If anything, the Cubeo are rather conscious of the limitations of power. We have seen this in how little power they attribute to the Ancients. *Kúwai* is a more telling illustration of the point, for this being ordinarily fails when he is truly manipulating power, while his successes are in the ordinary relations of teaching people useful things. In the Cubeo allocation of moderate powers among men and supernatural beings, men get their fair share, so to speak.

The native term for power is *parié*, a term that applies to the strength and vigor of a warrior, the magical potency of the ancestor flutes and trumpets, the awesome fierceness of the jaguar, as well as to the clearly magical powers of the shaman or of the layman who has learned how to cure and to practice sorcery. The term simply means "able" and is the verb in the common expression "I can do it." Thus, the distinction we might draw between natural and supernatural powers is not one that is recognized by the Cubeo.

The shaman is the principal holder of *parié*. He may be known as *pariékokü* (man of power) or as *yaví* (jaguar). By either term the Cubeo conjure up the image of power. As *pariékokü* it is power in a neutral sense; as *yaví* it is power in the aspect of dread. Every *yaví* is a *pariékokü* but not every *pariékokü* is a *yaví*. The *yaví* is the supreme shaman, the one who can take the form of a jaguar, who consorts with jaguars, who maintains the jaguar as a dog. The *pariékokü* is one who has learned how to cure as well as to kill but, not being a jaguar, is a second-class practitioner. Every sib has its *pariékokü*, but *yavís* are scarce. To distinguish between the *yaví* and the *pariékokü*, the Cubeo say of the former *urána pariékokü*, *urána* meaning "big." It is because of this Cubeo usage that I have thought it advisable to discuss shamanism under the heading of "power."

The power of the shaman is called *parúkü*, a noun form with the connotation of a substance. When a shaman has accomplished an exceptional act it is his *parúkü*, it is said, that enabled him to do it. The great shamans control the weather, for the most part unpleasantly. They bring storms, hail, fog, strong winds. They can lower the depths of a river as great as the Vaupés. When the river bottom of the smaller Cuduiarí is exposed, however, the attribution is to natural causes. The play of the shaman with weather and the river level is only a demonstration of his power and has no sinister motive. Shamanistic power also includes the control of tutelary spirits. Generally, a shaman controls a number of insect spirits who do his bidding, in a minor capacity, however, as scouts and as messengers. A shaman on the Cuduiarí once found a little girl who had blundered into the forest and become lost. He claimed he had sent an insect to look for her.

Another demonstration of shamanistic power is in the battles the shamans wage against one another. A *yaví*, I was told, has a different kind of *umé*, one that he can send to attack the *umé* of another. An injured *umé* sickens and dies and so does its owner. The people I spoke to did not believe that an ordinary person could be attacked through his *umé*. As a result of these shamanistic battles some strong *yavís* emerge with extraordinary reputations for power and aggressiveness. The *yavi* is the single truly aggressive figure among the Cubeo. The ordinary *pariékokü* is not. The fact of being called "jaguar" puts the shaman beyond the human pale and allows him scope for unbridled ferocity. The benevolent acts of the *yaví*, his skill as a curer, his ability to find things, and inexplicably his ability to ripen fruits — the subject of ancestral rites — weigh relatively little against his reputation as a "killer."

The relationship between the *yaví* and the jaguar never became fully clear to me, perhaps because my information came only from laymen. No *yaví* was willing to talk to me about his work. Some informants said flatly that every jaguar was a *yaví* or the dog of a *yaví*, or a jaguar into which a *yaví*'s soul had entered. When a *yaví* dies his ghost spirit (*dekókü*) becomes a jaguar. According to this view, the jaguar is feared because he is not an animal but a fiercely predatory man. Other informants explained that there are both ordinary jaguars and jaguars who are *yavís*. Both views agreed on the point that the fierceness of the jaguar is of human origin. Those who believed in ordinary jaguars said those were the kind that might run from a man. The *yaví* is ordinarily in human form and assumes the jaguar form by putting on a jaguar skin. One man said that it is not the man inside but the jaguar skin that eats the victim. There is also the view that it is the *umé* of the *yaví* that assumes a jaguar form and prowls about at night devouring people. One *yaví*, it is said, had his daughter pick the bits of human flesh from his teeth with the fang of a serpent. This young woman would steal from the manioc gardens. The women caught her at it and beat her. The next night the *umé* of her father ate them all. Another feature of the *yavís* is that they are never solitary. They travel in packs and they form a college for the training of recruits.

The story is told of an attack on a house at dawn by *pwányavíwa* (jaguar people) who ate up all the people but one man who had hidden on a rafter. Having eaten, the jaguars took off their skins and went outside to fetch water. The man jumped down and threw all the skins into the fire. When the jaguars returned they rushed to save the burning skins. Those that succeeded left the house as jaguars and those that did not had to leave as humans.

A short time ago a *Bahúkiwa* was clawed by a jaguar. He returned home bleeding from his wounds and died. The people said that the jaguar had eaten the body and had returned only the *umé* for proper burial.

The shaman, whether *yaví* or *pariékokü*, chooses his calling. It does not choose him. There is nothing to suggest that the Cubeo shaman is an unstable personality in the way in which Siberian and many North American Indian shamans are. That is to say, among the Cubeo there is neither trance nor other form of "hysterical" behavior. The *yaví*, who cultivates the reputation of himself as a jaguar, is seemingly an aggressive antisocial type, in marked contrast to the favored Cubeo personality. I heard of only one woman who had become a shaman, and she was a transvestite who made such a nuisance of herself bothering women that the shamans who had prepared her stripped her of her powers. Any youth may become a shaman if he is accepted by the school of shamans, submits to the rigors of the novitiate, and passes an examination. As a young man he will not be a *yaví*. He becomes more malevolent and more dangerous with age. As an elder he finally acquires the power to appear as a jaguar.

The novitiate lasts from one month to five. None of my laymen informants could describe it in detail. The novitiate consists of four sections: abstinences, insertions of magical substances into the body, learning of songs and ritual, and examinations. The abstinences include sexual relations and the eating of fish, broiled game flesh, and, inexplicably, pineapple. One informant said that the novice, who is expected to become thin, lives on nothing but manioc and water.

The insertions described below are the actual sources of the shaman's power: (1) *duvaíyo*, spines, the center stems of the leaf of the *amhókükü* tree, are softened and laid on the underside of the forearms until drawn in; (2) *hokúwe*, another spine, is inserted in the chest and in the palms of the hands; (3) *kenádox*, crystals of quartz, are inserted into the stomach; (4) *kwitóbo*, eagle feathers, are inserted up the nostrils to lodge in the head; (5) *dúpa*, the resin of the *amhókükü* tree, is powdered and inhaled to lodge in the heart;[4] (6) *kúria*, another snuff made from the bark of the *kuriákü* tree, is inhaled and produces a narcotic effect. My notes are not clear on whether *kúria* remains permanently in the body or is taken only for the narcotic effect. The *duvaíyo*, the *hokúwe*, and the *kenádox* later serve the shaman as his own weapons to use against other shamans and to shoot into the body of a victim.

After the insertions have been made, the novice is taught songs

---

[4] Koch-Grünberg's information was that *dúpa* was a white stone, excrement of a great mythical eagle. However, I was given a piece of *dúpa* and it is a resin.

and curing ritual, including handling of the shaman's rattle. The bark of the *kuriákü* tree is then prepared in a narcotic drink, also called *kúria*, which teacher and novice take together while singing the shamanistic songs. The instruction period concludes when shaman and novice sit side by side and under the influence of *kúria* sing and shake the rattle from dawn to sunset. At sunset a storm arises and passes quickly. Novice and teacher then go to the river to bathe; they rinse their mouths with water, return to the house, and eat. The novice spends five more days in isolation, repeating the insertions, and then he returns for his examination. He drinks *kúria* and sings until clouds come up. Then the teacher says to him, "Now you understand." He sings some more until the storm breaks, and the examination is over.

Curing is not a highly developed art. The shamans are the first to acknowledge their limitations. They claim only to be able to remove spines (*duvaíyo*) and crystals (*kenádox*) that another shaman has "shot" into the body. A common term for curing is *duvaitüwü* (to extract spines). The repertoire of sorcery techniques, not to mention the poisons that sorcerers and malevolent people use, go beyond the assured skills of the curer. Thus there are many ailments which the Indians must be prepared to accept as irremediable. Under the circumstances, the anxious despair into which an ailing Indian falls when ill is readily understood. At the same time, the Cubeo are eager to accept medical treatment for any ailment, regarding such treatment as superior to that offered by the *yaví*.

I witnessed only one full curing treatment which, I was assured, was standard. The patient, an old man who died shortly thereafter, was carried from his hammock and seated on a low stool at the front plaza. The medicine man, who was referred to as *yaví*, a respect term only since he was not credited with the power to be a jaguar, held a rattle hung with parakeet feathers. He asked that two black earthenware pots filled with water be brought to him. He then went off to some bushes, from which he gathered leaves and kneaded them into the water. While doing this he secretly dropped a fistful of black spines into each of the two pots. The spines sank to the bottom. He approached the patient, lighted a long ceremonial cigarette, and blew tobacco smoke at all parts of the body where the ailment might lodge. As he blew the smoke he gestured with his right hand in a motion of waving away breath from his mouth. After each blow he stood up and sent what seemed to be breath and smoke off in the direction of the river and in the direction of the forest. The blowing was accompanied by a shaking of the rattle and was followed by chanted phrases I could not hear but which I was told much later were spells to send the illness away. When the blowing was finished the *yaví* poured water from the earthenware pot into the blackened calabash, scooping into it with his left hand the palm spines. He poured the water over the head of the old man, taking pains to get it into the ears, the patient helping by rolling his head. The black spines now lay scattered on the ground near the old man. The *yaví* went about carefully picking them all up. The entire community had gathered to watch the cure and the *yaví* asked them to help gather the spines. The people did not dare touch the spines. Cautiously, without coming too near, they pointed them out. Having gathered all the spines after a very careful search, the *yaví* went off to the brush at the edge of the plaza. He returned rubbing his hands together and making blowing sounds with his mouth in all directions. He poured once more, this time from the second pot, shaking his rattle but uttering no sound. When he had disposed of the second collection of spines the cure was finished. For reasons of magical secrecy no one interpreted to me what was being done. Later, after the old man had died, I was told that the diagnosis had been unfavorable. The quantity of *duvaíyo* spines found was great, indicating a serious ailment, and the shaman thought that the ailment (*ihé*) was probably not curable.

For minor ailments such as headache, hangover, indigestion, mild bronchial disturbances, and the like, blowing with tobacco smoke is all that is required, and many an old man has the knowledge and preparation to do that. For hangover, smoke is blown onto the top of the head; for stomachache onto the abdomen, and for bronchial disturbances onto the chest. Minor ailments of this sort are treated by kinsmen, who receive no payment other than a small gift. Imported *yavís*, however, may demand as much as a machete or a musket for their services.

If curing seems unspectacular, the arts of killing or of causing serious illness are to the Cubeo mind extraordinarily well developed. As the Indians see it, most deaths, illnesses, and misfortunes are products of human malevolence. I doubt that any Cubeo seriously believes in dangerous encounters with *abúhuwa*. All, however, live in dread of sorcery. Fear of the *yaví* as jaguar seems genuine enough. Yet despite tales of packs of human "jaguars" going from house to house devouring people, actual incidents of assault by jaguars against people are rare. The Indians, in fact, say that since the establishment of a police garrison at Mitú on the Vaupés the *yavís* have become cautious and no longer attack people. The *yaví* has his distant method of killing and is feared for that. But even this fear, strong as it is, is as nothing compared with the fear of the nonprofessional sorcerer. The arts of sorcery, which include the arts of poisoning, are known to all men and are believed to be used by all men. What restrains native fear of the *yaví* is the Cubeo conviction already referred to, that mischief must be motivated by understandable feelings of anger, envy, hatred. In theory, the *yaví*, being outside the human pale, may act from motives not understood by the victim. But in fact, the Cubeo find it difficult to envisage this, and they seek to account for how a victim might have stirred up the animosity of the *yaví*. They console themselves with the thought that as long as they avoid trouble with the *yaví* they will be all right. Among the nonprofessionals, on the other hand, they have no difficulty in locating motives.

The *yavís* use esoteric means for killing at a distance. First they send a frightening dream of death as a warning, and follow that with objects such as have already been mentioned which are "shot" into the victim's body from a distance. Some use a method of killing that my informant said was introduced by Indians from the Rio Negro in Venezuela. Known as *dokübéwoinu* (dirt killing), it causes a slow and anguished death, and is used mainly as a retaliation against death from sorcery. The shaman takes from the corpse of the victim parings of nails and bits of foot callous, scurf from behind the ears, a bit of forelock hair, fingernails and toenails, and scrapings from the teeth. All this is mixed with boiled capsicum. When the brew is heated the intended victim suffers stomach cramps. It is brought to a boiling point and allowed to subside and the victim's pain subsides also. Boiling continues for three days. On the third day the medicine man sits over the pot and sings, commanding his victim to eat parts of his own body. The *yaví* accompanies his instructions with gestures. The victim now vomits continually. Then the brew is boiled vigorously and the medicine man does a staggering dance around the pot. His victim staggers and bites his tongue. Now, the spirit of the victim appears over the pot in the form of a butterfly. Caught in the vapors it falls into the pot. The medicine man immediately breaks the pot and the victim falls to his death. He has been made to eat his teeth, his penis, his testicles, and his fingers. What I have described is the short method of killing. The long method lasts ten days, during which time the sorcerer calls on his tutelary spirits, each of which is known as *ihékowakü dekókü* (sickness-bringing spirit). The *umé* of a sorcerer is never human; it takes the form of an insect or of several insects, not to mention the jaguar in the case of a true *yaví*. The insect spirits that arrive to fall into the pot are *tatárako* (butterfly), *utáwe* (firefly), *henohenóri* (bee), and *utcíkü* (wasp).

The common shamanistic form of killing is *dúwai*. The shaman usually kills when the victim is asleep. The death takes place in a dream and such a death is known as *dekóbaiwu* (dream death). There are other forms of professional shamanistic killing. Blowing in the house is one. If the shaman blows his breath and tobacco smoke in the same manner as in curing, but within the house, then someone in the house will sicken and may die. For this reason curing takes place on the plaza. Yet having explained this, my informant added that more important was intent. A shaman could treat someone within the house and his blowing would cause no harm if he did not want it to. Boiling nail cuttings from fingers or toes in a capsicum pepper broth kills by a similar principle but with less attention to painful detail than in the previously described method of killing a sorcerer or poisoner. The shaman prepares this brew deep in the woods where he cannot be seen. He must, however, have been able to obtain the cuttings from his intended victim. Finally, a shaman has a stone bull-roarer. As he whirls it the victim suffers as if struck with a machete.

The Indians claim to use a number of plant poisons which go by the *lingoa geral* term *marakimbára*, and in Tucanoan by the term for "illness," *ihé*. *Turú* is a leaf cultivated as a poison. The leaf is shredded and the fibers made up into a small packet that is dipped into a calabash of chicha until the infusion is strong. If the *turú* is used fresh it kills quickly and if allowed to dry for five days or so it produces only illness, the symptoms of which are diarrhea and excretion of blood. *Turú* is administered at a drinking party shortly after midnight. All in the house are implicated in *turú* poisoning since only the victim must drink the fatal chicha.

Koné nonedwaíye is a cultivated leafy plant similar to *turú* but one that produces a fatty exudation, and is intended to poison by entering the body through the urethra. At a drinking party the poisoner waits for his victim to leave the house to urinate. He then secretly places the substance on the urine. Symptoms of pain in the groin and in the genitals accompanied by a discharge of pus occur within three months and are fatal.

Yapíbü kowaíye (poison for swelling the abdomen) is another cultivated plant from which an infusion is put into chicha or porridge. Symptoms occur after a year and are fatal. For ten days the victim has fever and pain in his limbs. These symptoms subside and return.

When the rains come the abdomen swells. After days of steady rain the swollen abdomen bursts.

Yokaíhye (leaf poison) is reputed to be so poisonous a leaf that it is never touched with the bare hand. The leaf is boiled in water and allowed to dry. Its powder is wrapped in a leafy bag and dipped in any liquid to form an infusion. Some of this liquid spilled on the victim leaves a black spot that quickly disappears. Shortly thereafter the victim dies.

Pothaíye is a berry poison. Its extract is put in chicha or at the end of a stick if it is to be poked up the victim's nose when he is asleep. It causes a slow death by wasting.

Dyóka is a forest plant that kills only children but will sicken adults. A moist packet is allowed to drip over the forehead of the sleeping victim. There is said to be a remedy for this.

There are many other *ihé* products that were not identified to me by name. Some, from the end of a stick, are inserted into the nostrils of a sleeper. People who specialize in this are night wanderers called *parébohe abúhuwa* (very powerful *abúhuwa*). They can see in the dark and are difficult to observe. They lack specific motive for their deeds and may be regarded as male witches. It is these witches who are tortured by having their flesh torn with fishhooks — one tear for each victim — when they are caught.

Another *ihé* product is *pená*, an ash that comes from a secret site

Fig. 13. Petroglyph: *Kómi* playing the ancestral trumpet, Alligator (*Pedíkwa* sib).

at the Isana River. This is so potent that only the smallest amount will kill. The poisoner carries it under the fingernail of his index finger held in place with pitch. He may flick it into a calabash of chicha or drop it on a stool, where it will enter the anus of a victim and kill him within a month. The symptoms are headache, fever, stomach cramps, constipation, and wasting. The following tale accounts for the origin of *pená*. There was a drinking party on the Isana River and the people were dancing with *Bekǔpwänwa*. Suddenly *Kómi*, a short, fat man, flew into the house on two sticks. He caught a little boy and ate him alive and then another. The people became angry and tried to beat *Kómi* to death with clubs. He said to them, "If you shed my blood you will all die quickly. If you kill me in the house you will all die quickly." *Kómi* told them to take him to a creek called *Manánkanihye*, where they were to build a fire and throw him in. They did this and *Kómi* was reduced to ashes. Every bird and insect that flew near the fire fell into it and was burned. When the fire cooled, a little boy took some bone ash, although his father had warned him not to touch it, and dropped some at the canoe landing. An old man passed over it and immediately fell sick, then another. They tried it on animals and saw it was a good "poison." It comes to the Cuduiarí from Arawakan Indians by way of the Querarí.

Curare (*himá*) is known as a powerful poison that may be used only in war and not as a secret potion.

As a far from effective prophylactic against all poisons that may be administered at drinking parties and other group gatherings, the people wear as pendants packets made of a leaf called *hutcǔdü*, that gives a certain amount of protection against sorcery and poisoning.

The attitude of the Cubeo that human malevolence is difficult if not impossible to guard against must be contrasted with their optimism when it comes to dealing with nonhuman spirit beings. Thus, it will be recalled how the spells and "blowing" against the spirits that threaten the newborn infant can be safely entrusted to any sib elder; he need not possess special powers, only the knowledge. The technique of "blowing" has, oddly enough, full magical efficacy in the hands of the layman but is altogether uncertain when used by a medicine man. The point, of course, is that the layman uses simple magic against a manageable nonhuman adversary, whereas the medicine man is called in to pit himself against a formidable human adversary. The human adversary is formidable in Cubeo eyes for two reasons: it acts out of directed passion and it is devious. The nonhuman spirit world, by contrast, is stirred up to a generalized anger.

The river anaconda is angered at newborn children and at menstruating women but not at any particular child or woman. The anger of spirits is, finally, direct. Men are always suspected of conspiring, but nonhuman spirits never do.

Finally, Cubeo religion includes a concept of inanimate power, of power resident in substances, places, and personal states of being. I found no articulate Cubeo theory as to inanimate power. *Parúkü* is clearly personalized power and *parié* is limited in its applicability to objects intimately associated with the Ancients, the flutes and trumpets in particular. But clearly there is power in pigments, feathers, animal bones, plants, the toenail of the armadillo (which the medicine man uses to bring rain), human hair, leg ligatures, and a host of ceremonial objects. With respect to these substances it is clear that we are dealing with assorted beliefs and practices that are both old and widespread throughout the tropical forests of South America, not to mention beliefs that are close to universal.

Genipa (*vei*) is the most potent pigment. It is applied to the hands and feet as gloves and socks and is run coarsely down the back to create a deliberately crude covering rather than a design. The Cubeo are sensitive to neatly executed designs and normally take great pains with body painting, using special sticks as well as die rollers to stamp a design. The crudeness of genipa painting is to differentiate it from body decoration and to emphasize its purely magical character. Men do use genipa paint, but it is primarily a protective pigment for women and children. A menstruating woman will always coat her back with genipa as a safeguard against animal spirits. She will coat her hands with it when handling sacred substances such as coca and tobacco. Applied to infants, genipa wards off influences that might impede growth. Women say only that genipa is good for the skin, but this is typical evasiveness.

Red pigment (*monhá*) has more of a decorative function. It is applied by men and women with great care. Applied in spots it is jaguar magic to protect infants, and applied crudely it is a protection of sorts against the *yaví*.

It was never clear to me whether the love charm *pedídya*, a blossom worn in the hair, was intended to work by magic or merely by suggestion. The most effective love potions, carefully safeguarded by the women even against the prying anthropologist, are secret and magical.

Among ceremonial objects the *behórü* is a rattle lance some three meters long with a hollow chamber at the top in which pebbles have been placed. It can bring rain, one informant said, but it was not used by the Cubeo for that purpose. It is a ceremonial pennant and it accompanies the dead as a walking stick in the afterlife. Dancing staffs are hollowed cylinders that are stamped on the ground to produce a booming sound and are known as the "good sticks." They have a beneficent effect upon a dance, but whether by magic or by association is not clear. The elaborate coronets of feathers (*mápena*) are apparently sacred. They are handled with great care and kept in a special box. While a woman will touch the *mápena* she will not actually handle them. I did not, however, learn the Cubeo theory of their sacredness. Musical instruments may be regarded as quasi-sacred because they invoke birds and insects but are subject to no taboos (except for the ancestral flutes and trumpets). Flageolets embody the butterfly (*tatárako*). They are played by sounding *ta tara ta tara*, the sound, the Cubeo say, of the butterfly. The large eight-reed Panpipe is *kavá* — the vulture whose hovering form the Cubeo visualize as overhanging the mourning ceremony. Woven ligatures (*ñiknáwa*) worn by men below the knee and daubed with a salmon-pink pigment have several magical effects.[5] Worn at drinking parties they both hasten intoxication and promote long life. They flesh out the calf — a symbol of growth and for the Cubeo aesthetically pleasing.

The association between intoxication and long life as expressed in the ligature seems more than casual. For the Cubeo, intensity of feeling is the goal of ceremonial life. Excitement is one form of the sacred for the Cubeo; perhaps it is the most important expression of sacredness they know. This is borne out by the prominence of excitants in Cubeo religion. Tobacco, coca, *mihí*, chicha, capsicum peppers, all have sacred value for the Cubeo. The potency attributed to an excited state cannot be said to be magical nor can it be attributed to spirits. They have a bird as the spirit of intoxication but this bird does not cause intoxication — it presides over it. The religious significance of intensification of feeling is not an instrumental one in any narrow sense of the word. One can only state this as an impression, since the Cubeo did not put it into words. Intensification of feeling stands for them simply as an assertion of life. That is why, it seems to me, the Cubeo can assert that the salmon-colored ligature is for long life and for drunkenness both.

---

[5] Women also used to wear these garters in the days before the petticoat became common.

12

Conclusion: Principles and Patterns

Cubeo is a representative of that group of horticultural societies whose economies serve subsistence needs in the main. Such societies, commonly described as "simple," lack formal structures of social status and of power. Their social structures are built around relatively small segments, and they have religious doctrines and patterns of ceremonial organization that correspond to the primitiveness of social and economic relations.

Such a description does no more, however, than set a most general frame for the discussion of the type. We now know that the term "simple society" does little justice to the variety and intricacy of social relationships and of patterns of thought that even so materially impoverished a society as the Arunta of Australia possesses. Closer to our area, we are aware of the diversity and intricacy of social relationships among such "marginal" cultures as represented by the Ge-speaking Indians of central Brazil. The more closely a people are studied the more evident does it become that even for very broad descriptive purposes the old rubrics — simple or complex, seminomadic, egalitarian, segmentary, subsistence economy, to mention but a few of the more common — are inadequate to identify the true state of affairs. We need to locate in greater analytic depth the social and cultural principles upon which such broadly characterized societies are founded.

The emphasis in anthropology has, indeed, shifted from the descriptive to the analytical account of a society. In the analytical account the concern is with the structure of relationships, that is, with the more fundamental principles and patterns of social behavior. In deriving such principles and patterns we are now ready to go beyond those elementary and very general theoretical doctrines according to which culture is an apparatus for satisfying basic human needs. By now this doctrine impresses us as both obvious and tautological. Cultural anthropology seeks a characterization of distinctive cultural types rather than a generalized characterization of Culture or Society. In its recognition of the distinctiveness of cultures, cultural anthropology is close to history in method and aim. In its search for general principles it is close to sociology. The proper route of cultural anthropology, therefore, lies somewhere between the poles of generality and of uniqueness. Thus, in the summation of principles and of patterns that I am about to present, my aim is to find a level of analytic abstraction that is specific enough to characterize and to identify the Cubeo and yet has enough generality to provide a basis for identifying the broader sociocultural type to which the Cubeo may belong. The justification for a level that is between the generalizing and the particularizing is that it offers promise of greater analytic refinement than a level at either pole. The problem is to move as closely as possible to the ultimate uniqueness of a cultural configuration without losing the capability for comparative study. After all, one can profitably move up the scale from the particular to the general, but there is no good way of moving down. The aim of the present analysis, therefore, is to depict what is specifically Cubeo and yet allow bases for two successively broader typological characterizations, namely, tropical forest economies of South America and "simple" horticultural economies in general.

LINKAGE AND AUTONOMY

With respect to social structure, the most fundamental Cubeo principle involves a relationship between the apparent opposites of linkage and of autonomy. That is to say, the Cubeo will find a way to assert their independence of each group of which they are a part. The clearest example of this principle is the relationship between phratry and sib. What this relationship brings out is not an antagonism between opposing principles of collectivism and of individualism but rather a complementarity. The phratry does not impede the autonomy of the sib. On the contrary, it fosters this autonomy. It does so by fostering a strong sense of sib identity; for the consciousness of sib identity is actually heightened by the enforced relationship of sibs with one another, particularly in ceremony. Since the phratry represents a fraternal federation, promoting peace and security, the political and economic autonomy of a small and therefore potentially weak segment encounters no additional external threat. Thus, as we have seen, the phratry, by providing a zone of peace and security, facilitates sib fission, which may be regarded as a still further development of autonomy.

For the Cubeo, autonomy and linkage are equally strong attractions, and I think it is fair to say that they cannot visualize one without the other, or one as stronger than the other. The compulsions to form and to proliferate linkages are balanced, so to speak, by provisions for maintaining the identity and the potential autonomy of each component segment. No linkage is established that will interfere with autonomy, and, in fact, many linkages are established for the purpose of providing greater autonomy. Ceremonial friendship is a case in point, illustrating the way in which a self-initiating and hence autonomous paired relationship grows out of and complements, as well as extends, patterned relationships that have traditionally been established by kinship and by sib membership. In viewing Cubeo social structure, one is inclined to suspect that when relationships have become too solidly established, a way is found to assert the autonomous complement of that relationship. The striking oscillation between phratric solidarity and sib isolationism observed in the drinking parties may perhaps also be attributed to this very strong Cubeo tendency to assert autonomy wherever collectivism looms large. We shall return to oscillation as another principle of Cubeo social structure. At this point, we may review the principal linkage-autonomy relationships that have been described for the Cubeo. The following relationships are included, going from the largest to the smallest segments and fragments of segments.

1. *Tribe-phratry.* This is not an actual but only a potential relationship, since the Cubeo tribe has virtually no structural significance. If the principle that we have described as to the nature of linkage-autonomy is correct, it would follow that if the tribe were ever activated as a sociopolitical entity, the phratries would emerge as even stronger entities. This, however, is only an academic speculation. More pertinent is the hypothesis that the Cubeo phratry is weak because it lacks a higher, a more collective, counterpart against which to assert itself.

2. *Sib-phratry.* In this relationship we see the classic statement of linkage-autonomy. The phratry as the collective entity heightens the significance of the sib as the autonomous counterpart. The implica-

tion of this statement would be that the development of the sib organization out of perhaps some more amorphous form of patrilineal,
patrilocal organization is to be attributed to the process of federation
itself. That is to say, by confronting a series of equivalent segments,
each segment undertakes to assert its own clear identity. A sib, after
all, is a unilinear descent group that has undertaken to differentiate
itself categorically from like groups by means of such obvious symbolic devices as a name, a common tradition, and a theory of common
descent. In the absence of federation this process of categorical self-
identification would probably not occur. The process of sib formation, as a consequence of federation, is alleged in this instance for the
Cubeo only. It may, however, prove to be a more general process.
Elsewhere in the tropical forest the clan organization (parallel to the
Cubeo sib) is associated with moieties. The apparent exception of
the Witotoans is in all probability simply a matter of incomplete information.

3. *Independents and Satellites.* It is at this social level that the
issues of linkage-autonomy can be most readily analyzed. From the
standpoint of those who have removed themselves some distance from
the sib, the issue is simply that of autonomy with its counterpart, a
circumspectly defined linkage to the main body of the sib. The issue
of autonomy arises specifically in relation to the authority of the
headman, limited though such authority may be. The Satellites and
Independents do not disengage themselves from the sib; they are content simply to assert their autonomously considered degree of independence from the headman. The differentiated form of the Satellite
and Independent house may be a practical expedient for building a
small house. Nevertheless, it does illustrate graphically the point of
linkage-autonomy, since the square house, as has been demonstrated,
does not meet the requirements for total autonomy with respect to
sib functions.

4. *Sib-household.* The household, as has been demonstrated, has
its clearly defined zone of autonomy. It has its own compartment in
the maloca; it prepares its own food; it has its own manioc plantation; and it contributes its identified share of the chicha to both intrasib and intersib drinking parties. No one who has lived any time at
all among the Cubeo can fail to be acutely aware of the assertion of
autonomy, within the context of linkage, of each household. A sib-
lineage and a lineage-household relationship along the linkage-
autonomy gradient did not emerge clearly enough in my study to be
included in this discussion.

5. *Patrilocal household–wife.* The demand of a newly wed wife for

her own manioc garden is still another demonstration of linkage-autonomy. Much early marital discord can be attributed to a woman's assertion of independence from her mother-in-law's claim upon her labor. Her manioc plantation is a zone of autonomy vis-à-vis her mother-in-law as well as vis-à-vis her husband.

6. *Sib males and the children's play pack.* This age-grade relationship is still another example of linkage-autonomy. The young boys attach themselves as individuals or as a body to the adult males in economic and in ceremonial activities, but always have the option of detachment and of re-forming themselves as an autonomous play pack.

7. *Ceremonial friendship.* This, as we have already mentioned, may be regarded as a mode of autonomous selection among more distant kin of relationships that are parallel to the prestructured ties between siblings. The sibling relationship is the traditional linkage and the ceremonial friendship is its autonomous counterpart.

8. *Concept of Growth.* The capacity of a society to continue to grow through the proliferation of linkages must also be related to cultural concepts that define the values of social growth. It is clear that linkages do have positive value for the Cubeo. There is great satisfaction in multisib drinking parties and ceremonies that bring together a great many people from many sibs. This suggests some appreciation for growth of the phratry. As for the sib, the feeling for its growth is even more strongly expressed. There is always fear that it will diminish in size and there is pleasure in contemplating that one's own sib is larger than another. But these feelings that one comes upon for growth of phratry and of sib are rather indefinite. They are not clearly voiced, they are not embodied in specific ritual or traditions, and concern for growth is not delegated to any effective authority. The headman may be charged with holding the community together, but he is not expected to make it grow. On the other hand, the cultural concept of growth that is stressed is that of the individual body, of corporeal growth. The clearly articulated Cubeo concern is that a body grow big and fat, that the limbs, the forearms, and the calves, in particular, should bulge. The ancestral cult and postnatal magic including the naming ceremony play on this theme of corporeal development. The ancestral cult does, of course, bring out the value of potency, but again the emphasis is upon personal sexual power and not explicitly upon growth of the sib. I know of no Cubeo magic that deals specifically with growth in numbers. An interest in such growth is only implied. In short, the point to be made is not that **the Cubeo lack interest in social growth, but that they place their**

main emphasis upon the person and not upon the community. Such an emphasis, needless to say, tends to favor autonomy over linkage.

It is evident that the foregoing discussion of linkage-autonomy is in many respects simply a restatement of the familiar concept of segmentation. There are, however, significant differences that justify the use of other terminology. Segmentation as defined by Nadel (1953, p. 177) refers to a more limited set of relationships than have been included here. As an example of segment he describes a "hierarchical structure being arranged in an order of progressive inclusiveness, as lineages, for example, build up clans, and clans build up a tribe, or as several village communities form a district, and several districts the state. . . ." From the standpoint of this definition, Cubeo society is, of course, segmentary. The concept of segmentation, however, is purely objective, and as such is pertinent to the purposes of social anthropology. However, the term "segmentation" carries no cultural connotations, since it does not define the point of view of the members of the culture. Therefore it is inadequate for the aims of cultural anthropology. The concept of linkage-autonomy, on the other hand, expresses a cultural, a Cubeo, point of view and indicates how this point of view is embodied in social structure. This Cubeo point of view, which places a value both upon extending relationships and maintaining autonomy, goes beyond the structural patterns that are commonly included under the concepts of segmentation. It is a more inclusive concept.

LATERAL AND HIERARCHICAL RELATIONSHIPS

All social structures are regulated by bonds of relatively equivalent status relationships, as well as by bonds of nonequivalent or unequal status relationships. The former, existing on roughly the same social plane, are called lateral, and the latter, existing on different social planes, are called hierarchical. Hierarchy is always a culturally defined term and represents a clear-cut distinction of relative worth. Lateral is also a culturally defined term, but laterality is not a clearly set relationship of status equivalence. Hence it must be modified by the adjective "relative." The ranking of sibs is a clear example of hierarchy among the Cubeo, whereas kinship relations, including ceremonial friendships, are lateral. However, since kinship relations also embody formal principles of hierarchy, such as generation, seniority, consanguinity, and affinity they are lateral only by contrast with the strongly hierarchical distinctions of authority, power, prestige, and rank. Societies differ with respect to the relative role these two principles have in the social structure. That of the Cubeo is very strongly lateral and only weakly hierarchical. Even the ranking of sibs has ritualistic rather than political significance. Rank confers prestige but no power. On the other hand, it does confer economic privilege of a sort by granting to the high ranks superior river rights. But the Cubeo themselves do not make an issue of this economic distinction. Political authority, as we have shown, is relatively slight. In kinship, age, generational, and descent seniority elicit some respect and provide for ritual precedence. Such precedence is a prestige point. But the prestige accrues less in everyday affairs than upon formal occasions. Thus, from the Cubeo point of view virtually all relationships between persons and between groups are lacking in dominance-subordination, whereas only in rituals, that is, only upon the plane of the sacred, are there distinctions of worth and of respect. Even these are rather minor, involving only ritual precedence. The ritual pattern itself is not hierarchical. Now segmentation, as Nadel has observed, is a hierarchical form of organization, yet in the case of the Cubeo, segmental hierarchy has little cultural significance. Since the phratry has no organization of leadership it is not, in actuality, a "higher" segment. For all secular purposes the sibs deal with one another as equals.

The principal characteristic of a strong lateral structure, such as that of the Cubeo, is its considerable flexibility in forming new linkages and in rearranging old ones. Hierarchical structures, on the other hand, are dependent upon, or subject to, the authority of a higher-ranking segment. The new linkages that any Cubeo household is free to establish are limited far more by personal preferences than by inviolable principles. Sib exogamy is such an inviolable principle, but phratric exogamy is somewhat different. It involves not the "dread" of incest but rather the sentiment of confraternity. Cubeo flexibility responds to the absence of political constraint. Sibs can move about, and can, if they wish, change phratric affiliation.

FISSILITY

From the two preceding principles of sociocultural structure there follows a third, ease of fission. Every segment of the entire social structure has the capability of detaching itself from the larger body. The factions that have actually broken off include sib clusters, sibs, households, and individuals. Fission is an objective social process, a by-product of Cubeo cultural principles of autonomy and social equality. It is promoted, as well, by another cultural principle that we have not yet discussed. That principle I would describe as a low tolerance for psychic discomfort. That is to say, in the absence of political constraint and of economic necessity the Cubeo find it easier to leave an uncomfortable situation than to endure it.

PERIODICITY

Since the sibs join together on the basis of linkage-autonomy and upon lateral rather than hierarchical lines, some loosening of bonds would seem to be inevitable. The periodicity in drinking parties is the only measure we have of changes in the strength of attachment of sib bonds. These parties, we have noted, follow a cycle starting from full attendance and a very high state of mutual confidence and ending in a series of parties that are poorly attended and are conducted in an atmosphere that is dismal and heavy with distrust. Eventually confidence is restored and a new cycle begins. The period from high to low runs about one year. Periodicity is not a cultural principle; it is a consequence of several other cultural principles. As already suggested, linkage-autonomy and lateralization play a part in this periodicity because they allow relationships to find a "natural" level. That is to say, there is no formal authority that can step in to restore good relations when the social climate has been poisoned by drunken quarrels and by accusations of sorcery. Periodicity is perhaps to be regarded as an incomplete form of fission at the level of the phratry. Since the phratry is a stronger exponent of autonomy than is the sib, it develops only a few of the pressures that might lead to actual fission. As for other principles of Cubeo culture involved in the periodicity of sib bonds, we have already mentioned the low tolerance for psychic discomfort, and have described its relevance to fission of the sib. In the context of the drinking party, and indeed in the context of all collective activities, this principle can be stated in still another way: that collectivity demands its appropriate atmosphere of good feeling. We have seen this principle strongly at work in the mourning ceremony, where the atmosphere of grief, grimness, hostility, suspicion, and fear is systematically and ritually transformed to one of excitement and gaiety. We have also observed that the Cubeo do not harbor grudges for long. When a feeling begins to subside they allow it to subside. When a more neutral atmosphere forms, a new cycle of good feeling can begin.

POLARITY - COMPLEMENTARITY

The complementary role of conceptual opposites is, of course, a universal type of cultural patterning. Cultural distinctions occur in variations of the pattern. Under any circumstances, the general pattern of polarity-complementarity produces a mode of order and hence of social cohesiveness. In Cubeo life, polarity-complementarity is very strongly expressed. Its most prominent area is the male-female polarity. From a purely sociological point of view, the male-female opposition would seem to be a reflection of the patriliny-patrilocality of the sib, in which the women are outsiders as wives and outsiders-to-be as sisters and daughters, while the men are the permanent group. To this basic social condition the Cubeo add a variety of symbolic modes of opposition. Those that have been described include opposing but complementary roles in all ritual. In the ancestral cult and in mourning ceremonies these distinguishing roles of men and women are very sharply delineated. In ritual, men supply order, while women give spontaneity. Since female spontaneity in ritual is evidently complementary to masculine formalism, it is to be understood that we are dealing here with a somewhat dramatized rather than with a "pure" spontaneity. Generally speaking, and using the Durkheimian categories broadly, the men represent the sacred side of life and the women the profane. However, in the case of the Cubeo the female as profane is a complement of the sacred and not altogether outside of it.

From a more secular point of view, the male-female distinction can be expressed in terms of a collectivist-sectionalist dichotomy: the men represent the collectivism of the sib, the women the sectionalism of the individual household. The contrast between the gregariousness of the male play pack and the solitariness of the little girls is perhaps the most pointed demonstration of this distinction. Another illustration of this pattern is in the form of the dance in which the girls slip under the linking yokes of the men's arms, occupying, so to speak, interstices of the dance pattern. The collectivist-sectionalist distinction is also clear in economic activities. Hunting and fishing are commonly collective, whereas female-prepared food, that is, manioc cake and tapioca porridges, are largely sectional (household). If we were to attempt a hypothetical linking together of the various patterns of Cubeo culture we could argue that the principle of linkage-autonomy is related to the broad principle of male-female polarity-complementarity, on the grounds that the male side in relation to the female side stands for linkage, while the female side in relation to the male side stands for autonomy.

The second most important area in which polarity-complementarity can be observed is ritual. There is no need to review the obvious distinctions between sacred and profane in ritual matters. What is of special interest is the Cubeo pattern of setting all ritual within an emotional framework that moves from calm to frenzy, from order to chaos, from sobriety to intoxication, from a slow tempo to an excited tempo. A Dionysian frenzy is without doubt the desired culmination of Cubeo ritual, but the culmination is not the entire ritual. The pattern is that of a traversal of the emotional spectrum. Again it seems possible to relate ritual emotion as an example of polarity-complementarity to the previously described principle of linkage autonomy. The basis for this connection is brought out most clearly in the mourning ceremony. In this most solemn of Cubeo rituals the initial phases express symbolically the social patterns of masculine solidarity, of sibness, and of phratric solidarity. In the course of interaction with what has been described as "female spontaneity," and in the course of the excitement generated by dancing, dramatization, drinking chicha, and taking *mihí*, the clear social pattern of collectivity is broken down and the participants, having lost sib identity so to speak, appear finally in the guise of nonsib or autonomous dancers. In other words, the zone of ritual calm is parallel to the aspect of linkage, and the zone of ritual frenzy is parallel to the aspect of autonomy. A curious feature of this relationship, one that suggests an extension of the pattern, is the Cubeo characterization of the intrasib or domestic mood as calm, that is, based on food, and the intersib mood as frenzied, that is, based on the drinking parties. The significance of this distinction between intrasib and intersib moods is that, as we have already observed, the appearance of a phratric context stimulates, at the same time, the assertion of autonomy. A parallel pattern appears on those infrequent occasions when an intrasib drinking party is held. Such a drinking party follows a more moderate emotional scale, with far less intoxication, but it seems to have a similar result in accenting first the autonomy of the individual household and, finally, through some drunken disorder, the autonomy of the individual.

In this connection, it is interesting to consider that the women, who are on the side of the sectional as opposed to the collective, may and indeed do drink, but they, in contrast to the men, are under no obligation to become intoxicated. Masculine intoxication is ritual but feminine intoxication is secular and hence of minor significance.

The relationship between the patterns of calm-frenzy and linkage-autonomy appears also in the juridical area. Here, as we observed, justice is carried out not in an atmosphere of calm deliberation but in an atmosphere of high excitement, as befits a situation in which the collectivity of the sib has been broken both by commission of the crime and by the act of expelling the offender. The juridical is not a ritual area. The example, however, demonstrates the continuity of ritual polarity-complementarity with a more general patterning of mood.

PATTERNING OF MOOD

The point has been made repeatedly that the Cubeo will undertake no significant action unless the mood is appropriate. The previous example of the juridical process is illustrative. Punishment or vengeance must correspond with appropriate anger. Ritual acts and dances are omitted when the mood is wrong. All collective enterprises of the sib, such as hunting, fishing, foraging, and housebuilding, require a mood of geniality. When such a mood begins to break, a fairly rapid chain reaction ensues. The sense of collectivity weakens and this, in turn, darkens the mood. This cycle of mood periodicity has been discussed in the context of the drinking party. In a different context it applies to other major collective efforts such as housebuilding, which also follows a cyclical rhythm of spurts of work alternating with lulls. The fishing cycle is still another example of Cubeo dependence on mood.

OVER-ALL PATTERN

Some examples of linkage of smaller patterns have been presented to suggest at least the possibility of describing Cubeo society in some broader and more inclusive terms. The problem, however, is that the concept of pattern is a hypothetical construction based upon calling of attention to analogies or parallelisms. The method of pattern construction is largely intuitive and the demonstration of its validity is largely a matter of presenting a credible argument. Despite these self-evident scientific shortcomings there can be little doubt that the presentation or analysis of a culture without the concept of pattern must involve a serious distortion of reality. The aim of a theoretical construction that would present a culture in terms of over-all pattern is to provide appropriate bases for a more sophisticated culture typology than anthropology presently possessses. Pattern need not be accepted only as a statement of uniqueness, although the scientific value of a unique configuration is undeniable. Each general cultural pattern may ultimately be unique, but since uniqueness is a relative concept the possibility of some more general typology is a real one. Thus the hypothetical statement of a Cubeo over-all pattern should have more than specific applicability.

What kind of model, then, does Cubeo culture follow? Socially the root model is that of the solidarity of brothers. It is around this root concept that the characteristic principles of Cubeo kinship and sib and phratric organization develop. The solidarity-of-brothers concept is, as we have seen, both set off from and bound to all other relations by the universal human doctrine of order: polarity-complementarity. Since primogeniture, though recognized, is minor, the male sibling solidarity is in effect nonhierarchical; it is basically lateral. And it is this fraternal model, we might say, that gives the strong egalitarian cast to Cubeo society. The ancestral cult, in all its aspects, is the particular Cubeo phrasing of the sacred character of male sibling solidarity. It is not a worship of the past, nor does it single out for special distinction any particular ancestral line except from the standpoint of the phratry. But the phratry, having mainly a ritual rather than a corporate character, has only a limited effect upon the patterning of Cubeo life. The ancestral tradition does differentiate the sibs. The ancestral cult, on the other hand, serves rather to promote the lateral solidarity of the male siblings who are the roots of the sib.

The significance of the social pattern based upon the solidarity of the male siblings has been noted by Radcliffe-Brown as characteristic of primitive societies organized in patrilineal lineages. It is indeed a fundamental and elementary social pattern subject to a wide range of variations. In the case of the Cubeo, their entire elaboration of kinship, lineage, sib, and phratry follows very closely the lines of the elementary pattern. If the close approximation of a social structure to an elementary basic pattern may be taken as a mark of simplicity, then on this score Cubeo social structure may be characterized as "simple." It is understood, of course, that male sibling solidarity is only the focal point of a larger social pattern that includes the polarity-complementarity relationships of affinity-consanguinity, and the male-female as well as the near-distant relationship.

If Cubeo social structure can be derived from an elementary model, so can its emotional structure, or ethos. The Cubeo ethos seems to be based upon the doctrine of harmonizing each particular mode of emotional expression with an appropriate social activity. Stated generally, this relationship of appropriateness between mood and activity is not novel. It seems, in fact, altogether natural. Cultures, however, as we well know, do not necessarily pattern themselves quite so naturally. Civilizations, in particular, place the emphasis upon the social action and expect the mood to be disciplined or to be subordinated to the social occasion. The Cubeo, on the other hand, expect a rather high degree of emotional spontaneity. In this respect they correspond oddly to the eighteenth-century notions of "natural man." In secular affairs the spontaneity of correspondence between emotion and action is much greater than in ritual. In ritual the effort is made to establish the correspondence between feeling and the concept of the sacred. Ritual in primitive society generally expresses in a symbolic or highly compressed form the fundamental cultural themes of a society. We have repeatedly shown the integration of ritual with social structure. Cubeo ritual, similarly, reveals not only the role of emotionality in Cubeo life but exhibits that spectrum of emotionality that has greatest significance for the Cubeo.[1] It is indeed in ritual, as Ruth Benedict has demonstrated in *Patterns of Culture*, that the ethos of a culture is most vividly displayed. Cubeo ritual, as has been seen, dramatizes the interplay between formal pattern and spontaneity. The most vivid example of this interplay is the interaction between men as sacred and women as a laity during the mourning ceremony. The effect of this interplay is to add significance to the spontaneity of emotion, and at the same time to give emotional zest to the formal ritual pattern. In short, what seems an inescapable conclusion about Cubeo culture is that neither form nor action can be comfortably tolerated unless charged with a proper feeling or emotion.

The relationship between form and emotion and social action and emotion is but one part of the pattern. The pattern also includes the emotional preferences. It is not simply that the Cubeo prefer to run a gamut, since an emotional gamut is a range within a particular plane. In ritual the emotional gamut moves from sobriety and order, as we have already explained, to intoxication and disorder. On a smaller scale, the ritual pattern moves from slow to fast. In the mourning ceremony these related planes of emotional modulation seemed to find their focus in a sexual rhythm, culminating in what is almost literally an orgasmic excitement. From this there may be reason to conclude that it is coitus, a very elementary biological

---

[1] It is to be understood, of course, that the roles of emotionality in secular life are not the same as they are in the sacred realm. In secular life moderation is more appropriate than excitement or intensity.

model, that underlies an important aspect of the Cubeo ethos. What is surprising about finding coitus as a model for ritual ethos is not that this obvious pattern has been drawn upon, but that it is not drawn upon more often. Among the Carajá of central Brazil, I am informed, the coital ritual pattern is explicitly recognized, each phase of the dance being named from a phase of sexual intercourse.[2] It is quite possible that I simply failed to discover the same explicit relationship among the Cubeo. The explicitness that I did discover, though, is in their assertion that ritual excitement, whether produced by drugs, alcohol, or the ritualization of sex, is a necessary complement to the ritual magic of the below-the-knee ligature of long life. This identification of emotional intensity with life itself is also an obvious and therefore a simple relationship. In sum, we can say that the main features of Cubeo ethos draw upon very obvious and simple biopsychological models and — this is the significant point — adhere rather closely, almost literally, to them. Since the social pattern also draws upon a very elementary model we must conclude that the sociocultural pattern as a whole is built upon the simplest of social and biopsychological models. Needless to say, even the bare and incomplete account of Cubeo life that has been presented suggests that the elements of over-all pattern described here do not encompass the "totality" of the culture. In all probability, however, no concept of pattern can ever encompass a total social and cultural system. From the point of view of culture theory the question is a different one. The proper question is: Does the theory of pattern provide an adequate approach to an understanding of the culture?

We can attempt to answer this question by applying the concept of pattern that has been presented to an analysis of two fundamental cultural problems: the problem of social homeostasis and the problem of ecological adaptation. Strictly speaking, equilibrium and adaptation are one problem. It is simply that this problem can be approached from two sides.

SOCIAL HOMEOSTASIS

The assumption of social homeostasis is that a cultural system consists of relationships and interactions that are so patterned that their net effect is to perpetuate the system, generation after generation. It is understood, of course, that homeostasis, or equilibrium, is a relative condition only, since no society today is a precise duplicate of

---

[2] Personal communication from Dr. William Lipkind.

what it was yesterday. Moreover, the concept of homeostasis, like that of pattern, is a theory of society. As a theory it rests upon further theoretical assumptions as to what are the significant relationships, what are the normal patterns, and what are the disharmonious and stressful interactions. In the final analysis, a theory of homeostasis deals primarily with the ways in which a society handles conflicts and stresses. From a broad perspective, one can say that Cubeo society depends rather heavily upon what might be called "mood management" for equilibrium. Its homeostasis rests a good deal less upon networks of reciprocal obligations and upon formal exchanges of goods than, let us say, in Melanesian societies. The clearest illustration of this Cubeo equilibrium principle is in the role of the headman. In Cubeo culture ·he is not an economic redistributor (the drinking parties cannot be regarded as an economic exchange) but a regulator of community sentiment and of good feeling. However, the nature of Cubeo equilibrium is best considered at each particular level of social integration.

Cubeo society may be presented diagrammatically as encompassing five orbits of relationship, arranged in order of progressively weaker bonds of unity. The innermost orbit is represented by the male siblings, the nucleus of the sib; the second orbit is the sib itself; the third orbit is the phratry; the fourth, the affinal kin; and the fifth and outermost, the tribe. The brother-sister relationships and the husband-wife relationships may be regarded as within the confines of the first and second orbits.

Each orbit has its own characteristics of equilibrium. To take them in reverse order: Tribal unity is so tenuous that fragmentation into subtribal units is of little consequence. New combinations are readily formed and whatever disturbance this may cause is very temporary. Tribal continuity rests upon tradition and common language and customs, on the one hand, and upon the phratric organization, of which it is a summation, on the other. With respect to tribe, the question of equilibrium is more pertinently not what holds the tribe together, but rather what there is to disperse it. Tradition and common customs and language are little more than bonds of inertia. Once set, they hold unless some stronger force intervenes. Against what counterforces are the relatively weak bonds of tradition to contend? The answer is that there are no such counterforces arising from within the society, since tribal unity has no tasks to accomplish that could involve stresses and strains. Paradoxically, the very absence of a tribal leadership is a source of unity. By virtue of the linkage-autonomy principle, strong tribal leadership would provoke fission and would then have to become remarkably strong to overcome the disruptive forces it had set in motion.

Between in-laws, the linkages are more diversified and hence are stronger than those between fellow tribesmen. The system of exchange marriages creates a particularly close set of bonds, because it draws upon the powerful nuclear bonds between brother and sister and supplements these with preferential marriage into the sib of the mother. There seems to be a potentiality for moiety formation in the Cubeo system. But this potentiality is never realized because of geographic distances and the wide ranges of marital choice, intratribal as well as extratribal. In the case of affinal sibs, the thesis of inherent antagonism is counterbalanced by the brother-sister tie. When that tie is dissolved, as by death or divorce, the antagonisms may begin to loom large, and what were formerly close ties will begin to dissolve. In this orbit of in-laws, however, equilibrium does not really demand fixed ties, since the affinal relationships are eminently interchangeable.

In the orbit of the phratry, the bonds are more impressively substantial, based as they are upon tradition, upon the fiction of blood kinship, and upon contiguity, hospitality, and ceremonial participations. These bonds of attraction are all the more impressive because there is so little to oppose them. There is no phratric leadership and there are no secular tasks to provoke possible conflict of interest. Nevertheless, latent hostilities dramatized in the mourning ceremony and made seriously real in charges of sorcery have the capability of wrecking phratric unity. To offset the powerfully disruptive force of sorcery there are few specific institutional mechanisms that the Cubeo can call upon. They rely instead upon a cooling-off period of sib separation. The excited parties separate until the original fear and anger have drained off. But why the antagonisms between the sibs in the first place? Actually, the issues that disturb friendly relations between members of different sibs are fundamentally no different than those that turn sibmates against one another. They are largely the private issues of adultery and of personal insult, aggravated by intoxication and given a grim setting by the cultural theory of sorcery. Occasionally the hostile reaction is against a sib headman who is overly assertive. This situation is duplicated within the sib as well. It is not the issues, then, but their cultural context that is significant.

When men of a sib quarrel, it is relatively easy for the headman to isolate the grievance so that only the two principals are involved. In cases of adultery the device of shifting the blame upon the woman safeguards sib solidarity. On the other hand, when the disputants are of different sibs it is relatively easy for the issue to embroil the sibs as entities and correspondingly difficult to confine the issue to the actual principals. The fiction of phratric consanguinity notwithstanding, the sib is still, in Cubeo thought, a natural unit that holds within itself the constant potentiality of antagonism toward the fellow sib. The fact that each sib arrives at a drinking party or other ceremony armed and as a unit is the symbolic expression of latent antagonism. The ritual theme of dissolving the semblance of sib unity through intoxication is presumably counteractive to sib solidarity and antagonism. Yet this counteraction via intoxication contains the paradox of bringing the undercurrents of antagonism to the surface. To be sure, when a quarrel occurs in the late stages of a drinking party it often is isolated because the other sibmen may not be fully aware of what is going on. The safety device does work, to a degree and for a time. Moreover, some men are known to be quarrelsome by temperament and are consequently ignored. Granted all these mitigating circumstances, it is easy for a man to involve his own sib in a dispute with another. When illness and death occur, one conclusion is inevitable. That is found in the expression "*they* want *us* to die." This theme recurs in the funeral orations. Perhaps it is because the Cubeo sibs have a history of separate though related origins and a tradition of past antagonisms that present-day intersib hostility can flare, and is expected to flare, even though the issues that disturb them are, at bottom, trifling. However, in conformity with the minor nature of the disputes is the absence, in recent times, of intersib warfare. The disputes result in coolness and social distance and not in organized fighting. In summary, phratric unity is readily disturbed but never very seriously. It is restored by the process described under "Periodicity." It is because the issues are not irreconcilable that the social "governor" that restores peace by separation can work so well

The orbit of the sib has the same general form as the orbit of the phratry, with the formal difference that the sib has a leader whereas the phratry has no leadership at all. In the sib, moreover, all the ties are substantially firmer than in the phratry. Since the cultural view holds that sib unity is a natural expectation and since there are no important issues dividing sibmates, we are faced with a truly difficult theoretical problem in accounting for sib fission. The common explanation, that fission of local groups in simple societies is due simply to insufficiency of food in the immediate locality, does not apply to the Cubeo, who, at least in modern times — a period of population decline — are not confronted by land shortage. There is, in deed, reason to doubt the sufficiency of the ecological thesis generally. Insofar as Cubeo culture is concerned the question is clearly a complex one. If we were to postulate a simple explanation at all it would be to the effect that the Cubeo experience is close to the irreducible level of stress and strain inherent in community living. In the absence of strong restraints the people respond to these stresses by leaving. This explanation is perhaps not too far wrong. It is inadequate, however, for our purpose, which is to delineate the formal principles of homeostasis in a "simple" tropical forest horticultural society. There is no need to repeat in detail the powerful forces that hold sibmen together. They include the totality of binding forces that exist in Cubeo culture. In the institution of the male play pack they draw in addition upon the psychological attractions that are formed by the closest of associations developed over the period from early childhood to adulthood. It is not until marriage that the paternal bonds of sibship begin to weaken -- and even then only moderately.

As in the case of the phratry, the stresses within the sib result from adultery, personal insult, and resentment of authority. Can the prevalence of adultery be attributed simply and directly to the extraordinarily wide extension of exogamy that severely curtails courtship? Actually, the adulterous men are not the unmarried. It is almost always the married man who seduces or is seduced by a sib brother's wife. The unmarried, as we have noted, find sexual outlet more commonly in onanism, homosexual play, and near incest. These unorthodox modes of sexual activity reaching into early adulthood seem to produce a sexual maladjustment that is most manifest in the early stages of marriage. It is consequently the young wives and the older, more mature married men who are the most common adulterous partners. The role of exogamy is indirect but nonetheless strong; it may be regarded as a natural cause of adultery and hence of internal discord. There is also an apparent symbolic cause: the Cubeo symbolic view of a woman as separatist and as disruptive of sib unity. Indeed, this would seem to be the Cubeo woman's natural role. But this natural role gains in consequence of being placed in a traditional and symbolic setting. In such a setting the expectations are intensified and it is easier for the persons to overcome scruples.

We have seen that the Cubeo regard female adultery as more or less natural but that they regard male adultery more seriously as a sign of hostility. Adultery implies sibling rivalry, which the Cubeo acknowledge, but they have no specific theory to account for it. In status-conscious societies, status rivalry is a common institutional cause of conflict between brothers. Since the Cubeo lack status rivalry the explanation must be sought in subinstitutional relationships. The nature of food pathology illustrates one form of psychic conflict that disturbs the relationship of sibmates. In incidents of food pathology the subject was often deprived of a father, a particularized and personal tie, and displayed his resentment in a calculatedly resentful way. It may be said generally of the Cubeo that they hold to exceptionally high standards of personal warmth. When these standards are not met, as often in practice they cannot be, the people are unduly disturbed. Thus, it is not difficult for a man to feel that a brother has let him down and so seek vengeance in adultery. In a more general vein, it can be said that the solidarity of the sib has its natural psychological limts. Adultery, theft, and nonsharing are in Cubeo culture the most common manifestations of such discord. That fraternal discord may be more than superficial would be indicated by the accusations of sorcery that sometimes flash between brothers.

Unlike the phratry, the sibs have an officer whose job it is to deal with discord. The headman has no authority, but he has tact and the prestige of office. His difficulty is that since he cannot allocate punishments, assess injuries, and award compensation, he must deal only with the intangible and volatile aspects of mood. He can either soothe outraged feelings or exacerbate them, smooth over the difficulty or force a showdown and the departure of the culprit. The function of public opinion in an intrasib dispute is essentially to ratify a determination to expel a culprit. The Cubeo will prefer to overlook offenses within the sib as much as possible. But when the issue is out in the open the most likely way for equilibrium to be restored is for someone to leave. The departure of an offender is not an example of fission. When feelings have cooled he will return. Sib fission is exemplified by the Independents and the Satellites, composed of sib sections who are simply dissatisfied with the headman or with their fellows. Thus fission contributes to equilibrium by draining away the malcontents. Curiously, while the departure of the disaffected removes an immediate cause of potential stress, it leaves in its wake another form of stress in the form of a more diffuse sentiment of dismay that all is not well with the sib. The headman is well equipped to deal with this more generalized feeling, however.

The normal point of cleavage in the sib is the small group of blood brothers. True brothers form the most solid of all Cubeo linkages. The fraternal group is truly the core of Cubeo social structure. Yet this innermost orbit is far from indestructible. The Vaupés region is spotted with social "ions," free-floating men who, with their wives and children, circulate from community to community attaching themselves temporarily to different families, since the true nuclear family is not a self-sufficient unit. The strength of individual autonomy and its psychological counterpart in the form of low tolerance for psychic discomfort is capable, apparently, of breaking the firmest social connections Cubeo culture has devised.

Whether Cubeo social equilibrium is to be evaluated as static or as dynamic will depend upon the time perspective by which it is viewed. In sociological perspective one sees autonomy counterbalancing linkage, fission offsetting fusion. Tribe has only the vaguest suggestion of a higher level of integration, while phratry is a headless configuration, largely a ritual federation subject to dissolution and to re-formation. By freezing time, the sociological perspective has the inherent bias, however, of presenting social forces as in balance. On the other hand, the sociological perspective has the merit of being empirically true to the research design. That is to say, the study of a single society at a fixed point in time and for which only vague glimmerings of history are available provides few empirical grounds for any perspective other than the sociological.

The historical perspective on the Cubeo is then largely conjectural. It is, however, a necessary perspective both for the sake of offsetting the bias of artificial timelessness and for raising questions about Cubeo culture that would have relevance for a comparative study. In historical perspective, the Cubeo phratry, with its ranked sibs, the allocation of preferred river sites to the high-ranking, and the honorific prerogatives of high sib rank, suggests possibilities for further social and political development. Though the phratric organization is largely of a ritual nature, it is conceivable that a ritual organization provides a pattern for an eventually tighter integration through political and economic means. Some of the potential political means are already visible. Relations with the Macú point to an understanding of the dominance-subordination relationship on a political and economic plane. Recurrent alarms on the river that a headman is seeking political headship over all the sibs illustrate, to be sure, an acute Cubeo sensitivity to the danger of political control, but they also demonstrate that the possibility of overlordship is not altogether unreal. If then Cubeo culture has this potential for political evolution, what has impeded it? In the light of the foregoing analysis the answer is surely not simple. Since culture is an organization of patterns, its growth cannot be understood in terms of the action of single variables such as the influence of slash-burn cultivation, dependence on bitter manioc, or the tropical rain forest environment. Each of these conditions is relevant to an understanding of Cubeo culture. But even taken together they do not account for the principal patterns of Cubeo culture, which have a natural history of their own. The question, however, is not whether cultural patterns have a natural history, but only whether the ecological and the technological theories are adequate accounts of the natural history of a culture.

ADAPTATION

Thus, the problem of cultural adaptation to an environment cannot be dealt with simply and one-sidedly by describing the hypothetical shaping of a culture to the environment. Adaptation is a study of interaction. Generally speaking, highly specialized environments demand highly specialized and hence relatively predictable cultural responses. The tropical forest is not an example of a highly specialized economic environment judged empirically by the diversity of cultural patterns it has sustained. Bitter manioc is clearly a cumbersome crop, its high yield and relative ease of cultivation being offset by its very heavy demands on labor, specifically on that of women. It can be argued, therefore, that this crop offers a poor economic base for social and political development. Yet the Northwest Amazon also is familiar with maize, yams, and sweet manioc, not to mention beans and squash and gourd. These crops have traditionally sustained high cultures. Can we explain in ecological terms why the Northwest Amazon tribes chose to specialize in bitter manioc rather than maize and beans, as did, for example, the lowland Maya? It would seem that here is a case of cultural choice in which preferences for quick yield, minimum care in cultivation, strong sexual division of labor, and perennial harvest rather than the problems of storage and seasonal periodicity may have been compelling factors. Since the Cubeo social system placed no great demands upon an expanding economic productivity the "easy" adaptation to nature was always feasible. The main patterns of Cubeo life do not stress the disciplines of prolonged and closely managed effort. The habitual rhythms of masculine labor are discontinuous and varied. Leadership is based on the principle of mood regulation rather than on dedication to an ideal or submission to authority. High cultures are based on strongly disciplined and collective ways of life. By contrast, the Cubeo values greater emotional spontaneity and personal autonomy. An economy, needless to say, will in the end transform cultural values as well as the personal character of the members of a culture. Before it can do so, however, it must be given a chance, so to speak, by the culture. There is nothing in physical nature that dictates the form of an economy beyond the requirement that it satisfy subsistence needs. In the case of the Cubeo the simplicity of the economy, and the corresponding simplicity of the culture as a whole, would seem to be far more a product of its fundamental patterns and principles of organization than of an external nature. If this conclusion is correct, it would suggest that the simple horticultural societies, as a type, are not mere victims of inhospitable environments but rather that they constitute a range of cultural systems with characteristic modes of equilibrium and adaptation that do not readily foster economic expansion and higher levels of social and political integration. This statement leads to one other conclusion, namely, that a culture is only partly a functional system adapted to the satisfaction of basic needs. With respect to these satisfactions, most societies have surplus capacity, a great deal of room for maneuver and for improvisation. Much of the form of a culture represents a style of life that need not, indeed cannot, be explained simply in terms of function, equilibrium, or adaptation. A style of life then must be studied in its own terms since it too is part of the diversity of nature.

Bibliography

Archivo do Amazonas, "Os Exploracoes e os Exploradores do Rio Vaupés," Vol. I, No. 2, Manaos, 1906.

Bauer, Peter Paul, *NW Amazonien*, Brünn, 1919.

Beuchat, H., and P. Rivet, "La Famille Betoya ou Tucano," *Mémoires de la Société Linguistique de Paris*, XVII (1911), 117–36, 162–90.

Colombia, *Censo General de la Población, 1938*, Vol. XV, Bogotá, 1942.

Coudreau, H. A., *La France Equinoxiale*, 2 vols., Paris, 1886–87.

Farabee, William C., *The Central Arawaks* (University of Pennsylvania Museum, Anthropological Publications, Vol. IX), Philadelphia, 1915.

Fulop, Marcos, "Aspectos de la Cultura Tukana: Cosmogonia," *Revista Colombiana de Antropologia*, III (1954), 99–137.

————, "Notas Sobre los Terminos y el Systema de Parentesco de los Tukano," *Revista Colombiana de Antropologia*, IV (1955), 123–64.

Giacone, S. S., P. Antonio, *Os Tucanos e Outras Tribus do Rio Uaupés Afluente do Negro-Amazonas*, Sao Paulo, 1949.

Goldman, Irving, "Tribes of the Uaupés-Caquetá Region," *Handbook of South American Indians*, III (Smithsonian Institution, Washington, 1948), 763–98.

Greenberg, Joseph, "The General Classification of Central and South American Languages," *Selected Papers, International Congress of Anthropological and Ethnological Sciences*, Philadelphia, 1960, pp. 791–94.

Gumilla, J., *Historia, Natural, Civil y Geografica de las Naciones del Rio Negro*, 2 vols., Barcelona, 1791.

Hardenburg, W. S., *The Putumayo: The Devil's Paradise*, London, 1912.

Humboldt, Alexander J. von, *Personal Narrative of Travels to the Equinoctial Regions of America, 1798–1804*, 3 vols., Bonn and London, 1852.

Kirchoff, Paul, "Verwandschaftsorganization der Urwaldstämme Südamerikas," *Zeitschrift für Ethnologie*, LXIII (1931), 85–191.

Koch-Grünberg, Theodor, *Anfaenge der Kunst im Urwald*, Berlin, 1905.

————, "Die Maskentänze der Indianer des oberen Rio Negro und Yapura," *Archiv für Anthropologie*, IV (1906[a]), 293–98.

————, "Die Indianerstämme am oberen Rio Negro und Yapura und ihre sprachliche Zugehorigkeit," *Zeitschrift für Ethnologie*, XXXVIII (1906 [b]), 166–205.

————, *Zwei Jahre unter den Indianern*, 2 vols., Berlin, 1909.

————, "Betoya Sprachen Nordwest Brasiliens," *Anthropos*, X–XI (1915–16), 114–58, 421–49.

Krause, Fritz, "Tanzmaskennachbildungen vom Mittleren Araguaya," *Jahrbuch des Stadtischen Museums für Volkerkunde zu Leipzig*, III (1910), 97–122.

Lehmann, Walter, review article on Krause, *Zentralblatt für Anthropologie*, XVI (1911), 100.

Lowie, Robert, *Primitive Society*, New York, 1920.

————, "The Tropical Forests: An Introduction," *Handbook of South American Indians*, III (Smithsonian Institution, Washington, 1948), 1–56.

————, "Social and Political Organization of the Tropical Forest and Marginal Tribes," *Handbook of South American Indians*, V (1949), 313–68.

Martius, Carl Friedrich von, *Beiträge zur Ethnographie und Sprachenkunde Amerikas zumal Brasiliens*, 2 vols., Leipzig, 1867.

Mason, J. Alden, "The Languages of South American Indians," *Handbook of South American Indians*, VI (Smithsonian Institution, Washington, 1950), 157–318.

Medina, Jose Toribio, *The Discovery of the Amazon According to the Account of Friar Gaspar de Carvajal*, New York, 1934.

Meggers, Betty J., and Clifford Evans, *Archeological Investigations at the Mouth of the Amazon* (Bureau of American Ethnology, Bull. 167), Washington, 1957.

Métraux, Alfred, "The Hunting and Gathering Tribes of the Rio Negro Basin," *Handbook of South American Indians*, III (Smithsonian Institution, Washington, 1948), 861–68.

————, "Religion and Shamanism," *Handbook of South American Indians*, V (1949), 559–600.

Murphy, Robert F., *Headhunters Heritage*, Berkeley, Calif., 1960.

Nadel, S. F., *The Foundations of Social Anthropology*, Glencoe, Ill., 1953.

Nimuendajú, Curt, "Reconhocimento dos Rios Icana, Ayarí, e Vaupés," *Journal de la Société des Américanistes de Paris*, XXXIX (1950), 126–86.

————, *The Tukuna* (ed. Lowie, University of California Publications in American Archaeology and Ethnology, Vol. XLV), Berkeley, 1952.

Park, Willard Z., "Tribes of the Sierra Nevada de Santa Marta," *Handbook of South American Indians*, II (Smithsonian Institution, Washington, 1946), 865–86.

Plazas Olarte, Humberto, *Los Territorios Nacionales*, Bogotá, 1944.

Preuss, Theodor K., *Religion und Mythologie der Uitoto*, 2 vols., Göttingen, 1921–23.

Rice, Hamilton, "The River Vaupés," *The Geographical Journal* (London), XXV (1910), 682–700.

————, "Further Explorations in the North-West Amazon Basin," *The Geographical Journal*, XLIV (1914), 137–68.

Spruce, Richard, *Notes of a Botanist on the Amazon and Andes* (ed. Wallace), 2 vols., London, 1908.

Steinen, Karl von den, *Unter den Natürvölkern Zentral-Brasilens,* Berlin, 1894.

Steward, Julian, "Western Tucanoan Tribes," *Handbook of South American Indians,* III (Smithsonian Institution, Washington, 1948), 737–48.

————, "The Witotoan Tribes," *Handbook of South American Indians,* III (1948), 749–62.

————, "Culture Areas of the Tropical Forests," *Handbook of South American Indians,* III (1948), 883–900.

————, "South American Cultures: An Interpretive Summary," *Handbook of South American Indians,* V (1949), 669–772.

————, and L. C. Faron, *Native Peoples of South America,* New York, 1959.

Stradelli, E., "Leggenda dell' Jurupary," *Bolletino della Società Geografica Italiana* (Rome), XXVII (1890), 659–89.

Tessmann, Gunter, *Indianer Nordost-Perus,* Hamburg, 1930.

Wallace, Alfred Russell, *A Narrative of Travels on the Amazon and Rio Negro,* London, 1870.

Whiffen, Thomas W., *The Northwest Amazons: Notes on Some Months Spent Among Cannibal Tribes,* London, 1915.

Ypiranga Monteiro, Mario, "Pubertätsritus der Tucano Indianer," *Zeitschrift für Ethnologie,* LXXXV (1960), 37–39.

Afterword

It has been sixteen years since this book was published. During those years I have returned several times to the Cuduiarí to gather material for a second book dealing mainly with high-ranking *Hehénewa* sibs. The new book is still some distance away, however, and this seems a good time to bring the reader up to date on the current status of anthropological investigations in the region and on the present condition of the Cubeo.

In 1963 *The Cubeo* was the only systematic ethnography of any tribe of the Vaupés. That condition is now happily changed. The area has attracted many scholars whose field studies of Tukanoan and other peoples have given us, for the first time, a comprehensive account of its cultural features. Of particular importance for the sake of a better understanding of the Cubeo is the fact that most new field studies have dealt with a variety of Tukanoan-speaking communities. The entire Tukanoan language family of the Vaupés, as we now know, represents a single culture that is expressed, however, in variant forms. More than that, all other Tukanoan speakers of this region, except for the Cubeo, are bound together by their forms of marriage into a single society. A rule of language exogamy requires each tribe or "language aggregate" (Jackson, 1972) to take a wife from another, preferably Tukanoan, family. Consequently, what we customarily designate as a "tribe" is more like a clan or a fraternity of related clans — a phratry. The collection of Tukanoan-speaking communities, even though each has its own and distinct language, has then the character of a structurally well-organized society. The Cubeo, who are still a tribe in the traditional sense, with a common language and with marriages between phratries of that same language, stand apart from the greater Tukanoan social system. Even so, they recognize their cultural affinity to it. From the scholarly perspective there is no doubt that the total Tukanoan picture must be grasped if any of the component groups are to be understood in depth.

A recent unpublished study of several communities of Macú adds an essential ingredient to the comprehensive picture of Tukanoan cultures. As readers of *The Cubeo* know, the Macú, who speak an isolated tongue, have traditionally lived in a special symbiotic relationship with this tribe and with others in the region. Before that study was done they were the least known and the least understood of all peoples in the Vaupés area.

Not directly in the Vaupés but part of the necessary comparative picture are Arawakan, Cariban, and other language groups. In recent years these too have been the subject of systematic study. I append a bibliography of recent published and unpublished works on this general region that have come to my attention.

When I had completed my second sojourn on the Cuduiarí in May, 1970, the Cubeo were a tribe deeply and perhaps irrevocably divided by religious and cultural convictions. One part, approximately half, had converted to Evangelical Protestantism, and the rest had remained nominally or actively under the jurisdiction of the Catholic mission at Mitú. Most of the communities on the Cuduiarí, many on the Vaupés, but only a few on the Querarí, were Catholic. The Querarí was an Evangelical stronghold. Everywhere, however, Catholic and Evangelical villages were close neighbors, and, as a rule, all sibs and phratries were divided between the two faiths. At that time the distinctions between the two factions were more than religious. In 1968, the Catholic mission of the Vaupés had already decided on a drastic change of policy from that of active conversion to that of respect for and even encouragement of native traditions, including religious and ritual practices. By 1970, as I shall explain shortly, the new Catholic policy had begun to show results in native cultural revival. The *Hehénewa* and their *Bahúkiwa* neighbors on the Cuduiarí were then beginning to restore long-lapsed rituals and were heading toward a full resumption of traditional ways.

The Evangelical communities, on the other hand, had already abandoned all the highly visible features of Cubeo culture and were moving toward complete cultural obliteration. They had of course abandoned the maloca, as had most of the Catholics. But in a deeper break with the past they had given up smoking tobacco, chewing coca, drinking chicha, and taking hallucinogens, along with all rituals, dancing, and singing. Under severe pressure from their young American Evangelical guardians, they broke almost all social relations with their Catholic kinsmen and tribesmen. They did not intermarry and they rarely visited. They had become a separate and foreign entity and had removed themselves from the Cubeo. It is the Catholic remnants that now form the Cubeo tribe. Needless to say, their self-removal had markedly affected the entire pattern of traditional relationships of marriage, phratry, and sib.

For a number of the Catholic communities of the Cuduiarí the spring of 1970 was a cultural divide of another sort. Before that time each had reached its own condition of equilibrium between the traditional past and the pressures and promises of the commercial future. The maloca was gone in most places and only such relatively inconspicuous family rituals as protecting an infant from its first connections with the foodstuffs of adults had remained. Periodic drinking parties in honor of plants and fish were still held, but the mourning rites and ancestral cult celebrations, because they were conspicuously public, had been given up along with traditional ornaments and body painting. Indeed, my first impression of Cubeo communities when I revisited them in December 1968 was that they had reached an advanced state of deculturation. The clusters of small square-shaped huts that replaced the majestic maloca seemed crowded, disorderly, and altogether alien to the Cubeo ethos. Almost all native crafts had been abandoned in favor of store-bought hammocks, garments, dishes, pots and pans, chairs and tables. The general aspect of a typical hut, with its littered and untended front plaza and its unkempt interior, was that of a shanty.

Needless to say, this first impression of cultural decay failed to register the deeper currents of ethnicity. Even the loss of the maloca, which I had judged to be of central importance in Cubeo social and religious life, was in fact less significant than I had imagined it would be. The Cubeo managed dances on a smaller scale, and they arranged their small huts — if they so desired — to correspond with traditional standards of placing senior and junior ranks. What was not practiced went underground, so to speak, in the memories of the elders.

My field work tapped the underground currents and brought them to the surface. Photographs I had brought back from the 1939–40 field period stirred them to an astonishing degree. One picture, especially, of *Hehénewa* in full ceremonial dress lined up abreast ready to take part in the last series of dances that terminate the mourning rituals, became an icon of a sort, adorning a wall of the hut of an elder of the senior lineage. The interviews and the recording sessions revived lapsed chants and traditions for the older people, at the same time educating the young in the past culture of their parents and grandparents. This phase of my field work was different from the first. Then my insistence on specifics and on texts had become tiresome to my informants. This time, as events soon demonstrated, I had provoked catharsis.

When I concluded the recording of the songs of the mourning rites, the *Hehénewa* community decided to hold a true ceremonial to deal with the death of a sibsman who had died during the previous year. In preparation for this, they arranged for instruction in songs, dances, ritual procedure, and the making of bark-cloth masks and other emblems of animal spirits. A grouping of huts was quickly transformed into a maloca as though the huts had been artfully arranged (as undoubtedly they had been) for that purpose. Only two communities — *Hehénewa* and *Bahúkiwa* — were involved; the sacred trumpets representing the *Xudjikü* and *Xudjiko* ancestral spirits were omitted. In other respects it was a full-fledged ceremony. The *óyne,* I was then told, had been neglected for the last twenty years. "We will now continue it," they vowed. A year later, according to information I have from Kaj Arhem, the ceremonies of whipping the boys and playing the sacred ancestral trumpets had also resumed along the Cuduiarí.

But side by side with the resumption of older rituals and the reconstruction in some places of malocas goes the trend to modernize. Wealthier Cubeo own outboard motors; some households have sewing machines; some communities have formed marketing cooperatives; others are selling maize, hogs, and chickens in Mitú as entrepreneurs. The younger people have a vision of belonging to both worlds, that of the Cubeo and that of the outside. They combine a new ethnic consciousness with the admiration for western education and technology. In 1970 they were better informed on our moon-voyaging astronauts than I was. It seems fitting, therefore, that the two communities on the Cuduiarí that began the cultural renascence are also the most forward-looking, that they are the two with native teachers in the Catholic schools, and that these teachers are now engaged with me in collaborative ethnographic research.

I returned to the Vaupés in June 1979 for further field work and to observe the course of culture change over the past decade. On culture change, there are several interesting developments to report. First, the Colombian government is considering the abrogation of its long-standing agreement with the Summer Institute of Linguistics. If SIL were to leave the field the result would likely be a weakening of the Evangelical influence in the Vaupés and a consequent retardation of deculturation.

Related to this possibility has been the formation of an all-native regional council for the Vaupés, *Consejo Regional de Indígenas del Vaupés.* Founded in 1974 in response to a growing sense of ethnicity, CRIVA now includes all tribes of the region. It is headed by Pedro Rodríguez, a Cubeo of the *Hehénewa* sib and my principal field collaborator. CRIVA is concerned with cultural restoration, but also with the achievement of enhanced political and economic status within the overall administration of the Vaupés. One of its main aims, now under official consideration, is the establishment within the *Comisaría del Vaupés* of a relatively autonomous native reserve. Young natives have already been appointed to important administrative posts within the *Comisaría,* and the native population is now the majority political constituency within the government of the *Comisaría.* A young Cubeo, the grandson of Mandú Pedrero (*Bahúkiwa*), in whose community I lived during my earliest sojourn on the Cuduiarí, is the first of the tribe about to enter university studies. He expects to be an agronomist and to devote himself to the native cause.

The formation of CRIVA has given further impetus to the curiously complex pattern of cultural development. On the one hand, cultural revival has continued to gain momentum. In June there were three large malocas on the Cuduiarí, and every important ritual that had previously been allowed to lapse had been reinstated, including the ancestral cult with its ancestral trumpets. But at the same time, the socioeconomic system is modernizing even more rapidly. The maloca is now largely a ceremonial center surrounded by nuclear family housing. As a result, there is a loss of traditional family collectivism. The economy has turned to cash and to diversification. The normally intricate integration of ritual and society seems to be coming apart and reforming itself. What is now emerging is a new pattern of ritual collectivity and of social individualism.

Bibliography of Recent Works on Vaupés and Adjacent Areas

Arhem, Kaj, "The Life Cycle: Description given by Makuna Indian of Caño Komoyaka," unpublished paper, n.d.

———, "Fishing and Hunting among the Makuna: Economy, Ideology and Ecological Adaptation in the Northwest Amazon," *Annals, Göteborg Etnografiska Museum,* Arstrick, Sweden, 1976.

Bernal, Villa, *Guía Bibliográfica de Colombia de Interés para el Antropólogo,* Bogotá, 1970.

Bidou, Patrice, "Rapport la Première Année du Troisième Cycle," unpublished paper (Cubeo analysis), n.d.

———, "Representation de l'Espace dans les Mythologies Tatuyo," *Journal de la Société des Américanistes,* LXI (1972), 45–105.

———, "Les Fils de l'Anaconda Celestes (les Tatuyo). Étude de la Structure Socio-politique," unpublished doctoral thesis, Laboratoire d'Anthropologie Sociale, Paris, 1976.

———, "Naître et Être Tatuyo," *Actes du XLIIᵉ Congrès International des Américanistes,* II (1977), 105–20.

Biocca, E., G. Galeffi, E. G. Montalvo, and G. B. Marini-Bettolo, "Sulle Sostanzi Allucinogene Impregate in Amazonia, Nota 1, Osservazioni sul Paricá dei Tukano e Tariana del Bacíno del Río Vaupés," *Annale di Chímica,* LVI (1964), 1175–78.

Bödiger, Ute, "Die Religion der Tukano im Nordwestlichen Amazonas," doctoral dissertation, University of Cologne, 1965.

Bolens, Jacqueline, "Indians and Missionaries on the Río Tiquié, Brazil-Colombia," *Archives for Ethnography,* L (1966), 145–97.

———, "Mythe de Juruparí. Introduction a une Analyse," *L'Homme,* VII (1967), 50–66.

Brüzzi Alves da Silva, P. Alcionilio, *A Civilizacao Indigena do Vaupés,* Missao Salesiana do Rio Negro, São Paulo, 1962.

———, "Estructure da Tribo Tukano," *Anthropos,* LXI (1966), 191–203.

———, "A Familia Linguistica Tukano," *Acts of the Thirty-ninth International Congress of Americanists,* V (1970), 155–64.

Gasché, Jürg, "L'Habitat Witoto: 'Progress' et 'Tradition,'" *Journal de la Société des Américanistes,* LXI (1972), 177–214.

———, "Les Fondements de l'Organisation Sociale des Indiens Witoto et l'Illusion Exogamique," *Actes du XLIIᵉ Congrès International des Américanistes,* II (1977), 141–61.

Goldman, Irving, "Perceptions of Nature and the Structure of Society: The Question of Cubeo Descent," *Dialectical Anthropology,* I (1966), 287–92.

———, "Time, Space, and Descent: The Cubeo Example," *Actes du XLIIᵉ Congrès International des Américanistes,* II (1977), 175–83.

Guyot, Mireille, "La Maison des Indiens Bora et Miraña," *Journal de la Société des Américanistes,* LXI (1972), 141–76.

———, "Structure et Evolution Chez les Indiens Bora et Miraña, Amazonie Colombienne," *Actes du XLIIᵉ Congrès International des Américanistes,* II (1977), 163–74.

Hugh-Jones, Christine, "Social Classification among the South American Indians of the Vaupés Region of Colombia," unpublished doctoral dissertation, University of Cambridge, 1977.

———, "Skin and Soul. Social Time and Social Space in Piraparaná Society," *Actes du XLIIᵉ Congrès International des Américanistes,* II (1977), 185–204.

———, *From the Milk River,* Cambridge, 1979.

Hugh-Jones, Stephen, "Why Shamans Are Jaguars," unpublished paper, n.d.

———, "Male Initiation and Cosmology amongst the Barasana Indians of the Vaupés Area of Colombia," unpublished doctoral dissertation, University of Cambridge, 1974.

————, "Like the Leaves on the Forest Floor . . . Space and Time in Barasana Ritual," *Actes du XLIIe Congrès International des Américanistes,* II (1977), 205–16.

————, *Palm and Pleiades,* Cambridge, 1979.

Instituto Lingüístico de Verano, *Folclore Indígena de Colombia,* vols. I and II, División Operativa de Asuntos Indígenas, Ministerio de Gobierno, República de Colombia, Bogotá, 1974, 1976.

Jackson, Jean, "Language, Marriage, and the Tribe: The Bará of the Vaupés, Colombia," unpublished paper, 1971.

————, "Bará Cousin Terminology and Prescribed Language Aggregate Exogamy," paper presented at the seventieth annual meeting of the American Anthropological Association, New York, 1971.

————, "Marriage and Linguistic Identity among the Bará Indians of the Vaupés Area of Colombia," unpublished doctoral dissertation, Stanford University, 1972.

————, "Language Identity of the Colombian Vaupés Indians," in R. Bauman and J. Sherzer, eds., *Explorations in the Ethnography of Speaking,* New York, 1974.

————, "Recent Ethnography of Indigenous Northern Lowland South America," in B. Siegel, ed., *Review of Anthropology,* IV (Palo Alto, Cal., 1975), 307–40.

————, "Relations between Tukanoans and Makú of the Central Northwest Amazon," unpublished paper, 1976.

————, "Vaupés Marriage: A Network System in an Undifferentiated Lowland Area of South America," in *Regional Analysis,* Vol. II: *Social Systems,* ed. C. Smith, New York, 1976.

————, "The Bará: Individual and Group Identity in Tukanoans of the Northwest Amazon," unpublished paper, 1977.

————, "Bará Zero Generation Terminology and Marriage," *Ethnology,* XVI (1977), 83–104.

Jacopin, Pierre-Yves, "Habitat et Territoire Yukuna," *Journal de la Société des Américanistes,* LXI (1972), 109–40.

————, "Quelques Effets du Temp Mythologique," *Actes du XLIIe Congrès International des Américanistes,* II (1977), 217–32.

Landaburu, J., "Mission Linguistique auprès des Indiens Andoke du Rio Caquetá (Amazonie Colombienne)," *Journal de la Société des Américanistes,* LIX (1970), 165–70.

Langdon, Thomas A., "Food Restrictions in the Medical System of the Barasana and Taiwano Indians of the Colombian Northwest Amazon," unpublished doctoral dissertation, Tulane University, 1975.

Lathrap, Donald W., *The Upper Amazon,* London, 1970.

Migliazza, Ernesto, "Fonologia Makú," *Boletím do Museu Paraense Emilio Goeldi,* n.s., Antropologia, No. 25, Belém, 1965.

————, "Esboço Sintactico de um Corpus da Lingua Makú," *Boletím do Museu Paraense Emilio Goeldi,* n.s., Antropologia, No. 32, Belém, 1966.

Moser, Brian, *The Cocaine Eaters,* London, 1967.

————, and Donald Tayler, "Tribes of the Piraparaná," *Geographical Journal,* CXXIX (1963), 437–49.

Oliveira, Adelia Engracia de, "A Terminologia de Parentesco Baniwa — 1971," *Boletím do Museu Paraense Emilio Goeldi,* n.s., Antropologia, LVI (1975), 1–34.

Persson, Lars, *Indiansk Moleri Fron Amazonas,* Moderna Museet, Stockholm, 1973.

Reichel, Alicia Dussan de, *Problemas y Necessidades de la Investigación Etnologica en Colombia,* Ediciones de la Universidád de los Andes, Antropología 3, Bogotá, 1965.

Reichel-Dolmatoff, Gerardo, "A Brief Report on Urgent Ethnological Research in the Vaupés Area, Colombia," *International Committee on Urgent Anthropological and Ethnological Research,* Bull. 9 (Vienna, 1967), 53–62.

———, *Amazonian Cosmos: The Sexual and Religious Symbolism of the Tukano Indians,* Chicago, 1971.

———, "The Cultural Context of an Aboriginal Hallucinogen 'Banisteriopsis Caapi,'" in P. Furst, ed., *Flesh of the Gods,* London, 1972.

———, "Cosmology as Ecological Analysis: A View from the Rain Forest," *Man,* n.s., II (1975), 307–18.

———, *The Shaman and the Jaguar: A Study of the Narcotic Drugs among the Indians of Colombia,* Philadelphia, 1975.

Reid, H., "Comparative Discussion of Makú and Tukanoan Social Structure," unpublished paper, 1977.

Saake, W., "Erziehungsformen bei den Baniwa," in Hans Becher, ed., *Beiträge sur Völkerkunde Südamerikas,* Hanover, 1964.

Salser, J. K., Jr., "Cubeo Phonemics," *Linguistics,* LXXV (1971), 74–79.

Schauer, Stanley, *Aspectos de la Cultura Material de Grupos Etnicos de Colombia,* Ministerio de Gobierno, Bogotá, 1973.

Schindler, Helmut, "Die Stellung der Carijona im Kulturareal Nordwest-Amazonien," *Acts of the Fortieth International Congress of Americanists,* Rome-Genoa, 1972.

———, "Warum kann Man den Hurari mit den Gwaruma erschlagen?" *Zeitschrift für Ethnologie,* XCIX (1973), 246–76.

———, "Carijona and Manakini," in E. B. Basso, ed., *Carib-Speaking Indians — Culture, Society and Language,* Tucson, 1977.

———, "Mutterliche Abwendung von einem Zweijährigen Säuglings — ein Besipiel von den Karihona," *Homo,* XXIX (1978), 88–108.

Silverwood-Cope, Peter, "A Contribution to the Ethnography of the Colombian Makú," unpublished doctoral dissertation, Cambridge University, 1972.

Smith, R., *Southern Barasano Grammar,* Summer Institute of Linguistics Language Data Microfiche AM 3, Huntington Beach, Cal., n.d.

Sorensen, Arthur P., Jr., "Multilingualism in the Northwest Amazon," *American Anthropologist,* LIX (1967), 670–84.

———, "The Morphology of Tukano," unpublished doctoral dissertation, University of Michigan, 1970.

———, "Multilingualism in the Northwest Amazon: Papurí and Pirá-Paraná Régions," *Acts of the Thirty-ninth International Congress of Americanists,* V (1970), 331–36.

Soto Holguin, Álvaro, "Mitos de los Cubeo," *Acts of the Thirty-ninth International Congress of Americanists,* VI (1972), 59–65.

Torres Laborda, A. *Mito y Cultura entre los Barasana, un Grupo Indígena Tukana del Vaupés,* Bogotá, 1971.

Uscategui, Mendoza W., "Notas Etnobotánicas sobre el *Ají* Indígena," *Revista Colombiana de Antropología,* XII (1963), 89–96.

Velthen, Lucia Hussak van, "Plumária Tukano — Tentativa de Análise," *Boletím do Museu Paraense Emilio Goeldi,* n.s., Antropologia, LVII (1975), 1–29.

Waterhouse, Viola, ed., *Sistemas Fonológicos de Idiomas Colombianos,* Ministerio de Gobierno, Bogotá, 1972.

Index